D0050605

COURAGE

IN A

DANGEROUS

WORLD

COURAGE

IN A

DANGEROUS

WORLD

The Political Writings of Eleanor Roosevelt

EDITED BY ALLIDA M. BLACK

COLUMBIA UNIVERSITY PRESS | NEW YORK

COLUMBIA UNIVERSITY PRESS

Publishers Since 1893
New York   Chichester, West Sussex
Copyright © 1999 Columbia University Press
All rights reserved
Library of Congress Cataloging-in-Publication Data
Roosevelt, Eleanor, 1884–1962.
    Courage in a dangerous world : the political writings of Eleanor
Roosevelt / edited by Allida M. Black.
      p.   cm.
    Includes bibliographical references and index.
    ISBN 0-231-11180-0 (cloth : acid-free paper). — ISBN
0-231-11181-9 (pbk.)
      1. Roosevelt, Eleanor, 1884-1962—Political and social views.
    2. United States—Politics and government—1933–1953—Sources.
    3. United States—Politics and government—1953–1961—Sources.
    I. Black, Allida M. (Allida Mae), 1952–   . II. Title.
E807.1.R48A3   1999
973.917'092—dc21
                         98-33807
                          CIP

For
Frances Seeber
Kate Wittenberg

It depends on what each of us does, what we consider democracy means and what we consider freedom in a democracy means and whether we really care about it enough to face ourselves and our prejudices and to make up our minds what we really want our nation to be, and what its relationship is to be to the rest of the world.

The day we know that then we'll be moral and spiritual leaders. . . .

You are going to live in a dangerous world for quite a while I guess, but it's going to be an interesting and adventurous one. I wish you the courage to face it. I wish you the courage to face yourselves and when you know what you really want to be and when you know what you really want to fight for, not in a war but in order to gain a peace, then I wish you imagination and understanding. God bless you. May you win.

—ELEANOR ROOSEVELT
"Freedom and Human Rights"

CONTENTS

Part III. The Home Front: 1939–1945

Part IV. The United Nations and Human Rights: 1945–1953

ACKNOWLEDGMENTS

Eleanor Roosevelt left a paper trial six and a half miles long. She kept everything, more than two and a half million pages. Letters, memos, manuscripts, columns, reports, photographs, and audio and video tape fill more than 3,000 archival boxes. She took pride in her career, selected her words carefully, and worked to expand her audience. She did not concern herself with filing, collating, or sorting papers. While she knew she would be studied, I suspect she never imagined how invaluable her archives would become or how many students and scholars would want to study her written legacy. Even if she had, she would not have organized the papers before turning them over to the Franklin D. Roosevelt Library. Such a painstaking task would have taken too much of her time.

Frances Seeber brought order to this chaotic paper trail. First as archivist, and later as Assistant Director, of the Franklin D. Roosevelt Library, she organized the collection, prepared the finding aids, and, after mastering it herself, taught her fellow archivists how to decipher ER's often illegible scrawl. Reflecting ER's outreach, she made the key decision to open correspondence ER received from forgotten Americans seeking her help or damning her policies. She made the Eleanor Roosevelt papers reflect Eleanor Roosevelt. Her skill, dedication, and patient responses to endless questions enabled researchers to look past the icon and find the woman and the politician.

Kate Wittenberg also looked past the icon. As editor in chief of Columbia University press, she took a chance on an unknown graduate student writing on a popular topic in a very crowded field and stuck with her through the throes not only of finishing the dissertation and expanding it for publication but also through the emotional roller-coaster of the current academic job market. As my editor, she improved my prose, strengthened my argument, championed political history, and expanded my word limit. A fine scholar in her own right, she advocated the concept of a document collection before her editorial board.

This book is for them, with respect for their professionalism and gratitude for their friendship.

I also benefited from the wise counsel of a community of archivists, historians, teachers, and activists.

Lynn Bassanese, Karen Burtis, John Ferris, Bob Parks, Mark Renovitch, Nancy Snedeker, and Ray Teichman made visiting the FDR Library a joy. They set the standard by which all archivists should be judged. I also profited from the advice of John Sears of the Franklin and Eleanor Roosevelt Institute as well as the strong support of Library Director Verne Newton. Susan McElrath of the Mary McLeod Bethune Archives let me ghost walk through Bethune's home.

Other scholars took time away from their own work to review the documents reproduced here. Maurine Beasley, James MacGregor Burns, Patrice Curtis, John D'Emilio, Rose Gladney, Lewis Gould, June Hopkins, John Howard, Linda Lear, Edie Mayo, Gaylord Neely, Leo Ribuffo, Roy Rosenzweig, Gail Savage, and John Sherwood helped wean me away from repetitive documents. Helen Veit, Charlene Bickford, June Hopkins, and Don Gastwirth read more than one should ask a friend to undertake. Nancy Beck Young took time away from her study of Wright Pattman to search Lyndon Johnson's papers for me. Hallie Galligan, Paul McHugh, and Jill Kiah tracked down elusive documents when I could not make another trek to Hyde Park or the Library of Congress. I also thank my students in the Roosevelt seminars I taught for The George Washington University and George Mason University for the singular and passionate arguments they made in behalf of specific documents.

Blanche Wiesen Cook, in the true spirit of ER, gave her time, heartfelt support, and honest criticism. From discussing sources, debating interpretation, and agonizing over deletions to jovial celebrations of life's personal whimsy, she gave me a daily example of what a colleague should be. I thank her for her great spirit and for her own splendid work.

Ralph Carlson first supported this project by publishing *What I Hope To Leave Behind: The Essential Essays of Eleanor Roosevelt*. I thank him for his willingness to see the project continue in a different form with a different house, for Carlson Publishing, and for his friendship.

Nowell Briscoe inroduced me to ER's writings and, twenty-five years later, his interest remains keen and his support constant.

Leslie Bialler copyedited the manuscript applying his unique blend of syntactical, political, and basketball commentary.

Finally, I thank my partner Judy Beck for our home, our collaboration, and her dedication to the principles ER articulated within these pages. In the darkest times, she gives me hope.

A NOTE ABOUT STYLE

The following distinction has been made regarding article titles. If the article was so titled by ER, and/or printed originally with that title, then it is enclosed within quotation marks. If the article has been given a title by the editor, no quotation marks are used.

Ellipses within the articles designated deleted text. In "My Day,'" discussions of ER's personal life and family activities were deleted. In the longer essays, anecdotes and examples that she often repeated were deleted after their first appearance in this volume. *The Moral Basis of Democracy* begins with chapter 4. The first three chapters briefly reviewed the history of the American Revolution and early republic and were deleted because of space limitations.

COURAGE

IN A

DANGEROUS

WORLD

An Actor, Not a Hostess

Eleanor Roosevelt cast a long shadow over the twentieth-century landscape. Her life spanned such dramatic issues as the first Red Scare, the Great Depression, two world wars, the Holocaust, the creation of the United Nations, the cold war, McCarthyism, the demise of colonialism, the civil rights movement, the resurgence of feminism, and the rise of the imperial presidency. Her legacy as first lady, delegate to the United Nations, Democratic party leader, humanitarian, and social activist made her an icon to millions, many of whom would agree on nothing other than their respect for her. Her supporters iconographized her as "the conscience of the nation," "FDR's eyes and ears," and "the first lady of the world." Her detractors derided her as "that woman," a "gadfly," a communist, and "an unfit mother."[1]

As Blanche Wiesen Cook and other historians, including myself, reconstruct Eleanor Roosevelt's life, ER's writings, with the notable exception of her autobiography, are out of print. We interpret ER while ER's interpretations of world events, the words she chose to create her own legacy, are confined to the Roosevelt archives in Hyde Park. Despite the efforts of her biographers to let ER speak for herself, the irony is stark. The words of this private woman who took great efforts to underplay, if not deny, her influence while her husband lived, only to become one of the nation's most influential columnists and political advisers after his death, are now largely unheard. The woman who found indepen-dence in journalism and who took such great pride in that aspect of her career that she always carried her writers' union card in her wallet is now dependent upon others to tell you what she said.[2]

Eleanor Roosevelt left a voluminous paper legacy. She wrote, without a ghost writer, four autobiographies, seven monographs, seven children's books, and more than 550 articles. She delivered more than fifty speeches a year for more than thirty years. In February 1933, she began a monthly column which existed in a variety of forms until her death in November 1962. On December 30, 1935, she began "My Day," a 500-word column published five days a week, which ran continuously until September 27, 1962. And she wrote more than 100,000 letters.[3]

The questions she posed, the challenges she faced are those which have con-fronted the major social and political movements from the time of the late-nine-teenth-century progressives to contemporary neoconservatives. The Eleanor Roosevelt who emerges from these pages is a woman grappling with the com-plexities of a changing world and an ever-increasing awareness of the responsi-bilities incumbent upon anyone living in a democracy. The record she left is the record of American democracy struggling with its conscience and its critics.

Eleanor Roosevelt was forty-eight years old when she became first lady in 1933. By the time she moved to 1600 Pennsylvania Avenue, she had raised a fam-ily, taught school, managed a business, coordinated statewide and national polit-ical campaigns, chaired investigative committees and statewide reform organi-zations, become a respected lobbyist, launched her career as a journalist, and had developed a reputation in her own right as a skilled politician who refused to abandon her commitment to democratic ideals.

ER did not want to check these accomplishments at the White House door. Although she actively supported her husband's campaign for the presidency, she did not want to be first lady. Fearful that she would lose the independence she had worked so hard to achieve and that her goals would be subsumed into her husband's agenda, ER wanted a job of her own—a job in which she could be an actor, not just a hostess. Franklin D. Roosevelt declined her offers of help and initially refused to consider her requests for substantive assignments. Although other first ladies had been active behind the scenes, they had concealed their in-fluence from the public, leaving ER no overt precedent to follow for public ac-tivism on behalf of social change and public policy. Ever the realist, she expect-ed criticism for setting her own example. What she did not know was how she would convince the American people to support her own version of "bold per-sistent experimentation."[4]

ER used the press adroitly. In the simplistic, self-effacing style that became her trademark in press conferences and in print, she initially refused to discuss her accomplishments, hid her political skills, refrained from speculating on what her influence on future generations might be, and focused instead on the human side of policies her husband promoted. Yet, as the 300,000 letters ER received in response to "I Want You To Write To Me" proves, her motherly solicitations helped create a reservoir of support for the challenge she posed to convention and helped create her own constituency. By 1940 she became one of America's most syndicated columnists, with a circulation equal to such famous journalists of the era as foreign correspondent Dorothy Thompson, political analyst Walter Lippmann, and Roosevelt critic Westbrook Pegler; and polls listed her as one of the ten most influential people in Washington.[5]

Always aware of her traditional obligations as FDR's wife, she nevertheless chafed at the restrictions this identity placed on her. Thus, a quiet tension runs through ER's pronouncements. The documents reprinted reflect not only her participation in a specific political momentum, but also her entanglement in an intricate cultural web in which her identity became "a matter of paragraph and presentation" and her recollections "understated, self-deprecating, monuments to discretion and silence."[6]

However, as the war crises facing the nation increased, ER found this deference more difficult to present. The seeming inability of liberals to realize fascism's dangers and to implement effective reform angered her. Yet rather than succumb to bitterness or accept lukewarm liberalism, she used her pen to attack the politics of fear and temerity. She survived what Carolyn Heilbrun has called "the female moratorium" and placed her "life outside the bounds of society's restraints and ready-made narratives."[7] With a unique mixture of stubbornness, courage, tenacity, idealism, compassion, and pride, ER, to a great degree, transcended cultural stereotypes and political compromise to reinvent her life. And in the process she helped redirect American politics and redefine American liberalism.

ER was not a complacent Democrat. She believed in democracy more than the Democratic party. She also perfected her craft as she clarified her politics. The more than fifty lectures she delivered each summer before packed houses frequently helped her develop points she would later present more fully in magazine articles, essays, and political monographs. By the time she left the White House, worried that her political influence had died along with FDR, she saw herself as more journalist than political leader. However, disturbed by the domestic and international crises the cold war presented, ER quickly used her publications to challenge American complacency and invigorate political debate.

The more Eleanor Roosevelt saw of the world, the more she reevaluated her politics and the more her vision of the world changed. As she aged, she began to view democracy in broader terms. Not content to rest upon assumptions, she made the transition from progressive to social feminist to New Dealer to disgruntled liberal. While she still believed in the progressive ideals that characterized her early writings and the legislative programs introduced by the New Deal, by the late forties a new more realistic assessment of American society began to appear in her articles and speeches. Disappointed with the tepid commitment to reform displayed by most liberals, she dedicated the last twenty years of her life to explaining complex social issues to a complacent audience. Increasingly, racial justice, economic security, quality education, affordable housing, civil liberties, human rights and vigilant resistance to communism formed the core of her philosophy. Even more reluctant to promote someone else's agenda, Eleanor Roosevelt refined and presented her own—one that defined the tenets of liberalism, human rights, and the politics of inclusion.

In 1962 ER ruefully wondered "what has happened to the American dream." She worried that the nation had lost its vision and feared that America was in great danger of becoming a nation of self-satisfied hypocrites. "We are facing the greatest challenge our way of life has had to meet without any clear understanding of the facts." That saddened her immensely. "One can fight a danger only when one is armed with solid facts and spurred on by an unwavering faith and determination."[8]

No longer living in anyone's shadow, a confident, confrontational but increasingly infirm ER dedicated a great part of her seventy-eighth year to *Tomorrow Is Now*, her final call to arms. Published posthumously in 1963, the manifesto stands in stark contrast to the self-depreciating naivete that had permeated her earliest columns. Emboldened by her political experiences and convinced that the nation had abandoned its moral and political responsibility, an angry, exhausted ER struggled to call the nation's attention to the problems she believed needed attention and to offer her own solutions to these crises.

She understood that *Tomorrow Is Now* was her last chance to speak her mind and she committed herself to the project with passion. She chastised Americans who refused to see how desperate the situation was, bluntly telling her readers that "it is today that we must face the future of the world." Nor did she spare her own party from her scorn. "Staying aloof is not a solution," she lectured moderates, "but a cowardly evasion."[9]

Collected from archives, libraries, and manuscript collections across the nation, this anthology offers a generous sample of ER's writings and speeches and provides many of the tools necessary to reconstruct her politics. The articles select-ed trace ER's development as journalist, politician, activist, diplomat, and edu-cator and clearly demonstrate the ease with which she flowed from one role to another. Organized into six thematic sections—The New Deal Years, The World at War, The Home Front, The United Nations and Human Rights, The Cold War Abroad, and The Cold War at Home—the articles are arranged chronologically within each topic to reflect the development of ER's thought.

Part I, The New Deal Years, highlights the issues ER believed central to achieving true democratic reform—informed public participation; humane, re-sponsive government policy; strong commitment to education; and recognition of the specific needs and contributions of minorities, women and youth—and traces ER's development as an activist for democracy. Here, ER, as she became more comfortable in the role of first lady, expanded her focus from promoting FDR's policies to advocating controversial social and political policy central to her political vision, such as the "Subsistence Farmsteads" of Arthurdale, West Vir-ginia, and the impact the 1937 Ecnomy Act had on women workers. A common image runs throughout the articles, speeches, and columns—ER's increasing re-fusal to accept halfhearted solutions to human problems. Whether the subject was Social Security, government support of the arts, WPA wages, or the Amer-ican Youth Congress, she pressured her husband's administration to practice what it preached and called for Americans to make their demands known. Pro-moting the National Youth Administration, defending the Federal Theater Pro-ject, championing Marian Anderson, or advocating self-help cooperatives, ER insisted that the four freedoms her husband championed should not be seen merely as goals for the world but must be translated into the lives of individu-als.[10] To do otherwise was to "couple" freedom "with stupidity."[11]

Such outspokenness inspired harsh attacks. When the *New Yorker* parodied her activities in its now-famous cartoon depicting two coal miners responding to her visit "with undisguised horror," ER criticized those who thought "there certainly was something the matter with a woman who wanted to see so much and to know so much." They suffered from a "kind of blindness" that was both selfish and self-defeating. Her strong conviction offset the hurt such criticism inflicted and encouraged her to continue to speak out. She urged her readers to follow her lead. "It is a man's ceaseless urge to know more and to do more which makes the world move, and so, when people say woman's place is in the home, I say, with enthusiasm, it certainly is, but if she really cares about her home, that caring will take her far and wide."[12]

ER insisted that democracy had "a moral basis" that must be applied in the political arena if the nation was to survive the economic and international crises challenging its security. This required the informed, active participation of all citizens. No one should hide behind complacency or apathy. For democracy to flourish, each citizen must make the "greatest sacrifice"—reflection and commitment. "We must know what we believe in, how we intend to live, and what we are doing for our neighbors." Reaching this decision was just the first step. Action was the second. "We must fulfill our duties as citizens, see that our nation is truly represented by its government, see that the government is responsive to the will and desires of the people." The nation "must maintain a standard of living which makes it possible for the people really to want justice for all, rather than to harbor a secret hope for privileges because they cannot hope for justice."[13]

When she entered the White House, Eleanor Roosevelt did not understand the problems African Americans faced. Yet as she toured the nation during the 1930s, she realized that the Depression effected different groups in different ways. After working with civil rights leaders Walter White, Mary McLeod Bethune, and A. Philip Randolph, ER recognized the pernicious effects of racism and pressured the administration to speak out against racial discrimination and acts of racist violence. In Birmingham for the convening of the 1938 Southern Conference on Human Welfare, she spoke out against the poll tax, protested segregation, and pressured state officials to treat sharecroppers more equitably. Her confrontation with a young Bull Connor, whose 1963 attack on Birmingham's Civil Rights activists would stun the nation, prodded Lorena Hickok to ask teasingly, "how did you get out of B'Ham? Have they torn you limb from limb yet?"[14]

By the late 1930s, ER saw civil rights as the litmus test for American democracy. She would declare throughout World War II that there could be no democracy in the United States that did not include democracy for African Americans. In *The Moral Basis of Democracy* she asserted that people of all races have inviolate rights to "some property." "We have never been willing to face this problem, to line it up with the basic, underlying beliefs in Democracy." Racial prejudice enslaved African Americans and continued to hobble them: "no one can claim that . . . the Negroes of this country are free."[15] When the Daughters of the American Revolution refused to allow Marian Anderson to perform in Constitution Hall, ER discussed her decision to resign from the organization in "My Day."

ER realized that such continuous demands for democratic conduct did little to ease the pain African Americans encountered on a daily basis and she tried very hard to understand the depths of their anger. "If I were a Negro today, I think I would have moments of great bitterness," she confessed to readers of *Negro Digest*. "It would be hard for me to sustain my faith in democracy and to build up a sense of goodwill toward men of other races." She certainly could appreciate African Americans' rage because she knew that if she were African American, her anger would surface. Nevertheless, she hoped she could channel her fury constructively because "there now remains much work to be done to see that freedom becomes a fact and not just a promise for my people."[16]

Part II, The World at War, traces ER's evolution from strong anti-war activist to public lobbyist for military resistance. As the war with Germany neared, ER struggled to reconcile her own anti-war sympathies with the information FDR presented on German conduct. She detested Franco and Hitler, but she had a longstanding commitment to anti-war activism. Throughout the twenties, she campaigned tirelessly for America's entry into the League of Nations and the World Court, passionately endorsed the Women's International League of Peace and Freedom (WILPF), co-chaired the Edward Bok Peace Prize Committee, lobbied in support of the Kellogg-Briand Treaty, and circulated memoranda discussing economic reform as a deterrent to war to all her New York State Democratic Women colleagues. In the 1930s, she had supported the efforts of the National Conference on the Cause and Cure of War, arguing that "the war idea is obsolete," helped finance the Quaker-run Emergency Peace Committee, joined the advisory board of the American Friends Service Committee, keynoted the 1937 No-Foreign War Crusade, and praised those Loyalists who resisted Franco. She so admired Carrie Chapman Catt's work for WILPF that she told FDR that Catt was the greatest woman she had ever known.

In 1938, she published This Troubled World, in which she argued that negotiation and economic boycott, rather than military conflict, were the best ways to curtail aggression and that the nation could "profit" from a careful review of the mistakes made by the League of Nations. Returning to her plea for informed participation, she concluded "we have to want peace, want it enough to pay for it, pay for it in our own behavior and in material ways. We will have to want it enough to overcome our lethargy and go out and find all those in other countries who want it as much as we do."[17]

However, this passionate commitment to peace did not mean an unswerving allegiance to fascism or isolationism or acquiescence to the facist offensive. Indeed, as fascist aggression increased, ER became more outspoken in her opposition to isolationist policies and in support of "cash and carry" and "lend lease." When FDR phoned her at 5 A.M. September 1, 1939, to tell her that Germany had invaded Poland, ER knew that the United States would eventually enter the war and began to assess the role she would have to play. "I . . . could not help feeling that it was the New Deal social objectives that had fostered the spirit that would make it possible for us to fight this war," she later admitted. Well aware of the role she played in fostering these objectives, ER could not easily avoid recognizing that she would have a major part in defining the domestic conduct of the administration's war effort.

She recognized that "to win the war" Americans would "have to fight with our minds, for this is as much a war for the control of ideas as for control of material resources." As the "My Day" columns show, her challenge was to highlight the ideas she thought essential to winning both the international war against fascism and the domestic war against intolerance and prejudice. As she wrote for the *Saturday Review*, "if those who say that to win the war we must hate, are really expressing the beliefs of the majority of the American people, I am afraid we have already lost the peace, because out main objective is to make a world in which all the people of the world may live with respect and good will for each other in peace."[18]

ER's ability to see the complex relationships between war and peace, propaganda and education, and consensus and dissent placed her in an uncomfortable position politically and personally. The peace movement wanted her to be its voice within the administration and the administration expected her to defend its position with its anti-war critics. But rather than letting these expectations confine her, ER, as her stance on conscientious objectors reveals, worked to find a position she could advocate with conviction. And when the horrors of Pearl Harbor, the Holocaust, and Hiroshima became known, she discussed them in the context of foreign and domestic policy.

Part III, The Home Front, reflects the many ways war reinforced ER's desire to make democracy more effective at home. Refusing to believe that the emergencies of wartime justified postponing domestic reform, ER also refused to accept that the war warranted total suspension of political criticism, arguing "that curtailing these liberties may be a greater danger than we are trying to avert." Consequently, she worked to restrain the zeal with which the administration reprimanded its critics, telling audiences and officials alike that "intolerance has its roots in fear."

Worried that a battle-fatigued "civilian morale" might degenerate into attacks on non-white, non-Christian citizens, ER became more outspoken in defense of Jews and African Americans. "Race, religion, and prejudice" must be confronted and Jim Crow "abolished." Freedom must "become a fact, not a promise." "We who believe in democracy," she told readers of *The Nation*, "should not so much be concerned with stamping out the activities of those few groups or individuals as with developing among the people in this country a great sense of personal responsibility toward a democratic way of life. . . . We do not move forward by curtailing people's liberty."[19]

Still, the lists of those she defended had important and significant gaps. In fact, there were times when her silence was so notable that she could reasonably be accused of turning her back on her principles. What is clear is that at the beginning of the war, ER and FDR held opposite views of the rights of Japanese Americans. Less than a week after Pearl Harbor was bombed, ER toured the West Coast; praised a plea for racial tolerance by Mayor Harry Cain of Tacoma, Washington; posed with Japanese Americans for photographs that would be distributed over the Associated Press wire service; and editorialized against retribution. FDR, on the other hand, determined to capitalize on the procedures he had utilized to monitor his critics throughout the 1930s, immediately summoned aides to discuss the wholesale detention of Japanese and, if necessary, German Americans.

ER opposed internment. She worked closely with Attorney General Francis Biddle to ensure, first, that she understood how the Constitution applied to internment and, second, that the Justice Department presented a strong case against the policy to FDR. However, once FDR signed Executive Order 9066 and internment began, ER fell silent.

ER waited until late 1943 to address internment publicly. By then the vast majority of the Japanese American population had been removed from the West Coast and those interned in the Poston, Arizona, and Manzanar, California, camps had either struck or rioted in protest of their incarceration. Worried that the policy might backfire, FDR asked ER to visit the Gila River camp. She agreed and announced that she would inspect the camps and report her findings to the nation. Yet instead of discussing the psychological and political climate of the camps or the concerns about racism and resettlement the internees raised during their meeting with her, ER wrote columns praising the internees' attempts to beautify their small plots of land.

Despite this lapse into public acquiescence, a decidedly anguished tone resonates through her other depictions of internment life. When ER tried to present the administration's case that loyal Japanese Americans were interned for their own protection, as hard as she tried she could not completely suppress her own doubts about this argument. When she tried to justify the administration's demands for immediate relocation, she introduced as many arguments questioning this statement as she did endorsing it. Finally, she lambasted those West Coast xenophobes who believed that "a Japanese is always a Japanese" by declaring that such "unreasonable" bigotry "leads nowhere and solves nothing."[20]

Part IV, The United Nations and Human Rights, traces ER's determination not to repeat this behavior. Just as FDR's death liberated her to speak her mind on Democratic domestic policies, it also allowed her to address international issues with which she disagreed. Yet once again she defied traditional liberal boundaries.

Keenly aware of ER's political stature, Harry Truman appointed her to the first American delegation to the United Nations. ER considered this the most important position of her life and dedicated a great part of her remaining seventeen years to promoting and defending the institution and its policies. As the U.S. representative to the Social, Humanitarian and Cultural Committee of the General Assembly (Committee III), she guided the drafting and adoption of the Universal Declaration of Human Rights. Modeled after the Declaration of Independence, the Magna Carta, and the Declaration of the Rights of Man, this document—more than any other contained in this volume—reflects ER's vision of the world. From the first sentence of the preamble—"the recognition of the inherent dignity and of the equal and inalienable rights of all members of the human family is the foundation of freedom, justice and peace in the world"—to the last article, the document resonates with ER's commitment to human rights and informed participation. Insisting that citizenship confers rights with responsibility, the document concludes "everyone has duties to the community in which alone the free and full development of his personality is possible."[21]

Yet as ER revealed in *Foreign Affairs*, drafting the Declaration was politically perilous process. It took three years of contentious committee debate before a unanimously supported document could be presented to the General Assembly. ER chaired these meetings with a deft blend of discipline and compassion, often challenging grandstanding critics to make their point quickly or be ruled out of order. She then "mapped out our strategy very carefully," reviewing every word of the document with each voting member, diligently marshaling their support. Her diligence prevailed, convincing the Soviets to abstain rather than be the lone voice opposing the Declaration.

ER considered the Declaration her finest achievement and became its most outspoken champion at home and abroad. Conceding that the Declaration carried no sanctions for those nations which violated its provisions and that it could only serve as a model for nations to emulate, ER nevertheless declared it "of outstanding value" because it "put into words some inherent rights" that must be recognized for individual "security and dignity" to prosper. By making rights less intellectual and more "tangible," the Declaration not only set "before men's eyes the ideas which they must strive to reach" but also gave them standards that "could be invoked before law."[22]

Human rights was a volatile political concept and the United States and the Soviet diplomatic corps remained extremely leery of supporting documents that mandated its signatories compliance with economic and political rights. The Soviets insisted American commitment to human rights was a sanctimonious pronouncement of a racist society while Americans argued Soviet support of economic guarantees was merely backdoor communism. When the General Assembly instructed Committee III to present a binding covenant on economic and social rights to the United Nations, the two superpowers continued their entrenched posturings. Once again, as her statements before the committee show, ER demanded the hearings move forward while searching for common ground.

Yet ER was not always a patient negotiator. Although she was an instructed delegate to the United Nations and technically had to clear her remarks regarding foreign policy with the State Department, ER often chafed at its reservations. When readers compare her formal remarks with the extemporaneous speeches included in this collection, ER's inclination to link social and economic rights with political rights—a position with which the state department disagreed—is very apparent. Americans must realize that they are "responsible for what we have done in developing our own country but for what we have stood for as a democracy." Urging the nation to live up to its professions, she argued that it was hard to promote democratic values if the nation acted in an undemocratic fashion.[23]

Part V, The Cold War Abroad, shows that ER applied the same independence when it came to defining her view of American foreign policy. Rather than succumbing to a zealous cold warrior position or supporting unquestioned collaboration with the Soviet Union, as "Why We Are Cooperating with Tito" demonstrates, ER carved out her own positions. She told readers of *Look* that while "it takes patience and equal firmness and equal conviction to work with the Russians," she "admire[d] the Russians' tenacity." Moreover, she urged Americans "to divorce out fear and dislike of the American communists, as far as possible from our attitude as regards . . . the Soviet government." Once America insists that Russia not aid American communists, "we can work with Russia as we have with the socialist government in Great Britain."[24]

Grounded in an unyielding commitment to the United Nations, she argued that the world must see itself as a global community that shared certain inalienable rights. Just as she demanded civil rights at home, she defended the rights of refugees, Jews, and women to a life defined by self-determination and peace, and championed their "First Need: Resettlement." Traveling to India and the Middle East, she tried to make Americans understand the religious underpinnings of the different cultures and to prepare both societies for the precarious nature of young democracies. Lastly, she urged the world to reject propaganda and the shun what she would later call "the politics of fear." "Are we so weak in the United Nations, are we as individual nations so weak that we are going to forbid human beings to say what they think and fear whatever their friends and their particular type of mind happens to believe?"[25]

ER argued that Americans and the world must learn from the mistakes of the past, from war and discrimination and impoverishment. To focus only on success distorts the record and offers an unrealistic guide for the future. This is "not an easy lesson for any of us to learn, but one that is essential to the preservation of peace."[26] Diplomatic and military leaders needed to recognize that containment has not worked as well as it should have because it has been presented as a "negative objective," selfishly and erratically applied.[27] Angered by the Bay of Pigs, ER declared the CIA should have studied the lessons of Korea before it decided to attack Cuba. The government must weigh the moral impact of an action as precisely as it calculates its diplomatic objective. "We owe to ourselves and to the world, to our own dignity and self-respect, to set out own standards of behavior, regardless of what other nations do."[28]

Determined to motivate as many Americans as possible, she refused to limit her appeals to those Americans who only read newspapers or popular magazines. Consequently, when Professor Houston Baker asked her to join with Margaret Mead, Gunnar Myrdal and other academics interested in public policy and foreign affairs who planned to address the major dilemmas facing the nation, she not only agreed to introduce the volume but also, as "What Are We For?" demonstrates, adapted her writing style to a more sophisticated audience.

Part VI, The Cold War at Home, concludes the anthology. This, the most overtly political and partisan of the six sections, shows ER's increasing frustration with the temerity of American political leaders. Beginning with her letter to Harry Truman outlining her most pressing postwar concerns to correspondence with critics regarding the stances she took on the Taft-Hartley Act, the Alger Hiss case, and federal aid to parochial schools to her bitter assessment of the social progress made in the seventeen years since the end of war, the articles here are the most candid of all ER's publications.

Truman was not the only national Democratic leader to feel ER's displeasure. Although ER had been a staunch supporter of Henry Wallace as FDR'S vice president during his third term and as Truman's Secretary of Commerce, when Wallace decided to run for president as a third party candidate in 1948, she bluntly reprimanded her friend. Although she did not question his conviction, she did question his political acuity. "He has never been a good politician, he has never picked his advisors wisely, . . . and [he has] oversimplified the problems that face us today."[29] She next strove to keep liberals within the Democratic Party, telling them that, as "Liberals in This Year of Decision," she needed their help to push the party away from the politics of fear and loyalty tests and back in the direction she thought it must take for democracy to flourish.

As Democrats retreated to the "vital center" politics of the Truman adminis-tration, ER spoke out against the politics of fear the cold war generated with strongly worded "My Day" columns on loyalty oaths, the House Un-American Activities Committee, the Smith Act, Southern resistance to the 1954 *Brown v. Board of Education* decision, and the Civil Rights Acts of 1957 and 1960. She de-livered the keynote address to Americans for Democratic Action and urged the formation of a bipartisan liberal lobby concerned with results rather than image. Refusing to red-bait, she declared "the day that I am afraid to sit down in a room with people I do not know because 5 years from now, someone will say, 'You sat in the room and five people were Communists, and so you are a Communist,' that will be a bad day for democracy." Americans "must be sure enough of our-selves, of own convictions, to sit down with anyone and not be afraid of listen-ing to what they have to say, and not be afraid of containment by association."[30]

When the Democrats renominated Adlai Stevenson to run against Dwight D. Eisenhower in 1956, ER traveled the country speaking out in Stevenson's behalf. Her address to a Charleston, West Virginia rally reveals more than just her sup-port of Stevenson. Rather, it and Carl Rowan's interview serve as the perfect prism through which to assess her views of both the Eisenhower administration and cold war politics. She bemoaned Republican capitulation to strident cold war politics and challenged recalcitrant Democrats to remain true to democra-tic principles. When Eisenhower won reelection, she continued to criticize his foreign and domestic policies and urged the Democrats stop aping Republican policies and return to their liberal roots. And she immediately began to label Richard Nixon a "man who will do anything to get elected."[31]

The strains associated with McCarthyism did not moderate ER's position on racial justice. Moreover, as she became more familiar with the unique problems African Americans faced, ER abandoned her position as a defender of equal treatment to become a staunch advocate of integration and nonviolent protest.

ER had joined the board of directors of the National Association for the Ad-vancement of Colored People (NAACP) in 1945. Indeed, she spent the last sev-enteen years of her life arguing that the rights to vote, to work, to fair housing and quality education, and to organize in protest of discriminatory practices were crucial to democracy's success. And, as the correspondence with Lyndon John-son, then the Majority Leader of the Senate, illustrates, she used her column to pressure party leaders to consider her position. When the white mobs attacked African Americans and white students on the Freedom Rides, ER "found it intol-erably painful to accept the fact" that such violence could occur in the United States. "This was the kind of thing the Nazis had done to Jews in Germany."[32]

Discrimination women faced in the workplace and within the political arena also concerned ER. Influenced by her work with the Women's Trade Union League, the National Consumers League, and the League of Women Voters, she supported working women and lobbied for safer working conditions and minimum wage legislation. Yet despite all the criticism ER received for her activism, she never questioned that women had a unique political responsibility—to shape the values of their families and neighborhoods and the policies of their government. Convinced that women focused more on results than policy and wanted reform more than recognition, ER pushed American women to speak out, organize, and enter the public arena. After the Democrats returned to the White House in 1961, ER pressured John Kennedy to appoint more women to executive positions within the federal government. The president responded by establishing the Presidential Commission on the Status of Women and asking her to serve as its chair. Although her health kept her from taking as active a role as she wished, ER spent part of the last year of her life urging government recognition of the needs and talents of women. She ultimately rescinded her opposition to the Equal Rights Amendment and supported Pauli Murray and Esther Petersen's draft detailing the discrimination American women encountered. Although the commission did not succeed in its immediate goal of changing Kennedy's behavior, it did help birth the National Organization for Women and prepared the way for the national campaign in support of the ERA.

ER understood how difficult these attitudinal and policy changes were. The longer Americans looked to past stereotypes as guidelines for political behavior, the longer democracy would be delayed. And as she began to spend more time with young people in and out of the classroom, she became convinced that youth would take the necessary risks to eradicate prejudice and expand democracy.

Party leaders disappointed her. By 1960, concerned that John Kennedy did not have the experience, temperament, or character to become president, ER tried for a third time to rally Democrats behind Adlai Stevenson, proposing a Stevenson-Kennedy ticket. Although JFK left the convention with the nomination, he did not leave with ER's support. As the "My Day" columns reveal, she did not give her blessing easily, but only after he came to her home, Val-Kill, to answer her questions. Satisfied that he appreciated her viewpoint, ER became the honorary co-chair of New Yorkers for Kennedy, embarked on a sixteen-city campaign tour, and used her column to urge anxious voters to support the Democratic candidate. After the election, she continued to use the forum to defend his selection of Robert Kennedy as attorney general and to counsel caution to an impatient president-elect.

Clearly, Eleanor Roosevelt—ever aware of democracy's shortcomings—nevertheless envisioned a world in which it might flourish. Whether speaking to students, teachers, reform associations, the general public, members of Congress, political conventions, or career diplomats, ER never wavered from her commitment to participatory democracy, human rights, and the United Nations. The more of the world's injustice she witnessed, the more resolute her belief in democracy became. Yet hers was not a blind faith nor a naive abdication of responsibility. ER always understood that democracy could not succeed without hard work, sacrifice, and compassion. As this collection reveals, she urged the world to look beyond national boundaries and political rivalries, to consider rival points of view, to read, to think, and to act—to have the courage necessary to live in a dangerous world.

Notes

1. Joseph P. Lash, *Eleanor and Franklin: The Story of Their Relationship Based on Eleanor Roosevelt's Private Papers* (New York: Norton, 1970); Ruby Black, *Eleanor Roosevelt: A Biography* (New York: Duell, Sloan and Pearce, 1940); Katie Louchheim, ed. *The Making of the New Deal: The Insiders Speak* (Cambridge: Harvard Universiy Press, 1983); and George Wolfskil and John A. Hudson, *All but the People: Franklin D. Roosevelt and His Critics* (New York: Macmillan, 1969).

2. Recent ER biographies include Blanche Wiesen Cook, *Eleanor Roosevelt: A Life, Volume I* (New York: Viking, 1992); Allida M. Black, *Casting Her Own Shadow: Eleanor Roosevelt and the Shaping of Postwar Liberalism* (New York: Columbia University Press, 1996); Doris Kearns Goodwin, *No Ordinary Time: Franklin and Eleanor Roosevelt and the Homefront in World War II* (New York: Simon and Schuster, 1994); and Mollie Sommerville *Eleanor Roosevelt as I Knew Her* (Washington: EPM Publications, 1996).

3. See appendix for complete list of ER's publications.

4. Franklin D. Roosevelt, "Address at Oglethorpe University," May 22, 1932 in *The Public Papers and Addresses of Franklin D. Roosevelt*, vol 1, 1928–1932 (New York: Random House, 1938), 639.

5. For full discussion of ER's use of the media see Frances Seeber," 'I Want You to Write to Me': The Papers of Anna Eleanor Roosevelt," *Prologue* 2 (Summer 1987): 95–105, and Maurine H. Beasley, *Eleanor Roosevelt and the Media* (Urbana: University of Illinois Press, 1987).

6. Herbert Leibowitz, *Fabricating Lives: Explorations in American Autobiography* (New York: Knopf, 1990), xix and xxiii.

7. Carolyn Heilbrun, *Writing A Woman's Life* (New York: Ballantine. 1988), 30.

8. "What Has Happened to the American Dream" (Part V, article 13).

9. *Tomorrow Is Now* (Part VI, article 30).

10. Part I, articles 12–15.

11. "Insuring Democracy" (Part I, article 6).

12. "In Defense of Curiosity" (Part I, article 6).

13. *The Moral Basis of Democracy* (Part X, article 15).

14. Lorena Hickok to Eleanor Roosevelt (Part I, article 10).

15. *The Moral Basis of Democracy* (Part X, article 13).

16. Eleanor Roosevelt, "Freedom: Promise or Fact" (Part III, article 8).

17. *This Troubled World* (Part II, article 2).

18. Roosevelt *The Autobiography of Eleanor Roosevelt*, 230 and "Must We Hate to Fight?" (Part III, article 7).

19. "Fear is the Enemy," *The Nation* 150 (10 Feb. 1940): 173.

20. "Challenge to American Sportmanship" (Part III, article 10).

21. "Universal Declaration of Human Rights" (Part IV, article 1).

22. "The Promise of Human Rights" (Part IV, article 2).

23. "The UN and the Welfare of the World," *National Parent-Teacher* 47 (June 1953): 14–16, 35.

24. "The Russians Are Tough" (Part V, article 2).

25. "Human Rights and Human Freedoms" *The New York Times Magazine* (March 21, 1946): 21.

26. "The Russians Are Tough" (Part V, article 2).

27. "What Are We For?" (Part V, article 11).

28. "What Has Happened to the American Dream" (Part V, article 13).

29. "Plain Talk about Wallace" (Part VI, article 8).

30. "Address to Americans for Democratic Action" (Part VI, article 12).

31. "Ike—Nice Man" (Part VI, article 23).

32. "The Social Revolution" (Part VI, article 30).

PART I

The New Deal Years: 1933–1940

1.   "The State's Responsibility for Fair
      Working Conditions"
      Scribner's Magazine, March 1933

No matter how fair employers wish to be, there are always some who will take advantage of times such as these to lower unnecessarily the standards of labor, thereby subjecting him to unfair competition. It is necessary to stress the regulation by law of these unhealthy conditions in industry. It is quite obvious that one cannot depend upon the worker in such times as these to take care of things in the usual way. Many women, particularly, are not unionized and even unions have temporarily lowered their standards in order to keep their people at work. If you face starvation, it is better to accept almost anything than to feel that you and your children are going to be evicted from the last and the cheapest rooms which you have been able to find and that there will be no food.

Cut after cut has been accepted by workers in their wages, they have shared their work by accepting fewer days a week in order that others might be kept on a few days also, until many of them have fallen far below what I would consider the normal and proper standard for healthful living. If the future of our country is to be safe and the next generation is to grow up to healthy and good citizens, it is absolutely necessary to protect the health of our workers now and at all times.

It has been found, for instance, in Germany, in spite of the depression and the difficulty in making wages cover good food, that sickness and mortality rates have been surprisingly low amongst the workers, probably because of the fact that they have not been obliged to work an unhealthy number of hours.

Limiting the number of working hours by law has a twofold result. It spreads the employment, thereby giving more people work, and it protects the health of the workers. Instead of keeping a few people working a great many hours and even asking them to share their work with others by working fewer days, it limits all work to a reasonable number of hours and makes it necessary to employ the number of people required to cover the work.

Refusing to allow people to be paid less than a living wage preserves to us our own market. There is absolutely no use in producing anything if you gradually reduce the number of people able to buy even the cheapest products. The only way to preserve our markets is to pay an adequate wage.

It seems to me that all fair-minded people will realize that it is self-preservation to treat the industrial worker with consideration and fairness at the present time and to uphold the fair employer in his efforts to treat his employees well by preventing unfair competition.   □

2.   *"I Want You to Write to Me"*

Woman's Home Companion, August 1933

The invitation which forms the title of this page comes from my heart, in the hope that we can establish here a clearing house, a discussion room, for the millions of men, women and young people who read the *Companion* every month.

For years I have been receiving letters from all sorts of persons living in every part of our country. Always I have wished that I could reach these correspondents and many more with messages which perhaps might help them, their families, their neighbors and friends to solve the problems which are forever rising in our personal, family and community lives, not only with my ideas but with the ideas of others.

And now I have a department in this magazine which I can use in this way. The editor of the *Woman's Home Companion* has given me this page to do with exactly as I will; but you must help me. I want you to tell me about the particular problems which puzzle or sadden you, but I also want you to write me about what has brought joy into your life, and how you are adjusting yourself to the new conditions in this amazing changing world.

I want you to write to me freely. Your confidence will not be betrayed. Your name will not be printed unless you give permission. Do not hesitate to write to me even if your views clash with what you believe to be my views.

We are passing through a time which perhaps presents to us more serious difficulties than the days immediately after the war, but my own experience has been that all times have their own problems. Times of great material prosperity bring their own spiritual problems, for our characters are apt to suffer more in such periods than in times when the narrowed circumstances of life bring out our sturdier qualities; so whatever happens to us in our lives, we find questions constantly recurring that we would gladly discuss with some friend. Yet it is hard to find just the friend we should like to talk to. Often it is easier to write to someone whom we do not expect ever to see. We can say things which we cannot say to the average individual we meet in our daily lives.

To illustrate the changing nature of our problems it is interesting to remember that less than twenty years ago the outstanding problem of the American homemaker was food conservation, or how to supply proper nourishment for her family with one hand while helping to feed an army with the other! Ten years ago the same mothers were facing the problem of the post-war extravagance and recklessness; how to control the luxurious tastes of their children, the craving for gayety, pleasure, speed which always follows a great war. Today in millions of homes parents are wrestling with the problem of providing the necessities of life for their children and honest work for the boys and girls who are leaving school.

At almost stated intervals the pendulum swings, and so far the American people have each time solved their problems. And solve them we will again, but not without earnest consultation and reasoning together. Which is exactly where this page enters the national picture.

Let us first consider one or two typical problems. You all know that in May the entire nation celebrated Child Health Week. I was among those who spoke on the basic foundations on which the health of a child is built. A few days after I gave this radio talk I received a letter from a mother who wanted to know how she could supply nourishing food and proper clothing for her three children when her husband was earning exactly fifty-four dollars a month!

Again, a couple who had read something I had said about modern methods in education wrote asking what trades or professions would offer the best opportunities for young people in the next few years.

You will note that both of these earnest letters came from parents. This is encouraging, for there never was a time when the sympathy and tolerance of older people were more needed to help the younger people adjust themselves to a very difficult world.

In the hands of the young people lies the future of this country, perhaps the future of the world and our civilization. They need what help they can get from the older generation and yet it must be sympathetically given with a knowledge that in the last analysis the young people themselves must make their own decisions.

Please do not imagine that I am planning to give you advice that will eventually solve all your problems. We all know that no human being is infallible, and on this page I am not setting myself up as an oracle. But it may be that in the varied life I have had there have been certain experiences which other people will find useful, and it may be that out of the letters which come to me I shall learn of experiences which will prove helpful to others.

And so I close my first page to and for you, as I opened it, with a cordial invitation—I want you to write to me.   □

3.   ## "Old Age Pensions"

A Speech Before the D.C. Branch of the American Association for Social Security, the Council of Social Agencies, and the Monday Evening Club.

Social Security, February 1934

I do not feel that I have to discuss the merits of old age pensions with my audience. We have come beyond that because it is many years now since we have accepted the fact, I think, pretty well throughout the country, that it is the right of old people when they have worked hard all their lives, and, through no fault of theirs, have not been able to provide for their old age, to be cared for in the last years of their life. We did it at first in what I consider a terrible way— through poorhouses—but now we have become more humane and more enlightened, and little by little we are passing old age pension laws in the various states.

The state that I am most familiar with is New York. A pension law was passed there during my husband's administration. I would like tonight—because there is a law here under consideration for the District of Columbia, and because *I feel that the law should be as nearly a model law as possible because the eyes of the nation will be focused on it*—to discuss a few of the things that have come up in the administration of our law there.

No fixed sum is specified either in New York or in Massachusetts. I think that is a very good thing because it allows the investigation of every individual case by trained workers. It saves money, I believe, to the taxpayers and yet allows the needs of each case to be met. But it requires a good administration and it means that you are more dependent on having really good trained case workers; otherwise you will have unequal administration and unfairness in many ways, and, of course, the minute you have that, you have unfairness on the part of the people who are benefitting.

But we have an age limit: the age limit is 70 in New York State and I think that is a bad feature. I have found that in many cases where people have appealed to me much suffering might have been saved if it had been possible to have more elasticity. There are people at 70 who are better able to get along than some people at 65 or even 60, and it seems to me that in considering a law there should be some arrangement made for flexibility as to age and some other consideration besides age alone.

I also think that our law has another disadvantage: it is dependent on yearly appropriations. The expense is met half by the locality and half by the state. I believe that we should depend, when this becomes universal, on some method of insurance—some fund which is paid into over a whole period of a person's life, or earning life at least.

The reason that I am not discussing the necessity for this law is that I feel that most of us have had personal experiences which have brought that necessity home to us. But I will tell you what first made me feel what it would mean if old people could have enough money to stay on in their own homes: There was an old family—two old sisters and two old brothers—who had lived on a farm not far from us in the country just as long as I could remember. I was away a great deal and I didn't see them often, but on Election Day either my husband or I usually drove them to the polls, and we always talked about farm conditions and whatever the happenings in their lives had been during the year. Well, I did not see them for two or three years. Then, one Election Day, I went to get them and I found one old lady in tears because that day one surviving brother had been taken to the insane asylum because the worry of how they were going to get enough to eat and enough to pay their taxes had finally driven him insane, and she was waiting to go to the poorhouse. The other old sister had already gone, and the other brother had died.

Well, I can hardly tell you how I felt. In the first place, I felt I had been such a bad neighbor that I did not know just what to do. I felt so guilty, and then it seemed to me as though the whole community was to blame. They had lived there all their lives; they had done their duty as citizens; they had been kind to the people about them; they had paid their taxes; they had given to the church and to the charities. All their lives they had done what good citizens should do and they simply had never been able to save. There always had been someone in the family who needed help; some young person to start; somebody who had gone to the city and who needed his rent paid. Somehow or other there was always some demand and no money was saved. And if I had needed any argument to settle the question for me—that the community owes to its old people their own home as long as they possibly can live at home—these old neighbors would have supplied it. And I think it costs us less in the end. We may, of course, run our poorhouses very inexpensively; we may find that institutional care is inexpensive, but I think our old people will live at home as cheaply as they possibly can.

We can hardly be happy knowing that throughout this country so many fine citizens who have done all that they could for their young people must end their days divided—for they usually are divided in the poorhouse. Old people love their own things even more than young people do. It means so much to sit in the same old chair you sat in for a great many years, to see the same picture that you always looked at!

And that is what an old age security law will do. It will allow the old people to end their days in happiness, and it will take the burden from the younger people who often have all the struggle that they can stand. It will end a bitter situation—bitter for the old people because they hate to be a burden on the young, and bitter for the young because they would like to give gladly but find themselves giving grudgingly and bitterly because it is taking away from what they need for the youth that is coming and is looking to them for support. *For that reason I believe that this bill will be a model bill and pass without any opposition this year.* ☐

4. **"Subsistence Farmsteads"**
Forum, April 1934

It was a bright and sunny day in a mining camp in West Virginia, and a relief worker was walking down between two rows of houses, talking to a stranger as she went.

"In this house here, where we are going now," she said, "lives a young couple with two children. They have done remarkably well with the garden they started. He was a farmer before he came to the mines, and she is a very energetic young woman. She has canned dozens and dozens of things and sold all she is able in a nearby town. But their neighbors are not so fortunate. Right next door there is a family where the children undoubtedly have tuberculosis."

By this time we had reached the steps. We found the interior of the house clean, although the young woman who let us in apologized for the fact that her children were rather dirty, and her kitchen full of the mess which canning creates. It was easy to see that here was a young woman who was trying hard to bring up a healthy family and who had the standards of good and well-planned farm living in her mind. Before we had talked ten minutes, she asked the relief worker eagerly, "Is there any chance that we can get some land?" She knew that an effort was being made to persuade either the state or the mining companies to divide some land amongst the unemployed miners and she was most anxious to remove her children from the danger of tuberculosis and the family across the way, where the men spent a good deal of time drinking.

The case worker answered, "Yes, we hope that something will be done." As she emerged, she sighed a little and said, "I wonder when it will be done or if it will be done in time to serve any of these people." They had never heard of "Subsistence Farms" but they were the kind of people ideally suited to go and live on one.

II

The objective of subsistence farming is not to compete with regular farming or add to the burden of agricultural overproduction. The idea is that families engaged in subsistence farming consume their own garden products locally instead of sending them to distant markets. They are not expected to support themselves entirely by raising food, like the successful commercial farmers of the country. The plan is that they shall be situated near enough to an industry for one member of the family to be employed in a factory a sufficient number of days in the year to bring in the amount of money needed to pay for the things which the families must have and cannot produce for themselves. In this way farming will be helped by industry, and industry will be helped by farming. There will be no competition with agriculture nor with industry. Industry must be centralized in order to clear up the congested slum areas of our big cities. Subsistence farms will make possible shorter hours of work in the factories as well as the decentralization of crowded populations.

This new self-supporting manner of American living is being projected under the direction of the Division of Subsistence Homesteads of the Department of the Interior. Last spring $25,000,000 was appropriated for study and practical illustration of this idea of new social and economic units. We have several models to build upon in this country, and there is always the example of the self-sufficiency of village life in France. Round about the country various model projects are being planned. In Monmouth County, New Jersey, a community is being projected for two hundred families of Jewish needle workers from nearby crowded manufacturing cities. A factory is to be built for their use; the best soil is to be set aside for homesteads; and the less fertile land is to be devoted to cooperative agriculture to serve solely the consumption of this community.

III

Recently I have observed at first hand the subsistence-farming project near Reedsville, West Virginia. In that state a great many mines have closed down; some will probably never reopen; some may reopen for a certain number of days a week during part of every year. It is being urged upon the owners of these mines that they use the land which they own above the ground for this new type of subsistence farm. The miners can still work in the mines even though their jobs may not be steady day in and day out.

The government experiment near Reedsville is designed to provide for 125 families especially chosen from those miners who are permanently out of work. The West Virginia College of Agriculture had made a study of unemployed miners' families and found that many of them had come to the mines only within the last few years and because they were attracted by the very high wages paid. The high wages, alas, lasted in some cases not even long enough to pay for the cheap car bought on the installment plan, and these homes are devoid of all improvements. Living conditions in the mining villages are so bad that many of the families who have come from farms long to get back again. There is good land available for the Reedsville project, with watershed hills and a certain amount of valley bottom, typical of much of the West Virginia farming land. A factory will supply the industry, and every homestead will have five acres. There will be some land suitable for pasture only, which will be owned by the community and operated on model cooperative principles. The houses, while very simple, are being planned to meet the needs and aspirations of comfort of the people who are going to live in them. They want certain very definite things, among these a chance to be clean, a shower or a bathtub in every house, a suitable tub in which to wash clothes, enough room so that each member of the family can have a bed of his own. These desires suggest some of the things which the miners lack in their present houses.

Some of the men who have been building the foundations for the first fifty houses, which are now nearing completion, will probably occupy them. . . . Each farm family will plan for crops suited to its own land: the man who chooses to live down in the valley will grow one thing, and the man on the hillside another. Both men will have, during the first year, the advantage of expert advice and direction from the State College of Agriculture.

These new farming families will all remain on public relief until the factory is opened and the first crops are harvested; but when a family makes its first payment the title to the land will pass to the individual homesteader. In twenty or thirty years the individual will own it free and clear of debt. This plan varies in different projects.

Plowing was going on near Reedsville all through last autumn. Now roads are being built. The question of the type of government which the community wishes to set up is a difficult one, but it is hoped that some way will be found to organize a town-meeting type which may be changed easily to fit into the state government at the end of the first year.

There are in the vicinity a number of high schools which can accommodate the children who will be sent to them. An old barn is to be converted into a local grammar school and made attractive under the direction of the Department of Education. In this building a number of experiments will be tried: for instance, it may be possible to give more vocational guidance and more handicraft work than is usually done in schools. It may also be feasible to have a nursery school to which the mothers themselves may come for a couple of hours at definite times during the week to cooperate with the teachers and learn how best to feed and discipline their children.

All these things are being discussed, and some will be actually tried out. There is the possibility that 1 2 5 families will be too few for this community of graduate miners, and that the population will have to be enlarged. Eventually there may be two or three factories instead of one, but in any case the farms will be kept out of competition with those farms which are run for profit.

IV

If the West Virginia experiment succeeds it may be the model for many other similar plans throughout the United States. It is easy to see in advance, however, that the people living on these subsistence farms will be far more secure than the unemployed people living today in towns, whether small or large. It is possible, too, that on these farmsteads home crafts of different kinds may be started which will furnish added income. . . .

If directed from some central point where good designs and color schemes may be furnished by really good artists, and the products marketed in some cooperative way, a limited but still a good and remunerative occupation may be furnished to those who stay at home on the farms and yet can find spare time to do hand work.

We shall know more about subsistence farming when the first new projects have been working for a number of years. Already there is hope that this program will solve the difficulties of a good many people throughout our country who are now suffering from unemployment or the inability to better the poor standards of living imposed on them by slums and congested areas.   □

5.   "The New Governmental Interest in the Arts"

A Speech Before the Twenty-Fifth Annual Convention of the American Federation of Artists"

American Magazine of Art, September 1934

I think that we all of us now are conscious of the fact that the appreciation of beauty is something which is of vital importance to us, but we are also conscious of the fact that we are a young country, and we are a country that has not had assurance always in its own taste. It seems to me, however, that we are now developing an interest and an ability to really say when we like a thing—which is a great encouragement to those of us who think that we want to develop in a democracy a real feeling that each can have a love of art, and appreciate that which appeals to him as an individual, and that he need not be afraid of saying when he doesn't know a great deal: "Well, I like that, I may be able to develop greater appreciation as I know more, but at least I have reached a point where I know that I like this." I have been tremendously impressed by the interest which has developed since art and the Government are beginning to play with each other. I have been interested in seeing the Government begin to take the attitude that they had responsibility toward art, and toward artists. I have also been interested in the reaction of the artists to an opportunity to work for the Government. I have had a number of letters, saying, "I have been working on a Government project. It is the first time that I ever felt that I, as

an artist, had any part in the Government." I think it is a wonderful thing for
the Government, and I think it is a wonderful thing for the people—for the
people of the country in general—because through many of these projects I
think there are more people today throughout the country conscious of the fact
that expression—artistic expression—is something which is of concern to
every community.

Just a few days ago in talking with a rather varied group of women, I found
that those who came from other and older countries had all been to the Corco-
ran Art Gallery to see the exhibition there. Two of the Americans had been—but
two had not been, and one of them said she hadn't even heard there was such a
thing. Finally, they said that they would make an effort to go, and one of the
women who came from a country across the ocean replied, "But you must not
miss it. It is the most significant thing in Washington." I was very much interested that that should come to a group of American women from a foreigner. From
my point of view, it is absolutely true, for in a way that exhibition expresses what
many of us have felt in the last few years but could not possibly have either told
or shown to anybody else. That is the great power of the artist, the power to
make people hear and understand, through music and literature, or to paint
something which we ordinary people feel but cannot reveal. That great gift is
something which, if it is recognized, if it is given the support and the help and
the recognition from people as a whole throughout this country, is going to
mean an enormous amount in our development as a people. So I feel that if we
gain nothing else from these years of hard times, if we really have gained the acceptance of the fact that the Government has an interest in the development of
artistic expression, no matter how that expression comes, and if we have been
able to widen—even make a beginning in widening—the interest of the people
as a whole in art, we have reaped a really golden harvest out of what many of us
feel have been barren years. I hope that as we come out of the barren years, those
of us who can will give all the impetus possible to keeping up this interest of the
Government, and of the people in art as a whole.

I hope that in all of our communities, as we go back to them, we will try to
keep before the people the fact that it is money well spent to beautify one's
city, to really have a beautiful public building. I could not help this afternoon,
when my husband was giving a medal of the American Institute of Architects
to a Swedish architect, thinking of the story which has been told by the Government that he must finish this beautiful building in three years. When the
three years were up he told them he couldn't finish it, that he must go on and
take the time to really make it his ideal, the thing he had seen in his dreams—
he did not like what he had done. And it was not the Government officials who

said, "Go ahead and make this thing as beautiful as you can make it"—it was the people of the country who insisted that if he wanted ten years, he should have ten years—and he should make of this thing something that really was the expression of a "love"—a piece of work that was done because he loved to do it.

That is something I hope someday we shall see over here, and that is what this Federation is fostering, I know. I hope that in every community throughout this country, that spirit can be fostered which makes a piece of work worthwhile because you love to do it, regardless of the time you put into it, and because it is worth everything that you can put into it to give to the world a really perfect thing. All that I can do tonight is to wish you all great success in the work that you are doing, and hope that those of us who are only learning and who need much teaching, will sometime be able to help you. Thank you.   ☐

6.   "In Defense of Curiosity"

The Saturday Evening Post, August 24, 1935

A short time ago a cartoon appeared depicting two miners looking up in surprise and saying with undisguised horror, "Here comes Mrs. Roosevelt!"

In strange and subtle ways, it was indicated to me that I should feel somewhat ashamed of that cartoon, and there certainly was something the matter with a woman who wanted to see so much and to know so much.

Somehow or other, most of the people who spoke to me, or wrote to me about it, seemed to feel that it was unbecoming in a woman to have a variety of interests. Perhaps that arose from the old inherent theory that woman's interests must lie only in her home. This is a kind of blindness which seems to make people feel that interest in the home stops within the four walls of the house in which you live. Few seem capable of realizing that the real reason that home is important is that it is so closely tied, by a million strings, to the rest of the world. That is what makes it an important factor in the life of every nation.

Whether we recognize it or not, no home is an isolated object. We may not recognize it, and we may try to narrow ourselves . . . to our immediate home circle, but if we have any understanding at all of what goes on around us, we soon see how outside influences affect our own existence. Take, for example, the money we have to spend. The economic conditions of the country affect our income whether it is earned or whether it is an income which comes to us from invested capital. What we are able to do in our home depends on the cost of the various things which we buy. All of us buy food, and food costs vary with conditions throughout the country and world.

It took us some time to realize that there was a relationship between the farm situation and the situation of the rest of our country, but eventually wage earners in the East did feel the results of the lack of buying power on the farms in the Middle West. To keep an even balance between the industrial worker and the agricultural worker is an extremely difficult thing. Every housewife in this country should realize that if she lives in a city and has a husband who is either a wage earner or the owner of an industry, her wages or her profits will be dependent, not only on the buying power of people like herself but upon the buying power of the great mass of agricultural people throughout the country. The farm housewife must realize, too, that her interests are tied up with those of the wage earner and his employer throughout the nation, for her husband's products can only find a ready market when the city dweller is prosperous.

There is ever present, of course, the economic question of how to keep balanced the cost of living and the wages the man receives. The theory of low wages and low living costs has been held by many economists to be sound, for they contend what money one has will provide as much as high wages do in countries where living costs are also high.

We have gone, as a rule, on the theory in this country, particularly in eras of prosperity, that high wages and high costs make for a higher standard of living, and that we really obtain more for our money, even though our prices are higher.

This question is argued back and forth, and the method by which one or the other theory shall be put into practice is an equally good field for arguments.

It may seem like an academic discussion, but any housewife should know that it is the first way in which her home brings her in touch with the public questions of the day.

The women of the country are discovering their deep concern as to the policies of government and of commercial agencies, largely because these policies are reflected in many ways in their daily lives. . . .

This correlation of interests is something that every woman would understand if she had the curiosity to find out the reason for certain conditions instead of merely accepting them, usually with rather bad grace.

To go a bit further afield, trouble with sheep in Australia may mean higher cost on winter coats, and a low standard of living in a foreign country may affect our own standards. The child whom we cherish within our home may suffer from health conditions quite beyond our control, but well within the control of the community or state. Having grown to manhood, this same child may be taken away from us and die defending his country and its ideals. Unless we have seen our home as part of this great world, it will come to us as somewhat of a shock that the world crowds in upon us so closely and so much.

So many of us resent what we consider the waste of war, but if in each home there is no curiosity to follow the trend of affairs in various nations and our own conduct toward them, how can we expect to understand where our interests clash or to know whether our Government's policies are fair and just or generally selfish?

Out of the homes of our nation comes the public opinion which has to be back of every Government action. How can this public opinion be anything but a reaction to propaganda unless there is curiosity enough in each home to keep constant watch over local, state, national and international affairs?

Therefore, anyone who fully appreciates the value of home life must, of necessity, reach out in many directions in an effort to protect the home, which we know is our most valuable asset. Even the primitive civilizations reached out from the home to the boundaries of their knowledge, and our own pioneer homes reached back into the countries from which they came and out into the new lands which they were discovering and subduing to their needs.

It is man's ceaseless urge to know more and to do more which makes the world move, and so, when people say woman's place is in the home, I say, with enthusiasm, it certainly is, but if she really cares about her home, that caring will take her far and wide.

People seem to think that having many interests or activities must mean restlessness of spirit which can only indicate dissatisfaction and superficiality in an individual. It may be that an interest in the home may lead one to dissatisfaction with certain phases of civilization, but the fact that one is active or busy does not necessarily mean that one is either restless or superficial. Some of the people who are the most occupied remain unhurried in what they do, and have the ability to relax and rest so completely in the time which is free, that they are less weary and give less appearance of hurry than many who fritter away hours of the day in unpurposeful activity.

Repose and a feeling of peace is an absolute necessity to a home. . . . Repose is not a question of sitting still. It is a kind of spiritual attitude; no superficial human being can have it; real repose requires depth, a rich personality. The person possessing it can create a feeling that life flows smoothly and peacefully. Though they may never sit with folded hands, you may be able to sit with them and experience complete relaxation. It is something that comes from the soul, and no home gives complete satisfaction unless the persons making it can create this atmosphere. Repose, however, does not mean stagnation. . . .

It is perfectly obvious, of course, that intellectual curiosity, which makes you read history and science, will add greatly to your knowledge. Artistic curiosity will open up innumerable new fields in painting and sculpture and music and drama. If you have an opportunity to travel, you can add enormously to what you have already read in books or what you have experienced in art, by seeing with your own eyes some of the artistic masterpieces of the world in architecture and sculpture and in painting, by hearing great musicians and artists perform in their own countries.

You may even reconstruct for yourself, by seeing old cities and old country sides, civilizations that have gone before us. . . .

A great soul may go down to the depths, but he can also soar to the heights, . . . [and have] the power of rising to heights above the average mind. These things, however, will hardly be understood if, in addition to intellectual curiosity, you do not have what we will call emotional curiosity, because without that, these things will not become alive to us or speak of the human element which has gone into all of them, and which alone makes them speak to us from generation to generation in a language which we can understand. . . .

Young people say to me sometimes, "I have tried so hard to talk to So-and-So," and I know at once that they have not, as yet, discovered curiosity. Curiosity will make you take such an interest in finding out what So-and-So has to offer as a human being that you will soon find conversation flowing easily. Curiosity will prevent your being closed behind a barrier, and will add, day by day, to your imagination and make your contacts increasingly easy. . . .

For instance, I was traveling on a train once, and I noticed, across the aisle, a woman in tears. Our eyes met, and she came over to sit beside me. I soon found myself listening as the whole pitiful drama of her life unfolded before me. Her husband had been in the Army, but had left it when they married, and they had gone back on the vaudeville stage, where they had worked before. Two children had come to them, whom her mother cared for. As vaudeville actors do, they traveled from place to place, winter and summer, sometimes making fairly good money, sometimes having pretty lean years, always spending everything they had, but, on the whole, it was a gay life, and a happy one, for they loved each other. Then the dread disease of tuberculosis took hold of the man, and the Government took him back and gave him care in a Western hospital. She had to go on the road alone, to feed and house her mother and the children, and give her husband the little extras which meant so much to him. Now and then she would manage to get to see him. Six months before, they had a happy day together, and then came the telegram telling her that he was desperately ill, and, taking all she had, she went, only to see him die and to bring his body home. She was a realist and did not dramatize her situation, so tears were few, and even in her sorrow there was a certain gaiety, for she said, "We had good times, and I hope the children will have them too. Now I must be getting back to work."

Without curiosity, I would never have heard that story and I would have missed the lift which you get when you meet with courage that faces heartache and a future of hard work and anxiety and still can be gay, for this will mean much to you when your own road is rough, as it is sooner or later for every traveler in this most interesting world.

In its simplest form, curiosity will help you to an all-around education. That is why little children are so often living question marks. They naturally desire to know about the world in which they live, and if they lose that curiosity, it is usually because we grown people are so stupid.

. . . . It is quite easy to see a great many things and yet to be so lacking in curiosity and in understanding that one does not know what they mean.

I went to a play once, and in a part which was really tragic, the audience laughed. It was not the playwright's fault, nor yet the actor's, but what was shown upon the stage was so foreign and inexplicable to that particular audience that, instead of seeming tragic, it seemed funny. Laughter and tears are closely allied, but on this particular occasion, it was not nervous laughter, the laughter that verges on tears, but quite patently an inability to believe that a situation such as that play described could exist. On the whole, that particular audience had never been curious about that particular phase of life.

In addressing a fairly rich city audience, I tried to describe certain conditions of life in a distant part of our own country, and thinking if I chose something which all of them possessed, and which was entirely lacking in the homes of the families I was trying to picture, it would mean something to them. I said that until the depression had forced us to set up relief and to find some projects on which women could work, there were innumerable families throughout certain portions of the country that had never known what it was to sleep upon a mattress. I was met with blank faces, and before I said another word, I realized that my audience was thinking, "Well, what did they sleep on?" because it had never occurred to them that it was possible to sleep on anything but a mattress . . . [and] that anyone did [sleep] without a mattress was absolutely impossible for that audience to comprehend.

It is not always our own fault when we lack curiosity, for our environment may have prevented its development. The lack of curiosity in parents will often mean that they will try to eliminate it in their children, and thus keep their homes from stimulating the youthful urge to acquire knowledge.

A few years ago, when I was conducting a class in the study of city government, we took up one of the functions of the government—namely, public health. This is closely allied to housing, so I suggested that our group visit some of the different types of tenements. There was considerable concern among some of the mothers, for fear some illness might be contracted. It apparently never occurred to them that hundreds of young people lived in these tenements all the time, nor that, very likely, there entered into their sheltered homes daily people who served as delivery boys, servants, and workmen, who spent much of their time in tenements; so, even if the sheltered children did not visit them, the tenement home radiated out all that was good in it and all that was bad in it and touched the home on Park Avenue. No home is isolated, remember, so why should we not have a curiosity about all the homes that must in one way or another affect our own?

On visiting the various types of tenements, I found again that the lack of curiosity makes a poor background for real understanding. To these children of the rich, I had to explain what it meant to sleep in a room which had no window, what it meant to pant on fire escapes in hot July with people draped on fire escapes all around you, what it meant for a women with her husband and eight children to live in three rooms in a basement, and why a toilet with no outside ventilation could make a home unhealthy and malodorous.

Lack of curiosity in these young people meant lack of imagination and complete inability to visualize any life but their own, and, therefore, they could not recognize their responsibility to their less-fortunate brothers and sisters.

It is a far cry from Marie Antoinette playing at farm life in the Petite Trianon to our comfortable, sheltered young boys and girls, who have always had economic security and at least all the comforts and some of the luxuries of life, but, fundamentally, neither Marie Antoinette nor these children of ease knew real curiosity, so they rarely touched the realities of life. They knew only their own conditions, and they might as well have been blindfolded for all they saw as they walked their particular paths in life.

. . . . Perhaps you will tell me that you live in a small place where nothing ever happens, so you can have but few interests. This is not so.

The great experiences of life are the same wherever you live and whether you are rich or poor. Birth and death, courage and cowardice, kindness and cruelty, love and hate, are no respecters of persons, and they are the occasions and emotions which bring about most of the experiences of life. You cannot prevent unhappiness or sorrow entering into any life—even the fairy godmother of the legend could not give freedom from these experiences—but curiosity will insure an ever-recurring interest in life and will give you the needed impetus to turn your most baleful experience to some kind of good service. . . .

It is curiosity which makes scientists willing to risk their lives in finding some new method of alleviating human suffering, often using themselves as the best medium of experimentation. It is curiosity which makes people go down under the water to study the life on the floor of the ocean, or up into the air and out and over new and untried trails to find new ways of drawing this old world closer together.

I often wonder, as I look at the stars at night, if someday we will find a way to communicate and travel from one to the other. . . . Perhaps the day will come when our curiosity will not only carry us out of our homes and out of ourselves to a better understanding of material things, but will make us able to understand one another and to know what the Lord meant when He said, "He that hath ears to hear, let him hear." And we might well add: "He that hath eyes to see, let him see."   □

7.   "The Negro and Social Change"

A Speech before the National Urban League

Opportunity, January 1936

It is a pleasure to be with you tonight to celebrate this twenty-fifth anniversary of the Urban League, because of the purpose for which the League was founded—better understanding and cooperation of both the white and Negro races in order that they may live better together and make this country a better place to live in.

Much that I am going to say tonight would apply with equal force to any of us living in this country. But our particular concern tonight is with one of the largest race groups in the country—the Negro race.

We have a great responsibility here in the United States because we offer the best example that exists perhaps today throughout the world, of the fact that if different races know each other they may live peacefully together. On the whole, we in this country live peacefully together though we have many different races making up the citizenry of the United States. The fact that we have achieved as much as we have in understanding of each other is no reason for feeling that our situation and our relationship are so perfect that we need not concern ourselves about making them better. In fact we know that many grave injustices are done throughout our land to people who are citizens and who have an equal right under the laws of our country, but who are handicapped because of their race. I feel strongly that in order to wipe out these inequalities and injustices, we must all of us work together; but naturally those who suffer the injustices are most sensitive of them, and are therefore bearing the brunt of carrying through whatever plans are made to wipe out undesirable conditions.

Therefore in talking to you tonight, I would like to urge first of all that you concentrate your effort on obtaining better opportunities for education for the Negro people throughout the country. You *must* be able to understand the economic condition and the changes which are coming, not only in our own country, but throughout the world, and this, without better education than the great majority of Negro people have an *opportunity* to obtain today, is not possible. And without an improvement which will allow better work and better understanding, it will be difficult to remove the handicaps under which some of you suffer.

I marvel frequently at the patience with which those who work for the removal of bad conditions face their many disappointments. And I would like to pay tribute tonight to the many leaders amongst the colored people, whom I know and admire and respect. If they are apt at times to be discouraged and downhearted, I can only offer them as consolation, the knowledge that all of us who have worked in the past, and are still working for economic and social betterment, have been through and will continue to go through many periods of disappointment. But as we look back over the years, I have come to realize that what seemed to be slow and halting advances in the aggregate make quite a rapid march forward.

I believe, of course, that for our own good in this country, the Negro race as a whole must improve its standards of living, and become both economically and intellectually of higher calibre. The fact that the colored people, not only in the South, but in the North as well, have been economically at a low level has meant that they have also been physically and intellectually at a low level. Economic conditions are responsible for poor health in children. And the fact that tuberculosis and pneumonia and many other diseases have taken a heavier toll amongst our colored groups, can be attributed primarily to economic conditions. It is undoubtedly true that with an improvement in economic condition it will still be necessary not only to improve our educational conditions for children, but to pay special attention to adult education along the line of better living. For you cannot expect people to change overnight, when they have had poor conditions, and adjust themselves to all that we expect of people living as they *should* live today throughout our country.

This holds good for *all* underprivileged people in our country and in other countries. For instance, not long ago I was talking to a woman from England, a social worker, who told me that she had found it was not sufficient to give people better housing, to give them better wages; that you also had to have some leadership and education in how to live in those houses and how to use the better wages. And I have seen that proved in the last few years in some of the mining sections of our country. The stock is good American stock, but they have had long years of hard times, and some of the communities that I happen to know have been given good houses and a little economic security, but no leadership. And another community that I know has had both education from nursery school up, and leadership, and adult education. And someone said to me the other day in comparing a number of communities, that the particular community where this leadership has been given was Paradise compared to all the others.

So that I think I am right when I say that it is not just enough to give people who have suffered a better house and better wages. You must give them education and understanding and training before you can expect them to take up their full responsibility.

I think that we realize the desirability today of many social changes; but we also must realize that in making these changes and bridging the gap between the old life and the new, we have to accept the responsibility and assume the necessary burden of giving assistance to the people who have not had their fair opportunity in the past.

One thing I want to speak about tonight because I have had a number of people tell me that they felt the Government in its new efforts and programs was not always fair to the Negro race. And I want to say quite often, it is not the intention of those at the top, and as far as possible I hope that we may work together to eliminate any real injustice.

No right-thinking person in this country today who picks up a paper and reads that in some part of the country the people have not been willing to wait for the due processes of law, but have gone back to the rule of force, blind and unjust as force and fear usually are, can help but be ashamed that we have shown such a lack of faith in our own institutions. It is a horrible thing which grows out of weakness and fear, and not out of strength and courage; and the sooner we as a nation unite to stamp out any such action, the sooner and the better will we be able to face the other nations of the world and to uphold our real ideals here and abroad.

We have long held in this country that ability should be the criterion on which all people are judged. It seems to me that we must come to recognize this criterion in dealing with all human beings, and not place any limitations upon their achievements except such as may be imposed by their own character and intelligence.

This is what we work for as an ideal for the relationship that must exist between all the citizens of our country. There is no reason why all of the races in this country should not live together each of them giving from their particular gift something to the other, and contributing an example to the world of "peace on earth, good will toward men."   □

8.   "Are We Overlooking the Pursuit of Happiness?"
Scribner's Magazine, March 1936

With a committee actually appointed in Congress to consider the efficiency and reorganization of the government's business in Washington, I suppose we may expect a careful survey of all the functions of the federal government departments, and a reclassification to bring into a better grouping such things as are related to each other.

With this in mind, it has long seemed to me that fathers and mothers in this country would be deeply interested in the creation of a department in the Federal Government which dealt directly with the problems touching most closely the homes and the children of the nation.

All government departments touch our homes and our general welfare in one way or another, but certain things very obviously touch more closely than others the daily life of the home. Health, for instance. The Public Health Service does much to cooperate with the various state departments of health and now through the new Social Security Act, we shall be able to do much more than ever before for our handicapped and crippled children, our blind children and for dependent children either living at home with a widowed or deserted mother, or orphaned and living in foster homes or in institutions.

All social welfare measures touch the home very closely. Take the question of old age pensions. This has direct bearing on the employment of youth, for if we take out of the labor market the older people there naturally will be more opportunity for the young. Added to that, many and many a home where young people love their parents has become embittered by the fact that so much had to be given up in order to take care of the old people. I remember a story my mother-in-law used to tell me of an old Scotch farmer who remarked to her that one father and mother could take care of any number of children, but any number of children never could take care of one old father and mother!

It is all very well to think that young people are selfish. I have seen them struggle many a time to do what they felt was right for parents, and as their children grew up they wanted to give them opportunities for education or recreation or even provide them with proper food for building healthy bodies for the future, and the drag of the responsibility for the older people became almost more than human nature could stand.

For the old people who have lived so long a life of independence, how bitter it must be to come for everything they need to the youngsters who once turned to them!

From every point of view, it seems to me that the old age pension for people who so obviously could not lay aside enough during their working years to live on adequately through their old age is a national responsibility and one that must be faced when we are planning for a better future.

Unemployment insurance in many homes is all that stands between many a family and starvation. Given a breathing spell, a man or woman may be able to get another job or to re-educate himself in some new line of work, but few people live with such a wide margin that they have enough laid aside to face several months of idleness.

Next comes education and we are certainly coming to realize that education is of vital importance. Many of us who have completely accepted the idea that our system of education is perfect in this country have made a mistake in not realizing that nothing in the world is ever perfect and that we should watch and constantly study public education to make it more responsive to the needs of our day.

We must equalize educational opportunities throughout the country. We must see that rural children have as good a general education as city children can acquire, and the advantages of both groups must if possible be made interchangeable. No city child should grow up without knowing the beauty of spring in the country or where milk comes from, how vegetables grow and what it is like to play in a field instead of on a city street. No country child who knows these things should be deprived, however, of museums, books, music and better teachers because it is easier to find them and to pay for them in big cities than it is in rural districts.

With more leisure time, we are discovering that the arts are a necessity in our lives, not only as a method of self-expression, but because of the need for enjoyment and occupation which requires appreciation of many things which we could never hope to understand when we toiled from dawn till dark and had no time for any aspirations.

The arts are no longer a luxury but a necessity to the average human being and they should be included in any department which includes health, social security and education. It seems to me also that crafts and recreation should come under this department.

All these things belong together, they deal with the daily lives of the people.

We are entering a period when there are vast possibilities for the creation of a new way of living. It only requires sufficient imagination and sufficient actual knowledge on the part of all those who are considering this reorganization of government to bring into the government picture today one of the objectives laid down by our forefathers for government, but which seemed in the past too impossible of achievement to receive consideration.

The attainment of life and liberty required most of our energy in the past, so the pursuit of happiness and the consideration of the lives of human beings remained in the background. Now is the time to recognize the possibilities which lie before us in the taking up and developing of this part of our forefathers' vision. Therefore, I hope that the parents in this country will take enough interest in the new reorganization plans to realize that the interests of youth which lie close to their hearts can best be served by a federal department which will include such things as I have suggested and which touch primarily the homes and the youth of America.   □

9.   Married Persons Clause of the Economy Act

My Day, July 24, 1937

Hyde Park—I am particularly happy today that the Senate has followed in the steps of the House and sent the bill repealing the so-called married persons clause of the Economy Act to the President for his signature. The bill has worked a great deal of hardship among government employees. It was probably very necessary as an emergency economy measure, but it is very satisfactory to feel Congress considers the emergency to be at an end.

The other day I received an appeal from an organization which has as its purpose the removal of any married woman whose husband earns enough to support her, from all employment. Who is to say when a man earns enough to support his family? Who is to know, except the individuals themselves what they need for daily living or what responsibilities are hidden from the public eye?

There are few families indeed who do not have some members outside of their own immediate family who need assistance.

Added to this, who is to say whether a woman needs to work outside her own home for the food of her own soul? Many women can find all the work they need, all the joy they need and all the interest they need in life in their own homes and in the volunteer community activities of their environment. Because of this I have received many critical letters from women complaining that other women who did not need paid jobs were taking them. That they were working for luxuries and not for necessities, that men who had families to support were being kept out of jobs by these selfish and luxury-loving creatures.

I have investigated a good many cases and find that, on the whole, the love of work is not so great. Those who are gainfully employed are usually working because of some real need. There are a few, however, who work because something in them craves the particular kind of work which they are doing, or an inner urge drives them to work at a job. They are not entirely satisfied with work in the home.

This does not mean they are not good mothers and housekeepers. But they need some other stimulus in life. Frequently they provide work for other people. If they suddenly ceased their activities many other people might lose their jobs. As a rule, these women are the creative type.

It seems to me that the tradition of respect for work is so ingrained in this country that it is not surprising fathers have handed it down to their daughters as well as their sons. In the coming years, I wonder if we are not going to have more respect for women who work and give work to others than for women who sit at home with many idle hours on their hands or fill their time with occupations which many indirectly provide work for others but which give them none of the satisfaction of real personal achievement. □

10.   ## The Southern Conference on Human Welfare
Birmingham, Alabama, November 1938

Excerpts from ER's speech, November 22, 1938, as reprinted in
Report of the Proceedings of the Southern Conference on Human Welfare

We are the leading democracy of the world and as such must prove to the world that democracy is possible and capable of living up to the principles upon which it was founded. The eyes of the world are upon us, and often we find they are not too friendly eyes.

I very much hope we are going to study the real basis of democracy—universal education—so that every individual will be able to bear his responsibility fully.

We must be proud of every one of our citizens, for regardless of nationality, or race, every one contributes to the welfare and culture of the nation.

The future of democracy rests with the nation's youth. Face the question with open minds and above all make sure a thing is true before accepting it as true. On this alone we stake our hopes for democracy.

Correspondendence Regarding Above Event

Henry Grady Hotel, Atlanta
November 23, 1938

Dearest Hick:

Yesterday I had no time to breathe! I made a stop to walk over a proposed Negro playground. A half an hour on a panel on women's labor conditions, a lunch in which I had to argue at length with Governor Bibs Graves on the poll tax and the right of the Negro to vote. Then for two hours a youth panel, then two columns to write, and a visit from Lucy Mason and Josephine Wilkins (President of the Georgia League of Women Voters) and then dined at 6:15 with Mr. and Mrs. Donald Cower, speech in a packed auditorium and questions for over an hour—Dress, pack, and we fell on the train more dead than alive. The city invoked an old ordinance and required segregation at all meetings held in churches and it caused most vigorous protest. I felt very uncomfortable and some of the questions I longed to answer not as a visitor should!

Hickok's reply

November 28, 1938

Your Wednesday letter, written in Atlanta, was at the apartment last night. How did you finally get away with the trip to B'ham? Have they torn you limb from limb yet? ☐

Marian Anderson and the Daughters of the American Revolution

My Day, February 27, 1939

Washington—I am having a peaceful day. I drove my car a short distance out of the city this morning to pilot some friends of mine who are starting off for a vacation in Florida. I think this will be my only excursion out of the White House today, for I have plenty of work to do on an accumulation of mail, and I hope to get through in time to enjoy an evening of uninterrupted reading. I have been debating in my mind for some time, a question which I have had to debate with myself one or twice before in my life. Usually I have decided differently from the way in which I am deciding now. The question is, if you belong to an organization and disapprove of an action which is typical of policy, should you resign or is it better to work for a changed point of view within the organization? In the past, when I was able to work actively in any organization to which I belonged, I have usually stayed until I had at least made a fight and had been defeated.

Even then, I have, as a rule, accepted my defeat and decided I was wrong or, perhaps, a little too far ahead of the thinking of the majority at that time. I have often found that the thing in which I was interested was done some years later. But in this case, I belong to an organization in which I can do no active work. They have taken an action which has been widely talked of in the press. To remain as a member implies approval of that action, and therefore I am resigning. . . . □

12. The Federal Theater Project

My Day, June 20, 1939

Hyde Park—After my ride, I sat in the sun and read the newspapers, completely forgetting I had an appointment with Mrs. Hallie Flanagan at noon. She appeared on time, however, and I confess that I am just as concerned as she is about the proposed ending of the Federal Theatre Projects. There seems to be nothing I can do to help. Apparently the House of Representatives has decided that it doesn't matter what happens to people who have definite talents of a particular kind. Only 5 percent of people on the Federal Theatre Project are non-relief, so apparently the 95 percent can starve, go on local relief, or dig ditches, if they can find ditches to dig.

I know that this project is considered dangerous because it may harbor some Communists, but I wonder if Communists occupied in producing plays are not safer than Communists starving to death. I have always felt that whatever your beliefs might be, if you could earn enough to keep body and soul together and had to be pretty busy doing that, you would not be very apt to have time to plot the overthrow of any existing government.

However, the wisdom of Congress must never be questioned and I can only hope that in the Senate some changes may be deemed wise. If this is an era, as some people think, of civilization, then this project may serve as an instrument to that end. . . .   □

13.   ## Women, Politics, and Policy

My Day, June 16, 1939

New York—There was one item in the paper yesterday which extremely interested me. It appears that Governor Herbert Lehman signed a bill introduced in the New York State Legislature this past term by Assemblyman Jane H. Todd, a Republican, which makes it permissible to have equal representation of the sexes on all political committees.

This representation, so far as the Democratic party in New York State is concerned, has been acknowledged and considered advisable for a number of years. It is quite true that there have been cases where, on county committees and on other positions, certain gentlemen have objected to giving women equal representation and, therefore, in such places there have been few if any women active in the party. Since this bill is not mandatory, however, I cannot see how it really changes the present situation a great deal.

I feel quite sure that in the case of coveted positions at state conventions there will be considerable objection if any group of women attempt to obtain fifty-fifty representation! However, I suppose that having a permissive law, rather than party rule, is a step forward for the women, and I congratulate Miss Todd and the Governor on achieving this.

A number of people have written me in opposition to my stand that married women should be allowed the privilege of working. They plead with me to consider how cruel it is that these married women, with husbands well able to support them, should be taking jobs away from young people. They insist that most of these married women are simply doubling good incomes and acquiring luxuries for themselves. They think they are taking the bread out of the mouths of single women who are helping to support members of their families.

It sounds a bit hysterical, so let us consider the question calmly. Basically, is it wise to begin to lay down laws and regulations about any particular group? If we begin to say that married women cannot work, why shouldn't we say next that men with an income of more than a certain sum shall not work, or that young people whose parents are able to support them have no right to look for jobs? It seems to me that it is the basic right of any human being to work.

Many women, after marriage, find plenty of work in the home. They have no time, no inclination or no ability for any other kind of work. The records show that very few married women work from choice, that they are working only because a husband is ill or has deserted them, or there are special expenses caused by illness or educational requirements in the home. There may even be fathers, mothers, sisters or brothers to be supported. It seems to me that it is far more important for us to think about creating more jobs than it is for us to worry about how we are going to keep any groups from seeking work.   □

14.   WPA Wages

My Day, August 8, 1939

Hyde Park—I am reminded daily of the statements which I heard when WPA was cut off by Congress last spring: "If people have to, they will find jobs. It will be cheaper to support people on straight relief than on WPA. We have got to be practical about this situation and cease being sentimental about the unemployed. Business is ready to take up the slack, if it feels that Congress is not subservient to the President and it gets some laws they want."

Well, I wish the Congressmen who enacted the bill which is now being put into effect would answer some of the questions which come to me. Perhaps, you, in your various communities will get them to do so, now that they are at home.

A woman writes me: "I have a family of six. Our WPA pay has been $42.50 a month. We haven't saved anything on that, could you? Now, it is coming time to get the children ready for school and there is a new rule as to the hours we work a month and then we lay off thirty days. How do we live, Mrs. Roosevelt, and how can we get clothes so as to send the children to school?"

Here is another statement: "Many men laid off have only one or two days coming to them, not two weeks as so often stated, and they wait for that. Their regular paychecks are never large enough to cover all their living expenses. They cannot apply for home relief for thirty days and it may be four to six weeks before they get any help. As I write, another 'pink slip' has just come for a youngster who supports his invalid mother and his sister on less than $17 a week and who yesterday, a week before payday, had to borrow money to come to work. A finer worker I have never known, unusually bright, energetic and dependable, indispensable to the work he has been doing." How can the men who have enacted this legislation go home and face their wives and children, when they decreed starvation for other men's wives and children?

They have said they were legislating against communistic activities in the WPA. Such crass stupidity is beyond belief. They have made ten potential Communists for every one now existing and have increased by great numbers the members of the "radical" organizations they dislike.

"I am a veteran of the last war, my father, his father, and his father before him fought in the wars and I think that I am a loyal and true American, yet I am not sure that I wouldn't rather have a full stomach and shelter under some other regime than to be hungry and homeless under the present one."

This isn't an academic discussion, this is actually what happens to human beings. Mr. Legislators, what are your answers?   □

15.   ## "The Moral Basis of Democracy"
Howell, Soskin and Company 1940

. . . I am hoping in this little book to be able to give a clearer definition of the thinking of one citizen in a Democracy. By so doing it may be possible to stimulate the thoughts of many people so that they will force themselves to decide what Democracy means to them—whether they can believe in it as fervently as they can in their personal religion; whether it is worth a sacrifice to them, and what they consider that sacrifice must be.

4

What are our problems today?

I have reviewed the past and pointed out the association of a Christ-like life to the Democratic ideal of government, inaugurated to produce a Democratic way of life.

Now, let us look at our country as it is today and see if, from this examination, we can get a better understanding of some of our problems, and some of the decisions which we have got to make in the near future.

First of all we are a great nation of 130,000,000 people. We cover about three million, seven hundred thousand square miles, including our outlying dependencies such as the Philippines, Puerto Rico, the Virgin Islands, etc. Our people stem from every nation in the world. We include Orientals, Negroes, Europeans, Latin Americans. We are in truth the melting pot of the world. Our solidarity and unity can never be a geographical unity or a racial unity. It must be a unity growing out of a common idea and a devotion to that idea.

Our national income last year, 1939, was $69,378,000,000. It went down as low as $40,074,000,000 in 1932 in contrast with the peak in 1929, which was $82,885,000,000.

We are slowly climbing out of the economic morass we fell into, but so long as we have the number of unemployed on our hands which we have today, we can be sure that our economic troubles are not over and that we have not found the permanent solution to our problem.

There is going to be almost an entire continent of vast natural resources under the direction of an opposing philosophy to ours, and an opposing economic system. Either we must make our economic system work to the satisfaction of all of our people, or we are going to find it extremely difficult to compete against the one which will be set upon on the Continent of Europe.

We hear a good deal of loose talk about going to war. As a matter of fact we are already in a war—an economic war and a war of philosophies. We are opposing a force which, under the rule of one man, completely organizes all business and all individuals and takes no chances except with such uncontrollable phenomena as weather, fire, flood or earthquake. This one man in Europe has no limit on what he can spend for the things he desires to bring about. If he wants quantities of armament, he simply goes ahead and has quantities of armament. His nation has functioned on an internal currency. When he has need for things from outside, he has obtained them by barter of his manufactured goods or by simply taking the gold which he needed to buy goods from other nations, from those who happen to have it in his own country or from some other country that he decided to take over.

His people receive the wages *he* decrees, they work the hours *he* decrees, they wear the clothes *he* allows them to wear, they eat the food *he* allows them to have. They go away or do not go away for vacations according to his caprice, and they take no vacations outside of their own country without his permission, and even when a visit outside their own country is permitted, they can take only a specified sum of money with them.

An effort to set up similar conditions is quite evidently being made in Japan in the Far East. Our entire continent must be aroused to what it will mean if these ideas are successful. Our Democracies must realize that from the point of view of the individual and his liberty, there is no hope in the future if the totalitarian philosophy becomes dominant in the world.

Here, in this country, it seems to me that as the strongest nation in the battle today, we have to take an account of just what our condition is; how much Democracy we have and how much we want to have.

It is often said that we are free, and then sneeringly it is added: "free to starve if we wish." In some parts of our country that is not idle jest. Moreover, no one can honestly claim that either the Indians or the Negroes of this country are free. These are obvious examples of conditions which are not compatible with the theory of Democracy. We have poverty which enslaves, and racial prejudice which does the same. There are other racial and religious groups among us who labor under certain discriminations, not quite so difficult as those we impose on the Negroes and the Indians, but still sufficient to show we do not completely practice the Democratic way of life.

It is quite obvious that we do not practice a Christ-like way of living in our relationship to submerged people, and here again we see that a kind of religion which gives us a sense of obligation about living with a deeper interest in the welfare of our neighbors is an essential to the success of Democracy.

5

We are, of course, going through a type of revolution and we are succeeding in bringing about a greater sense of social responsibility in the people as a whole. Through the recognition by our government of a responsibility for social conditions much has been accomplished; but there is still much to be done before we are even prepared to accept some of the fundamental facts which will make it possible to fight as a unified nation against the new philosophies arrayed in opposition to Democracy.

It would seem clear that in a Democracy a minimum standard of security must at least be possible for every child in order to achieve the equality of opportunity which is one of the basic principles set forth as a fundamental of Democracy. This means achieving an economic level below which no one is permitted to fall, and keeping a fairly stable balance between that level and the cost of living. No one as yet seems to know just how to do this without an amount of planning which will be considered too restrictive for freedom. The line between domination and voluntary acquiescence in certain controls is a very difficult one to establish. Yet it is essential in a Democracy.

For a number of years we seemed to be progressing toward a condition in which war as a method of settling international difficulties might be eliminated, but with the rise of an opposing philosophy of force, this has become one of our main problems today. It brings before us the question of whether under the Democratic theory we can be efficient enough to meet the growing force of totalitarianism with its efficient organization for aggression.

This question is of special interest to youth, and added to the question of unemployment, it creates for them the main problem of existence.

The youth which is coming of age in our country today is living under a government which is attempting to meet a great many internal problems in new ways, and with methods never before tried. These ways are questioned by a great many people; but few people question the fact that the problems are with us and must be faced.

Youth seems to be more conscious than anyone else of the restrictions of opportunity which have come with our form of civilization. Some of these restrictions may be due to the development of the nation to a degree which leaves few physical frontiers to master; some of them may be due to a lack of social development, to a system which hasn't kept pace with the machine and made it possible to use advantageously more leisure time. Such malfunctioning makes it impossible to lessen the burden of labor without curtailing the volume of work, so that many people are left with nothing to do, and therefore without the wherewithal for living.

Nowhere in the world today has government solved these questions. Therefore, as their elders leave the stage, it remains for youth to find a way to face the domestic situation, to meet the conditions which confront their country in this relationship with the other countries of the world.

It is not enough to adopt the philosophies and methods which have appeared in other countries. These difficulties have been met elsewhere by deciding that one man who orders the lives of great numbers of people can best arrange for the equable distribution of the necessities of life. From the point of view of our Democratic philosophy and our belief in the welfare of the individual this has fatal drawbacks.

Youth must make a decision. It will have to decide whether religion, the spirit of social cooperation, is necessary to the development of a Democratic form of government and to the relationship which human beings must develop if they are to live happily together. If it is, youth will have to devise some means of bringing it more closely to the hearts and to the daily lives of everyone.

It is not entirely the fault of any of the churches, or of any of the various religious denominations that so many people, who call themselves Catholic, Protestant or Jew, behave as though religion were something shut up in one compartment of their lives. It seems to have no effect on their actions or their growth or on their relationship to their surroundings and activities.

Leaders of religious thought have tried for generations to make us understand that religion is a way of life which develops the spirit. Perhaps, because of the circumstances which face us today, the youth of this generation may make this type of religion a reality. I think they might thus develop for the future of this country and of the world a conception of success which will change our whole attitude toward life and civilization.

6

Youth wishes to do away with war. But youth and the men and women of Democracy will have to set their own house in order first, and show that they have something to offer under a Democratic form of government which is not offered by any other philosophy or any other theory of government.

It will be an exciting new world if it is created on these principles. It will not mean that great changes take place overnight, because people have been born for generations under conditions which it will take generations to change; but a new concept held by the youth of today as a basic meaning of Democracy, and its foundations in a religion, which shows itself in actual ways of life, will, I think, change the future generations.

We cannot expect, of course, that any development will go on without some setbacks, and we are at present in one of the most serious of retrogressions. If any of the young people of 1917 and 1918 could return to us today they would undoubtedly feel that the sacrifice of their lives had been valueless. Yet, I have a feeling that perhaps in the long run that sacrifice will be the one thing that will drive the young generation of today into doing something which will permanently change the future. They know that a gesture of self-sacrifice is not enough; that they cannot in one war change the basic things which have produced wars. They know that they must begin with human beings and keep on, each in his or her own particular sphere of influence, building up a social conscience and a sense of responsibility for their neighbors. They have begun to build bridges between the youth of their own nation and the youth of other nations. These bridges may be stronger because of the fiery trials so many young people are going through today. The value of human liberty may have a more tangible meaning to the next generation than it has in the present because for so many human beings it has temporarily disappeared.

The challenge of today is, I think, the greatest challenge that youth has faced in many generations. The future of Democracy in this country lies with them, and the future of Democracy in the world lies with them as well. The development of a dynamic Democracy which is alive and actively working for the benefit of all individuals, and not just a few, depends, I think, on the realization that this form of government is not a method devised to keep some particular group that is stronger than other groups in power. It is a method of government conceived for the development of human beings as a whole.

The citizens of a Democracy must model themselves on the best and most unselfish life we have known in history. They may not all believe in Christ's divinity, though many will; but His life is important simply because it becomes a shining beacon of what success means. If we once establish this human standard as a measure of success, the future of Democracy is secure.

7

The war-ridden, poverty-stricken world of today seems to be struggling essentially with problems of economics and its ills seem to be primarily materialistic. Yet, I believe that we do not begin to approach a solution of our problems until we acknowledge the fact that they are spiritual and that they necessitate a change in the attitude of human beings to one another.

War is the result of spiritual poverty. People say that war is the cause of a great many of our troubles; but in the first analysis it is the fact that human beings have not developed the ability to rise above purely selfish interest which brings about war. Then war intensifies all of our social problems and leaves us groping for the answers.

As we look at France today we realize that her plight is partly due to the fact that some of her people actually believed that the Communists were more of a menace than the Fascists. Both were an equal menace, for their hold on the people comes from the same sources—discontent and insecurity. The people who were comfortably off never looked below the surface in France to find out why the Communists could get such a hold on the imagination of people in a country which has supposedly so much liberty and equality.

Some people say salvation can come only through a form of selfish interest which brings about the realization by those who have their share of the good things of life, that nothing which they have in a material sense will be preserved unless they share it with those less fortunate; that some charitable way will be found to distribute more equably the things which the people as a whole lack. This would be a reaction to fear, of course, and it does not seem to me a final answer.

Somehow or other, human beings must get a feeling that there is in life a spring, a spring which flows for all humanity, perhaps like the old legendary spring from which men drew eternal youth. This spring must fortify the soul and give people a vital reason for wanting to meet the problems of the world today, and to meet them in a way which will make life more worth living for everyone. It must be a source of social inspiration and faith.

It is quite true, perhaps, that "Whom the Lord loveth, He chasteneth"; but nowhere is it said that individual human beings shall chasten each other, and it seems to me that all of us are sufficiently chastened by the things which are beyond our power to change. We can do nothing about death, or physical disabilities which science does not understand and cannot therefore remedy; nor can we help the maladjustments of various kinds which lie in the personality and not in the physical surroundings of the individual.

So the chastening will come to us all, rich and poor alike. But hunger and thirst, lack of decent shelter, lack of certain minimum decencies of life, can be eliminated if the spirit of good will is awakened in every human being.

8

I am not writing a political thesis, otherwise I might explain how we have been groping for a way during the past few years, to achieve some of these ends through government. In this little book, however, I am trying to go a little bit deeper and point out that court decisions, and laws and government administration, are only the results of the way people progress inwardly, and that the basis of success in a Democracy is really laid down by the people. It will progress only as their own personal development goes forward.

When I have occasionally said to people that perhaps some of us had too much of this world's goods, and that we are thereby separated too widely from each other and unable to understand the daily problems of people in more limited circumstances, I have often been met by the argument that these more privileged people are the ones who open up possibilities and new vistas for others. They are the people, I am told, who because of greater leisure have developed an appreciation of art; they build art galleries and museums, and give to other people an opportunity to enjoy them. They are the people who could envision the possibilities of scientific research, thereby building up great research laboratories where students make discoveries which increase our knowledge along so many lines. They are the people who create foundations which help the unfortunates of the world. All this is true, and we must be grateful for it, but perhaps it is time to take a new step in the progress of humanity.

I wonder if part of our education does not still lie before us and if we should not think of educating every individual to the need of making a contribution for these purposes which have been recognized only by a small group in the past as their contribution to society. The development of art, science, and literature for the benefit of our country as a whole is a concern of the whole country, not of a privileged few. I wonder if the support for these things should not come through an infinite number of small gifts rather than through a few great ones.

I recognize the fact that this development is slow and in some ways may be a question of years of evolution, particularly until we approach the better understanding of people of different races and different creeds. This country is perhaps the best example, however, of the fact that all people can learn to live side by side. We have here representatives of almost every nation and almost every religious belief.

There have been times when waves of bigotry and intolerance have swept over us. There is still a lack of true appreciation of the contributions made by some of these nations to the development of our culture, but the fact remains that, by and large, we live happily and understandingly together and gradually amalgamate until it is hard to distinguish what was once a separate nationality and what is today entirely a product of the United States of America.

This should give us courage to realize that there can be a real development of understanding among human beings, though it may take a great many years before there is sufficient change throughout the world to eliminate some of the dangers which we now face daily. There must be a beginning to all things and it seems to me the beginning for a better world understanding might well be made right here. Our natural resources are very great, and are still far from being fully developed. Our population is mixed and we are still young enough to be responsive to new ideas and to make changes fairly easily.

Some people feel that human nature cannot be changed, but I think when we look at what has been achieved by the Nazi and Fascist dictators we have to acknowledge the fact that we do not live in a static condition, but that the influences of education, of moral and physical training have an effect upon our whole beings. If human beings can be changed to fit a Nazi or Fascist pattern or a Communist pattern, certainly we should not lose heart at the thought of changing human nature to fit a Democratic way of life.

9

People say that the churches have lost their hold and that therein is found one of our greatest difficulties. Perhaps they have, but if that is true, it is because the churches have thought about the churches and not about religion as a need for men to live by. Each man may have his own religion; the church is merely the outward and visible symbol of the longing of the human soul for something to which he can aspire and which he desires beyond his own strength to achieve.

If human beings can be trained for cruelty and greed and a belief in power which comes through hate and fear and force, certainly we can train equally well for gentleness and mercy and the power of love which comes because of the strength of the good qualities to be found in the soul of every individual human being.

While force is abroad in the world we may have to use that weapon of force, but if we develop the fundamental beliefs and desires which make us considerate of the weak and truly anxious to see a Christ-like spirit on earth, we will have educated ourselves for Democracy in much the same way that others have gone about educating people for other purposes. We will have established something permanent because it has as its foundation a desire to sacrifice for the good of others, a trait which has survived in some human beings in one form or another since the world began.

We live under a Democracy, under a form of government which above all other forms should make us conscious of the need we all have for this spiritual, moral awakening. It is not something which must necessarily come through any one religious belief, or through people who go regularly to church and proclaim themselves as members of this or that denomination. We may belong to any denomination, we may be strict observers of certain church customs or we may be neglectful of forms, but the fundamental thing which we must all have is the spiritual force which the life of Christ exemplifies. We might well find it in the life of Buddha, but as long as it translates itself into something tangible in aspirations for ourselves and love for our neighbors, we should be content; for then we know that human nature is struggling toward an ideal.

Real Democracy cannot be stable and it cannot go forward to its fullest development and growth if this type of individual responsibility does not exist, not only in the leaders but in the people as a whole.

It is vitally important in the leaders because they are articulate. They should translate their aspirations and the means by which they wish to reach them, into clear words for other people to understand. In the past I think they have never dared to voice all their dreams, they have never dared to tell all the people their hopes because of the fear that the people would not be able to see the same vision. Unless there is understanding behind a leader, and a compelling desire on the part of the people to go on, he must fail.

This Democratic experiment of ours is in its infancy; in fact, real Democracy has never been realized, because it involves too much individual responsibility, and we have been slow to accept it.

Democracy does not imply, of course, that each and every individual shall achieve the same status in life, either materially or spiritually; that is not reasonable because we are limited by the gifts with which we enter this world. It does mean, however, that each individual should have the chance, because of the standards we have set, for good health, equal education and equal opportunity to achieve success according to his powers; and this opportunity should exist in whatever line of work, either of hand or head, he may choose to engage in. It also means that through self-government each individual should carry his full responsibility; otherwise the Democracy cannot be well balanced and represent the whole people.

I think that our estimate of success is going to change somewhat and that the man or woman who achieves a place in the community through service to the community will be considered a more successful individual than anyone who gains wealth or power which benefits himself alone. Changing the standards of success is going to mean more to the future of youth than anything else we can do, so perhaps this is the time for us to consider what is the future of youth.

10

There are two questions which young people in our country have to face.

What are we prepared to sacrifice in order to retain the Democratic form of government?

What do we gain if we retain this form of government?

Let us consider first the sacrifices that we make in a real Democracy. Our basic sacrifice is the privilege of thinking and working for ourselves alone. From time immemorial the attitude of the individual has been one of selfishness. As civilization has advanced people have thought of their families, and finally of a group of people like themselves; but down in our hearts it has always been the interest which you and I had in ourselves primarily which has motivated us.

If we are able to have genuine Democracy we are going to think primarily of the rights and privileges and the good that may come to the people of a great nation. This does not mean, of course, that we are going to find everyone in agreement with us in what we think is for the good of the majority of the people; but it does mean that we will be willing to submit our ideas to the test of what the majority wishes.

That is a big sacrifice for Democracy. It means that we no longer hold the fruits of our labors as our own, but consider them in the light of a trusteeship. Just as the labor itself must be put into avenues which may no longer be bringing us what at one time we considered as satisfactory returns, but which are serving some socially useful purpose in the community in which we live.

This does not mean that we will work any less hard. It does not mean that we will use less initiative or put less preparation into the field of work in which we are entering. It does mean, however, that we will execute to the best of our ability every piece of work which we undertake and give our efforts to such things as seem to us to serve the purposes of the greatest number of people.

The second sacrifice which we make for Democracy is to give to our government an interested and intelligent participation. For instance, if a city, town or county meeting is called, we will not find something more interesting or attractive to do that evening. We will go to the meeting, take part in it and try to understand what the questions and issues are. Thus we start the machinery of Democracy working from the lowest rung upward.

We often make the mistake of believing that what happens at the bottom makes no difference. As a matter of fact, it is what we do at the bottom which decides what eventually happens at the top. If all the way down the line every able-bodied citizen attended to his duties, went to the community meetings, tried to find out about the people who were going to hold office, knew the questions that came before them, there would be a radical change in the quality of people who take active part in political work.

We must have party machinery because there must be people who attend to such things as calling meetings, sending out notices, going from door to door to distribute literature or bring the issues to the voters before Election Day. These issues can be presented in many different ways, according to the understanding and the feeling of the people who present them. It would not be so difficult to find people to run for office if we knew that the citizens as a whole were going to know something about them and their ideas, and were going to vote not on a traditional basis, but according to their actual knowledge of the questions at stake and the personalities of the candidates. There would be less opportunity for calumny, for unfairness, and for the acceptance of untrue statements if, every step of the way, each individual took his responsibility seriously and actually did his job as a citizen in a Democracy.

There is no reward for this kind of citizenship except the reward of feeling that we really have a government which in every way represents the best thought of all the citizens involved. In such a Democracy a man will hold office not because it brings certain honors and considerations from his constituents, but because he has an obligation to perform a service to Democracy.

Perhaps the greatest sacrifice of all is the necessity which Democracy imposes on every individual to make himself decide in what he believes. If we believe in Democracy and that it is based on the possibility of a Christ-like way of life, then everybody must force himself to think through his own basic philosophy, his own willingness to live up to it and to help carry it out in everyday living.

The great majority of people accept religious dogmas handed to them by their parents without very much feeling of having a personal obligation to clarify their creed for themselves. But, if from our religion, whatever it may be, we are impelled to work out a way of life which leads to the support of a Democratic form of government, then we have a problem we cannot escape: we must know what we believe in, how we intend to live, and what we are doing for our neighbors.

Our neighbors, of course, do not include only the people whom we know; they include, also, all those who live anywhere within the range of our knowledge. That means an obligation to the coal miners and sharecroppers, the migratory workers, to the tenement-house dwellers and the farmers who cannot make a living. It opens endless vistas of work to acquire knowledge and, when we have acquired it in our own country, there is still the rest of the world to study before we know what our course of action should be.

Again a sacrifice in time and thought, but a factor in a truly Democratic way of life.

Few members of the older generations have even attempted to make themselves the kind of people who are really worthy of the power which is vested in the individual in a Democracy. We must fulfill our duties as citizens, see that our nation is truly represented by its government, see that the government is responsive to the will and desires of the people. We must make that will and desire of the people the result of adequate education and adequate material security. We must maintain a standard of living which makes it possible for the people really to want justice for all, rather than to harbor a secret hope for privileges because they cannot hope for justice.

If we accomplish this, we have paved the way for the first hope for real peace the world has ever known. All people desire peace, but they are led to war because what is offered them in this world seems to be unjust, and they are constantly seeking a way to right that injustice.

These are the sacrifices future generations will be called upon to make for a permanent Democracy which has a background of spiritual belief.

II

And now, what do we gain from Democracy?

The greatest gain, perhaps, is a sense of brotherhood, a sense that we strive together toward a common objective.

I have sat with groups of people who for a few short minutes were united by the ideas and aspirations that had been presented to them by leaders able to express their vision or their dreams.

Those few minutes have made clear to me the possibility of strength that someday might lie in a moral feeling of unity brought about by a true sense of brotherhood.

By achieving improvement in our own small sphere, we would gain, too, a tremendous satisfaction in realizing that we were actively participating in whatever happens in the world as a whole. The decisions at the top would be ours, because, in the first place, we had started choosing our men at the bottom and had thus brought about a real representation at the top. The new world which we conceived could become a reality, for these men, the leaders, would share the vision of the people.

It would be no Utopia, for the gains made by Democracy, which are the gains made by human beings over themselves, are never static. We fight for them and have to keep on fighting. The gains are slow and won in day by day effort. There is no chance for boredom or indifference because of a lack of further heights to climb. In such a society the heights are always before one, and the dread of slipping backward ever present.

One of the gains of Democracy would be that constant sense of vigilance and alertness which makes of life an adventure and gives it a continuous appeal. We cannot remove sorrow and disappointment from the lives of human beings, but we can give them an opportunity to free themselves from mass restrictions made by man.

There is nothing more exciting in the world than to be conscious of inwardly achieving something new; and anyone who puts into practice the life of Christ on earth, cannot fail to feel the growth in his own mastery over self. Under the Democracy based on such a religious impulse, there would still, of course, be leaders, and there would still be people of initiative interested and prodding other people to attempt the development of new ideas, or to participate in new enjoyments which they had not before understood or experienced.

Under such a Democracy the living standard of all the people would be gradually rising. That is what the youth of the next generation will be primarily interested in achieving, because that is the vital gain in Democracy for the future, if we base it on the Christian way of life as lived by the Christ.   □

16.   "Women in Politics"

Good Housekeeping, January, March, April 1940

We are about to have a collective coming of age! The women in the United States have been participants in government for nearly twenty years. I think it behooves us to look back on this period in which we have been serving our apprenticeship and decide what our accomplishments have been, how much good our education has done us, and whether we really are able to consider ourselves full-fledged citizens. . . .

Twenty years ago, when we were granted the right of suffrage, some people thought that women were going to revolutionize the conduct of government. Yet all we were given was the right to vote. Men had had the vote on a fairly universal basis ever since the country was established—without achieving Utopia. Everyone knew that corruption still existed, and that the gentlemen did not always devote themselves to their civic duties in the unselfish and ardent manner that might be expected in a democracy. In 1919, however, this fact did not seem to prevent the belief that all desirable reforms would come about by the granting of suffrage to women. Alas and alack, the reforms just did not happen!

Perhaps it would be as well to mention also that some of the dire results prophesied if women were given the vote haven't come about, either.

Let us see what women have actually done in public life thus far.

It is fair, I think, to speak first of some of the women who were leaders in the fight for suffrage because of their influence on the thought of the men and women of the period, even though they may not actually have held public office. By studying them, I think we can get a very good idea of the qualities women must bring to public life.[1] . . .

Available facts about women who have actually occupied political office during the past twenty years are incomplete, and it is extremely difficult to get accurate information. . . .

---

[1] Anna Howard Shaw, Carrie Chapman Catt, Inez Millholland.

There are certain trends, however, that even incomplete figures seem to show. In the past ten years fewer women have been elected to Congress and to state legislatures. The peak was reached in 1929, when thirty-eight states could boast of 149 women in state legislatures. In 1939 there were only twenty-eight states having women representatives, and the total was only 129 women.

However, the change is so very slight that I think we may consider it a temporary fluctuation, indicating nothing more than that women haven't yet gained real confidence in themselves in that type of competition. Besides, as we shall see, the number of women in appointive positions is steadily increasing.

In the United States Senate, Gladys Pyle, Republican of South Dakota, was elected in November 1938 for an unexpired term, which ended January 3, 1939. And three other women Senators were appointed to finish out unexpired terms and then retired. Mrs. Hattie Caraway, Democrat of Arkansas, is the one woman who has really served as a United States Senator. She was first appointed to succeed her husband in 1931, and then elected in 1932 and reelected in 1938. She has, I think, gained confidence in her ability and is respected by men in political life. At first one heard that she was under this or that influence; that she was a rubber stamp; that she did little thinking for herself; but of late one hears a great deal more about her being a useful member of the Senate and having a mind of her own. There is no doubt that she has grown and that her record can bear comparison with that of any of her colleagues.

In the House of Representatives, we have had twenty-one women members. Jeannette Rankin served before the adoption of the federal suffrage amendment. Her state of Montana had passed a suffrage act of its own. She will always be remembered for her inability to vote for war. One of the dramatic incidents reported in the newspapers of the day was how she burst into tears and refused to cast her vote in favor of war. I was not present, but I have always had a certain sympathy with the gesture even though it was futile.

Of these twenty-one members, eleven have been Republicans and ten Democrats. In the short session of the 71st Congress, nine women's names were carried on the rolls of the House of Representatives. This is the largest number carried at any one time. Since then the number has been steadily decreasing, till today there are only four women members of the House: Mary Norton of New Jersey, Caroline O'Day of New York, Edith Nourse Rogers of Massachusetts, and Jessie Sumner of Illinois. Three of these women I know well; all are good, hardworking members and on a par with the men who have served with them.

I always think of Mary Norton as being primarily interested in welfare work, though she has grown far beyond those first interests. Caroline O'Day has fixed ideas on the subject of war, which nothing could change. . . . Edith Nourse

Rogers still has her interest in World War soldiers, and she still looks charming in her old Red Cross uniform.

I remember also Ruth Hanna McCormick Simms, who, as a member of the House of Representatives, did credit to a family that has often served the public. And Mrs. Florence Kahn of California was an able and witty member, who would be welcomed back by the House with open arms. The picture is much the same in state legislatures.

We have had only two women state governors, both Democrats—Mrs. Nellie Tayloe Ross of Wyoming and Mrs. Miriam A. Ferguson of Texas. I met Mrs. Ferguson once and then only for a few minutes; but it is generally conceded that her job was that of being her husband's mouthpiece. This is pardonable in private life, but extremely unwise in public life, where every individual should stand on his or her own feet. . . .

We will find on the rolls of both the elective and appointive officials, according to the laws of their respective states, a number of women as secretaries of state, state treasurers, state auditors—which looks as though women are better mathematicians than they are credited with being!

In the appointive positions, the trend shows an upward curve in both state and federal governments. This would seem to prove me correct in my surmise that women are not yet prepared to go out and stand up under the average political campaign. In addition men rarely are inclined to give them nominations for elective positions if there is a chance to elect a man; so, frequently, a woman is beaten for an elective office before she starts to run.

In the old days men always said that politics was too rough-and-tumble a business for women; but that idea is gradually wearing away. There is more truth in the statement that men have a different attitude toward politics than women. They play politics a little more like a game. With the men, it becomes a serious occupation for a few weeks before election; whereas women look upon it as a serious matter year in and year out. It is associated with their patriotism and their duty to their country.

There are moments when I think that women's fervor to work continuously does not make them very popular with the gentlemen! . . . [2]

In 1933 about thirty-five women came into important positions in Washington, and in the last six or seven years there has been an increase in the number

[2] ER praised Mabel Walker Willebrandt and Dr. Mary Harris's efforts to reform women's prisons; Dr. Louise Stanley's leadership in the Department of Home Economics; Mary Anderson's tenure as head of the Women's Bureau in the Department of Labor; Katharine Lenroot and Grace Abbott's management of the Children's Bureau in the Department of Labor.

of women appointed to more important offices. Strange as it may seem, I think this is due to the work of a woman who never held any office, except that of Vice-Chairman of the Democratic National Committee in charge of the Women's Division—Miss Molly Dewson.

Miss Dewson was interested in politics because of what she thought women could achieve through political organizations. She began her career in Boston, at the age of twenty-three, as a supervisor of the Girls' Parole Department of Massachusetts. She made her contact with state legislatures while she worked for the Consumers' League. She came into partisan political work during a national campaign. When that was over, she stayed on in the National Democratic Committee, and I think virtually all the men, from the President and Postmaster General Farley to most of the other heads of Departments, will concede that there has rarely been a woman more active in getting women into political positions! She was almost uncomfortably honest, at times somewhat brusque; but she had a sense of humor and a loyalty and devotion that made many people admire her and grieve when she was transferred from political work to the Social Security Board and when, finally, because of illness, she had to retire from active work.

Many women in Washington today hold positions because of ability and preparation that has little or no connection with political work. They have been distinguished along some special line, and frequently they came in long before the present administration. But those who came in during this administration owe a great deal to Molly Dewson, and women as a whole should be grateful for the fact that she never backed a woman whom she did not think capable of holding the job she was trying to get. The record of women in office during the past few years shows that her judgment was, on the whole, good.

We have, for instance, the first woman member of a President's Cabinet—the Secretary of Labor, Miss Frances Perkins. Most of us find it difficult to recall the names of former Secretaries of Labor. I happen to remember one or two; but I find, when I ask my friends about them, that the only Secretary of Labor whom they know much about is Frances Perkins, the present incumbent. They do not always sing her praises; but they do know that she exists—first, because she had a career before she held her present office; next, because she has held an extremely difficult position in a most trying period and, on the whole, has acquitted herself well. She has never really learned to handle the press, so her newspaper contacts are bad. This is partly because she is suspicious of reporters, and those around her, trying to protect her, accentuate this suspicion. I cannot say that this attitude is never justified; but with her keen intuition and her wide experience and contact with human nature, she should be able to distinguish between the fine and trustworthy correspondents and those who cannot be trusted. Newspaper correspondents are no different from other human be-ings—they are good and bad. Years ago Louis Howe told me that no group of people has a higher standard of ethics, and I still believe that to be true . . .[3]

In the Labor Department we find Miss Mary La Dame, special assistant to the Secretary of Labor. Everyone knows the name of Mrs. Lucille Foster McMillin, on the Civil Service Commission. She, like Mrs. Ellen Woodward, formerly head of the women's and professional projects under the Works Progress Administra-tion, and now on the Social Security Board, would impress you first as a very feminine woman with charm and social distinction; but both of them know how to be good executives and work hard. They may carry their sympathetic under-standing of human problems with them in their working hours, but they also carry level heads and a keen intelligence, which makes them acceptable mem-bers of any men's conference. . . .[4]

In 1939 there were approximately fifty-five women in major positions throughout the federal government. The number of women in clerical, fiscal, and professional positions has grown to 162,518. . . .

Two other women, while not actually holding public office, have done so much to affect the thinking of both men and women on political questions that I feel they should not be forgotten. One is Anne O'Hare McCormick, who was chosen last year as the woman of distinction for 1939. She has established a record in her interviews with important people who make world policies today. Her fairness, her ability to understand varying points of view and to report the essence of a conversation have won her distinction and a following among think-ing people everywhere. Her analysis and presentation of world situations has helped clarify many difficult and universally interesting points.

The other woman is Dorothy Thompson, also a political writer of distinction, swayed perhaps by her own emotions, personal interests, and past experience, but still with such a gift of expression that she has a great following.

All these women are blazing trails for women in the future, and by the suc-

[3] Only two women served in the diplomatic corps (Ruth Bryan Pohde, Minister to Denmark and Mrs. J. Borden Harriman, Minister to Norway) and in the federal judiciary (Florence Allen on the Ohio Supreme Court and Genevieve R. Cline on the U.S. Customs Court in New York City).
[4] ER praised the work of Katherine Blackburn (Bureau of Press Intelligence), Jo Coffin (Printing Office), Rose Schneiderman (Advisory Committee of the National Recovery Administration and Secretary to the Commissioner of Labor for New York State), Marian Bannister (Office of the Treasurer), Jewell W. Swofford (United States Employment Compensation Commission), Laura S. Brown and Lucy Howorth (Veterans Administration), Marion J. Harron (Board of Tax Ap-peals), and Florence Kerr (WPA).

cess or failure of their work they will either increase the possibility of women's participation in government or make the public less anxious to place women in positions of responsibility.

To me it seems that those who have borne the brunt of the fight thus far are rather shining examples of what women can do in the political arena if they really work, and I think it will be interesting to watch not individual women, but the accomplishment of women as a whole in the field of public affairs.

Now . . . , I think it is only fair to deal with that perennial question: "What have women accomplished for human betterment with the vote?"

Of course, I never felt that there was any particular reason why we should expect miracles to occur as a result of giving women the right to vote. It was denied them for so long that men acquired great interest in public questions and women felt these questions were not their responsibility. Therefore, women for many years have been accustomed to centering their interests in the home or in allied activities. They have left the administration of government almost exclusively in the hands of men.

Changing the habits of thought of any group of people, men or women, is not a rapid process, so I am not in the least surprised, at the end of twenty-one years of suffrage, that the answer to: "What have women accomplished by their vote?" is frequently a shrug of the shoulders.

Women have used this suffrage . . . approximately as much as men have. There is a great percentage of people, eligible to vote, who do not vote on election day, and there is no proof that they are predominately either men or women. And, strange though it may seem, women apparently make up their minds on public questions in much the same way that men do.

I think it is fairly obvious that women have voted on most questions as individuals and not as a group, in much the same way that men do, and that they are influenced by their environment and their experience and background, just as men are. . . .

You will find . . . women divided in the same groupings that have divided men, and they approach any question before the electorate in much the same way. There are liberals and conservatives among the women as well as among the men. As far as I can judge, only one thing stands out—namely, that on the whole, during the last twenty years, government has been taking increasing cognizance of humanitarian questions, things that deal with the happiness of human beings, such as health, education, security. There is nothing, of course, to prove that this is entirely because of the women's interest, and yet I think it is significant that this change has come about during the period when women have been exercising their franchise. It makes me surmise that women who do take an interest in public questions have thrust these interests to the fore, and obliged their fellow citizens to consider them. Whereas in the past these human problems have remained more or less in the background, today they are discussed by every governing body.

No revolution has come about because women have been given the vote, and it is perfectly true that many women are not thrilled by their opportunity to take part in political-party work. They probably do not like it so well as the men do, for we do not find them competing for places on party committees or for actual recognition in the political positions.

The women, however, are gradually increasing their activities. There are more women in civil-service positions and there are more women in rather inconspicuous, but important positions in city, state, and federal governments where technical knowledge is required.

When I went to Washington, I was so much impressed by the work they were doing that I started to have parties for women executives in various departments, and I discovered an astonishing number of women doing very important work, but getting comparatively little recognition because government is still a man's world.

As a result of all this, however, I find the influence of women emerging into a more important sphere. There was a time when no one asked: "What will the women think about this?" Now that question comes up often. It is true that we had more women in elective positions a few years ago; but I think the change is so slight that it is just a temporary fluctuation, and due to the fact that women haven't yet gained real confidence in themselves in that type of competition. Women are quite willing to compete in an examination that tests their knowledge even though there is still a prejudice against appointing them to certain positions because of their sex. To come out and fight a political campaign, however, is still difficult for most women. That is one reason why a woman who does hold an office, either elective or appointive, so often obtains it at her husband's death or as a result of his interests. She is continuing work she might never have taken up on her own initiative.

We have had, of course, a few failures among women who have taken office either because men have urged them to do so, or because they have followed in their husbands' footsteps. When a woman fails, it is much more serious than when a man fails, because the average person attributes the failure not to the individual, but to the fact that she is a woman. . . .

Their achievements certainly do not justify their having the suffrage; but then there are people who question whether men's achievements justify their having the suffrage. I think Mr. Hitler and Mr. Mussolini quite openly question this and are perhaps rather successfully curtailing the independence of both men and women, for the good of the human race and the state, so they say! We do not agree with that point of view; but the dictators have persuaded a good many people to accept it. I think we in this country feel that suffrage is not a question of achievement, but merely a right granted to individuals, and women, because they are individuals, have this right in exactly the same measure as men.

Let us acknowledge, too, the fact that women frequently try to stay out of fights which have to be made to get rid of corruption in politics. As far as I know, it was very largely a group of young men, perhaps assisted by a few women, who cleaned up the Kansas City, Missouri, situation and finally proved that the political-boss system under Mr. Pendergast—or anybody else, for that matter— rarely brought about an honestly run government. The same thing might be said about the Hines case in New York City. These political bosses, who used their political power for personal gain, were the result of a system. Probably Mr. Pendergast and Mr. Hines are kind and good in many ways according to their own lights. They happened to fall on times which were evil for them because the public conscience has changed as to what is right and wrong in positions of public responsibility. These men may feel that they were unjustly singled out, for many other men have done much the same things they have done, but the conscience of the public was not yet aroused against them. I fear, however, that we cannot claim that women have any greater part in this change than have men.

Looking for concrete achievements, I feel we can really credit to the women only one over this period of years, and that is the one already mentioned—the government's attitude of concern for the welfare of human beings. On the whole, more interest is now taken in social questions. The government is concerned about housing, about the care of citizens who temporarily are unable to take care of themselves, about the care of handicapped children, whether handicapped by poor homes or by straitened circumstances. This is a general change, which I attribute to the fact that men had to appeal for the vote of the women and have therefore taken a greater interest in subjects they feel may draw women to their support.

There are, of course, many men who have been conscious of the need for some changes; but a big majority of them have of late been moved to action in certain situations to which they had given little thought in the past. Women have become better educated, and women have taken more active part in helping to educate men connected with government to think in terms of human betterment. Therefore, I should say that, while one could claim no particular accomplishment, there has been a tremendous change in the outlook of government, which can be attributed to the fact that women have the ballot.

When people ask: "Have women in politics advanced temperance or other moral reforms?" I always point out that they have been as divided on moral questions as on political questions. They did not have the vote when the prohibition amendment was originally passed. The Women's Christian Temperance Union group undoubtedly worked for the passage of this amendment and against its repeal; but other groups of women were undoubtedly a factor in its ultimate repeal. Many of the best workers in the women's organizations for repeal worked because they felt a moral obligation to something greater than prohibition. They sensed the fact that we were developing a group of lawbreakers in this country, and, sad to say, many of the leaders of public thought were offenders in this respect. These leaders said that breaking a law was justified if you felt that a law did not represent the will of the majority. I always felt that anyone had a right to work to have the law changed, but that we should live up to it as long as it remained on the statute books. However, I think that my stand was distinctly a minority stand, and as far as women are concerned, they were divided on this as on many other moral questions.

What the future holds, none of us knows; but in this country we now hold that women have the same rights as men have. They do not have to justify their achievements as a group. I think we might legitimately ask whether as a democracy we have gone forward in the past twenty-one years, and take it for granted that if we have, it means that the majority of the women, as well as the majority of the men, have justified their right to suffrage.

Where are we going as women? Do we know where we are going? Do we know where we want to go?

I have a suggestion to make that will probably seem to you entirely paradoxical. Yet at the present juncture of civilization, it seems to me the only way for women to grow.

Women must become more conscious of themselves as women and of their ability to function as a group. At the same time they must try to wipe from men's consciousness the need to consider them as a group or as women in their everyday activities, especially as workers in industry or the professions.

Let us consider first what women can do united in a cause.

It is perfectly obvious that women are not all alike. They do not think alike, nor do they feel alike on many subjects. Therefore, you can no more unite all women on a great variety of subjects than you can unite all men.

If I am right that . . . women have caused a basic change in the attitude of government toward human beings, then there are certain fundamental things that mean more to the great majority of women than to the great majority of men. These things are undoubtedly tied up with women's biological functions.

The women bear the children, and love them even before they come into the world. . . .

This ability to be objective about children is one thing women have to fight to acquire; never, no matter what a child may do or how old he may be, is a woman quite divorced from the baby who once lay so helpless in her arms. This is the first fundamental truth for us to recognize, and we find it in greater or less degree in women who have never had a child. From it springs that concern about the home, the shelter for the children. And here is the great point of unity for the majority of women.

It is easy to make women realize that a force which threatens any home may threaten theirs. For that reason . . . as women realize what their political power might mean if they were united, they may decide now and then to unite on something which to them seems fundamental. It is quite possible, in the present state of world turmoil, that we may find women rising up to save civilization if they realize how great the menace is. I grant you that things will have to be pretty bad before they will do it, for most women are accustomed to managing men only in the minor details of life and to accepting the traditional yoke where the big things are concerned.

I have heard people say that the United States is a matriarchy—that the women rule. This is true only in nonessentials. Yes, the husbands spoil their wives; they let them travel and spend more money than foreign women do, but that is because money has come to us more easily in the past and therefore we have spent it more easily. The French woman who is her husband's business partner has more real hold on him than the American woman who travels abroad alone has on her husband. She buys all the clothes she wants without knowing whether her husband will be able to pay the bills, because she is completely shut out of the part of his life that holds most of his ambition and consumes the greater part of his time.

This country is no matriarchy, nor are we in any danger of being governed by women. I repeat here what I have so often said in answer to the question: "Can a women be President of the United States?" At present the answer is emphatically "No." It will be a long time before a woman will have any chance of nomination or election. As things stand today, even if an emotional wave swept a woman into this office, her election would be valueless, as she could never hold her following long enough to put over her program. It is hard enough for a man to do that, with all the traditional schooling men have had; for a woman, it would be impossible because of the age-old prejudice. In government, in business, and in the professions there may be a day when women will be looked upon as persons. We are, however, far from that day as yet.

But . . . if we women ever feel that something serious is threatening our homes and our children's lives, then we may awaken to the political and economic power that is ours. Not to work to elect a woman, but to work for a cause.

There may be a women's crusade against war, which will spread to other countries. I have a feeling that the women of the United States may lead this crusade, because the events of the last few months have left us the one great nation at peace in the world. Some of our South American neighbors have as much potential greatness as we have, but are not yet so far developed. We women may find ourselves in the forefront of a very great struggle some day. I think it will take the form of a determination to put an end to war for all time.

It is obvious that American women cannot do this alone; but throughout the world this might prove a unifying interest for women. When they get to the point of feeling that men's domination is ruining their homes then they will use whatever weapons lie at hand.

I think we in this country should be prepared for something of this kind. That is why I said that we must become more conscious of ourselves as women and of the force we might wield if we were ever to have a women's cause. . . .

The consideration of future possibilities for peace seem to me of paramount importance; but other things of worth enter into our present considerations. Great changes in our civilization have to be considered, and the women are going to weigh the effect of these changes on the home. I believe women can be educated to think about all homes and not so much about their own individual homes. If certain changes have to be made in industry, in our economic life, and in our relationship to one another, the women will probably be more ready to make them if they can see that the changes have a bearing on home life as a whole. That is the only thing that will ever make women come together as a political force.

Women should be able to weigh from this point of view all questions that arise in their local communities. They should vote with that in mind. But when it comes to standing for office or accepting administrative positions, they should realize that their particular interests are not the only ones that will come up, and that, while they may keep their personal interests, they must prove that as persons they can qualify in understanding and in evaluating the interests of the men, too.

Now let us consider women in the other phases of activity where they wish to be persons and wipe out the sex consideration.

Opposition to women who work is usually based on the theory that men have to support families. This, of course, is only saying something that sounds well, for we know that almost all working women are supporting someone besides themselves. And women themselves are partly to blame for the fact that equal pay for equal work has not become an actuality. They have accepted lower pay very often and taken advantage of it occasionally, too, as an excuse for not doing their share of their particular job.

If women want equal consideration, they must prepare themselves to adjust to other people and make no appeals on the ground of sex. Whether women take part in the business or in the political world, this is equally true.

A woman who cannot engage in an occupation and hold it because of her own ability had much better get out of that particular occupation, and do something else, where her ability will count. Otherwise, she is hanging on by her eyebrows, trying to exploit one person after another, and in the end she is going to be unsuccessful and drag down with her other women who are trying to do honest work.

In the business and professional world women have made great advances. In many fields there is opportunity for them to work with men on an equal footing. To be sure, sometimes prejudice on the score of sex will be unfair and a woman will have to prove her ability and do better work than a man to gain the same recognition. If you will look at the picture of Mrs. Bloomer, made a hundred years ago, and think of the women today in factories, offices, executive positions, and professions, that picture alone will symbolize for you the distance women have traveled in less than a century.

In the political field they haven't gone so far. This field has long been exclusively the prerogative of men; but women are on the march. I do not think that it would be possible or desirable to form them into a separate women's political unit. Too many questions arise in government which are not fundamentals that stir women as women. Women will belong to political parties; they will work in them and leave them in much the way that men have done. It will take some great cause that touches their particular interests to unite them as women politically, and they will not remain united once their cause is either won or lost.

I do not look, therefore, for a sudden awakening on their part to a desire for greater participation in the government of the nation, unless circumstances arise that arouse all the citizens of our democracy to a feeling of their individual responsibility for the preservation of this form of government. Otherwise, I think it will be a gradual growth, an evolution.

There is a tendency for women not to support other women when they are either elected or appointed to office. There is no reason, of course, why we should expect any woman to have the support of all women just because of her sex; but neither should women be prejudiced against women as such. We must learn to judge other women's work just as we would judge men's work, to evaluate it and to be sure that we understand and know the facts before we pass judgment.

Considering women as persons must begin with women themselves. They must guard against the temptation to be jealous. That little disparaging phrase one sometimes hears, which suggests that a woman has failed because she is a woman! A woman may fail; but women must begin to impress it upon everyone that a woman's failure to do a job cannot be attributed to her sex, but is due to certain incapacities that might as easily be found in a man. . . .

There is one place, however, where sex must be a cleavage in daily activity. Women run their homes as women. They live their social lives as women, and they have a right to call upon man's chivalry and to use their wiles to make men do the things that make life's contacts pleasanter in these two spheres. Sex is a weapon and one that women have a right to use, because this is a part of life in which men and women live as men and women and complement, but do not compete with each other. They are both needed in the world of business and politics to bring their different points of view and different methods of doing things to the service of civilization as individuals, with no consideration of sex involved; but in the home and in social life they must emphasize the difference between the sexes because it adds to the flavor of life together.

Some people feel that the entry of women into industry has brought about the fact that there are not enough jobs. But we don't need to eliminate workers, we need to create jobs. We certainly haven't reached a point of satiety when all around us we can see that work needs to be done. Let us, therefore, as women unite for great fundamental causes; but let us insist on doing the work of the world as individuals when we wish to be modern versions of Mrs. Bloomer, and let us function only as women in our homes. We need not feel humiliated if we elect to do only this, for this was our first field of activity, and it will always remain our most important one.

We must be careful, however, to remain in the home not as parasites, but because our abilities lie along the lines of domestic life. Remember that a home requires all the tact and all the executive ability required in any business. The farmer's wife, for instance, must get into her day more work than does the average businessman. Many a woman runs the family home on a slender pay envelope by planning her budget and doing her buying along lines that would make many a failing business succeed.

It will always take all kinds of women to make up a world, and only now and then will they unite their interests. When they do, I think it is safe to say that something historically important will happen. □

17.   ## "Insuring Democracy"

Collier's, June 15, 1940

I do not think that I am a natural-born mother. . . . I did have a sense of duty and of obligation and that was fostered in me by my mother and then by my grandmother. If I ever wanted to mother anyone, it was my father and not my baby brothers. That sense of obligation to smaller and weaker children remained with me through my school years and gained great impetus through my first year of teaching some classes of small girls in a New York City settlement house. There I saw with my own eyes some of the disadvantages of conditions brought about by economic insecurity.

I think I approached my own motherhood with a keen sense of responsibility but very little sense of the joy which should come with having babies. It was a long time before I gained enough confidence in my own judgment really to enjoy a child. . . .

I remember that it took all of my courage, and the fact that everybody else in the house had the flu, to trust myself to move the youngest of our five children into my own bedroom and take complete responsibility for him when he had an attack of bronchial pneumonia. I could get only one trained nurse and she had complete care of one of the other children who had double pneumonia. Practically everybody in the city and in the house was laid low, and so I had to rise to the occasion, otherwise I doubt if I would have felt like trusting myself to carrying that amount of responsibility without direction from others close at hand all the time!

But all children, it seems to me, have a right to food, shelter, and equal opportunity for education and an equal chance to come into the world healthy and get the care they need through their early years to keep them well and happy. And though one may not trust oneself to direct their lives, every mother should encourage them to self-confidence and should give them the feeling that whatever happens in life, there is a place where they can turn for understanding and help.

If you have this feeling about your own children, you should have it about all children, and for that reason I have always been interested in the problems of the children in our communities. Under the standards which we have set to guide us in the upbringing of our children, we used to be very individualistic, with, however, certain strongly marked influences such as those of the church, and group traditions in which we had grown up. For instance, in New England the customs of the Pilgrims shaped the child's education, just as later the Quakers had a great deal to do with the character and upbringing of the young Philadelphians.

Thirty years ago the President of the United States felt that we needed to bring together, to formulate standards for our guidance, the people who had some influence on the general thought of what should be done for the children of the nation. This became the first White House Conference on Children under President Theodore Roosevelt. Since then there have been three others—1919, 1930 and 1940.

As Miss Katharine Lenroot, of the Children's Bureau in the Department of Labor, says:

> The 1909 conference called by President Theodore Roosevelt stated a principle that is now recognized in all parts of the country: that the home is the place for children and that no child should be deprived of his home for reasons of poverty alone. The stimulus of this conference led to the creation of the Federal Children's Bureau in 1912, a national center of research to serve the growing child-welfare movement.
>
> The 1919 conference called under President Woodrow Wilson's auspices formulated a set of child-welfare standards that have guided and still guide the programs of public and private children's agencies and state and federal legislation affecting children.
>
> The 1930 White House Conference on Child Health and Protection called by President Herbert Hoover brought together an outstanding series of reports describing the content and character of care and protection needed for children and revealed the limited extent to which such services were available for many children. The findings on medical care raised to a new level the recognition of the care needed for the health of mothers and children in the United States. The committee reports on hazardous occupations for minors laid the groundwork for the later regulation of the employment of minors in hazardous occupations under the Fair Labor Standard Act of 1938. The discussion throughout the country of the Children's Charter and other conference recommendations helped to pave the way for the inclusion in the Social Security Act of 1935 of the federal-state programs for aid to dependent children, for maternal and child-health services, for services for crippled children and for child-welfare services, and for the subsequent development of these programs in our states and territories.

The standards set up in these conferences are very much the same standards that any able and intelligent parent will set for himself in contemplating the upbringing of his own family. First we consider the health program, which brings us to the question of maternity and infancy care. As a result of the conference in 1919, the Sheppard-Towner Act was passed in August, 1921. It brought before the people statistics on the shocking loss of mothers and of infants during the first year after birth. The right of children to normal family life received recognition, and today mothers' pensions keep families together even in the face of economic disaster through the loss of fathers or the impairment of their earning capacity. In turn, we came to consider education and recreation. Today we are considering the more difficult question of the right of youth to work, and last and most difficult of all, though most important, we are considering the moral values which our children must acquire if they are to feel a sense of responsibility for themselves and their neighbors, and so develop the type of democracy which they have inherited into a more perfect instrument of self-government.

Again in Miss Lenroot's words:

> The 1940 conference has counted the gains made for children even during the years of economic depression and has planned, for the coming ten years, that we seek to provide for children in every community in the United States the essential services and benefits for the preparation of responsible citizens of a democracy. The conference emphasized the fact that the family has the primary opportunity and responsibility for the care of children and for introducing them to the experiences that lead to a full personal life and to successful community life. The report recognized the economic and social factors that condition family and community life. It points out the gains that can be made for children through joint planning and effort on the part of individuals and groups in each community, through the leadership of state agencies, and through federal action that provides for nationwide programs.

The people who attended the conference and who listened to the President's speech can go back to their own communities, influence public opinion and demand:

1. Some kind of medical program.
2. That all our citizens take an active part in shaping the policies in the public schools; that all of us know our public-school teachers and give them any help and assistance that they desire.
3. That all of us take an interest in recreation programs designed not only to be of value to children in school, but to help our young people who are unfortunate enough not to find suitable jobs immediately.
4. That in every community we set up, in conjunction with the nearest employment service, an auxiliary to help young people to obtain the most suitable jobs.

This last year we have come to realize that instead of thinking only of what should be done for the mother in pregnancy and at the birth of her child, we should find out what economic situation forced the mother and child at these crucial moments to be a burden on the community. Instead of being concerned with obtaining proper diets for small children through charitable agencies, we should be concerned with the education of the average girl and boy so they will make the most of their dollars, to learn through practical experience how to make use of food in order to keep well.

If we relate the immediate problems of the child to the problems of the family as a whole, we will find ourselves concerned with housing, medical and dental care, education and recreation. We will be interested in wages and hours for labor, and we will try to figure out an adequate family income.

We are beginning to realize that what the family can do must be supplemented by what the community can do for its children. Population and income studies show that in many cases the ability of a community to supplement the family income and to contribute to a child's well-being is particularly low in the areas where we have the greatest number of children.

Where the local income falls short I think the state or even the nation should be called upon to make this equality of basic rights applicable to every child.

We are learning that rural slums may be quite as bad as city slums. We are learning that it is not because of the adult members of the family alone that we must do away with these slums. The children born and brought up in them are apt to be conditioned for the future by their earliest environment. What happens to our children is the concern of the whole nation because a democracy requires a standard of citizenship which no other form of government finds necessary. To be a citizen in a democracy a human being must be given a healthy start. He must have adequate food for physical growth and proper surroundings for mental and spiritual development. . . . We must learn to reason and to think for ourselves. We must make our decisions on the basis of knowledge and reasoning power. In a democracy we must be able to visualize the life of the whole nation. When we vote for candidates for public office to be our representatives, we must decide on the qualities to be required of the men and women who are to hold public offices.

These men will not only decide what shall be done for us in the present day, but they will be laying the foundations on which our children will have to build.

Poor schools in our communities today mean poor citizens in these communities in a few years—men and women ill-prepared to earn a living, or to participate in government. A three-months school year in certain communities certainly does not give a child the same advantage he would have with a nine-months school year in another community.

One minority group of American children that I feel deserves particular attention are about five million Negroes, Indians, Mexicans and Orientals under sixteen years of age. They have all the handicaps of other children with the addition of a number of special handicaps of their own. Their families are usually in the lowest income groups and the restrictions put upon the opportunities offered them for health, for education, for recreation and later for employment, are very great because of prejudice and lack of understanding or appreciation of their needs and capabilities. This conference should set the example and perhaps start our thinking in a new way—in America good standards apply to all children regardless of race or creed or color.

Child labor has frequently flourished in underprivileged groups. Child labor, of course, is a menace not only to other young people but to all workers. We have been handicapped by the fact that many people have thought that the regulation of child labor would mean interference in the home and prevention of ordinary home training in work habits. This, of course, is not child labor, and there is much child labor in this country which we should make every effort to control. We are concerned about the children before they are born, but we should follow them through every step of their development until the children are firmly on their feet and started in life as citizens of a democracy.

Our particular task in this conference has been to emphasize the fact that children in a democracy are all-important and that in leaving unsolved many economic and social problems, which touch the lives of children, we have jeopardized the future of democracy. We feel we are more advanced than many other nations in this respect, but after looking at some pictures of the health work in schools for German children I think we are not as intelligent in this field as the German people have been for years past. . . .

I have often heard people say they would rather have a democracy, even if it had to be inefficient, than regimented efficiency. We love our freedom, but must we of necessity have freedom coupled with stupidity? Is it not possible to face our situation and recognize the inequalities in the economic background of America's children, inequalities in educational opportunities, in health protection, in recreation and leisure-time activities and in opportunities for employment?

I began by telling you how inadequate I felt when I was bringing up my children. I feel the mistakes I made serve to give me a little more wisdom and understanding in helping people who are trying today to preserve our democracy. We cannot direct youth altogether but we can give courage to the next generation and stand back of them so that they will feel our protection and good will.   □

18.   "Helping Them to Help Themselves"

The Rotarian, April 1940

Some of us who have been going around America are impressed with the fact that one type of organization might possibly be a real help in carrying people through hard times without needing so much Government assistance. It requires, however, a consciousness on the part of the whole community that there are difficulties to be solved and a willingness to set its shoulders to the wheel and help to solve them. The particular activity I have in mind is the self-help cooperative. To many people that is just a name and means very little, but to some people it means the preservation of self-respect, the development of a new skill or the practice of an old one, and a chance to start out again with a background of security.

The first self-help cooperative that I remember hearing much about was the one established in Richmond, Virginia. The principle of the self-help cooperative is that anyone, old or young, if he has need to do so, may come in and work, and that his work hours will be exchanged for scrip which can, in turn, be exchanged for commodities and services performed by others, also members of the cooperative. In 1938 in the Richmond Citizen's Service Exchange, 211,300 hours were worked by the members. For this work, scrip was issued to the workers and they exchanged it for food, clothing, shoes, bedding, and fuel wood.

In some places even shelter may be provided in this way, and frequently beauty-parlor work and barbering are done. In order to do this, all these activities must be carried on in the exchange, which means, for instance, that if you have a man who is capable of being a baker, . . . the community must be conscious enough of the need to furnish the bake oven and the materials for bread. The baker, in return for his hours of labor, may want to buy a suit. Some other person who gets his bread in exchange will have spent his hours of labor in repairing, cleaning, and pressing a suit which somebody in the community has not needed and has therefore turned in to the self-help cooperative to be renovated for someone who does need it. You see, you cannot start a self-help cooperative with nothing.

The more things the people who come in are able to do, the more things you have to get from the community in order to enable them to go to work. . . . But in the end these people who work in the exchange do not suffer from the stigma of being unemployed and on relief.

Of course, on the Works Projects Administration (WPA) there should be no sense of stigma, because one gives work in return for what he gets, but I am sorry to say that in many places I have found deep resentment at the attitude of those who interview WPA workers. On the other side of the picture, there is a resentment on the part of many people toward the WPA worker which prevents him from getting a job on the outside, which he could frequently fill and would give a great deal to obtain.

In the self-help cooperative these feelings are not present. What is furnished by the community is usually material which would otherwise be wasted, and, except in the case of money granted by the Government or by some other source to pay for trained supervision or for certain definite expenses which cannot be eliminated, there is very little direct tax in the way of cash taken from the taxpayer.

The Richmond Citizens' Service Exchange served as a model for the establishment in Washington, D.C., of a self-help exchange. . . . In 1939 this exchange gave work to between 600 and 680 people a month. In 1939, 422,554 hours of work were provided. It is interesting to see the ways in which those workers spent the scrip earned: 181,524 pieces were spent for meals and bread; 103,553 pieces for clothing and such household supplies as sheets, towels, and table linen; 27,354 for furniture and furniture repair; 15,884 for fuel; 13,023 for shoe repair; 10,547 for barbering and beauty-shop services.

In that list of scrip spent, which represents hours of labor, is the tale of the possibility of getting a new job. If you can get something to eat, even if it is not entirely adequate; if you can get new clothes and have your shoes repaired, and go to a barber or a hairdresser, you can start again on the job-hunting business in the frame of mind which gets a job.

Self-help, like WPA, is something to tide us over until the nations of this world solve their economic problems and recognize the fact that no civilization can possibly survive which does not furnish every individual who wishes to work a job at wages on which he can live decently.

I grew up in an era when I remember hearing many people say with some contempt that this or that individual felt the world owed him a living. The idea was that the individual in question was unwilling to work and that, therefore, society had no obligations toward him. I am inclined to agree with the idea, but we are up against a different problem now.

Most of the people who are out of work are ready and willing to work. You and I can pick out, of course, individuals who like to live on other people's labor and who perhaps have to be forced to work. The great majority of people who are not ill or too old are ready and anxious to work, however, and in this curiously complicated civilization which we have created through the centuries, there is no work for them to do. We ought to change that old saying and say that a civilization and an economic system which does not recognize its responsibility to answer this question of how work at a living wage can be furnished every individual, should be held in as great contempt as we used to hold the individual who had the attitude that he could go through life effortlessly and expect the world to look after him.

The self-help cooperative has no use for anyone who is not willing to do a good day's work, but the cooperative has this advantage—every age is served alike. In different parts of the United States self-help has been a spontaneous response of workers to prolonged unemployment. Both in Richmond and in Washington, D.C., it was initiated by people who saw that it might solve certain difficulties and wished to make a demonstration of what could be done; so that in these two instances it has not sprung up so clearly from the people themselves. I have seen it, however, with curious vitality, spring up in places where you would expect to find utter discouragement and loss of all initiative. Such things as this have happened: unemployed workers have borrowed idle tractors and asked nearby farmers if they would take their labor for unsold potatoes. It is just going back to the early days of America and using mother wit and neighborliness to keep alive.

During the last seven years, for the first time, these sporadic efforts of idle workers have been systematized and certain precise economic aims and definite techniques of operation have been worked out, and in certain of these the Government has supplied funds with which to buy necessary tools.

Self-help cooperatives should be looked upon as a protection for industrial workers who are subject to the present extremes which require in many industries at times a maximum of employment and at other times throwing great numbers of people back on their own resources. In another field, the Farm Security Administration, an effort has been made to help the small farmer provide himself with a broad base of real income by expanding his productive activities so as to supplement his cash income in good years and in bad years to make him more self-sustaining.

The last Government grants to these self-help cooperatives were made in 1936, and 125 exchanges are still in existence and going strong. The essential activities are always the production of food, the cutting of fuel wood, and the making of clothing, but many other things have been done in different parts of the country, such as dairying, poultry raising, fishing, plumbing, carpentry, baking, operating cafeterias and beauty shops, and repairing automobiles, radios, and shoes.

The Barter Theater in Abingdon, Virginia, was based on much the same barter idea which furnished the springboard for nearly all self-help cooperatives, and I have never forgotten a delightful story I heard told at a luncheon a year ago by Robert Porterfield. He told of looking out of the window and seeing a man and his wife and a cow standing outside the theater. Shortly the man came in and inquired how much milk would be needed for a ticket to the show. He was told and went out and brought the milk in. Mr. Porterfield asked if the farmer's wife was not to attend also, and he answered: "Sure, but I ain't doing her milking for her."

So you see, everybody must do his own work, but the cooperative spirit which underlies the whole movement is valuable education for a democracy. Every day you work you realize that you cannot work for yourself alone, but all the other workers must be producing too in order that you may barter for what you wish and need. The more you help the others, the more you really gain yourself. Good doctrine to inculcate in the citizens of a great democracy!

It seems foolish to have to repeat that the cooperative does not compete with factory production, but it is necessary to say so over and over again apparently. Industry has at times been fearful lest these self-help groups might become a menace, but after all, they need these workers at times and they need workers who have skills and who are accustomed to work with good equipment.

In a way, the running of a self-help exchange is insurance for industry that its workers will not come back rusty and have to be reeducated in their work when they are needed. What they produce in the exchange is for consumption among themselves. With no income they could not buy from outside. If they were not working in the exchange, they would be a complete charge upon the community. This would not perhaps be serious if it meant that you could take care of them through relief in the cheapest way possible for the short time and that then they would return at the call of industry to their usual jobs, but that is not what happens as a rule. If they are idle, they are underfed, their families lack food, a decent home, and a chance for recreation, and so disintegration begins. A young criminal may develop in a family which has never had that kind of a blot before; some of the children may develop tuberculosis. When a worker is called back, his background, his own condition, unfits him to be of any value.

This is the thing which too few people think about when they count the cost of giving men and women work in self-help exchanges or even on the WPA or any place which is not the usual form of employment in either urban or rural localities.

I do not see how it is possible to study the results of the self-help exchanges without being anxious to see this work supported and extended. True, there have been some failures, frequently because of lack of leadership or lack of knowledge on the part of the community or group working out their particular community problem. We need to give more study and thought to helping people to help themselves, and that is why I hope that communities all over the United States will take an interest in self-help cooperatives.   □

PART II

The Threat of War: 1935–1945

1. "Because the War Idea Is Obsolete"

From *Why Wars Must Cease*, edited by Rose Young, Macmillan, 1935

My first wish is to see this plague of mankind [war] banished from the earth.
—George Washington

Is the war idea obsolete?

I have asked many, many people if they thought that war itself was actually obsolete, and a great many have agreed that war should be obsolete, but invariably they insist that, for one reason or another, the continuation of war in the world is probably inevitable.

What I want to prove to you is that the war idea is obsolete, but that we haven't as yet recognized it. The day that the majority of people throughout the world recognize this truth, that day war itself will be obsolete.

We had a period in our own history which illustrates what I mean when I say that an idea may be obsolete, but that until the fact that it is obsolete is recognized it continues to be a menace. I am thinking of the time in our early history when the witch idea ruled the minds of the American people. From the beginning there were groups who fought it, saw it as an obsolete superstition and made a concerted effort to educate the people against it. But in spite of all they could do, the idea that human beings were witches held its ground for a time. Then suddenly the belief disappeared from the pages of our history. Almost overnight it was gone. What had happened was that the knowledge of science had grown so rapidly that people could no longer be fooled by the witch idea. It had become recognized as an obsolete idea. That does not mean that there are not instances, up to the very present, of people who are still ridden by a belief in witches. In New Mexico, not so many years ago, a young girl fell ill. She did not recover and her fiancé and a comrade set forth to wreak vengeance on an old woman who, the fiancé was convinced, had bewitched her. They tied a rope to each of the old woman's wrists, one young man took one rope, one took the other, both put their horses to a run, and they dragged the old woman over the rough road until they killed her. In Pennsylvania quite recently, a young man became so wrought up by his conviction that a witch had put a curse on him that he shot the supposed witch to death. If examples of this kind show how tenacious the witch idea is, they also show how obsolete it is. When people revert to it, as in the cases quoted, we now say they are crazy.

There was another time in our history when many of our best minds subscribed to the almost universal custom of settling personal disputes by force. Duels were fought to settle points of honor between individuals. There was a time, too, when police forces were not only less adequate than now, but in many parts of the country there were none at all, so an individual had frequently to protect his own life and property by the use of force.

But times have changed. We no longer fight duels. No city today is without its police force and nearly all rural districts are protected by some kind of peace officers. Though there are still crimes of violence, it is only in sporadic instances that the individual feels it is his responsibility to do his own protecting of himself and his property by reverting to force. In the affairs of our daily lives we are gradually learning to cooperate for peaceful existence and the old law of the jungle is becoming obsolete in the relations between individuals. We can say that, by and large, it has been accepted amongst private individuals that the war idea, or the use of force as the one means of settling a dispute, is obsolete insofar as private affairs are concerned.

But in the case of the affairs of nations the war idea, like the witch idea in the individual case, hangs on and is still put into practice with outmoded and long-drawn-out cruelty. We still have wars because the majority of people, considered as national groups, do not yet recognize that the war idea is obsolete. Wars . . . often give us instances of the danger of not recognizing crucial things, by dragging on over a long period beyond their finish simply because it is not recognized that the war has come to an end. Historians tell us that the Civil War actually was ended at Gettysburg and yet the fighting went on for more than a year after that bloody battle was fought and many more lives were sacrificed. They now tell us that in the World War the Allies had really won at the Marne, that from that date forward the end was sure, and yet the war continued four long years and every nation sacrificed hundreds of thousands of lives. It is even more terrible to contemplate the fact that on Armistice Day itself everybody in the high command knew that an armistice would be declared during the morning, and yet the firing went on till eleven o'clock and during those morning hours many lives were lost. History records many bloody battles which were fought for no better reason than that it was impossible to communicate with the combatants and tell them the war was over.

Let me define now what I conceive to be the meaning of the phrase "the war idea is obsolete" when applied to the affairs of nations and their inter-relations. An idea, or ideal, is obsolete if, when applied, it does not work. Going back into our own history again, we could not say that the war idea was obsolete at the time of our War of the Revolution, because we desired separation from England and we achieved it. There were two objectives for which the Civil War was fought. One was the question of the right of any one of our states, or a group of states, to secede and become a separate country—in other words, the question of the unity of this country. The other was slavery and its continued existence in this country. The Civil War freed the slaves and imposed upon those states which fought to secede the obligation to remain a part of the United States and preserve this country as a unified nation. The underlying cause of the Civil War, of course, was the quarrel between the agrarians and the industrialists, the agrarians being more numerous in the South and considering that slaves were necessary for their well-being, whereas the industrialists were more numerous in the North where slavery seemed unnecessary. This broader point, however, was probably not realized by the people who actually fought the war, though it stands out clearly to those who look back upon that war. On both points, however, we have to concede that the war idea was not obsolete at that time because, while we may think that both questions might have been settled more easily and efficaciously by joint agreement, still this war did accomplish what it set out to do, even though in a wasteful and costly manner.

The world conflagration which began in 1914 and ended in 1918, in which the great nations of Europe as well as the United States and Japan were involved, proved for the first time in our history that the war idea is obsolete as far as settling difficulties between nations is concerned. It did not achieve its objectives.

We were told the World War was fought, at least by our own country, to preserve democracy, to prevent the people of Europe from coming under the control of a despotic government which had no regard for treaties or the rights of
neutral nations, and, above all, to end all future wars. Judged by the actual accomplishment of objectives, these four years were absolutely wasted. Far from
preventing future wars, the settlements arrived at have simply fostered hostilities. There is more talk of war today, not to mention wars actually going on the
Far East and in South America, than has been the case in many long years. The
world over, countries are armed camps and many peacetime industries have
taken on potential value primarily as a preparation for war. How far forward the
preparations for war are projected is shown by the fact that across the water a
great leader tells his people that boys must be trained for war from the age of
eight. Some time ago I drove over the French battlefields. The fields were covered with green but there were curious hollows where before the war the
ground had been flat. The hollows were the remains of shell holes. The woods we
passed through looked green, too, for Mother Nature rapidly covers up the rav-
ages of man's stupidity, but the new growth was small and the old trees which
once upon a time had been the giants of the forest were now gaunt, bare stumps.
Out of the fields at evening came old men and boys. Apparently two generations
were missing in these French villages where placid rural life was again being carried on. One generation lay under the sod in the acres and acres of cemeteries
that fill the French countryside. The next generation was in military training,
getting ready to take the places of those who had already died for their country.
War maneuvers were in progress and the young men who had grown up since
the World War were learning to use bayonets and charge across the fields where
their fathers had died.

The same handing on of the war idea, the war tradition, is as apparent in one
great European nation as another. We are in danger of actual war today simply
because we cannot convince enough people that the war idea is obsolete.

We are perhaps in this country the very best example of the fact that the war
idea is obsolete and no longer accomplishes even part of what it sets out to do
in practice. Though the underlying cause of the Civil War has not been even yet
settled, though there still is a constant friction between agrarian and industrial
states because their interests still conflict, we do not tolerate the suggestion that
we should go to war about it. We acknowledge the fact that California has certain interests which we in the East do not share, but we know that, though probably no one will be completely happy, some sort of compromise will have to be
reached. We do not intend that any state from Maine to Arizona shall drag us into
civil war on local differences of opinion.

People are prone to say that history repeats itself and that today in the United States they can see the period of Roman decadence, if not actually repeating itself, at least drawing nearer and nearer. They are prone to say, too, that Greece and Rome were conquered by barbarians because they ceased to be able to fight. I doubt if these countries were conquered simply because they ceased to be as warlike as the barbarians. I think they were conquered because they ceased to be a forward-moving civilization. They had the opportunity and they failed. They came to a point where they declined physically, mentally and morally. It was not only that they could not fight from a physical standpoint, they were worthless and gradually decaying from every point of view.

If we do not find another way to settle our disputes and solve the problems of our generation, we will probably find our civilization disappearing also, but that will not happen because we are unable to fight, but because we do not find a substitute for war. There is no further use for war in business, or war between labor and capital, or war between the rich and the poor. The time for unbridled competition, or war, is at an end. We must cooperate for our mutual good.

It is high time to look realistically at this war idea. Many people in the past have felt that war brought a nation not only material gain when it was victorious, but certain moral gain. I have heard people of my generation say that war developed certain qualities of comradeship and loyalty and courage which nothing else could do so well, but we seldom hear the equally true statement that war also gave the opportunity for the development of greed and cupidity to an extent scarcely possible under any other conditions. There has never been a war where private profit has not been made out of the dead bodies of men. The more we see of the munitions business, of the use of chemicals, of the traffic in other goods which are needed to carry on a war, the more we realize that human cupidity is as universal as human heroism. If we are to do away with the war idea, one of the first steps will be to do away with all possibility of private profit.

It does not matter very much which side you fight on in any war. The effects are just the same whether you win or whether you lose. We suffered less here in America in the World War than did the people of European countries, but at least some of our families can share the feelings of those across the sea whose sons did not come back, and today as a country we are realizing that economic waste in one part of the world will have an economic effect in other parts of the world. We profited for a time commercially, but as the rest of the world suffers, so eventually do we.

The easy answer to it all is that human nature is such that we cannot do away with war. That seems to me like saying that human nature is so made that we must destroy ourselves. After all, human nature has some intelligence and the world's experience has already proved that there are ways in which disputes can be settled if people have intelligence and show good will toward one another. To do this on a national scale, as it is done on the individual, people must first be convinced that the war idea is obsolete. When people become convinced of this they will convince their governments and the governments will find the way to stop war.   □

2.   "This Troubled World"

H.C. Kinsey And Company, Inc., 1938

The Case as It Stands

The newspapers these days are becoming more and more painful. I was reading my morning papers on the train not so long ago, and looked up with a feeling of desperation. Up and down the car people were reading, yet no one seemed excited.

To me the whole situation seems intolerable. We face today a world filled with suspicion and hatred. We look at Europe and see a civil war going on, with other nations participating not only as individual volunteers, but obviously with the help and approval of their governments. We look at the Far East and see two nations, technically not at war, killing each other in great numbers.

Every nation is watching the others on its borders, analyzing its own needs and striving to attain its ends with little consideration for the needs of its neighbors. Few people are sitting down dispassionately to go over the whole situation in an attempt to determine what present conditions are, or how they should be met.

We know, for instance, that certain nations today need to expand because their populations have increased. Certain people will tell you that the solution of this whole question lies in the acceptance or rejection of birth control. That may be the solution for the future, but we can do nothing in that way about the populations that now exist. They are on this earth, and modern science has left us only a few places where famine or flood or disease can wipe out large numbers of superfluous people in one fell swoop. For this reason certain nations need additional territory to which part of their present populations may be moved; other nations need more land on which to grow necessary raw materials; or perhaps they may need mineral deposits which are not to be found in their own

country. You will say that these can be had by trade. Yes, but the nations possessing them will frequently make the cost too high to the nations which need them.

It is not a question today of the "free" interchange of goods. If standards of living were approximately the same, throughout the world, competition would be
on an equal basis and then there might be no need for tariffs. However, standards
of living vary. The nations with higher standards have set up protective barriers
which served them well when they were self-contained, but not so well when
they reached a point where they either wished to import or export.

When you take all these things into consideration, the size of this problem
is apt to make you feel that even an attempt to solve it in the future by education is futile. Faint heart, however, ne'er won fair lady, nor did it ever solve
world problems!

Peace plan after peace plan has been presented to me; most of them, I find,
are impractical, or not very carefully thought out. In nearly all of them someone
can find a flaw. I have come to look at them now without the slightest hope of
finding one full-fledged plan, but I keep on looking in the hope of finding here
and there some small suggestion that may be acceptable to enough people to insure an honest effort being made to study it and evaluate its possible benefits.

For instance, one lady of my acquaintance brought me a plan this past spring
which sounded extremely plausible. Her premises are: We never again wish to
send our men overseas; we wish to have adequate defense; we do not need a navy
if we do not intend to go beyond our own shores, with guns along our coasts as
an added protection. Therefore, we do not need an army, for our men are going
to stay at home. With our coast defenses strong, nobody will land here, so why
go the expense of an army? We do not need battleships or, in fact, any navy beyond submarines because we do not intend to own any outlying possessions.

In this way, said the lady, we will save vast sums of money which can be applied to all the social needs of the day—better housing, better schools, old age
pensions, workmen's compensation, care of the blind and crippled and other dependents. There is no limit to what we might do with this money which we now
spend on preparation for destruction.

It is a very attractive picture and I wish it were all as simple as that, but it
seems to be fairly well proved that guns along our coasts are practically useless.
No one, as far as I know, has ever devised an adequate defense by submarines and
airplanes, or calculated whether the cost of the development of these two forces
would really be any less than what we spend at present on our army and navy.

The greatest defense value of the navy is that its cruising radius is great
enough to allow it to contact an attacking force long before that force reaches
our shores. If we trusted solely to submarines and airplanes we would have to

have them in sufficient number really to cover all our borders, and this type of defense would seem to be almost prohibitive in cost for a nation with a great many miles of border to defend.

Has anyone sounded out the people of this country as to their willingness to wait until an attacking enemy comes within the cruising radius of our planes and submarines? Have we faced the fact that this would mean allowing an attacking enemy to come unmolested fairly near to our shores and would make it entirely possible for them to land in a nearby country which might be friendly to them, without any interference on our part? Have our citizens been asked if they are willing to take the risk of doing without trained men? We have always had a small trained army forming the first line of defense in case somebody does land on our borders, or attempts to approach us by land through a neighboring country. Our army has not been thought of as an attacking force; do we want to do away with it?

Are all the people in this country willing also to give up the outlying islands which have come into our possession? Some of them cost us more than they bring in, but others bring certain of our citizens a fair revenue. Can we count on those citizens to accept the loss of these revenues in the interests of future peace?

Perhaps this is part of what we will have to make up our minds to pay someday as the price of peace; but has any one as yet put it into concrete form to the American people and asked their opinion about it?

One of the things that is most frequently harped upon is the vast sums of money spent for war preparation in this country. Very frequently the statements are somewhat misleading. It is true that in the past few years we have spent more than we have for a number of preceding years because we had fallen behind in our treaty strength but, in a world which is arming all around us, it is necessary to keep a certain parity and these expenditures should be analyzed with a little more care than is usual.

For instance, few people realize that in the army appropriation is included all the work done under the army engineers on rivers and harbors, on flood control, etc. One other consideration which is frequently overlooked is that, because of the higher wages paid for labor in this country, whatever we build costs us more than it does in the other nations. One significant fact is that we only spend twelve percent of our national income on our army and navy, as against anywhere from thirty-five to fifty-five percent of the national income spent by nations in the rest of the world. It is well for us to realize these facts and not to feel that our government is doing something that will push us into a position which is incompatible with a desire for peace. We are the most peaceloving nation in the world and we are not doing anything at present which would change that situation.

One very intelligent friend of mine developed an idea the other day which seems to me common sense for the present time, at least. "Why do we talk," she asked, "about peace? Why don't we recognize the fact that it is normal and natural for differences to exist? Almost every family, no matter how close its members may be, is quarrelsome at times." Quarrelsome may be too strong a word, so we might better say that differences of opinion arise in the family as to conduct or as to likes and dislikes. Why should we expect therefore, that nations will not have these same differences and quarrels? Why do we concentrate on urging them not to have any differences? Why don't we simply accept the fact that differences always come up and concentrate on evolving some kind of machinery by which the differences may be recognized and some plan of compromise be worked out to satisfy, at least in part, all those concerned? Compromises, of course, have to be made; they are made in every family. There are usually some members of a family, who, by common consent, are the arbitrators of questions that arise, and who hold the family together, or bring them together if relationships become strained.

The League of Nations was an effort to find for the nations of the world a method by which differences between nations would automatically be brought before the court of public opinion. Some kind of compromise would be made and those involved would feel that substantial justice had been done, even though they might not at any one time achieve all of their desires.

Many of us have become convinced that the League of Nations as it stands today cannot serve this purpose. The reason for this is unimportant. The important thing now is that we should concentrate on finding some new machinery or revamping what already exists so that everyone will function within it and have confidence in its honesty.

The people of the United States have congratulated themselves on the fact that they have made a beginning towards the development of this machinery in their conferences with the representatives of the other American governments.

Perhaps we have a right to feel a sense of satisfaction for as a nation we have made a small beginning. We were cordially disliked throughout South America for years because we were the strongest nation on this continent. We took the attitude of the big brother for a long time and constituted ourselves the defender of all the other nations. We were not only the defender, however, we also considered it our duty to set ourselves up as the judge, and the only judge, of what should happen in the internal as well as the external affairs of our various neighbors.

To them it seemed a bullying, patronizing attitude. As they grew stronger, they resented it, but we went right on regardless of their feelings. During the past few years we have put ourselves imaginatively into their situation. The final result is that we have reached an amicable understanding and actually are in a fair way to get together and discuss subjects of mutual interest with little or no sense of suspicion and fear being involved in the discussion. This can, of course, be spoiled at any time by the selfishness of individual citizens who may decide that, as individuals, they can exploit some other nation on the North or South American continents. The restraint of these individuals will not be a question of government action, but of the force of public opinion which, it is to be hoped, will be able to control and exert a potent influence because of the sense of responsibility acquired by our citizens.

This is satisfactory, but there is still much to be done before we can feel that even here in the Americas we have a thoroughly sound working basis for solving all misunderstandings. We cannot be entirely satisfied with anything, however, which does not include the world as a whole, for we are all so closely interdependent today that we can only operate successfully when we all cooperate.

We have had the experience and can profit by the mistakes and the difficulties through which the League of Nations has passed. Every nation in the world still uses policemen to control its unruly element. It may be that any machinery set up today to deal with international difficulties may require policemen in order to function successfully, but even a police force should not be called upon until every other method of procedure has been tried and proved unsuccessful.

We have some economic weapons which can be used first and which may prove themselves very efficient as the guardians of peace.

Ultimate Objectives

What are our ultimate objectives and how shall we achieve them? First, the most important thing is that any difficulties arising should automatically go before some body which will publish the facts to the world at large and give public opinion an opportunity to make a decision. Then, a group of world representatives will have to decide with whom the fault lies. If their decision is not accepted by the nations involved and either nation attempts to use force in coercing the other nation, or nations—in opposition to what is clearly the majority opinion of the world—then and then only, it seems to me, the decision will be made that the nation using force is an aggressor nation. Being an aggressor, the majority of nations in opposition would be obliged to resort to some method designed to make that nation realize that they could not with impunity flout the public opinion of the majority.

We need to define what an aggressor nation is. We need to have a tribunal where the facts in any case may be discussed, and the decision made before the world, as to whether a nation is an aggressor or not. Then the steps decided upon could be taken in conjunction with other nations.

First of all, trade should be withdrawn from that nation and they could be barred as traders in the countries disagreeing with them. It would not seem probable that more than this economic weapon would have to be used but, if necessary in the end, the police force could be called upon.

In the case of a clearly defined issue where the majority of nations agreed, the police force would simply try to prevent bloodshed and aggression, and it would be in a very different position from an army which was attempting to attack a country and subjugate it. Even the use of a police force, which so many think of as tantamount to war, would really be very different and there would be no idea of marching into a country or making the people suffer or taking anything from them. It would simply be a group of armed men preventing either of the parties to a quarrel from entering into a real war.

Of course, I can imagine cases in which the police force might find itself in an unenviable position, with two countries engaged in a heated quarrel trying to do away with the police so they could get at each other!

All we can hope is that this situation will not arise and that the non-aggressor party to the quarrel, at least, may be willing to sit peacefully by and see the police force repulse the enemy without wishing to turn into aggressors themselves.

With all our agitation about peace, we lose sight of the fact that with the proper machinery it is easier to keep out of situations which lead to war than it is to bring about peace once war is actually going on.

I doubt very much whether peace is coming to us either through plans, even my own as I have outlined it, or through any of the theories or hopes we now hold. What I have outlined is not real peace, just a method of trying to deal with our difficulties a little better than we have in the past, in the world as it is today. We may, of course, be wiped off the face of the earth before we do even this. Our real ultimate objective must be a change in human nature for I have, as I said, yet to see a peace plan which is really practical and which has been thought through in every detail. Therefore, I am inclined to believe that there is no perfect and complete program for bringing about peace in the world at the present moment.

I often wonder as I look around the world whether any of us, even we women, really want peace. Women should realize better than anyone else, that the spirit of peace has to begin in the relationship between two individuals. They know that a child alone may be unhappy because he is alone, but there will be no quarreling until another child appears on the scene, and then the fur will fly, if each of them desires the same thing at the same time.

Women have watched this for generations and must know, if peace is going to come about in the world, the way to start is by getting a better understanding between individuals. From this germ a better understanding between groups of people will grow.

In spite of this knowledge, I am sure that women themselves are among the worst offenders when it comes to petty quarrels. . . .

At the moment we, as a nation, are looking across the Atlantic and the Pacific, patting ourselves on the back and saying how fortunate we are to be away from all their excitements. We feel a little self-righteous, and forget that we ourselves have been engaged in a war on the average of every forty years since our nation was founded. We even fought a civil war, complicated by the alignment of other nations with one side or the other, though no foreign soldiers actually came to fight on either side.

The people who settled in New England came here for religious freedom, but religious freedom to them meant freedom only for their kind of religion. They were not going to be any more liberal to others who differed with them in this new country, than others had been with them in the countries from which they came. This attitude seems to be our attitude in many situations today.

Very few people in any nation today are inclined to be really liberal in allowing real freedom to other individuals. Like our forebears we want freedom for ourselves, but not for those who differ from us. To think and act as we please within limits, of course, caused by the necessity for respecting the equal rights which must belong to our neighbors, would seem to be almost a platitudinous doctrine, yet we would frequently like to overlook these limits and permit no freedom to our neighbors. If this is our personal attitude, it is not strange that our national attitude is similar. We are chiefly concerned with the rights and privileges of our own people and we show little consideration for the rights and privileges of others. In this we are not very different from other nations both in the past and in the present.

I can almost count on the fingers of one hand the people whom I think are real pacifists. By that I mean, the people who are really making an effort in their personal lives to bring about an atmosphere which will be conducive to a solution of all our difficulties in a peaceful manner.

The first step towards achieving this end is self-discipline and self-control. The second is a certain amount of imagination which will enable us to understand situations in which other people find themselves. We may learn to be less indignant at any slight or seeming slight, and we may try to find some way by which to remove the cause of the troubles which arise between individuals, if we become disciplined and cultivate our imaginative facilities. Once we achieve a technique by which we control our own emotions, we certainly will be better able to teach young people how to get on together. . . .

When we once control ourselves and submit personal differences to constituted authorities for settlement, we can say that we have a will to peace between individuals. Before we come to the question of what may be the technique between nations, however, we must go a step farther and set our national house in order. On every hand we see today miniature wars going on between conflicting interests. As the example most constantly before us, take capital and labor. If their difficulties are settled by arbitration and no blood is shed, we can feel we have made real strides towards approaching our international problems. We are not prepared to do this, however, when two factions in a group having the same basic interests cannot come to an agreement between themselves. Their ability to obtain what they desire is greatly weakened until they can reach an understanding and work as a unit. The basis of this understanding should not be hard to reach if the different personalities involved could forget themselves as individuals and think only of the objectives in view, and of the best way to obtain them.

Granted that they are able to do this, then we can approach our second problem with the knowledge that more deeply conflicting interests are at stake but that those with common interests can state their case so the public may form their opinion. Here again, if you could take it for granted that on both sides a real desire existed amongst those representing divergent interests to consider unselfishly ultimate goals and benefits for the majority, rather than any individual gain or loss, it would undoubtedly be possible to reach a peaceful agreement.

Human beings, however, do not stride from peak to peak, they climb laboriously up the side of the mountain. The public will have to understand each case as it comes up and force divergent interests to find a solution. The real mountain climber never gives up until he has reached the highest peak and the lure of the climb to this peak is always before him to draw him on.

That should be the way in human progress—a peaceful, quiet progress. We cannot follow this way, however, until human nature becomes less interested in self, acquires some of the vision and persistence of the mountain climber, and realizes that physical forces must be harnessed and controlled by disciplined mental and spiritual forces.

When we have achieved a nation where the majority of the people is of this type, then we can hope for some measure of success in changing our procedure when international difficulties arise.

What we have said really means that we believe in one actual way to peace—making a fundamental change in human nature. Over and over again people will tell you that that is impossible. I cannot see why it should be impossible when the record of history shows so many changes already gone through. . . .

Human beings either must recognize the fact that what serves the people as a whole serves them best as individuals and, through selfish or unselfish interests, they become people of good intentions and honesty. If not we will be unable to move forward except as we have moved in the past with recourse to force, and constant, suspicious watchfulness on the part of individuals and groups towards each other. The preservation of our civilization seems to demand a permanent change of attitude and therefore every effort should be bent towards bringing about this change in human nature through education. This is a slow way and, in the meantime, we need not sit with folded hands and feel that no steps can be taken to ward off the dangers which constantly beset us.

Immediate Steps

We can begin, and begin at once, to set up some machinery. Our international difficulties will then automatically be taken up before they reach the danger point. One of our great troubles is that it is nobody's business to try to straighten out difficulties between nations in the early stages. If they are allowed to continue too long, they grow more and more bitter and little things, which might at first have been easily explained or settled, take on the proportions of a bitter and important quarrel.

We do not scrap our whole judicial machinery just because we are not sure that the people who appear before the bar are telling the truth. We go ahead and do our best to ascertain the truth in any given case, and substantial justice seems to be done in a majority of situations. This same thing would have to satisfy us for a time at least in the results achieved by whatever machinery we set up to solve our international difficulties.

I am not advocating any particular machinery. The need seems fairly obvious. To say that we cannot find a way is tantamount to acknowledging that we are going to watch our civilization wipe itself off the face of the earth.

For those of us who remember the World War, there is little need to paint a picture of war conditions, but the generation that participated in that war is growing older. To the younger group what they have not seen and experienced themselves actually means little.

. . . . Therefore, it seems to me that one of our first duties is constantly to paint for young people a realistic picture of war. You cannot gainsay the assertion that war brings out certain fine qualities in human nature. People will make sacrifices which they would not make in the ordinary course of existence. War will give opportunities for heroism which do not arise in every-day living, but that is not all that war will do.

It will place men for weeks under conditions which are physically so bad that years later they may still be suffering from the effects of the "period of adventure" even though they may not have been injured by shot or shell during this time of service. Upon many people it will have mental or psychological effects which will take them years to overcome. In many countries of the world there are people to attest to the changed human beings who have returned to them after the World War. Men who could no longer settle down to their old work, men who had seen such horrors that they could no longer sleep quietly at night, men who do not wish to speak of their experiences. It is a rather exceptional person who goes through a war and comes out unscathed physically, mentally or morally.

Secondly, it is one's duty to youth to point out that there are ways of living heroically during peacetimes. I do not imagine that Monsieur and Madame Curie ever felt the lack of adventure in their lives, for there is nothing more adventurous than experimentation with an unknown element. Their purpose was to find something of benefit to the human race. They jeopardized no lives but their own.

I doubt if Father Damien ever felt that his life lacked adventure; and I can think of a hundred places in our own country today where men or women might lead their lives unknown or unsung beyond the borders of their own communities and yet never lack for adventure and interest. Those who set themselves the task of making their communities into places in which the average human being may obtain a share, not only of greater physical well-being, but of wider mental and spiritual existence, will lead an active and adventurous life to reach their goal.

This will need energy, patience and understanding beyond the average, qualities of leadership to win other men to their point of view, unselfishness and heroism, for they may be asked to make great sacrifices. To reach their objectives they may have to hand over their leadership to other men, their characters may be maligned, their motives impugned, but they must remain completely indifferent if only in the end they achieve their objectives. Moral courage of a rare kind will be required of them.

In the wars of the past, deeds of valor and heroism have won decorations from governments and the applause of comrades in arms, but the men who lead in civic campaigns may hope for none of these recognitions. The best that can happen to them is that they may live to see a part of their dreams come true, they may keep a few friends who believe in them and their own consciences may bring them inner satisfactions.

Making our everyday living an adventure is probably our best safeguard against war. But there are other steps which we might well take.

Let us examine again, for example, the ever-recurring question of the need for armaments as a means of defense and protection and see if something cannot be done immediately. Many people feel the building of great military machines leads us directly into war for when you acquire something it is always a temptation to use it.

It is perfectly obvious, however, that no nation can cut down its army and navy and armaments in general when the rest of the world is not doing the same thing.

We ourselves have a long unfortified border on the north which has remained undefended for more than a hundred years, a shining example of what peace and understanding between two nations can accomplish. But we also have two long coastlines to defend and the Panama Canal, which in case of war must be kept open, therefore it behooves us to have adequate naval defense. Just what we mean by adequate defense is a point on which a great many people differ.

Innumerable civilians have ideas as to what constitutes adequate military preparedness and the people most concerned, our military forces, have even more definite ideas. Many people in the United States feel that we are still rendered practically safe by the expanse of water on our east and west coasts. Some people even feel, like Mr. William Jennings Bryan, that if our nation needed to be defended a million men would spring to arms overnight. They forget that a million untrained, unarmed men would be a poor defense. We must concede that our military establishments have probably made a more careful, practical study of the situation than anyone else, for they know they would have to be ready for action at once.

Whether we accept the civil or the military point of view on preparedness, we can still move forward. We can continue to try to come to an understanding with other nations on some of the points which lead to bad feeling. We can begin, first, perhaps, with the Central and South American nations and continue later with other nations, to enter into agreements which may lead to the gradual reduction of armaments. If we only agree on one thing at a time, every little step is something to the good. Simply because we have so far not been able to arrive at any agreement is no reason for giving up the attempt to agree. No one has as yet discovered a way to make any of the methods of transportation by which we all travel around the world, absolutely safe, but nobody suggests that we should do away with ships and railroads and airplanes. I feel that the people of various nations can greatly influence their governments and representatives and encourage action along the lines of reduction in arms and munitions.

Every international group that meets must bear in mind that they have an opportunity to create better feeling, but to move forward along this particular front also requires the backing of public opinion at home. This opinion may be formed in many little groups all over the world and may be felt in an ever widening circle of nations until it becomes a formidable force in the world as a whole.

Then there is the matter of private interests involved in the manufacture of arms and munitions. I know there are many arguments advanced against government ownership of the factories making arms and munitions. When you know the story of the part played by certain families in Europe whose business it has been to manufacture arms and munitions, however, you wonder if the arguments advanced against this step are not inspired in large part by those whose interests lie in this particular business?

It is true that a government can lose its perspective for a number of reasons. The need for employment may push them to overproduction, as well as fear of their neighbors, and they may manufacture so much that the temptation to use it may be great. Some governments today manufacture practically all they need for peacetime purposes and this is a safeguard, but for wartime use, all governments would have to fall back on private manufacturers who could convert their plants easily for the manufacturing of war materials. Some governments today encourage private manufacturers to produce arms and munitions needed in peacetime by buying from them, but the great danger lies in the uncontrolled private production which is used for export. The element of private profit is a great incentive towards the increase of this business just as it is in any other business. Governments are not tempted in the same way, for they do not manufacture for export or for profit.

It seems to me that we must trust someone and I think perhaps it is wiser to trust a government than the more vulnerable and easily tempted individual. Besides which, a democracy has it within its power to control any government business and, therefore, the idea that our government should control the manufacture of arms and munitions fills me with no great trepidation.

This control of the manufacture of arms and munitions is a measure which could be undertaken by one government alone. It does not have to wait for all the other governments to concur, and so I believe either in complete government ownership or in the strictest kind of government supervision, allowing such manufacture as will supply our own country but which will not create a surplus for exportation, thus removing the incentive for constantly seeking and creating new markets.

The next step will be the mutual curtailment, very gradually I am sure, of the amount of armaments the world over. This is a difficult step, because it requires not only an agreement on the part of all the nations, but sufficient confidence in each other to believe that, having given their word, they will live up to the spirit of the agreement as well as to the letter of it, and not try cleverly to hide whatever they have done from possible inspectors.

They will not, for instance, destroy a battleship and add a half dozen airplanes, telling the other members to the agreement that they have carried out the promised reduction, but forgetting to mention the additions to some other arm of their military service.

This lack of integrity, or perhaps we should call it more politely the desire to be a little more clever than one's neighbor, is what promotes a constant attitude of suspicion amongst nations. This will exist until we have accomplished a change in human nature and that is why for the present it seems to me necessary to have inspection and policing as well as an agreement.

The objection will be made that in the nations which are not democracies a government might build up a great secret arsenal; but in those countries this could be done today for most of them control the press and all outgoing information with an iron hand.

Outside of the democracies, government ownership is a much more serious danger on this account. If all nations were obliged to report their military strength to some central body, and this body was allowed to inspect and vouch for the truth of their statements, then all governments could feel secure against that hidden danger which is now part of the incentive for a constant increase in the defense machinery of every nation.

Here again we are confronted with the need of some machinery to work for peace. I have already stated that I doubt if the present League of Nations could ever be made to serve the purpose for which it was originally intended. This does not mean that I do not believe that we could get together. We might even begin by setting up regional groups in different parts of the world which might eventually amalgamate into a central body. It seems to me almost a necessity that we have some central body as a means of settling our difficulties, with an international police force to enforce its decisions, as long as we have not yet reached the point everywhere of setting force aside.

Joint economic action on the part of a group of nations will undoubtedly be very effective, but it will take time to educate people to a point where they are willing to sacrifice, even temporarily, material gains in the interests of peace, so

I doubt whether we can count at once on complete cooperation in the use of an economic boycott. To be a real weapon against any nation wishing to carry on war, it must be well carried out by a great number of nations.

Another small and perhaps seemingly unimportant thing might be done immediately. It might be understood that in wartime everyone should become a part of the military service and no one should be allowed to make any profit either in increased wages or in increased interest on their capital investment. This might bring about a little more universal interest in peace, and more active interest in the efforts to prevent war whether a man were going to the front or staying at home.

Of course, when we talk of "the front" in connection with future wars, we are taking it for granted that future wars will be much like those of the past, whereas most people believe that future wars will have no fronts. What we hear of Spain and China makes this seem very probable. Gases and airplanes will not be directed only against armed forces, or military centers, they may be used for the breaking of morale in the opposing nation. That will mean shelling of unfortified cities, towns and villages, and the killing of women and children. In fact this means the participation in war of entire populations.

One other element must be considered, namely, the creating of public opinion today. Wars have frequently been declared in the past with the backing of the nations involved because public opinion had been influenced through the press and through other mediums, either by the governments themselves or by certain powerful interests which desired war. Could that be done again today in our own country or have we become suspicious of the written word and the inspired message? I think that as a people we look for motives more carefully than we did in the past but whether issues could be clouded for us is one of the questions that no one can answer until the test comes.

I am inclined to think that if a question as serious as going to war were presented to our nation we would demand facts unvarnished by interpretation. Whether we even in our free democracy could obtain them is another question. Who controls the dissemination of news? Is the process totally, uncompromisingly devoted to the unbiased presentation of all news insofar as possible? Is it possible for groups with special interests to put pressure on the press and . . . to what extent?

This is an interesting study in every country where people are really interested in good will and peace. If these sources of information are not really free should not the people insist that this be one of our first reforms? Without it we can have no sound basis on which to form our opinions.

These are things we can work for immediately, but some of my friends consider that one point transcends all others and epitomizes the way to "peace."

Summary

We can establish no real trust between nations until we acknowledge the power of love above all other power. We cannot cast out fear and therefore we cannot build up trust. Perfectly obvious and perfectly true, but we are back again to our fundamental difficulty—the education of the individual human being, and that takes time.

We cannot sit around a table and discuss our difficulties until we are able to state them frankly. We must feel that those who listen wish to get at the truth and desire to do what is best for all. We must reach a point where we can recognize the rights and needs of others, as well as our own rights and needs.

I have a group of religious friends who claim that the answer to all the difficulties is a great religious revival. They may be right, but great religious revivals, which are not simply short emotional upheavals lifting people to the heights and dropping them down again below the place from which they rose, mean a fundamental change in human nature. That change will come to some people through religion, but it will not come to all that way, for I have known many people, very fine people, who had no formal religion. So the change must come to some, perhaps, through a new code of ethics, or an awakening sense of responsibility for their brothers, or a discovery that whether they believe in a future life or not, there are now greater enjoyments and rewards in this world than those which they have envisioned in the past.

I would have people begin at home to discover for themselves the meaning of brotherly love. A friend of mine wrote me the other day that she wondered what would happen if occasionally a member of Congress got up and mentioned in the House the existence of brotherly love. You laugh, it seems fantastic, but this subject will, I am sure, have to be discussed throughout the world for many years before it becomes an accepted rule. We will have to want peace, want it enough to pay for it, pay for it in our own behavior and in material ways. We will have to want it enough to overcome our lethargy and go out and find all those in other countries who want it as much as we do.

Sometime we must begin, for where there is no beginning there is no end, and if we hope to see the preservation of our civilization, if we believe that there is anything worthy of perpetuation in what we have built thus far, then our people must turn to brotherly love, not as a doctrine but as a way of living. If this becomes our accepted way of life, this life may be so well worth living that we will look into the future with a desire to perpetuate a peaceful world for our children. With this desire will come a realization that only if others feel as we do can we obtain the objectives of peace on earth, good will to men.   □

3.   Cash and Carry

My Day, February 3, 1939

Washington—You know that it is my policy to make this column primarily a chronology of the daily goings of the wife of the President. . . .

As far as possible, I never discuss questions of partisan politics, but now and then it seems to me that public questions arise which are of particular interest to women and which far transcend any partisan lines.

As I read a headline this morning, I could not help thinking of something which happened the day before the second Munich meeting. Today's headline reads: "Hoover Says Course Invites War." Naturally, any citizen has a right to state his opinion, but the rest of the country's citizens have a right to weigh that opinion. In Kansas City on the night that the President's second message was sent to Munich, a speech was made by this same eminent gentleman of today's headline before a gathering of Negroes. On that occasion he denounced the foreign policy of this Administration, I suppose because of the same fears which he now expresses that this policy might lead us into war.

Let us, as citizens, examine our present situation. We are the leading democracy of the world. Do our sympathies lie with the other democracies or do they lie with the totalitarian states? The present tempest in a teapot stirred up by the fact that a Frenchman flew in a test plane which France quite legally was going to buy from an airplane manufacturer in the United States. This is a new type of plane, but there are no secrets of government involved and any buyer is entitled to test the wares which he is about to buy. Germany is geared to produce a thousand planes a month; France to produce one hundred planes per month.

It seems evident why France would be interested in buying from us. It is also quite evident that Germany would naturally start a hue and cry that the United Sates was favoring France. Of course it is delightful to feel that no one anywhere near you can ever defend himself for a day if you decide you wish to do something. There is no real reason, however, why any particular nation should be protected in that amount of supremacy and dictatorship over the other nations. This is an open transaction, there is nothing secret about it; it is neither friendly nor unfriendly, it is pure commerce between two friendly nations.

I have fought for peace for many years. I want to see all the nations of the word reduce their armaments. Mr. Chamberlain has suggested it, but I have seen no acquiescence on the part of Mr. Hitler. Have you? Who is taking a belligerent attitude in the world today? The American people cannot afford to consider this as a partisan question and use it as such, and the women, above all, must think clearly on this subject for the future of those who they love many depend upon their influence.   □

4.   The Invasion of Poland

My Day, September 2, 1939

Hyde Park—At 5 o'clock this morning, our telephone rang and it was the President in Washington to tell me the sad news that Germany had invaded Poland and that her planes were bombing Polish cities. He told me that Hitler was about to address the Reichstag, so we turned on the radio and listened until 6 o'clock.

Curiously enough, I had received a letter on my return last evening from a German friend who roomed with me in school in England. In this letter she said that when hate was rampant in the world, it was easy to believe harm of any nation, that she knew all the nations believed things that were not true about Germany, did not understand her position, and therefore hated her. She begged that we try to see Germany's point of view and not to judge her harshly,

As I listened to Hitler's speech, this letter kept returning to my mind. How can you feel kindly toward a man who tells you that German minorities have been brutally treated, first in Czechoslovakia and then in Danzig, but that never can Germany be accused of being unfair to minorities? I have seen evidence with my own eyes of what this same man has done to people belonging to a minority group—not only Jews, but Christians, who have long been German citizens.

Can one help but question his integrity? His knowledge of history seems somewhat sketchy too for, after all, Poland possessed Danzig many years prior to the time that it ever belonged to Germany. And how can you say that you do not intend to make war on women and children and then send planes to bomb cities?

No, I feel no bitterness against the German people. I am deeply sorry for them, as I am for the people of all other European nations facing this horrible crisis. But for the man who has taken this responsibility upon his shoulders I can feel little pity. It is hard to see how he can sleep at night and think of the people in many nations whom he may send to their deaths.   □

5.   Wartime Sacrifice

My Day, July 3, 1940

Hyde Park—Tomorrow is the Fourth of July, and this year it seems to me that this particular date should have a very deep meaning for all of us.

Our forefathers wrote the Declaration of Independence and on that Declaration our Constitution was based. We fought as a young nation for the ideas that were expressed by the men who wrote this document. Though sometimes it seems as though, during the intervening years, we had forgotten all that document implies, the events of the last few months have made many of us think over carefully what are the things which really matter to us as individuals in the United States of America.

We will have to be very sure what we want for ourselves and our fellow citizens in order to really to organize our strength and live or die for the things in which we believe.

I personally want to continue to live in a country where I can think as I please, go to any church I please, or to none if that is my desire; say what I please, and within the limits of any free society, do as I please.

Long ago we decided here that if we held views opposing those of other people, it was against the interest of the country to try to persuade those others by force to agree with us. We could go on talking about our own ideas in the hope of eventually winning a majority, and it seems to me that this is the essence of democracy.

I am willing to be asked to sacrifice time and money for the good of the country as a whole. I am willing to be asked to share what I am able to earn with other less fortunate people, and I am willing to consider any curtailment of personal liberty which I can persuaded is for the good of the majority, but I want to be able to discuss it.

I want the right to work, and I want the opportunity to be extended to all my fellow citizens. I want them to have an equal opportunity for educational development, for health and recreation, which is all part of the building of a human being capable of coping with the modern world.

I want to have within my own hands the choice of my leaders, and if the majority opinion is against me at any time, I want the right to differ, while recognizing the necessity of cooperation on my part to prove fairly whether the majority opinion is right or not.

On this Fourth of July morning I hope each of us and every one of us will dedicate ourselves to the service of our country and the service of our fellow citizens, never forgetting that we hope through example to strengthen the ultimate brotherhood of man throughout the world.   □

6.   Should There Be a Referendum on War?

My Day, June 28, 1941

Eastport, Maine—I have just received a slightly delayed communication from my congressman, The Hon. Hamilton Fish. His letter, addressed to the people of the 26th Congressional District in New York State, interests me very much. He suggests in the first paragraph that "an undeclared war is an invention and creation of totalitarian nations, and a negation of democratic processes and our constitutional form of government."

Nowhere in the letter does he seem to suggest that, this being the case and we being a peace-loving people, we may find ourselves the victims of an undeclared war, whether we like it or not, even if we ourselves adhere scrupulously to the "democratic processes."

He encloses in this courteous note, a postal card which reads:
"The United States should:
Enter the war . . .
Stay out of the war . . ."

All I am asked to do is to check one of these statements, sign my name or not, as I like, and return my ballot within three days of receipt.

I understand from a newspaper item which I read that my congressman has received an overwhelming number stating flatly that the United States should stay out of war. That seems to me fairly natural.

If I thought I had a choice in the matter, I should answer wholeheartedly that I did not wish to enter any war anywhere in the world. But it seems to me that my congressman has oversimplified the question which confronts us at the moment.

We would like to stay out of war. The people of Norway, Holland and all the other countries in Europe, even France and Russia, and Germany itself, would probably have liked to stay out of war. But that wasn't even put before them as a choice. The war was suddenly upon them. It some cases, their government in the form of a dictator decreed it so. In others, because they woke up one morning and found soldiers of an enemy government marching down their streets.

I can think of a number of questions, Mr. Congressman, which you could have asked your constituents that would have been more enlightening to them and to you. Just as suggestions, why not ask "Shall the U.S. allow any enemy nation to obtain possession which may menace, under modern conditions of warfare, the safety of the U.S.?" or "Shall we accept restrictions on our trade or the abrogation of our right to travel in neutral waters throughout the world?"

We have always been a proud and independent people, Mr. Congressman. As a woman, I pray for peace not only now, but in the future. But I think we must look a little beyond next week to ensure an independent U.S.A. to our children. There is such a thing, too, as the moral values of a situation, and I do not think we are a nation that has given up considerations for right and wrong as we see it.   □

7.   ## The Bombing of Britain
My Day, July 28, 1941

Hyde Park—. . . . Today we have all been to church, and, on the whole, I think we will have a more peaceful day even for the President, than any day since he came, because the main things which were on his mind seem all to be in the morning paper.

I received a letter, the other day, sent me by an English Naval officer, written by his daughter in London. For two reasons I am quoting parts of the letter here. One is that it shows a confidence and companionship between two generations which is not often achieved. The other reason is that it shows what the spirit of youth can be and that two generations can work together, for the mother seems to be working as hard as this young woman is at tasks as dangerous and as nerve-wracking.

Here is part of the letter:

"April, 1941.

"Darling Daddy: It is difficult to put into words expressive enough a description of the raid of Wednesday night. . . For ten hours the din was incessant—guns, planes, fire bells and the tinkle of shrapnel, not to speak of bombs. We rocked like a ship all night. I did more work yesterday than I have for a long time. I went on duty at nine and we had lots of dirty ambulances to clean. We had carried eighty-one casualties during the night with six ambulances. Everything had a puncture or something amiss and we lost masses of equipment. No shortage of dead.

"I wasn't shocked, as I had expected to be. I have so often visualized it and have armed myself against it. . . We had sleep last night. There were two alerts, but people were so tired they didn't hear them. . . I am conscript now since April first. . .

"I wish Mummy would leave the RAR. She is always tired. . . . We are extremely lucky still to have our gas and water at home. The lights failed here and in thousands of instances. . . . The ambulances were mostly Green Line buses, which take nine cases. . . .

"A bomb fell thought St. Paul's again and exploded in the crypt where they had Easter Sunday services, which I went to a week ago. . . . We had a good dance down here on Easter Monday. It was jolly throughout and one forgot raids. Thank heaven no blitz interrupted. Cheerio and tons of love and kisses.

"From Marion"

☐

8.   # Pearl Harbor

My Day, December 8, 1941

Washington—I was going out in the hall to say goodbye to our cousins, Mr. and Mrs. Frederick Adams, and their children, after luncheon, and, as I stepped out of my room, I knew something had happened. All the secretaries were there, two telephones were in use, the senior military aides were on their way with messages. I said nothing because the words I heard over the telephone were quite sufficient to tell me that, finally, the blow had fallen, and we had been attacked.

Attacked in the Philippines, in Hawaii, and on the ocean between San Francisco and Hawaii. Our people had been killed not suspecting there was an enemy, who attacked in the usual ruthless way which Hitler has prepared us to suspect.

Because our nation has lived up to the rules of civilization, it will probably take us a few days to catch up with our enemy, but no one in this country will doubt the ultimate outcome. None of us can help but regret the choice which Japan has made, but having made it, she has taken on a coalition of enemies she must underestimate unless she believes we have sadly deteriorated since our first ships sailed into her harbor.

The clouds of uncertainly and anxiety have been hanging over us for a long time. Now we know where we are. The work for those who are at home seems to be obvious. First, to do our own job, whatever it is, as well as we can possibly do it. Second, to add to it everything we can do in the way of civilian defense. Now, at last, every community must go to work to build up protection from attack.

We must build up the best possible community services, so that all of our people may feel secure because they know we are standing together and that whatever problems have to be met will be met by the community and not one lone individual. There is no weakness and insecurity when once this is understood. □

9.   The Nazi Camps

My Day, September 25, 1942

New York—Yesterday afternoon I joined a broadcast to the women of Poland on the third anniversary of the loss of their country's freedom. Miss Dorothy Thompson, Mrs. Clare Booth Luce, Miss Pearl Buck and Miss Moore were extremely effective in their talks. I hope the broadcast will give some sense of future security to the women of Poland. I was glad to be able to say how deeply the women of this country sympathized with the suffering of the women in Poland.

Starvation and horror live with them day by day. I wonder more and more at the Nazi psychology when I read descriptions of what happens to people in the occupied countries under Nazi control. How can the Nazis hope to create loyal and friendly citizens in a country which they have conquered by cruel treatment? Certainly, if they want good will, they go about it in a strange fashion.

I have before me a description of the Ravensbruck Women's Preventive Camp. Part of the item reads: "People are regarded as ill only when they drop. Prisoners have to go barefoot in streets sprinkled with coarse gravel. In consequence prisoners get sore and festered heels, but they have to go on walking barefoot. No food is provided during the examination period so, if they bring some of their own, they go hungry until they are finally assigned to barracks. One of the punishments consists of transfer to punishment barracks where degenerates are detained. If a Polish woman talks to a Jewess, she is punished with 42 days in a dark cell. There is one month of quarantine on entrance to the camp. Kitchen work starts at 4:00 A.M. and included the carrying of heavy sacks of food from the lorries."

This is only the description of one camp, and I should not think it would tend to make the conquered people love their conquerors. The Nazi psychology is a strange one, because fear and suffering do not create love and loyalty.   ☐

10.   The Holocaust

My Day, August 13, 1943

Hyde Park—I talked a little while yesterday morning with a representative from the group which is trying to formulate plans to save the Jewish people in Europe. Some people think of the Jewish people as a race. Others think of them purely as a religious group. But in Europe the hardships and persecution which they have had to endure for the past few years have tended to bring them together in a group which identifies itself with every similar group, regardless whether it is religious or racial. The Jews are like all the other people of the world. There are able people among them, there are courageous people among them, there are people of extraordinary intellectual ability along many lines. There are people of extraordinary integrity and people of great beauty and great charm.

On the other hand, largely because of environmental and economic conditions, there are people among them who cringe, who are dishonest, who try to take advantage of their neighbors, who are aggressive and unattractive. In other words, they are a cross-section of the human race, just as is every other nationality and every other religious group.

But good or bad, they have suffered in Europe as has not any other group. The percentage killed among them in the past few years far exceeds the losses among any of the United Nations in the battles which have been fought throughout the war.

Many of them for generations considered Germany, Poland, Romania and France their country and permanent home. It seems to me that it is in the part of common sense for the world as a whole to protest in its own interest against wholesale persecution, because none of us by ourselves would be strong enough to stand against a big enough group which decided to treat us in the same way. We may have our individual likes and dislikes, but this is a question which far transcends prejudices or inclinations.

It means the right of survival of human beings and their right to grow and improve. You and I may be hated by our neighbors, but if we know about it we try to change things within us which brought it about. That it the way civilized people develop; murder and annihilation are never a satisfactory answer for the few who escape grow up more bitter against their persecutors, and a day of reckoning always comes, which is what the story of Moses in the bulrushes teaches us.

I do not know what we can do to save the Jews in Europe and to find them homes, but I know that we will be the sufferers if we let great wrongs occur without exerting ourselves to correct them.   □

11.   D-Day

My Day, June 6, 1944

Washington—So at last we have come to D-Day, or rather it reached us over the radio in the early hours of the morning on June the 6th. The first people I saw seemed very much excited. Curiously enough I have no sense of excitement whatsoever. It seems as though one had been waiting for this Day for weeks and dreading it and all the emotion is drained away.

All the preparation which has gone on, the endless photographing, the endless air-raids, the constant practicing of the men in landing, or in whatever their own specialty may be. This is not ended. The fact that boys you know have been waiting with an almost desperate feeling for this Day, when all their training would be tested, made you dread it and yet hope for it. The time is here and we live in safety and comfort and wait for the victory. It is difficult to make life seem real. To believe that the beaches of France which once you knew, are now places from which in days to come, boys in hospitals over here will tell you that they have returned, this is hard to take in. They will never go beyond the water of the beach, but all their lives perhaps they will bear the marks of the Day upon them. At that they will be the lucky ones, for many others won't return.

This is the beginning of a long, hard fight, a fight for ports where heavy materials of war must be landed, a fight for airfields in the countries where we must operate, day by day miles of country taken, and lost, and retaken—that is what we have to face, what the boys who are over there have been preparing for and what must be done before the day of victory. That day is coming surely. It will be happy and glorious day. How can we hasten it?

There is no way in which we can help except by doing our jobs better here than ever before, whatever they may be. Every unauthorized and unwarranted strike is an added danger to the boys over there, and a man or a woman leaving a war plant today adds to some soldier's load. But on the reverse side, we should remember that every employer who forces his employees into a position where they see no way out except to strike is equally guilty with the strikers. I have seen so many condemnations of strikers, but I have seen little recognition that there are always two sides to any dispute. Therefore the responsibility for whatever happens today which slows up production, which we need also desperately in every theatre of the war, lies never with one group alone.   □

12.   D-Day, Continued

My Day, June 7, 1944

There is a further effort which can be made, I think, to help both labor and management to face the present needs of war production. The Government, as represented by its leadership in Congress has the opportunity to do one important thing. If they pass legislation and made people secure in that these laws are actually being implemented, and that no citizen need fear if he continues in his present war time job, that he will not have adequate coverage during a period of unemployment following the closing of his war plant and the reconversion to civilian use, there will be less unrest among the workers.

In addition an assurance that transportation and opportunity for new work is now being planned for in every section of the country by industry and labor jointly, with the knowledge and cooperation of the Government, would vastly strengthen and hearten the people in their war production jobs. The carrying out of the provisions of the Baruch report as to the methods of reimbursement and disposal of surplus would give management their needed sense of security. This is the pattern of cooperation that the citizens need to see functioning in order to do their jobs with quiet minds in these crucial days.

Like everybody else I am spending more time that usual reading the papers and listening to the radio these days which is really not conducive to accomplishing much work.

I did, however, go up to the Senate Office Building yesterday afternoon to be present at the ceremony when the committee which had been appointed to write the account of what had happened to the Jews in Poland, presented their completed work in the form of "The Black Book of Polish Jewry," to Senator Wagner, Representative Bloom, Representative Cellar and Mr. Michael E. W. Straus, first assistant secretary of the Interior Department.

I hope that many people will see this book. The pictures speak more vividly than the written word. It is a horrible book, a book which explains the terrible statistics of the martyrdom of the Jews in Warsaw, and makes one ashamed that a civilized race anywhere in the world could treat other human beings in such a manner. All of us must pray for forgiveness.

In the evening my daughter, her husband and I were with the President when he read the prayer in which he hoped the nation would join him. It is a good prayer to read and reread in these coming days and I think he is right in saying that instead of one day of prayer, we need to keep on praying day by day until the long march to Berlin has been accomplished . . . .   □

13.   Conscientious Objectors

My Day, June 21, 1944

Hyde Park—Conscientious objectors feel that Great Britain has become "more enlightened" than the United States, since many of them over there have been able to pursue their own vocations, or do the work which themselves have chosen to do for the nation during the war period. The British conscientious objectors feel that they have been more useful and that they are treated with greater intelligence by their government and this opinion is shared by conscientious objectors here.

I can not help feeling very sorry for honest conscientious objectors, for I am quite sure than many a young man must find it bitter to let other young men of his own age die and fight and give up time in occupations they care little about.

It is only because of these young men, however, who are willing to fight that anyone can indulge himself in a personal viewpoint. Some day, perhaps, the world will be the kind of civilized place in which we can all live in safety according to our own lights. But it isn't that kind of place today, and so you and I are defended in our peaceful lives at home by those who will do what their Government asks of them, no matter what that task may be.

It is true that conscientious objectors have earned and saved much money for the Government. It is true that they have made the lives of patients in the state hospitals more bearable than they have ever been before. It is true that those who are willing to work in factories or military or medical establishments, and some of them actually in danger zones or in the field of battle, have done heroic deeds and are fine people. But they are doing what they want to do. They are not the same kind of citizens as are the men in the armed services. For this reason, Congress has not appropriated money to pay them or to help their dependents on the same basis as the men drafted into the armed services.

It is hard on the families, but that is the price of doing what one believes in. Some men go to prison and will not do anything during the period of war and that again is the price of doing what you believe in. When the day arrives when war is no more, these men may feel that they have hastened it. In the meantime, however, as the world is constituted today they might not be alive or they might be slaves to other more warlike people if some of their brothers were not willing to defend them against other warlike peoples.   □

14.   Total War

My Day, December 28, 1944

Hyde Park—For the first time since the early days of the war, the people in this country are being tested by the war news. It is harder to bear today, because in the early days we could say that we had not been a war-like nation, that we had not wanted to make war, that we had not prepared for it and that our Allies would therefore have to hold the fort until we were ready. No one could help us in the Pacific, and we took some pretty humiliating defeats. Yet the men we had in that area did a holding job which was magnificent, for it is harder to retreat and give way and keep morale high than it is to go forward.

Gradually, as we came into greater production, the picture in the Pacific changed. We have regained some of what we lost, and we have taken many more islands which the Japanese had occupied. We have inflicted blows from the air on their homeland. But all the time we have known that we had to do most of the aggressive work. China, after many years of war, was doing a magnificent defensive job, but we knew that we had to come to her assistance, important as she was to us because of her resistance.

I think we are probably better prepared in our minds for the long war in the Pacific than we at first were for the slow, hard fighting on the Italian peninsula. Very few people in this country remembered the mountainous terrain our men who have to fight through. Sunny Italy was all we thought about, not snow and ice, cold and rain and mountains, with the enemy on top, which had to be crossed. That has been a long, hard, mile-by-mile campaign.

Then we landed in France, and romped across that country with a liberated people cheering us on. The enemy fell back, but in pretty good order, shortening their supply lines with every day's retreat as we lengthened ours. When they reached a point where they decided to stand and counter attack, it was a surprise to us at home. Probably our generals knew that some day this point would have to be reached. Just when it would come they knew possibly no better than anyone else, since we cannot read other people's minds. But I imagine that our men hoped they would advance into Germany as fast as they had crossed France, and the loss of the territory which they fought so hard to gain must be a bitter disappointment to them.

There may be people here who would say—Why do we have to fight our way across Germany? But those are the people who have forgotten what happened in the last war. They do not remember the German army's boast that it was never beaten—that only the German people at home let the army down—or they would not suggest that we run the same risk again.

This is total war, and we fight in spirit with our men overseas. We know that we have to produce more if they need more; that there have to be nurses for the wounded and supplies of food for our men, as well as for the liberated peoples who are hungry and cannot help in their weakened condition. We civilians at home have so far been annoyed by the war, but still on the whole we are comfortable at home. Our great suffering has been in the loss of our dear ones. Now we may have to face some of the physical hardships of a nation making a really great war effort. No hardships will equal those endured by our men at the battlefronts. □

15. Equal Justice for All

My Day, April 30, 1945

New York—Representative Mary Norton of New Jersey is making a magnificent fight for the passage of the Fair Employment Practices bill. This bill would give us a permanent group in the government whose function it would be to see that, as far as employment goes throughout this country, there is complete equality of opportunity and treatment for all.

Many people have come to think of this bill as being of value only to certain minority groups. I think it is important for the public in general; to understand clearly that the bill, while it may be of value to these groups, is equally vital to each and every one of us who are citizens of the United Sates. If we do not see that equal opportunity, equal justice and equal treatment are meted out to every citizen, the very basis on which this country can hope to survive with liberty and justice for all will be wiped away.

Are we learning nothing form the horrible pictures of the concentration camps which have been appearing in our papers day after day? Are our memories so short that we do not recall how in Germany this unparalleled barbarism started by discrimination directed against Jewish people? It had ended in brutality and cruelty meted out to all people, even to our own boys who have been taken prisoner. This bestiality could not exist if the Germans had not allowed themselves to believe in a master race which could do anything it wished to all other human beings not of their particular racial strain.

There is nothing, given certain kinds of leadership, which could prevent our falling prey to this same kind of insanity, much as it shocks us now. The idea of superiority of one race over another must not continue within our own country, nor must it grow up in our dealings with the rest of the world. It is self-evident that there are people in certain parts of the world who, because of different opportunities and environment, have not progressed as far as other people in what we call civilization. That does not mean, however, that they will forever be inferior in our type of civilization. Given the same kind of opportunities, they may do better than we have done.

Looking at the war-torn world of today, we cannot say that our civilization has been perfect. We can only say that we have created greater material comfort for human beings and that we are struggling to find a way of living together peacefully and cooperatively in the future.

That is a great step forward, and we are taking it internationally; but we must also take it within our own borders. We cannot complain that the Germans starved and maltreated our boys if we at home do not take every step—both through our government and as individuals—to see not only that fairness exists in all employment practices, but that throughout our nation all people are equal citizens. Where the theory of a master race is accepted, there is danger to all progress in civilization.

16.   The Atomic Bomb

My Day, August 8, 1945

New York—The news which came to us yesterday afternoon of the first use of the atomic bomb in the war with Japan may have surprised a good many people, but scientists—both British and American—have been working feverishly to make this discovery before our enemies, the Germans, could make it and thereby possibly win the war.

This discovery may be of great commercial value some day. If it is wisely used, it may serve the purposes of peace. But for the moment we are chiefly concerned with its destructive power. That power can be multiplied indefinitely, so that not only whole cities but large areas may be destroyed at one fell swoop. If you face this possibility and realize that, having once discovered a principle it is very easy to take further steps to magnify its power, you soon face the unpleasant fact that in the next war whole peoples may be destroyed.

The only safe counter weapon to this new power is the firm decision of mankind that it should be used for constructive purposes only. This discovery must spell the end of the war. We have been paying an ever increasing price for indulging ourselves in this uncivilized way of settling difficulties. We can no longer indulge in the slaughter of young men. The price will be too high and will be paid not just by young men, but by whole populations.

In the past we have given lip service to the desire for peace. Now we meet the test of really working to achieve something basically new in the world. Religious groups have been telling us for a long time that peace could be achieved only by a basic change in the nature of man. I am inclined to think that this is true. But if we give human beings sufficient incentive, they may find good reasons for reshaping their characteristics.

Good will among men was preached by the angels as they announced to the world the birth of the child Jesus. He exemplified it in His life and preached it Himself and sent forth His disciples, who have spread that gospel of love and human understanding throughout the world ever since. Yet the minds and hearts of men seemed closed.

Now, however, an absolute need exists for facing a non-escapable situation. This new discovery cannot be ignored. We have only two alternative choices: destruction and death—or construction and life! If we desire our civilization to survive, then we must accept the responsibility or constructive work and of the wise use of a knowledge greater than any ever achieved by man before.   □

PART III

The Home Front: 1939–1945

1. "Keepers of Democracy"

The Virginia Quarterly Review, Winter 1939

Recently a radio broadcast was given, based on a story written by
H. G. Wells some years ago, called "War of the Worlds." For the purpose of
dramatization it was placed in the United States with the names of regions and
people who would naturally be involved if such a thing were to happen today.
The basic idea was not changed; these invaders were supernatural beings from
another planet who straddled the skyway and dealt in death rays, but it was dra-
matically done with many realistic touches.

I do not wish to enter into a discussion here as to whether the broadcasting
company should do dramatizations of this type, nor do I wish to cast aspersions
on people who may not have read the original book. But the results of this broadcast were the best illustration of the state of mind in which we as a nation find
ourselves today. A sane people, living in an atmosphere of fearlessness, does not
suddenly become hysterical at the threat of invasion, even from more credible
sources, let alone by the Martians from another planet, but we have allowed ourselves to be fed on propaganda which has created a fear complex. For the past few

years, nearly all of our organizations and many individuals have said something about the necessity for fighting dangerous and subversive elements in our midst.

If you are in the South someone tells you solemnly that all the members of the Committee for Industrial Organization are Communists, or that the Negroes are all Communists. This last statement derives from the fact that, being for the most part unskilled labor, Negroes are more apt to be organized by the Committee for Industrial Organization. In another part of the country someone tells you solemnly that the schools of the country are menaced because they are all under the influence of Jewish teachers and that the Jews, forsooth, are all Communists. And so it goes, until finally you realize that people have reached a point where anything which will save them from Communism is a godsend; and if Fascism or Nazism promises more security than our own democracy we may even turn to them.

It is all as bewildering as our growing hysterical over the invasion of the Martians! Somehow or other I have a feeling that our forefathers, who left their women and children in the wildernesses while they traveled weary miles to buy supplies, and who knew they were leaving them to meet Indians if need be, and to defend themselves as best they could, would expect us to meet present-day dangers with more courage than we seem to have. It is not only physical courage which we need, the kind of physical courage which in the face of danger can at least control the outward evidences of fear. It is moral courage as well, the courage which can make up its mind whether it thinks something is right or wrong, make a material or personal sacrifice if necessary, and take the consequences which may come.

I shall always remember someone, it may have been Theodore Roosevelt, saying in my hearing when I was young that when you were afraid to do a thing, that was the time to go and do it. Every time we shirk making up our minds or standing up for a cause in which we believe, we weaken our character and our ability to be fearless. There is a growing wave in this country of fear, and of intolerance which springs from fear. Sometimes it is a religious intolerance, sometimes it is a racial intolerance, but all intolerance grows from the same roots. I can best illustrate this fear by telling you that a short time ago someone told me in all seriousness that the American Youth Congress was a Communist organization and that the World Youth Congress was Communist controlled. This person really believed that the young people who were members of these organizations were attempting to overthrow by force the governments of the countries in which they belonged.

Undoubtedly, in the World Youth Congress there were young Communists, just as there are a group of young Communists and a group of young Socialists in the American Youth Congress, but this does not mean that either of these bodies is Communist controlled. It simply means that they conform to the pattern of society, which at all times has groups thinking over a wide range, from what we call extreme left to extreme right. The general movement of civilization, however, goes on in accordance with the thinking of the majority of the people, and that was exactly what happened in both the American Youth Congress and the World Youth Congress.

The resolutions finally passed by both bodies were rather sane and calm, perhaps a trifle idealistic and certainly very optimistic. There were amendments offered for discussion, and voted down, which many people might have considered radical; but since there is radical thinking among both young and old, it seems to me wiser to discuss and vote down an idea than to ignore it. By so doing we know in which direction the real trend of thought is growing. If we take the attitude that youth, even youth when it belongs to the Communist party, cannot be met on the basis of equal consideration and a willingness to listen, then we are again beginning to allow our fears of this particular group to overwhelm us and we are losing the opportunity to make our experience available and useful to the next generation.

I do not believe that oppression anywhere or injustice which is tolerated by the people of any country toward any group in that country is a healthy influence. I feel that unless we learn to live together as individuals and as groups, and to find ways of settling our difficulties without showing fear of each other and resorting to force, we cannot hope to see our democracy successful. It is an indisputable fact that democracy cannot survive where force and not law is the ultimate court of appeal. Every time we permit force to enter into a situation between employer and employee we have weakened the power of democracy and the confidence which a democratic people must have in their ability to make laws to meet the conditions under which they live, and, when necessary, to change those laws with due political process according to the will of the majority of the people.

When we permit religious prejudice to gain headway in our midst, when we allow one group of people to look down upon another, then we may for a short time bring hardship on some particular group of people, but the real hardship and the real wrong is done to democracy and to our nation as a whole. We are then breeding people who cannot live under a democratic form of government but must be controlled by force. We have but to look out into the world to see how easy it is to become stultified, to accept without protest wrongs done to others, and to shift the burden of decision and of responsibility for any action onto some vague thing called a government or some individual called a leader.

It is true today that democracies are in danger because there are forces opposed to their way of thinking abroad in the world; but more than democracies are at stake. When force becomes so necessary that practically all nations decide that they must engage in a race which will make them able to back up what they have to say with arms and will thus oblige the rest of the world to listen to them, then we face an ultimate Armageddon, unless at the same time an effort to find some other solution is never abandoned.

We in this country may look at it more calmly than the rest of the world, for we can pay for force over a longer period of time; and for a while at least our people will not suffer as much as some of the other nations of the world, but the building up of physical forces is an interminable race. Do you see where it will end unless some strong movement for an ultimate change is afoot?

Someone may say: "But we need only to go on until the men who at present have power in the world and who believe in force are gone." But when in the past has there been a time when such men did not exist? If our civilization is to survive and democracies are to live, then the people of the world as a whole must be stronger than such leaders. That is the way of democracy, that is the only way to preserve a rule of law and order as opposed to a rule of force.

We can read the history of civilization, its ups and its downs as they have occurred under the rule of force. Underlying that history is the story of each individual's fears. It seems to me a challenge to women in this period of our civilization to foster democracy and to refuse to fall a prey to fear. Only our young people still seem to have some strength and hope, and apparently we are afraid to give them a helping hand.

Someone said to me the other day that, acknowledging all the weaknesses of human nature, one must still believe in the basic good of humanity or fall into cynicism and the philosophy of old Omar Khayyam. I do still believe that there is within most of us a basic desire to live uprightly and kindly with our neighbors, but I also feel that we are at present in the grip of a wave of fear which threatens to overcome us. I think we need a rude awakening . . . to make us willing to sacrifice all that we have from the material standpoint in order that freedom and democracy may not perish from this earth.   □

2.   "Intolerance"

Cosmopolitan, February 1940

People keep asking: "Is a wave of intolerance sweeping over our country? Are we getting away from our traditional attitude that all races and religions are equal in the eyes of the law?"

The answer is obviously "Yes." A wave of intolerance most certainly is sweeping over us. But we need not behave as though it were a phenomenon which we had never before experienced, and we should not magnify it. On the whole, we are a tolerant people.

War anywhere develops intolerance everywhere. Notice how in this country today, because of the activities of a noisy minority, we see Germans who have lived here most of their lives, and who came to us because they believed in what the United States represented, suspected of disloyalty. The same is true for other refugees. War breeds fear and intolerance.

Intolerance has its roots in fear. Many of the people who have testified before the Dies Committee [House Committee on Un-American Activities]—White Camellias, Silver Shirts, Brown Shirts, or what have you—are examples of this fear. They are afraid that we cannot solve our problems in accordance with our own traditions, and so they turn to the solutions found in other countries and hide foreign ideologies under the names of American patriotism. They typify the very traits which true Americans have sought to eradicate ever since the Declaration of Independence and the Constitution were written.

Perhaps the wave of anti-Semitism is our greatest manifestation of intolerance today, though in some places anti-Catholicism runs a close second, and in others fear of the Negro's aspirations is paramount.

Persecution and confiscation of property, largely for the Jewish race, but also for Catholics and Protestants who do not agree entirely with the "powers that be," have swept parts of the world because of economic conditions and *fear*.

The ideas which crop up anywhere are bound to affect the rest of the world. Especially is this true when selfish foreign interests take advantage of our traditional freedom and put their ideas before us with little regard for truth. I want to tell you a story which illustrates the foolishness of such fears. A friend of mine told me of finding himself at a dinner given by the Chamber of Commerce in a small town at a time when the Ku Klux Klan was active in that section. On his right sat the treasurer of the organization, and to his surprise the man was a Jew. Beside the chairman sat the secretary, a Catholic.

"Is the Klan strong in this vicinity?" my friend asked the chairman.

"Yes; oh yes," was the reply.

"Then how is it that two of the officers of your organization are respectively a Jew and a Catholic?"

The answer came unhesitatingly: "But we know *them*. They are good fellows and important in our community."

I was in a western state some years ago when a general strike occurred, and I made the discovery that when people are made uncomfortable, the spirit of tolerance disappears. No longer are they interested in what is right or wrong; they want action and a return to comfortable living conditions. Every time we succumb to this degree of selfishness, we fail to live up to the citizenship of which our forefathers thought we would be capable.

All of us in this country give lip service to the ideals set forth in the Bill of Rights and emphasized by every additional amendment, and yet when war is stirring in the world, many of us are ready to curtail our civil liberties. We do not stop to think that curtailing these liberties may in the end bring us a greater danger than the danger we are trying to avert. I do not believe that people like Mr. Kuhn or Mr. Browder[1] can have great success in injuring us as a nation. They may well be undesirable citizens of the United States, however, because, as has been made evident, their first loyalty belongs to some other country. They may be good citizens of the other nation; they are not good citizens of the United States.

Under our present laws we can deal fairly with our own people and still safeguard ourselves against those who would destroy democracy. We should constantly guard our civil liberties, to be sure that all get equally fair treatment, and try to teach greater tolerance. Actually, complete tolerance has not been realized as yet. My husband's ancestress, Anne Hutchinson, could have testified that the early New Englanders were not very tolerant. In 1637 she was expelled from the Boston Church because "she broke from a covenant of works in favor of a covenant of grace."

These New Englanders had left their native land out of a desire to be free from such prejudices as existed there, yet they persisted in their own type of intolerance. They were a good example of the sort of people who believe in tolerance so long as the opposition agrees with them. We always have that kind of tolerance with us.

Then again, we had a long fight to establish the fact that the right of man to govern himself does not depend upon his material possessions. We believe that in a democracy a man should participate in government even if he owns very little of this world's goods.

Strange to say—though we rarely think about it—that fight isn't yet won. We disenfranchise many people every year.

In a minor degree, our present intolerances have existed for a long time. We not only accepted immigrants from the Old World; we welcomed them with open arms. Some of them came as political refugees and were the cream of the countries which they left, but a great many were sought primarily for

---

[1] Fritz Kuhn headed the pro-Nazi German-American Bund. Earl Browder served as Secretary General of the Communist Party of the United States.

their ability to do a heavy day's work with their hands and to live on a submarginal standard, and we assumed a rather superior attitude toward them. We called foreigners "wops," "hunkies" and other names, and thought it beneath us to study foreign languages. It was up to the people who came here to learn our language, or at least learn enough to understand the orders issued to them in the day's work.

By our very attitude we strengthened these people and weakened ourselves. Our children learned no new language, while theirs did. Our children had no special difficulty to overcome. Their children did, and in the end they gained thereby.

We would not see that the newcomers frequently had a heritage of culture and skill to give us. For instance, even today the great majority of our expert cabinetmakers are of foreign extraction, and one of our greatest experts on early American furniture is a Russian Jew.

No, we did not profit by the foreigners' skills as much as we might have done. In this attitude toward the many foreigners who now make up our nation lie the roots of some of our present-day intolerance.

I sometimes meet people in drawing rooms who talk about the unemployed as though the latter were a different race, and occasionally remark: "Well, if they cannot support themselves, they are probably better off out of the way. They are not doing the country any good."

I leave with the feeling that these people were not my people, yet often we had much the same background.

Some persons I talk to remind me of a social worker who once refused assistance to a woman who had three starving children. When I inquired the reason for her hardness of heart, she responded: "My dear lady, the children are illegitimate!" Unfortunately, starvation does not take this item of morals into account!

Real tolerance does not attempt to make other people conform to any particular religious or racial pattern. We are within our rights, of course, in refusing to go to church with another man if we do not like his church, but we are certainly not within our rights in condemning him because he attends that church.

I should say that our open manifestations of intolerance today are still of minor importance. The great majority of our people stand behind the leaders who insist on freedom of speech, freedom of assembly, freedom of the press, and equality before the law. We do not attain these freedoms everywhere, but we like to think we do. The Ku Klux Klan is pretty well discredited. Similar organizations are probably going the same way.

The best recent example of real tolerance that I can think of was the protection given the meeting of the German-American Bund in New York by Mayor LaGuardia, even when the speakers denounced the mayor and his actions.

This is the kind of tolerance that recalls the statement attributed to Voltaire: "I disapprove of what you say, but I will defend to the death your right to say it."

On the whole, we back the authorities when they try to clean up conditions in business and politics which are irreconcilable with our traditions. With better education, some of our other prejudices will pass, but one factor we *must* face: the economic situation. As yet we haven't done so.

As I have said, the economic situation is the reason for much of our intolerance today. People who are having a hard time will complain about certain races, or certain groups, because they fear the economic competition of certain individuals who, either because of racial background or because of former experiences, may succeed better than they have succeeded.

Every individual who sees himself sinking below the economic surface fears his neighbor who can survive.

Because of the economic situation there is not enough work for men, so it is suggested that women be barred from economic independence. First it will be married women who should be supported by men, then it will be all other women, "Because woman was created to be the slave of man and should be dependent whether she likes it or not."

In 1939, twenty bills were introduced in as many legislatures in the United States to prevent married women from holding some kinds of positions. This was the direct result of economic intolerance. We fear that we cannot solve our economic difficulties. If we act in accordance with these fears, the results will be retrogression in civilization, as we may discover by looking back in history.

We must solve our economic problems from the point of view of re-employment, or we can never hope to wipe out intolerance.

Businessmen say our failure to solve the problem of giving men work is the fault of certain policies of the government. They have asked for certain changes which it is to be hoped Congress will make, insofar as these changes tend to increase employment.

We might as well face the fact, however, that for many people a revival of business is not regarded primarily from the point of view of the re-employment of men, but is thought of as an opportunity to make more money. Re-employment is spoken of as a thing which will naturally follow business revival.

I confess to some trepidation where re-employment is not the first consideration; where it is not fully realized that earned wages for more people is our best way to create better markets, and thus to establish our economic system on a firm basis. If we put the making of money first, I am afraid we shall have the cart before the horse.

In my opinion, the solution of this problem of giving men a chance to earn a decent living is the most important consideration before us at the present time, because ending unemployment will, to a very great extent, end intolerance. □

3.   "Why I Still Believe in the Youth Congress"

Liberty, April 20, 1941

When you and I were young, there was no need for a youth congress. We sat and listened to our elders. We went out, when the time came to earn a living, and we found jobs—at low wages, to be sure, and with pretty hard working conditions; but that was what we expected to find. We did the jobs, and a surprising number of us managed to find new avenues opening up, new opportunities, new worlds to conquer. The rest of us lived and died in drab and difficult surroundings, with our enjoyments frequently curtailed to some rather elemental things. . . . Enough people went out and found new opportunities for us to forget those who did not.

The need for a government program to help unemployed people; the need for a government program to help youth get more training for a job; and the need for various groups to get together to discuss their own difficult situations, is why we have forums, workers' alliances, and a youth congress. That is why people do not see in a name just a happy group of youngsters, and why some people are afraid of them. In reality, it is not the youngsters . . . , but it is the circumstances which have led to these groups getting together which inspire people with fear. So far, these groups are not very strong, but nobody knows when they may be. That is why we find the comfortable people of the world looking at them warily. Between four and five million unemployed young people is the estimate made by the American Youth Commission. That means that there are more people unemployed today below the age of twenty-five than over. A serious problem for youth.

Let us stop for a minute to consider just what our attitude as older, responsible citizens in a democracy should be. We cannot deny that we have a certain responsibility, because the world as it is today was made by us. If we have wars in Europe and the Far East, it is not the young people of twenty or thirty who carry any of the responsibility. It is we who saw war, the last war of twenty years ago, who have been directing public affairs, . . . who must now wake up in the night and wonder just what kind of world we have built for the youth of today.

. . . . [W]e had better face the fact that at least youth has a right to ask from us an honest acceptance of our responsibility, a study of their problems, cooperation with them in their efforts to find a solution, and patience in trying to understand their point of view and in stating our own.

Like so many other countries in the world, we are seizing upon the fear of Communism as a good excuse for attacking anything we do not like. Of course we have Communists in this country, and of course they appeal to the youth. The Communist Party leaders are giving youth training; they will help them to live while they volunteer as workers in something which they believe is going to help other young people. They are giving them a feeling that they are important in the world, a wide brotherhood working to improve the conditions of their fellow human beings. We who believe in democracy could do just the same for youth if we would take the trouble; but we have either failed in intelligent understanding of youth, or we have been apathetic ourselves. . . .

Even when a reputable journalist like Mr. Fulton Lewis, Jr., starts out to give a report on a meeting of a youth group, he does not take the trouble to get the details of the picture accurately—and that is one of the things which make youth resentful. . . . If he would look back in the records, he would find that the Dies Committee subpoenaed no one before making a statement to Congress about the Communist control of the Youth Congress; that committee was then requested to allow some of the Youth Congress leaders a hearing, and did nothing about it until November, after the report had been made to Congress in the previous January. Then, not Mr. Cadden, who had been secretary for two years, but Mr. William Hinckley, who had been chairman two years before, was subpoenaed. Mr. Hinckley was notified that the hearings were postponed, and then one afternoon a telegram arrived at the office of the American Youth Congress asking Mr. Hinckley to appear before the committee in Washington the following morning.

At this hearing a request was made that Mr. Cadden and Mr. Jack McMichael, the present chairman of the Youth Congress, should testify with Mr. Hinckley because the latter was not familiar with many of the activities of the Youth Congress during the past two years. This was allowed. Mr. Lewis proceeds to say that I was at Mr. Cadden's elbow and helped him and his companions to plan their testimony, and that I suggested the tactics, and at midday recess and in the evenings dined them at the White House. That last statement is the only statement which is true. I went to the hearings, but I was not at Mr. Cadden's elbow, nor did I plan the testimony nor the tactics.

Then you come to the description of what Mr. Lewis called "the Youth Congress Institute of Citizenship." And again the statement is inaccurate; because the Youth Congress sponsored and arranged the Citizenship Institute, but the people who attended were not of necessity affiliated with the Youth Congress. . . .

These youngsters came from all over the United States, however, and from every type of background; and it was quite reasonable to suppose that among such a big group here would be at least an organized representation of the Communist group, and that, having been trained while many of the others had not, they could make themselves felt. There is nothing very surprising about that.

Now let us come down to the actual meeting. Mr. Lewis says that Mr. Cadden told him that about 1,900 of the 5,130 young people who registered came from New York City, and that other officials said that close to 4,500 of this group were from New York City. I am sure Mr. Cadden was speaking from his knowledge of the registration, but I have asked for the final check, and find that 2,212 young people came from New York City. I also found that thirty-eight states and the District of Columbia had representatives at this Institute.

As to the difficulties which my young cousin, Archie Roosevelt, and his friends had in being heard, I can only say that I think they showed very little intelligence if they really were interested in getting over their point of view and not merely interested in making a disturbance. My experience is that if you want to get over a point of view, you find out the correct way of being heard. These two young men attempted to present a resolution during a meeting which was scheduled for speeches only, and no discussion. When informed that it was not the time to present a resolution and that the Institute could pass no resolutions, Mr. McArthur or Peter Tropea threw a book of rules governing the Senate and the House at the chairman of the meeting, and were then hustled out by those who felt that the meeting should proceed as scheduled. The next morning, before the opening meeting, the rules governing the procedure were adopted. Everyone wishing to speak could send up his or her name and, in the order in which the slips were received, would be allowed to come to the platform and speak for two minutes. You can say a good deal in two minutes if you are willing to be concise and clear. Here was the chance for these two young men to put over their point of view; but they did not take advantage of the opportunity.

. . . I have attended a great many meetings in the course of a long life, and I have seen steamroller tactics used by adults, and I have yet to see those methods used in the American Youth Congress meetings. . . .

This was a serious crowd of young people. Most of them had barely enough money to come to Washington for the three days. They sat up all night in buses and in cars. The fact that 20 percent of those present were Negro youth simply means that Negro youth has many problems.

It did not mean that these youngsters were out on a spree, whether white or colored.

Now to the question of the meeting on the White House lawn. Many young people started to parade after spending the night in buses with very little sleep. It was raining and it was cold. The young people to be addressed stood without any protection. There was nothing in the weather to encourage enthusiasm or to inspire a mood in which reproof could be accepted without rancor. The President tried to be ingratiating and he certainly had a kindly feeling toward his audience. It is true the young people showed bad manners, but how many older people would have gone through that ordeal and have accepted criticism gracefully? I do not condone bad manners, nor do I condone disrespect for a high office; but only a fraction of those present showed such disrespect. I think all of us in public life understand the type of audience we are addressing, and we do not expect, under certain conditions, the kind of self-discipline and self-restraint which might be expected from older people or even from young people with different backgrounds. I wonder if older people would always be able to rise above the feeling of being baffled by their problems when those to whom they look for leadership and reassurance seem to fail them?

No, I do not condone bad manners, but I am experienced enough to understand them sometimes in both old and young. Youth should not be pampered, but they should be treated fairly and sympathetically. They must learn by their own mistakes, but we must not make them feel that their mistakes are irretrievable.

Now as to the hisses which greeted some of my statements. Why should anyone who goes before a group of people to express points of view which conflict with those held by some of the audience expect not to be hissed?

The Columbia University students mentioned in Mr. Lewis' article were quite right when they said: "Do we have to pay for her help by subscribing to what she says?" I never for a minute would expect such a thing. I hold no office which requires respect. The President does. That is why bad manners on the lawn of the White House was worse than bad manners in the auditorium. I did not go to answer questions for the Citizenship Institute as the President's wife. I went as Eleanor Roosevelt, to answer, as honestly as I could, questions that were going to be put to me as an individual. I had the obligation not to place the President or the administration in any difficulties through my answers. Outside of that, I had an obligation to be truthful and give whatever information I could. The young people had an obligation to listen to me because they had asked me to come, but no obligation whatsoever to agree, nor to suppress their feelings, whatever they might be.

The disturbance in the gallery of the Congress was, of course, unfortunate. Had these youngsters been older, they would have realized that it was very foolish and that it would bring them discredit. In addition, it would tend to create antagonism to the bill in which they were interested.

Mr. Lewis quotes Mr. Ernest Lindley as writing: "They [the American Youth Congress] have washed themselves out. It is doubtful whether even Mrs. Roosevelt could obtain a hearing of their case [in public opinion] after their performance here." This is perfectly true as far as newspapers and certain sections of public opinion are concerned, but they haven't washed themselves out with the young people. Whatever else the Institute did, it awakened in a great many young people a realization that there are others who are struggling with the same questions that they are struggling with. . . .

All the attacks made upon the Congress have only consolidated the feeling of "youth against the world." That is a danger, I think; because what we want to do is to have all ages work together to solve the problems of today. We have gone about obtaining this cooperation most stupidly. Whether we can retrieve what we have lost, and make these youngsters feel that the attacks that have been made upon them in the press do not represent the attitude of thinking and sympathetic older people, I do not know. If we cannot, then I think we have done a dangerous thing; because, whatever else this meeting did, it awakened a great many more young people to the fact that they were being attacked as young people, and that is not a good spirit to foster. . . .

The American Youth Congress may lose some of the groups which were affiliated with them, but they will be sorry if they lose any members, because I think it is important to join together in work on the main issues—namely, (1) to try to help young people to get jobs; (2) to try to advance the cause of civil liberties in this country; (3) to try really to study what will bring us more permanent peace in the future. . . .

I wish we could look at this whole question of the activities of youth-led organizations from the point of view of the wisest way for older people to help youth. We certainly cannot help by attacking them, or by refusing to co-operate when we are asked for financial assistance or for speakers to attend their meetings. Making inaccurate statements about them is not helpful. We must go and deal with them as equals, and we must have both courage and integrity if we expect respect and cooperation on the part of youth.

4.   # "Civil Liberties—The Individual and the Community"

Address to the Chicago Civil Liberties Committee, March 14, 1940
Reference Shelf, 1940

Ladies and gentlemen: . . . Now we have come here tonight because of civil liberties. I imagine a great many of you could give my talk far better than I could, because you have had first-hand knowledge in the things you have had to do in Chicago over the years to preserve civil liberties. Perhaps, however, I am more conscious of the importance of civil liberties in the particular moment of our history than anyone else, because as I travel through the country and meet people and see things that have happened to little people, I realize what it means to democracy to preserve our civil liberties. All through the years we have had to fight for civil liberty, and we know that there are times when the light grows rather dim, and every time that happens democracy is in danger. Now largely because of the troubled state of the world as a whole civil liberties have disappeared in many other countries. It is impossible, of course, to be at war and to keep freedom of the press and freedom of speech and freedom of assembly. They disappear automatically. And so in many countries where ordinarily they were safe, today they have gone and in other countries, even before war came, not only freedom of the press and freedom of assembly and freedom of speech disappeared, but freedom of religion disappeared and so we know that here in this country we have a grave responsibility. We are at peace. We have no reason for the fears which govern so many other peoples throughout the world, and, therefore, we have to guard the freedoms of democracy. Civil liberties emphasize the liberty of the individual. In many other forms of government the importance of the individual has disappeared. The individual lives for the state. Here in a democracy the government still exists for the individual, but that does not mean that we do not have to watch and that we do not have to examine ourselves to be sure that we preserve the civil liberties for all our people, which are the basis of our democracy. Now you know if we are honest with ourselves, in spite of all we have said, in spite of our Constitution, many of us in this country do not enjoy real liberty. For that reason we know that everywhere in this country every person who believes in democracy has come to feel a real responsibility to work in his community and to know the people of his community, and to take the trouble to try to bring about the full observance for all our people of their civil liberties.

I think I will tell you a little story that brought home to me how important it was that in every community there should be someone to whom people could turn, who were in doubt as to what were their rights under the law, when they couldn't understand what was happening to them. I happen to go every now and then to a certain mining community and in that mining community there are a number of people who came to this country many years ago. They have been here so many years that they have no other country. This is their country. Their children have been born here. They work here. They have created great wealth for this country, but they came over at a time when there was not very much feeling of social responsibility about giving them the opportunity to learn the language of the country to which they had come, or telling them how to become citizens, or teaching about the government of this country. I had contact with a family where the man had been here over thirty-five years, and the first time I went to see him in his house it came about this way. I was standing with a group of people, and a young girl with arms full of packages came along the road. She stopped to look at me and said, "Why, you are Mrs. Roosevelt. My mama say, 'She is happy if you come to her house.' " I said, "Where is her house?" "Up the run." So I walked with her and when I got to the house a Polish woman was sitting at the table. The girl walked in and said, "Mama, this is Mrs. Roosevelt," and the woman got up and threw both arms around me, and I was kissed on both cheeks. She told me she had been expecting me to come for a long time. She wanted me to come because she wanted me to see how really nice her house was, and we went through the four rooms and it was nice. She had made crochet pieces which decorated every table. The bedspreads were things of real beauty. We admired everything together. We came back to the kitchen and she said, "You eat with us?" and I said, "No, I just had breakfast." She wouldn't let me leave without eating something, so we had a piece of bread there together.

Six months later I came back and I went again to visit my friend. The minute I crossed the threshold I knew something had happened in that house. It was quite dark. In a few minutes the old man came through from the back room and said, "Mrs. Roosevelt, you have come. I have wanted to ask you something for a long time. The mine, it close down, no more work. I work on W.P.A. for a time and then they tell me I no citizen. Mrs. Roosevelt, I vote. I vote often. Why I no citizen?" There was nobody that stood out in the community that he dared trust, that he felt he could go to find out what his rights were, or what he should do. Well, of course, it was true that he had never become a citizen. His children were born in this country; they were citizens, but he was not. And they had lived, those two people by being allowed by the county to take in four old men who would have gone otherwise to the county poor house. Six people were living on the allowance of those four old men. The allowance was pitifully small. As I looked at the stove at what they were going to have for supper, I realized the woman wouldn't again say, "Sit down and eat." There wasn't enough for a stranger, and that was the breakdown of her morale. It hurt you. Something was wrong with the spirit of America that an injustice like that could happen to a man who, after all, worked hard and contributed to the wealth of the country. It should have been somebody's business, first of all, to see that he learned the English language well enough to find things out for himself. Secondly, when he was in trouble, to fight for his rights and to tell him how to go about to remedy what was wrong. I felt there was something wrong with any community where you had to wait many months for a stranger to come to listen to your story and help you straighten out what was a manifest injustice. He couldn't be on W.P.A. He could start out to become a citizen, and he could get relief and, at least, have the feeling that there was an interest on the part of someone in justice. I think that is, perhaps, one of the greatest things that the civil liberties committees do, and I wish we had one in every place throughout the country—one group of people who really care when things go wrong and do something when there is an infringement of the individual's rights.

There are many times when even with freedom of the press and freedom of speech, it is hard to get a hearing for certain causes. I often think that we, all of us, should think very much more carefully than we do about what we mean by freedom of speech, by freedom of the press, by freedom of assembly. I sometimes am much worried by the tendencies.   □

5.   "Social Gains and Defense"
       Common Sense, March 1941

The preservation of any gains at any time in a democracy depends primarily on the will of each individual to do his share toward that preservation. We are gradually waking up to the fact that living in a democracy is not an easy thing. We have taken a great deal for granted in the past. I think that many of us have felt that always, no matter what we did, some inherent rights were ours which would affect our way of life.

Well, we're waking up to the fact that a form of government which is called a democracy requires everybody to work every day and to live for that way of life and develop it through his efforts. We can't take anything for granted and we can't sit back and think it's somebody else's responsibility. And perhaps when we talk about whether we can keep certain social gains while the defense program is being developed and is going on, we'd better accept that basic fact first of all.

It depends on us as individuals. We can have what we want. But we'll have to pay for it in self-discipline, in sacrifice, in work, in determination to preserve certain things. I sometimes hear people make remarks which would indicate that they think one achieves things in this world without any effort. Of course we are going to pay for everything we get. It all depends upon whether we care enough to pay the price.

One way to preserve the gains we've made is to have mediums for discussion in which we can say frankly what we feel, what we think, and *Common Sense* is one of those mediums. It is essential, I think, to all social gains, that we realize that we can't simply maintain a status; we have to go on. If we stand still we slide back. And we must always examine everything at every step of the way. It's well to be critical of ourselves, of the things we do, but always to be critical with the objective of finding something better—not just to tear down but to suggest and to experiment with doing something better.

I feel very strongly that no one today, looking at our own country and really knowing it, can be satisfied. If you ask me if I want to merely "maintain" under the defense program, gains we have made in various lines of social service to the country in the last few years—or of social justice—I will say that I will not be satisfied just to maintain those gains. I feel that we still have many things to do before we can even begin to feel that we are really a democracy.

I do not see why, under the defense program, we cannot move forward. It seems to me that in housing alone there is a great opportunity for experiment in the next few years. There is an awareness, I think, of the things we may attempt to do. I don't think we can expect that every attempt will be successful, but we really have an opportunity to find out, under the defense program, what things must be done in the field of housing in a variety of situations. One thing which I am very much interested in at the moment is not merely whether we shall provide shelter but whether the government hasn't an obligation—when it draws people together in a community either temporarily or with the idea of permanency—to sit down with the state and local governments and work out opportunities for good living in that community. For instance, at this very moment, in Bremerton, Washington, there are something like twenty-five hundred children with no school available. That is not exactly a satisfactory way to plan a life for people who are doing a very essential work for the defense program.

There are places where there is no medical care whatsoever. And we are going to find that just as in the line of housing which we are bound to face, we are going to meet all kinds of new problems and decide just where the responsibility lies and find out how we are going to work it out. In this direction lie great opportunities for education for life in a democracy and its responsibilities.

Under the defense program we are, of course, confronted with the need for emphasizing certain kinds of production, and to certain people that production is a paramount obligation. We all acknowledge that that must be achieved. But I think it will be better achieved if at the same time we achieve for human beings a constantly increasing satisfaction in their way of life. If we establish that, I think we will find that a desire to produce for defense along the entire front will outstrip even the hopes of our most ardent planners. I think that people who feel that they are constantly moving forward in a way of life which they can see is better for them and for their families—a way which promises more opportunities for education, for recreation, for health—can have no hesitation then in deciding that what they have is worth defending.

I am entirely frank in saying that I can understand the point of view of many people in this country today who are not sure whether what they have is worth defending. Of course, you and I can look across the water and say that no matter what our conditions are they are worth defending in comparison with what we see in other lands. . . . But I have great sympathy with a woman who wrote me a most vituperative letter the other day. (I grieve to say that she did not sign her name. If she had I might have done something about her situation.) What made her write the letter was the significant thing. She said, "I am starving and my children are starving. What do I care—if Hitler will give me any kind of a living and promise it to me steadily—what do *I* care who is in power and who wins the war! I don't want my son to be killed when it doesn't seem to me to matter what happens."

There is a case for that woman, just as there was for a youngster who said to me once that it was all very well for those young people who had jobs and who had educations they hadn't had to work very hard to get, and who always had plenty to eat, to say that they were willing to defend the country. For his part, he had spent six years wandering over the country and he had never been able to find a job, except now and then for a day or so, and the country had not given him much of a home or much of a job or much of an education. And he did not see that it was best for him to defend a way of life that for him was not very good. Well, we don't agree; we say that even as it is it is better than domination by one man, or by a few men. We must understand their point of view, however, because only by understanding it, only by knowing what brings it about, are we going to move forward in our social gains. Only by knowing that we have to move forward, will we be prepared to broaden the base. And only when the base is broadened can all the people be certain that a way of life beneficial to them is at stake, and that therefore they have an individual responsibility to render service in the pattern of democracy. Then will they have something for which they are willing to work. Then will they have something for which they are willing to sacrifice.

Only with equal justice, equal opportunity, and equal participation in the government can we expect to be a united country—a country that is prepared to win out in any battle, the battle of economic production and of solving of our social questions, or the battle of ideas which is perhaps today the most important of all, for ideas know no barriers. It is only the knowledge that you are fighting for a better future which makes life worth living.   □

6.   "Race, Religion and Prejudice"

New Republic, May 11, 1942

Madame Chiang Kai-shek's recent articles force us all to realize that one of the phases of this war that we have to face is the question of race discrimination.

We have had a definite policy toward the Chinese and Japanese who wished to enter our country for many years, and I doubt very much if after this war is over we can differentiate between the peoples of Europe, the Near East and the Far East.

Perhaps the simplest way of facing the problem in the future is to say that we are fighting for freedom, and one of the freedoms we must establish is freedom from discrimination among the peoples of the world, either because of race, or of color, or of religion.

The people of the world have suddenly begun to stir and they seem to feel that in the future we should look upon each other as fellow human beings, judged by our acts, by our abilities, by our development, and not by any less fundamental differences.

Here in our own country we have any number of attitudes which have become habits and which constitute our approach to the Jewish people, the Japanese and Chinese people, the Italian people, and above all, to the Negro people in our midst.

Perhaps because the Negroes are our largest minority, our attitude towards them will have to be faced first of all. I keep on repeating that the way to face this situation is by being completely realistic. We cannot force people to accept friends for whom they have no liking, but living in a democracy it is entirely reasonable to demand that every citizen of that democracy enjoy the fundamental rights of a citizen.

Over and over again, I have stressed the rights of every citizen:

Equality before the law.

Equality of education.

Equality to hold a job according to his ability.

Equality of participation through the ballot in the government.

These are inherent rights in a democracy, and I do not see how we can fight this war and deny these rights to any citizen in our own land.

The other relationships will gradually settle themselves once these major things are part of our accepted philosophy.

It seems trite to say to the Negro, you must have patience, when he has had patience so long; you must not expect miracles overnight, when he can look back to the years of slavery and say—how many nights! he has waited for justice. Nevertheless, it is what we must continue to say in the interests of our government as a whole and of the Negro people; but that does not mean that we must sit idle and do nothing. We must keep moving forward steadily, removing restrictions which have no sense, and fighting prejudice. If we are wise we will do this where it is easiest to do it first, and watch it spread gradually to places where the old prejudices are slow to disappear.

There is now a great group of educated Negroes who can become leaders among their people, who can teach them the value of things of the mind and who qualify as the best in any field of endeavor. With these men and women it is impossible to think of any barriers of inferiority, but differences there are and always will be, and that is why on both sides there must be tact and patience and an effort at real understanding. Above everything else, no action must be taken which can cause so much bitterness that the whole liberalizing effort may be set back over a period of many years.   □

---

7.   **"Must We Hate to Fight?"**

The Saturday Review, July 4, 1942

Can we kill other human beings if we do not hate them? I suppose the answer must come from those in our fighting forces. Some young people will tell you that unless you hate the people of Germany and Japan, you cannot possibly win. On the other hand, many a young soldier going into the war, will assure you that he cannot hate the individuals of any race. He can only hate the system which has made those individuals his enemies. If he must kill them in order to do away with the system, he will do so, but not because he hates them as individuals. If those who say that to win the war we must hate, are really expressing the beliefs of the majority of our people, I am afraid we have already lost the peace, because our main objective is to make a world in which all the people of the world may live with respect and good will for each other in peace.

If we allow the hate of other men as individuals to possess us, we cannot discard hate the day we have won and suddenly become understanding and cooperative neighbors.

There will be no victory if out of this war we simply develop armed camps again throughout the world. We may in the interests of self-preservation cut down the actual race to obtain guns, planes, and battleships because no people will survive if it goes on, nor will those who survive have the wherewithal for the decencies of life. Even if we cut out all weapons of force, there can exist armed camps in the minds of people, which express themselves through the economic systems which we set up and through all the barriers which we set up between peoples to keep them from real understanding. If we really do not mean that after this war we intend to see that people the world over have an opportunity to obtain a satisfactory life, then all we are doing is to prepare for a new war. There is no excuse for the bloodshed, the sacrifices, and the tears which the world as a whole is now enduring, unless we build a new worthwhile world.

The saving grace for most of us is that hope does spring eternal in the human breast. We do believe that just around the corner is that solution to our problems which we have long been looking for and that human beings will never give up til they find the answers.

I believe that the solution will be easier to find when we work together, and when all the plans, all the abilities of people the world over, are concentrated on finding positive solutions, but if we hate each other then I despair of achieving any ultimate good results.

I will acknowledge that it is easier to urge upon our people that they hate those whom we now must fight as individuals, because it is always easier to build up contempt and dislike for that which is making us suffer than it is to force ourselves to analyze the reasons which have brought about these conditions and try to eliminate them.

In small ways we see over and over again that the child who is badgered and punished in youth grows up to treat anyone weaker than himself in much the same way. That is probably what we will do to the people of our nation as a whole when we tell them that in fighting to stamp out cruelty and hate, dominated by force, they must hate. Somehow as a whole the thousands in our fighting forces must preserve a belief and a respect for the individual and a hate only of the system, or else we will go down ourselves, victims of the very system which today we are striving to conquer.   □

8.   "Freedom: Promise or Fact"

Negro Digest, October 1943

If I were a Negro today, I think I would have moments of great bitterness. It would be hard for me to sustain my faith in democracy and to build up a sense of goodwill toward men of other races.

I think, however, that I would realize that if my ancestors had never left Africa, we would be worse off as "natives" today under the rule of any other country than I am in this country where my people were brought as slaves.

In a comparatively short period of time the slaves have become free men— free men, that is, as far as a proclamation can make them so. There now remains much work to be done to see that freedom becomes a fact and not just a promise for my people.

I know, however, that I am not the only group that has to make a similar fight. Even women of the white race still suffer inequalities and injustices, and many groups of white people in my country are slaves of economic conditions. All the world is suffering under a great war brought about because of the lag in our social development against the progress in our economic development.

I would know that I had to work hard and to go on accomplishing the best that was possible under present conditions. Even though I was held back by generations of economic inequality, I would be proud of those of my race who are gradually fighting to the top in whatever occupation they are engaged in.

I would still feel that I ought to participate to the full in the war. When the United Nations win, certain things will be accepted as a result of principles which have been enunciated by the leaders of the United Nations, which never before have been part of the beliefs and practices of the greater part of the world.

I would certainly go on working for complete economic equality and my full rights under a democratic government. I would decide which were the steps that I felt represented my real rights as a citizen and I would work for those first, feeling that other things such as social relationships might well wait until certain people were given time to think them through and decide as individuals what they wished to do.

I would not do too much demanding. I would take every chance that came my way to prove my quality and my ability and if recognition was slow, I would continue to prove myself, knowing that in the end good performance has to be acknowledged.

I would accept every advance that was made in the Army and Navy, though I would not try to bring those advances about any more quickly than they were offered. I would certainly affiliate with the labor movement because there is the greatest opportunity for men to work side by side and find out that it is possible to have similar interests and to stand by each other, regardless of race or color.

I would try to remember that unfair and unkind treatment will not harm me if I do not let it touch my spirit. Evil emotions injure the man or woman who harbors them so I would try to fight down resentment, the desire for revenge and bitterness. I would try to sustain my own faith in myself by counting over my friends and among them there would undoubtedly be some white people. □

9.   ## "Abolish Jim Crow!"

New Threshold, August 1943

A senator stood up in the Congress the other day after listening to a lengthy discourse on the poll tax, and spoke his mind on the discussion which was going on. Later he asked: "Are we fighting the Civil War all over again?"

Sometimes when I look at the Lincoln statue and read the things which he said, I think that we fought a bitter war which brought suffering to many people and yet achieved no answer to the question—are the colored people free in fact or only in word?

In that war we succeeded in establishing our unity. We would be one nation and not two and we said that all the people in our nation should enjoy equal rights and privileges, but in our hearts we never really believed what we said.

That is why we have to set to work to persuade our citizens not only to give lip-service to the results of the Civil War, but actually to put those results into practice, even though we are engaged in fighting a war to assure these same rights and privileges of freedom throughout the world.

A great many people believe that there should be no intermingling of races. Hitler has proved with bloody massacres that he holds this belief. Nevertheless, down through the ages, it has been proved over and over again that this is one of the questions which people settle for themselves, and no amount of legislation will keep them from doing so. We would not have so many different shades of color in this country today if this were not so. This is a question, therefore, that I think we have to leave to individuals, not only all over the United States, but all over the world, to handle.

There is no more reason to expect that there will be more intermarriage if the four fundamental basic rights of citizens are granted to all people in this country than there will be if they are withheld. In fact, I think it probable that there would be less.

An equal opportunity for education may raise economic standards as a whole—may make it possible for colored people to get equal pay, because they will have training equal to that of white people. There will be more self-respect; the dignity and pride of race will be enhanced and the bitterness of inferiority removed.

I am not writing from the point of view of the scientists, as their point of view is amply covered in many scientific books. I am trying to state the case clearly because we need firm ground to stand on as we fight this war.

Many a boy, when asked, still says he does not know what he is fighting for. While he knows we have to beat Hitler and the Japs, he will be glad when it is done and he is back home again. That would be all right if winning the war would settle all the racial questions, but it is after the war when we live together that they will become really important. In addition, if every boy was sure that he would be going back home again, he could decide later for what objectives he had fought and work for them, but if he is to die, he must be sure that what he died for is worthwhile to his parents, his brothers, his sisters, his wife or his sweetheart.   □

10.   "A Challenge to American Sportsmanship"
Collier's, October 16, 1943

I can well understand the bitterness of people who have lost loved ones at the hands of the Japanese military authorities, and we know that the totalitarian philosophy, whether it is in Nazi Germany or in Japan, is one of cruelty and brutality. It is not hard to understand why people living here in hourly anxiety for those they love have difficulty in viewing our Japanese problem objectively, but for the honor of our country, the rest of us must do so.

A decision has been reached to divide the disloyal and disturbing Japanese from the others in the War Relocation centers. One center will be established for the disloyal and will be more heavily guarded and more restricted than those in which these Japanese have been in the past. This separation is taking place now.

All the Japanese in the War Relocation centers have been carefully checked by the personnel in charge of the camps, not only on the basis of their own information but also on the basis of the information supplied by the Federal Bureau of Investigation, by G-2 for the Army, and by the Office of Naval Intelligence for the Navy. We can be assured, therefore, that they are now moving into this segregation center in northern California the people who are loyal to Japan.

Japanese-Americans who are proved completely loyal to the United States will, of course, gradually be absorbed. The others will be sent to Japan after the war.

At present, things are very peaceful in most of the Japanese Relocation centers. The strike that received so much attention in the newspapers last November in Poston, Arizona, and the riot at Manzanar, California, in December were settled effectively, and nothing resembling them has occurred since. It is not difficult to understand that uprooting thousands of people brought on emotional upsets that take time and adjustment to overcome.

Neither all the government people, naturally, nor all of the Japanese were perfect, and many changes in personnel had to be made. It was an entirely new undertaking for us, it had to be done in a hurry, and, considering the number of people involved, I think the whole job of handling our Japanese has, on the whole, been done well.

A good deal has already been written about the problem. One phase of it, however, I do not think has as yet been adequately stressed. To cover it, we must get our whole background straight.

We have in all 127,000 Japanese or Japanese-Americans in the United States. Of these, 112,000 lived on the West Coast. Originally, they were much needed on ranches and on large truck and fruit farms, but, as they came in greater numbers, people began to discover that they were competitors in the labor field.

The people of California began to be afraid of Japanese importation, so the Exclusion Act was passed in 1924. No people of the Oriental race could become citizens of the United States by naturalization, and no quota was given to the Oriental nations in the Pacific.

This happened because, in one part of our country, they were feared as competitors, and the rest of our country knew them so little and cared so little about them that they did not even think about the principle that we in this country believe in: that of equal rights for all human beings.

We granted no citizenship to Orientals, so now we have a group of people of whom have been here as long as fifty years) who have not been able to become citizens under our laws. Long before the war, an old Japanese man told me that he had great-grandchildren born in this country and that he had never been back to Japan; all that he cared about was here on the soil of the United States, and yet he could not become a citizen.

The children of these Japanese, born in this country, are citizens, however, and now we have about 47,000 aliens, born in Japan, who are known as Issei, and about 80,000 American-born citizens, known as Nisei. Most of these Japanese-Americans have gone to our American schools and colleges, and have never known any other country or any other life than the life here in the United States.

The large group of Japanese on the West Coast preserved their national traditions, in part because they were discriminated against. Japanese were not always welcome buyers of real estate. They were not always welcome neighbors or participators in community undertakings. As always happens with groups that are discriminated against, they gather together and live as racial groups. The younger ones made friends in school and college, and became part of the community life, and prejudices lessened against them. Their elders were not always sympathetic to the changes thus brought about in manners and customs.

There is a group among the American-born Japanese called the Kibei. These are American citizens who have gone to Japan and returned to the United States. Figures compiled by the War Relocation Authority show that 72 percent of the American citizens have never been to Japan. Technically, the remainder, approximately 28 percent, are Kibei, but they include many young people who made only short visits, perhaps as children with their parents. Usually the term Kibei is used to refer to those who have received a considerable portion of their education in Japan.

While many of the Kibei are loyal to Japan, some of them were revolted by what they learned of Japanese militarism and are loyal to the land of their birth, America.

Enough for the background. Now we come to Pearl Harbor, December 7, 1941. There was no time to investigate families or to adhere strictly to the American rule that a man is innocent until he is proved guilty. These people were not convicted of any crime, but emotions ran too high. Too many people wanted to wreak vengeance on Oriental-looking people. Even the Chinese, our allies, were not always safe from insult on the streets. The Japanese had long been watched by the FBI, as were other aliens, and several hundred were apprehended at once on the outbreak of war and sent to detention camps.

Approximately three months after Pearl Harbor, the Western Defense Command ordered all persons of Japanese ancestry excluded from the coastal area, including approximately half of Washington, Oregon and California, and the southern portion of Arizona. Later, the entire state of California was added to the zone from which Japanese were barred.

At first, the evacuation was placed on a voluntary basis; the people were free to go wherever they liked in the interior of the country. But the evacuation on this basis moved very slowly, and furthermore, those who did leave encountered a great deal of difficulty in finding new places to settle. In order to avoid serious incidents, on March 29, 1942, the evacuation was placed on an orderly basis, and was carried out by the Army.

A civilian agency, the War Relocation Authority, was set up to work with the military in the relocation of the people. Because there was so much indication of danger to the Japanese unless they were protected, relocation centers were established where they might live until those whose loyalty could be established could be gradually reabsorbed into the normal life of the nation.

To many young people this must have seemed strange treatment of American citizens, and one cannot be surprised at the reaction that manifested itself not only in young Japanese-Americans, but in others who had known them well and had been educated with them, and who asked bitterly, "What price American citizenship?"

Nevertheless, most of them realized that this was a safety measure. The Army carried out its evacuation, on the whole, with remarkable skill and kindness. The early situation in the centers was difficult. Many of them were not ready for occupation. The setting up of large communities meant an amount of organization which takes time, but the Japanese, for the most part, proved to be patient, adaptable and courageous.

There were unexpected problems and, one by one, these were discovered and an effort was made to deal with them fairly. For instance, these people had property and they had to dispose of it; often at a loss. Sometimes they could not dispose of it, and it remained unprotected, deteriorating in value as the months went by. Business had to be handled through agents, since the Japanese could not leave the camps.

Understandable bitterness against the Japanese is aggravated by the old-time economic fear on the West Coast and the unreasoning racial feeling which certain people, through ignorance, have always had wherever they came in contact with people who were different from themselves.

This is one reason why many people believe that we should have directed our original immigration more intelligently. We needed people to develop our country, but we should never have allowed any groups to settle as groups where they created little German or Japanese or Scandinavian "islands" and did not melt into our general community pattern. Some of the South American countries have learned from our mistakes and are now planning to scatter their needed immigration.

Gradually, as the opportunities for outside jobs are offered to them, loyal citizens and law-abiding aliens are going out of the relocation centers to start independent and productive lives again. Those not considered reliable, of course, are not permitted to leave. As a taxpayer, regardless of where you live, it is to your advantage, if you find one or two Japanese-American families settled in your neighborhood, to try to regard them as individuals and not to condemn them before they are given a fair chance to prove themselves in the community.

"A Japanese is always a Japanese" is an easily accepted phrase and it has taken hold quite naturally on the West Coast because of some reasonable or unreasonable fear back of it, but it leads nowhere and solves nothing. Japanese-Americans may be no more Japanese than a German-American is German, or an Italian-American is Italian. All of these people, including the Japanese-Americans, have men who are fighting today for the preservation of the democratic way of life and the ideas around which our nation was built.

We have no common race in this country, but we have an ideal to which all of us are loyal. It is our ideal which we want to have live. It is an ideal which can grow with our people, but we cannot progress if we look down upon any group of people among us because of race or religion. Every citizen in this country has a right to our basic freedoms, to justice and to equality of opportunity, and we retain the right to lead our individual lives as we please, but we can only do so if we grant to others the freedoms that we wish for ourselves.   □

11.   "Henry A. Wallace's *Democracy Reborn*"
The New Republic, August 7, 1944[2]

Democracy Reborn is a collection of the speeches and writings of Henry Wallace, some of which go back to 1932 and 1933, when he became Secretary of

---

[2] Although this article appeared after the 1944 Democratic Convention, at which Henry Wallace, Vice President during Franklin Roosevelt's third term, was replaced on the ticket by then-Senator Harry Truman, ER had actually submitted the article to *The New Republic* two weeks before the convention, in order to endorse his renomination.

Agriculture. This is a valuable collection; first, because it is a contribution to the understanding of a human being who has become a statesman; and second, because it drives into the minds of the American people certain truths which Mr. Wallace makes clear as no other statesman in this period has done.

The introduction written by the editor, Russell Lord, is an essential part of the book. Mr. Lord reveals the background and hereditary influence which illumines the personality of the Vice President. Some of his ideas are better understood today because of the knowledge of what his grandfather was, and Mr. Wallace's extensive training in journalism and in the technique of scientific experiment help one to understand the patience which he showed as Secretary of Agriculture. Mr. Wallace never was a politician and is not a very good one now, but he has long been a thinker and writer. That is why his speeches, until very recently, read much better than they sound. He has had to become a speaker.

If one were to pick out the one outstanding and continuing theme of all that Wallace says, it is his belief that whatever is done, must be done for the general welfare of the majority of the people. This belief colors his attitude on domestic as well as international problems.

You will hear people say that they are afraid of Henry Wallace because he is a dreamer, an impractical person, a mystic. No one who reads these speeches attentively would be afraid on any of these counts. They would recognize instead a man of curiosity, of deep religious feeling, not bound by any particular doctrine. They would know that he had to be practical because his scientific training was too intense to allow loose thinking. They would know that out of his background, nothing which was not truly American could possibly grow. He has traditional American attitudes on so many things that this fear of him which has been implanted in some people's minds, will seem strange to anyone who reads him carefully.

He is a realist. In 1933 he recognized the he could not embark on the realization of his own theory of abundance until he had cleared away the wreckage left by the past, and changed the political and economic philosophy which had preceded him. That is the attitude of a practical, straight thinking person.

There is a unity of thought in what he writes about the hopes the American people have for the future. It runs through every year of his life. Back in 1933 we find him saying:

> In brief, then, we wish a wider and better controlled use of engineering and science to the end that man may have a much higher percentage of his energy left over to enjoy the things which are non-material and non-economic, and I would include in this not only music, painting, literature and sport for sport's sake, but

I would particularly include the idle curiosity of the scientist himself. Even the most enthusiastic engineers and scientists should be heartily desirous of bending their talents to serve these higher human ends. If the social will does not recognize these ends, at this particular stage in history, there is grave danger that Spengler may be proved right after all, and a thousand years hence a new civilization will be budding forth after this one has long lain fallow in a relative Middle Ages.

And in 1944 we find the following:

Big business must not have such control of Congress and the executive branch of government as to make it easy for them to write the rules of the postwar game in a way which will shut out the men who have made such a magnificent contribution to the productive power of America during the war. We need them to furnish the jobs which are so important both to labor and to agriculture.

The big three—Big Business, Big Labor and Big Agriculture—if they struggle to grab federal power for monopolistic purposes, are certain to come into serious conflict unless they recognize the superior claims of the general welfare of the common man. Such recognition of the general welfare must be genuine, must be more than polite mouthing of the high-sounding phrases. Each . . . has unprecedented power at the present time. Each is faced with serious postwar worries. Each will be tempted to try to profit at the expense of the other two when the postwar boom breaks. Each can save itself only if it learns to work with the other two and with government in terms of the general welfare. To work together without slipping into an American fascism will be the central problem of postwar democracy.

The most revealing speech from the point of view of the man himself, his tenderness and sensitivity, is the one made at the commencement exercises of the Connecticut College for Women. His mind was wholly engrossed with the death of the son of his good friend, Milo Perkins, a boy whom he had known and loved. This boy had pointed out that though young men fight wars, it is fifteen or twenty years before they come to the position where they really control the postwar activity, or the political climate in which the results of the war are really accomplished. The boy wondered and doubted whether the older men in power would make the kind of a peace he was willing to fight for. Henry Wallace points out the responsibility of the older generation and then appeals to the youth coming out of college, urging them to grasp their responsibilities and carry out the duties which a people assume when they govern themselves.

In 1942 Mr. Wallace cited the four duties of the American people as he saw them. We were in the war and this was the people's pact:

The duty to produce to the limit.

The duty to transport these products as rapidly as possible to the field of battle.

The duty to fight with all that is in us.

The duty to build a peace—just, charitable and enduring.

In 1943 he defined the responsibilities of the peace. He lists for us the six assets which will be ours when the war comes to an end:

Manpower by the Million: skilled workers from war industries, military manpower and young people coming of working age.

The largest industrial plant capacity in the world.

The greatest resources, both natural and artificial, to make peacetime products—and thousands of new inventions waiting to be converted to peacetime use.

The largest scientific farm plant in the world.

The biggest backlog of requirements for housing, transportation, communications and living comforts.

The greatest reserve of accumulated savings by individuals that any nation has ever known.

Vice President Wallace found Mr. David Lilienthal's book on the TVA one of the most exciting books he had read in the past year. That in itself is another key to the personality of Henry Wallace. He warns us of the possible danger of American fascism. He knows our weaknesses, he knows our temptations, but he has a deep-seated faith in the common sense, idealism and purpose which our people have. As far back as 1940 he said, "There has continually flamed in the hearts of Americans the belief that this continent is different. On this new soil, we have thought, mankind would escape from the compulsions, the suspicions and the greeds of the Old World."

But Mr. Wallace knows that we have to grow with the times and he is trying to point out the way we must travel. I hope many people will read his collection of speeches, for I doubt that it would be possible in any other way to get the full impact of his belief that successful democracy must have an underpinning of religious belief, and that the future, which may be a glorious one, depends on what we in America think and feel and determine to do. He believes in individual responsibility, but he knows that unless we work for the good of the common man there is no future for any of us.   □

12.   # FDR's Death

My Day, April 17, 1945

Washington—When you have lived for a long time in close contact with the loss and grief which today pervades the world, any personal sorrow seems to be lost in the general sadness of humanity. For a long time, all hearts have been heavy for every serviceman sacrificed in the war. There is only one way in which those of us who live can repay the dead who have given their utmost for the cause of liberty and justice. They died in the hope that, through their sacrifice, an enduring peace would be built and a more just world would emerge for humanity.

While my husband was in Albany and for some years after coming to Washington, his chief interest was is seeing that the average human being was given a fair chance for "life, liberty and the pursuit of happiness." That was what made him always interested in the problems of minority groups and of any group which was at a disadvantage.

As the war clouds gathered and the inevitable involvement of this country became more evident, his objective was always to deal with the problems of the war, political and military, so that eventually an organization might be built to prevent future wars.

Any man in public life is bound, in the course of years, to create certain enemies. But when he is gone, his main objectives stand out clearly and one may hope that a spirit of unity may arouse the people and their leaders to a complete understanding of his objectives and a determination to achieve those objectives themselves.

Abraham Lincoln was taken from us before he had achieved unity within the nation, and his people failed him. This divided us as a nation for many years.

Woodrow Wilson was also stricken and, in that instance, the peoples of the world failed to carry out his vision.

Perhaps, in his wisdom, the Almighty is trying to show us that a leader may chart the way, may point out the road to lasting peace, but that many leaders and many peoples must do the building. It cannot be the work of one man, nor can the responsibility be laid upon his shoulders, and so, when the time comes for peoples to assume the burden more fully, he is given rest.

God grant that we may have that wisdom and courage to build a peaceful world with justice and opportunity for all peoples the world over. . . .   □

PART IV

The United Nations and Human Rights: 1945–1953

1.   **"The Universal Declaration of Human Rights"**
Adopted by the General Assembly of the United Nations,
December 10, 1948

Preamble

Whereas recognition of the inherent dignity and of the equal and inalienable rights of all members of the human family is the foundation of freedom, justice and peace in the world,

Whereas disregard and contempt for human rights have resulted in barbarous acts which have outraged the conscience of mankind, and the advent of a world in which human beings shall enjoy freedom of speech and belief and freedom from fear and want has been proclaimed as the highest aspiration of the common people,

Whereas it is essential, if man is not to be compelled to have recourse, as a last resort, to rebellion against tyranny and oppression, that human rights should be protected by the rule of law,

Whereas it is essential to promote the development of friendly relations between nations,

Whereas the peoples of the United Nations have in the Charter reaffirmed their faith in fundamental human rights, in the dignity and worth of the human person and in the equal rights of men and women and have determined to promote social progress and better standards of life in larger freedom,

Whereas Member States have pledged themselves to achieve, in co-operation with the United Nations, the promotion of universal respect for and observance of human rights and fundamental freedoms,

Whereas a common understanding of these rights and freedoms is of the greatest importance for the full realization of this pledge,

Now, Therefore,

The General Assembly

proclaims

This Universal Declaration of Human Rights

as a common standard of achievement for all peoples and all nations, to the end that every individual and every organ of society, keeping this Declaration constantly in mind, shall strive by teaching and education to promote respect for these rights and freedoms and by progressive measures, national and international, to secure their universal and effective recognition and observance, both among the peoples of Member States themselves and among the peoples of territories under their jurisdiction.

Article 1

All human beings are born free and equal in dignity and rights. They are endowed with reason and conscience and should act towards one another in a spirit of brotherhood.

Article 2

Everyone is entitled to all the rights and freedoms set forth in this Declaration, without distinction of any kind, such as race, colour, sex, language, religion, political or other opinion, national or social origin, property, birth or other status. Furthermore, no distinction shall be made on the basis of the political, jurisdictional or international status of the country or territory to which a person belongs, whether it be independent, trust, non-selfgoverning or under any other limitation of sovereignty.

Article 3

Everyone has the right to life, liberty and security of person.

Article 4

No one shall be held in slavery or servitude; slavery and the slave trade shall be prohibited in all their forms.

Article 5

No one shall be subjected to torture or to cruel, inhuman or degrading treatment or punishment.

Article 6

Everyone has the right to recognition everywhere as a person before the law.

Article 7

All are equal before the law and are entitled without any discrimination to equal protection of the law. All are entitled to equal protection against any discrimination in violation of this Declaration and against any incitement to such discrimination.

Article 8

Everyone has the right to an effective remedy by the competent national tribunals for acts violating the fundamental rights granted him by the constitution or by law.

Article 9

No one shall be subjected to arbitrary arrest, detention or exile.

Article 10

Everyone is entitled in full equality to a fair and public hearing by an independent and impartial tribunal, in the determination of his rights and obligations and of any criminal charge against him.

Article 11

(1) Everyone charged with a penal offence has the right to be presumed inno-

cent until proved guilty according to law in a public trial at which he has had all the guarantees necessary for his defense.

(2) No one shall be held guilty of any penal offence on account of any act or omission which did not constitute a penal offence, under national or international law, at the time when it was committed. Nor shall a heavier penalty be imposed than the one that was applicable at the time the penal offence was committed.

Article 12

No one shall be subjected to arbitrary interference with his privacy, family, home or correspondence, nor to attacks upon his honour and reputation. Everyone has the right to the protection of the law against such interference or attacks.

Article 13

(1) Everyone has the right to freedom of movement and residence within the borders of each State.

(2) Everyone has the right to leave any country, including his own, and to return to his country.

Article 14

(1) Everyone has the right to seek and to enjoy in other countries asylum from persecution.

(2) This right may not be invoked in the case of prosecutions genuinely arising from non-political crimes or from acts contrary to the purposes and principles of the United Nations.

Article 15

(1) Everyone has the right to a nationality.

(2) No one shall be arbitrarily deprived of his nationality nor denied the right to change his nationality.

Article 16

(1) Men and women of full age, without any limitation due to race, nationality or religion, have the right to marry and to found a family. They are entitled to equal rights as to marriage, during marriage and at its dissolution.

(2) Marriage shall be entered into only with the free and full consent of the intending spouses.

(3) The family is the natural and fundamental group unit of society and is entitled to protection by society and the State.

Article 17

(1) Everyone has the right to own property alone as well as in association with others.

(2) No one shall be arbitrarily deprived of his property.

Article 18

Everyone has the right to freedom of thought, conscience and religion; this right includes freedom to change his religion or belief and freedom, either alone or in community with others and in public or private, to manifest his religion or belief in teaching, practice, worship and observance.

Article 19

Everyone has the right to freedom of opinion and expression; this right includes freedom to hold opinions without interference and to seek, receive and impart information and ideas through any media and regardless of frontiers.

Article 20

(1) Everyone has the right to freedom of peaceful assembly and association.

(2) No one may be compelled to belong to an association.

Article 21

(1) Everyone has the right to take part in the government of his country, directly or through freely chosen representatives.

(2) Everyone has the right of equal access to public service in his country.

(3) The will of the people shall be the basis of the authority of government; this will shall be expressed in periodic and genuine elections which shall be by universal and equal suffrage and shall be held by secret vote or by equivalent free voting procedures.

Article 22

Everyone, as a member of society, has the right to social security and is entitled to realization through national effort and international co-operation and in accordance with the organization and resources of each State of the economic, social and cultural rights indispensable for his dignity and the free development of his personality.

Article 23

(1) Everyone has the right to work, to free choice of employment, to just and favourable conditions of work and to protection against unemployment.
(2) Everyone, without any discrimination, has the right to equal pay for equal work.
(3) Everyone who works has the right to just and favourable remuneration ensuring for himself and his family an existence worthy of human dignity and supplemented, if necessary, by other means of social protection.
(4) Everyone has the right to form and to join trade unions for the protection of his interests.

Article 24

Everyone has the right to rest and leisure, including reasonable limitation of working hours and periodic holidays with pay.

Article 25

(1) Everyone has the right to a standard of living adequate for the health and well-being of himself and of his family, including food, clothing, housing and medical care and necessary social services, and the right to security in the event of unemployment, sickness, disability, widowhood, old age or other lack of livelihood in circumstances beyond his control.
(2) Motherhood and childhood are entitled to special care and assistance. All children, whether born in or out of wedlock, shall enjoy the same social protection.

Article 26

(1) Everyone has the right to education. Education shall be free, at least in the elementary and fundamental stages. Elementary education shall be compulsory.

Technical and professional education shall be made generally available and higher education shall be equally accessible to all on the basis of merit.

(2) Education shall be directed to the full development of the human personality and to the strengthening of respect for human rights and fundamental freedoms. It shall promote understanding, tolerance and friendship among all nations, racial or religious groups, and shall further the activities of the United Nations for the maintenance of peace.

(3) Parents have a prior right to choose the kind of education that shall be given to their children.

Article 27

(1) Everyone has the right freely to participate in the cultural life of the community, to enjoy the arts and to share in scientific advancement and its benefits.

(2) Everyone has the right to the protection of the moral and material interests resulting from any scientific, literary or artistic production of which he is the author.

Article 28

Everyone is entitled to a social and international order in which the rights and freedoms set forth in this Declaration can be fully realized.

Article 29

(1) Everyone has duties to the community in which alone the free and full development of his personality is possible.

(2) In the exercise of his rights and freedoms, everyone shall be subject only to such limitations as are determined by law solely for the purpose of securing due recognition and respect for the rights and freedoms of others and of meeting the just requirements of morality, public order and the general welfare in a democratic society.

(3) These rights and freedoms may in no case be exercised contrary to the purposes and principles of the United Nations.

Article 30

Nothing in this Declaration may be interpreted as implying for any State, group or person any right to engage in any activity or to perform any act aimed at the destruction of any of the rights and freedoms set forth herein. □

2.   **"The Promise of Human Rights"**

Foreign Affairs, April 1948

The real importance of the Human Rights Commission which was created by the Economic and Social Council lies in the fact that throughout the world there are many people who do not enjoy the basic rights which have come to be accepted in many other parts of the world as inherent rights of all individuals, without which no one can live in dignity and freedom.

At the first meeting of the Economic and Social Council in London, early in 1946, a Nuclear Commission was named to recommend a permanent setup for the full Commission of Human Rights, and to consider the work which it should first undertake. These first members of the Nuclear Commission were not chosen as representatives of governments, but as individuals. Naturally, however, each government was asked to concur in the nomination from that country. There were nine members nominated, but two of them were not able to come; and one or two nations insisted on nominating their own representatives. I was one of the members of the original Nuclear Commission, and when we met at Hunter College, I was elected chairman. The other members were: Mr. Fernanda de Husse, Belgium; Mr. K. C. Neogi, India; Professor René Cassin, France; Dr. C. L. Haai, China; Mr. Dusan Brkish, Yugoslavia; Mr. Borisov, USSR.

The representative from the USSR was at first a young secretary from the Soviet Embassy. The other members of the Nuclear Commission did not realize that he was not the regular representative and was not empowered to vote. It was not until three days before the end of the meeting that the regular member, Mr. Borisov, arrived; and then we discovered that the representative of the USSR who had been attending the meetings actually had no right to vote, and such votes had to be removed from the record. The Commission was a little disturbed because a number of concessions had been made in order to obtain unanimity. Also, this change made it impossible for any decision to be unanimous, since the Soviet representative had been told that he could not commit his government by a vote on any subject and therefore registered no vote on the first recommendations for the Commission's organization and program of work.

The Commission made a number of recommendations. For instance, we agreed that persons should be chosen as individuals and not merely as representatives of governments. We agreed that there should be 18 members of the full Commission—an example of a minor point on which we had made concessions to the representative of the USSR, because originally the various members of the group had differed as to what the proper size of the Commission should be. I had been told that it made very little difference to the United States whether the Commission numbered 12 or 25, but it was felt the number should not be less than 12 because unavoidable absences might cut it down to too small a group; and it was felt also that the number should not be more than 25, for fear a large group might make our work very difficult to accomplish.

When I found out how many varieties of opinion there were, I made the suggestion as chairman that we might make the number 21, since we were apt to discuss some rather controversial subjects, and if there was a tie the chairman could cast the deciding vote. Most of the members agreed with this until we came to the representative of the USSR. He insisted that we should be 18, because our parent body, the Economic and Social Council, was made up of 18 members. As we did not feel that the size of the Commission was vitally important, and as he could not be induced to change, we agreed to recommend that the Commission consist of 18 members.

Among a number of other recommendations in our report we suggested that the first work to be undertaken was the writing of a Bill of Human Rights. Many of us thought that lack of standards for human rights the world over was one of the greatest causes of friction among the nations, and that recognition of human rights might become one of the cornerstones of which peace could eventually be based.

At its next meeting, the Economic and Social Council received our report, which I presented, and it was then studied in detail and a number of changes were made. The members of the Commission were made government representatives, chosen by their governments. The 18 governments to be represented on the Commission were chosen by the Economic and Social Council. The United States was given a four-year appointment and my government nominated me as a member. At present the following are represented on the commission: Australia, Belgium, Byelorussia, China, Chile, Egypt, France, India, Lebanon, Panama, the Philippines, Ukraine, the USSR, Yugoslavia, Uruguay, the United Kingdom and the United States.

The first session of the full Commission was called in January 1947. The officers chosen at that time, in addition to myself as permanent chairman, were Dr. Chang of China as vice-chairman and Dr. Charles Malik of Lebanon as rapporteur. In that first meeting we requested that the Division of Human Rights in the Secretariat get out a yearbook on human rights, and receive all petitions and acknowledge them. Since we were not a court, we could do nothing actually to solve the problems that the petitions presented, but we could tell the petitioners that once the Bill of Human Rights was written, they might find that their particular problems came under one of its provisions.

We considered some of the main points which should go into the drafting of the Bill of Human Rights, and we named a drafting committee which should present the first draft to the next meeting of the full Commission. This work was entrusted to the officers of the Commission, all of whom were available in or near Lake Success, and to Dr. John Humphrey, as head of the Division of Human Rights in the Secretariat. But when the Economic and Social Council received the report of this procedure considerable opposition to the appointment of so small a committee was expressed. As it had been understood in our meeting that the chairman of the committee was to call upon other members of the Commission for advice and assistance, I at once urged that the drafting committee be increased to eight members. This was done.

The drafting committee then met in June 1947. The delegate from the USSR, Mr. Koretsky, and the delegate from Byelorussia, neither of whom was authorized to vote on an unfinished document and both of whom lacked instructions from their governments, participated very little in the general discussion of the drafting committee, though they did agree to the principles that all men are equal and that men and women should have equal rights. The second meeting of the full Commission was called in Geneva, Switzerland, because some members felt strongly that the Human Rights Commission should hold a session in Europe. We were scheduled to meet on December 1, 1947, but as many of the members were delayed in arriving we actually met on December 2.

We mapped out our work very carefully. The position of the United States had been that it would be impossible in these initial meetings to do more than write a Declaration. If the Declaration were accepted by the General Assembly the next autumn, it would carry moral weight, but it would not carry any legal weight. Many of the smaller nations were strongly of the opinion that the oppressed peoples of the world and the minority groups would feel that they had been cruelly deceived if we did not write a Convention which would be presented for ratification, nation by nation, and which when accepted would be incorporated into law in the same way that treaties among nations are accepted and implemented. The Government of the United States had never, of course, been opposed to writing a Convention; it simply felt that the attempt would not be practical in these early stages. When it was found that feeling ran high on this subject, we immediately cooperated.

The Commission divided itself into three groups. The group to work on the Declaration consisted of the representatives of Byelorussia, France, Panama, the Philippines, the USSR and the United States. The group to work on the Convention was made up of the representatives of Chile, China, Egypt, Lebanon, the

United Kingdom and Yugoslavia. The third group, to work on methods of implementation, which would later, of course, be included in the Convention, consisted of the representatives of Australia, India, Iran, Ukraine and Uruguay.

At the first meeting of the Commission, the representative from Australia made the suggestion that a Court of Human Rights be created. There had been a good deal of discussion of this idea in previous meetings. The general feeling was, however, that this action could not be taken under the Charter as it now stands and would raise the problem of revision of the Charter.

At the start, the United Kingdom had brought to the drafting committee a Declaration and a Convention which included suggestions for implementation. The USSR, while still not committing itself to any vote, as the Soviet Government still insisted that until a finished document was prepared they could not vote on it, nevertheless was willing to participate in the discussions which concerned the writing of a Declaration. Their representative took an active part, particularly in the discussion and formulation of the social and economic rights of the individual which are considered in some detail in the Declaration.

This was a hard-working committee, and I was extremely gratified both at the willingness of the members to put in long hours and at the general spirit of cooperation. In spite of the fact that a good many of the members must frequently have been very weary, there was always an atmosphere of good feeling and consideration for others, even when questions arose which called forth strong differences of opinion

We finished our work at 11:30 P.M. on the night of December 17, and I think the documents which have now gone to all of the member governments in the United Nations are very creditable. A Declaration and a Convention were written. The group working on implementation made suggestions which, of course, must be more carefully considered before they are fully incorporated in the Convention. We now await the comments. These were requested in early April, so that the Human Rights Division of the Secretariat could go over them carefully and put them in shape for the drafting committee which will meet again at Lake Success on May 3, 1948.

The full Commission will meet at Lake Success on May 17, to give final consideration to this Bill of Human Rights, or Pact, as our Government prefers to have it called. The Economic and Social Council received the report of the documents written in Geneva, and sent them to the governments in January. They will now make their comments and suggestions. The final opportunity for consideration by the Economic and Social Council will come at its meeting next July, and the pact or charter which is finally adopted at that meeting will be presented to the General Assembly in the autumn of 1948.

II

Three Articles in the Declaration seem to me to be of vital importance. Article 15 provides that everyone has the right to a nationality; that is, all persons are entitled to the protection of some government, and those who are without it shall be protected by the United Nations. Article 16 says that individual freedom of thought and conscience, to hold and change beliefs, is an absolute and sacred right. Included in this Article is a declaration of the right to manifest these beliefs, in the form of worship, observance, teaching and practice. Article 21 declares that everyone, without discrimination, has the right to take an effective part in the government of his country. This aims to give assurance that governments of states will bend and change according to the will of the people as shown in elections, which shall be periodic, free, fair and by secret ballot.

Some of the other important Articles are broad in scope. For instance, Article 23 says that everyone has the right to work, and that the state has a duty to take steps within its power to ensure its residents an opportunity for useful work. Article 24 says that everyone has a right to receive pay commensurate with his ability and skill and may join trade unions to protect his interests.

Other Articles in the Declaration set forth rights such as the right to the preservation of health, which would give the state responsibility for health and safety measures; the right to social security, which makes it the duty of the state to provide measures for the security of the individual against the consequences of unemployment, disability, old age and other loss of livelihood beyond his control; the right to education, which should be free and compulsory, and the provision that higher education should be available to all without distinction as to race, sex, language, religion, social standing, financial means or political affiliation; the right to rest and leisure—that is, a limitation on hours of work and provisions of vacations with pay; the right to participate in the cultural life of the community, enjoy its arts and share in the benefits of science. Another Article asserts that education will be directed to the full physical, intellectual, moral and spiritual development of the human personality and to combating hatred against other nations or racial or religious groups.

If the Declaration is accepted by the Assembly, it will mean that all the nations accepting it hope that the day will come when these rights are considered inherent rights belonging to every human being, but it will not mean that they have to change their laws immediately to make these rights possible.

On the other hand, as the Convention is ratified by one nation after another it will require that each ratifying nation change its laws where necessary, to make possible that every human being within its borders shall enjoy the rights set forth. The Convention, of course, covers primarily the civil liberties which many of the nations of the world have accepted as inherent rights of human beings, and it reaffirms a clause in the Charter of the United Nations which says that there shall be no discrimination among any human beings because of race, creed or color.

The most important articles of the Convention are subjects with which every American high school student is familiar. Article 5 makes it unlawful to deprive a person of life except as punishment for a crime provided by law. Article 6 outlaws physical mutilation. Article 7 forbids torture and cruel or inhuman punishment. Article 8 prohibits slavery and compulsory labor, with exceptions permitted as to the latter in the case of military service and emergency service in time of disaster such as flood or earthquake.

A provision which is new in an international constitutional sense, though not new in practice to Americans, is Article 11, which guarantees liberty of movement and a free choice of residence within a state, and a general freedom to every person in the world to leave any country, including his own. Article 20 makes all sections of the Convention applicable without distinction as to race, sex, language, religion, political or other opinion, property status, or national or social origin; and Article 21 requires the states to forbid by law the advocacy of national, racial or religious hostility that constitutes incitement to violence. In general, every nation ratifying the Convention will have to make sure that within its jurisdiction these promised rights become realities, so it is the Convention which is of the greatest importance to the peoples throughout the world.

A possible stumbling block to general ratification of the Convention is the fact that some federal states, like the United States, operate constitutional systems in which the primary laws affecting individuals are adopted by the constituent states and are beyond the constitutional power of the federal government. The Convention provides, in Article 24, that in such cases these federal governments shall call to the attention of their constituent states, with a favorable recommendation, those Articles considered appropriate for action by them.

One of the questions that will come before the Human Rights Commission in May is whether all the Articles included in the Convention shall be submitted to the various nations for ratification in a single document, to be taken all in one gulp, so to speak, or shall be divided into separate conventions, in the thought that this procedure would avoid the rejection of the entire document because of objection to one or two articles, as might happen in many cases. Of course, it is quite evident that in the future there will have to be many conventions on special subjects, and that the work of the Human Rights Commission should be directed for years to come on those subjects as they arise. A convention on the subject of nationality and stateless persons seems to be knocking at our doors for consideration almost immediately.

III

As I look back at the work thus far of our Human Rights Commission I realize that its importance is twofold.

In the first place, we have put into words some inherent rights. Beyond that, we have found that the conditions of our contemporary world require the enumeration of certain protections which the individual must have if he is to acquire a sense of security and dignity in his own person. The effect of this is frankly educational. Indeed, I like to think that the Declaration will help forward very largely the education of the peoples of the world.

It seems to me most important that the Declaration be accepted by all member nations, not because they will immediately live up to all of its provisions, but because they ought to support the standards toward which the nations must henceforward aim. Since the objectives have been clearly stated, men of good will everywhere will strive to attain them with more energy and, I trust, with better hope of success.

As the Convention is adhered to by one country after another, it will actually bring into being rights which are tangible and can be invoked before the law of the ratifying countries. Everywhere many people will feel more secure. And as the Great Powers tie themselves down by their ratifications, the smaller nations which fear that the great may abuse their strength will acquire a sense of greater assurance.

The work of the Commission has been of outstanding value in setting before men's eyes the ideals which they must strive to reach. Men cannot live by bread alone.   □

3.   "Statement on Draft Covenant on Human Rights"

Department of State Bulletin, December 31, 1951

I am pleased that we are now undertaking to consider the substantive questions relating to the Draft Covenant on Human Rights in this Committee. It is particularly important at this time that the Assembly give adequate consideration to human rights. . . .

It is a tragic commentary on the status of civilization in the middle of the twentieth century that the systematic and deliberate denials of human rights by some governments are so widespread in certain areas of the world that they are almost taken for granted. The kind of callous brutality which would have shocked the conscience of mankind a century ago is now unfortunately a commonplace occurrence in those areas.

All members of the United Nations have a responsibility, individually and collectively, to see that the lights of freedom are not further extinguished throughout the world.

Every member has a responsibility to see that the rights of men are safeguarded, for no country is perfect in protecting the individual rights of its citizens.

Three years ago in this same city the General Assembly proclaimed the Universal Declaration of Human Rights. That Declaration has already become the yardstick by which all can measure the conduct of governments. The language of that Declaration has been written into the constitution of a number of states. The United Nations must now move ahead to develop new methods for advancing human liberty and for translating human rights and fundamental freedoms into action. One of these methods is the Draft International Covenant on Human Rights.

The task of drafting the Covenant, of putting human rights into treaty form, is not an easy one. We have been working in the United Nations on this draft Covenant since 1947.

I would like in particular to discuss the matter of economic, social, and cultural rights.

When the General Assembly last year called on the Commission on Human Rights to include economic, social, and cultural provisions in the Covenant on Human Rights, the United States fully cooperated in the five-weeks' session of the Commission this spring in Geneva in drafting these provisions. The United States delegation voted last year in the General Assembly against the inclusion of economic, social, and cultural rights in the same Covenant with civil and political rights. At no time, however, did my delegation to the Commission on Human Rights question the responsibility of the Commission to prepare a draft with these provisions for the consideration of the General Assembly. The United States delegation to the Commission felt that, as a member of a technical commission, we should cooperate in doing that which the General Assembly had asked us to do at that time.

We did vote at the end of the Commission session for a resolution introduced by the delegate of India requesting a reconsideration by the General Assembly of the question of including economic, social, and cultural rights in the same Covenant with civil and political rights. This resolution did not, however, interrupt the technical work of the Commission. This Indian resolution pointed out that economic, social, and cultural rights, though equally fundamental and therefore important, formed a separate category of rights from that of the civil and political rights in that they were not justiciable rights and their method of implementation was different.

At this session of the General Assembly we have before us a resolution of the Economic and Social Council inviting the General Assembly to reconsider its decision of last year. It is entirely appropriate for us in the General Assembly this year to reconsider this matter. In view of the importance of the Covenant on Human Rights, we must be willing to study and restudy the basic problems involved in the drafting of this document. There may be differences of opinion in this Committee on the question of whether there should be one covenant or two covenants, but at no time should anyone argue that this Committee should avoid a further consideration of this very important question.

Principal Provisions of the ECOSOC Resolution

The resolution of the Economic and Social Council points out that there are certain differences between the provisions on civil and political rights and the provisions on economic, social, and cultural rights and that these differences warrant a consideration of two covenants rather than a single covenant. The Council resolution also refers to the difficulties which may flow from embodying in one covenant two different kinds of rights and obligations.

Let us examine these differences which have been recognized by the Commission in a number of ways in drafting the provisions of the Covenant.

In the first place, article 19 of the draft Covenant recognizes that the economic, social, and cultural provisions are objectives to be achieved "progressively." This obligation is to be distinguished from the obligation applicable to the civil and political rights in the Covenant. In the case of civil and political rights, states ratifying the Covenant will be under an obligation to take necessary steps fairly quickly to give effect to these rights. A much longer period of time is clearly contemplated under the Covenant for the achievement of the economic, social, and cultural provisions. This is obvious and is, of course, to be expected.

For example, in the field of health, it would be necessary to undertake training programs for doctors and nurses, to establish experimental stations, build hospitals, obtain hospital beds, medical supplies, etc. Similarly, in the field of education, it will take a considerable period of time to train teachers, write school texts, obtain necessary supplies, build schools, et cetera. In these fields, it will take years to reach the objectives set forth in the Covenant. As you well know, my delegation fully supports the attainment of these objectives. I am simply stressing the longer period of time it will of course take and the long-range planning that will be necessary to achieve the objectives of the economic, social, and cultural provisions of the Covenant.

It has taken years to achieve progress in the United States in these fields, as it will no doubt take years to achieve further progress in these fields in my country as well as in other countries.

For example, with respect to education in the United States, which under our federal system is essentially a matter within the jurisdiction of our states, in 1900, in one-third of the United States, there was no compulsory school-attendance law and in only a few sections of the country was there legislation requiring compulsory school attendance until the age of 16. Fifty years later, all sections of the United States require school attendance for all boys and girls at least until the age of 16, and in some areas school attendance is required until the age of 17 or 18. Since 1910 we have increased our expenditures per student in our schools 300 percent.

In the field of health in the United States, it has taken us 30 years to reduce infant mortality by more than two-thirds. Pneumonia and tuberculosis, which were the two leading causes of death in the United States in 1900, now are in sixth and seventh places as causes of death.

I mention these instances, not to claim we have achieved our goals in these fields but simply to indicate that it takes a long time to move toward these economic, social, and cultural objectives. In contrast, in the case of civil and political rights, it is anticipated that these rights will be effectuated promptly. It is this time difference between these two types of rights that I am stressing.

A second difference between the civil and political provisions and the economic, social, and cultural provisions is the manner in which the obligation is expected to be performed. In the case of the civil and political rights, they can in general be achieved by the enactment of appropriate legislation, enforced under effective administrative machinery. On the other hand, it is recognized that economic, social, and cultural progress and development cannot be achieved simply by the enactment of legislation and its enforcement. Private as well as public action is necessary. The Commission on Human Rights repeatedly rejected the proposal by two members of the Commission to limit the achievement of economic, social, and cultural rights solely through state action. The Commission fully recognized the importance of private as well as governmental action for the achievement of these rights.

A third difference between the civil and political provisions and the economic, social, and cultural provisions relates to the difference in the implementation contemplated. Initially the Commission on Human Rights drafted provisions for the establishment of a Human Rights Committee to which complaints by one state against another state may be filed. The Commission did not then have time at its session this spring to decide whether this machinery should also be applicable to the economic, social, and cultural provisions, but there actually was general sentiment in the Commission that this complaint machinery should be limited to the civil and political provisions of the Covenant. It was felt by those with whom I discussed this matter in the Commission that this machinery is not appropriate for the economic, social, and cultural provisions of the Covenant, since these rights are to be achieved progressively and since the obligations of states with respect to these rights were not as precise as those with respect to the civil and political rights. These members of the Commission thought that it would be preferable, with respect to the economic, social, and cultural rights, to stress the importance of assisting states to achieve economic, social, and cultural progress rather than to stress the filing of complaints against states in this field.

Instead of a complaint procedure, a reporting procedure was devised by the Commission with respect to the progress made in the observance of the economic, social, and cultural provisions of the Covenant.

A fourth difference between the civil and political rights and the economic, social, and cultural rights relates to the drafting of these rights. The economic, social, and cultural provisions were necessarily drafted in broad language as contrasted to the civil and political provisions. For example, article 22 simply provides that "The States Parties to the Covenant recognize the right of everyone to social security." It was thought in the Commission that since economic, social, and cultural provisions were being stated in terms of broad objectives, general language would be adequate.

It seems to my delegation that these four basic differences between the civil and political rights and the economic, social, and cultural rights warrant the separation of the present provisions of the Covenant into two covenants, one covenant on civil and political rights and another covenant on economic, social, and cultural rights. By a separation of these rights into two separate covenants we would avoid a great deal of confusion that is naturally inherent in a combination of all these different provisions in one covenant.

Equality of Importance in the Two Groups of Rights

Of course, I realize that some members of this Committee argue for a single covenant to include all the provisions now before us. The principal argument urged by those pressing this view is that there should be no differentiations in importance between civil and political rights and economic, social, and cultural rights. In the proposal that I wish to make to the Committee there is no question raised with respect to the importance of one group of rights as against another group of rights. I consider each group of rights of equal importance. My proposal would maintain this equality of importance.

My delegation proposes that two covenants of equal importance be completed in the United Nations simultaneously and be opened for signature and ratification at the same time. Neither one nor the other covenant would be called the first or the second covenant. Each of the two covenants would be on human rights, one setting forth the civil and political rights, and the other setting forth the economic, social, and cultural rights. We would request the Commission on Human Rights to prepare both of these covenants for the consideration of the General Assembly next year.

If members of the Committee will look at the present text of the Covenant, they will observe how naturally its parts may be divided into two covenants. The provisions on civil and political rights are in parts I, II, and IV. These parts can constitute one covenant. The economic, social, and cultural provisions are in parts III and V. These parts can constitute another covenant. Part VI contains general provisions which should accordingly be repeated in both covenants.

The basic differences between civil and political rights and economic, social, and cultural rights warrant this division into two covenants. The option will, of course, remain open for countries wishing to ratify both covenants at once to do so. To insist on the inclusion of all the provisions in one covenant will delay the coming into force of any covenant on human rights. A separation of these provisions into two covenants would accelerate their ratification by many states.

I hope that this proposal that I have made will be supported and will facilitate reaching agreement in the Committee on the question of economic, social, and cultural rights. The situation this year is very different from the situation last year in the General Assembly. At that time we were considering the drafting of a first covenant on human rights, containing only civil and political rights. A covenant on economic, social, and cultural rights was proposed to be drafted at a later date. Now that the Commission on Human Rights has drafted provisions on economic, social, and cultural rights, we are in a position to visualize two covenants, simultaneously completed, one on civil and political rights and the other on economic, social, and cultural rights. This changed situation warrants a decision by the General Assembly calling for two covenants rather than one covenant.

I will not at this time discuss other aspects of the covenant. I may comment on these other matters later. I have devoted my attention in these remarks to the importance of drafting two covenants, one on civil and political rights, and the other on economic, social, and cultural rights, because I feel this to be the most important question facing us.   □

4.   "Reply to Attacks on U.S. Attitude Toward Human Rights Covenant"

Department of State Bulletin, January 14, 1952

This statement is a reply to the views expressed by Byelorussia, Czechoslovakia, Poland, the Ukraine, and the USSR concerning the United States in this Committee. My observations in this statement accordingly relate to these five countries.

I am interested that these five countries place so much stress on the unity of the provisions of the Universal Declaration of Human Rights in our debates here. In 1948 those five countries did not vote for the Declaration. At that time they were critical of it. Now they cite it for their own purposes. They seem to praise the Declaration one time and minimize its importance another time, so that I must question the sincerity of their reliance on the Declaration at this point.

The delegates of a number of the countries expressed concern that an "illusory" Covenant on Human Rights might be drafted in the United Nations. The term "illusory" is descriptive of the type of covenant which the delegates of these countries are seeking to have drafted in the United Nations. For example, the Soviet Union has repeatedly taken the initiative in the General Assembly and in the Commission on Human Rights for the elimination of any provision in the Covenant on implementation. In the General Assembly last year, the Soviet Union proposed that these articles be deleted on the ground that "their inclusion would constitute an attempt at intervention in the domestic affairs of states and would encroach on their States' sovereignty." This proposal was rejected in the Third Committee last year in a roll-call vote. Only the five members of this Committee now attacking the United States voted for this proposal. A similar proposal was rejected by the Commission on Human Rights at its 1951 session.

These countries protest that the implementation of the provisions of the Covenant would be "shameful." What nonsense is this? A Covenant on Human Rights would indeed be illusory if the proposal of the USSR were accepted to delete all implementation provisions from it. It seems to me that freedom must be preserved primarily as we were reminded yesterday. The right to think and freedom to speak freely are among the most important rights, and some of you may realize that these are rights that have become rather illusory in some countries.

Even Mr. Vishinsky himself acknowledges the lack of freedom in his country when he observes in the book he edited on *The Law of the Soviet State* that in his state "there is and can be no place for freedom of speech, press, and so on, for the foes of socialism." Thus he proclaims a so-called freedom for only those supporting the dictates of the state. Freedom is not really freedom unless you can differ in thought and in expression of your thought.

The speakers from these five countries insist over and over again a condition of perfection exists in their countries. It always seems to me that when things are so absolutely perfect that it would almost shine out and you would not have to express it so frequently. I can only say that I wish it were possible for all of us to be allowed to go to the Soviet Union, for example, to see for ourselves the actual conditions which exist there. It would be very helpful if even some impartial observers were allowed to report to us on the actual conditions existing there.

Now let me turn to the charge made by some of the delegates of these five countries that the United States is disregarding the interests of the Negroes in our country. Unfortunately there are instances of American Negroes being victims of unreasoning racial prejudice in my country. However, we do not condone these acts in the United States. We do everything possible to overcome and eliminate such discrimination and racial prejudice as may still exist. Racial discrimination in my country is irreconcilable with the fundamental principles of humanity and justice which are embodied in our Bill of Rights.

Affirmative steps are continually being taken to combat racial discrimination. Recently the President of the United States issued an Executive Order to insure protection against racial discrimination in employment under Government contracts.

The President has on several occasions established advisory commissions to provide evaluations of the progress being made in the United States. The recommendations of these commissions have served to spur further action to obtain the equality we are seeking in my country. Channing Tobias, now on the United States delegation to the United Nations, was one of the Negroes who served on some of these commissions. Some of the recommendations and reports of those commissions were quoted here which show that we do not hide anything that is wrong.

Acts of prejudice and discrimination by private individuals or groups in my country are more than merely deplored by the Government and by the vast majority of the people of the United States. Not only through laws but also by the process of education and in many other ways, efforts are constantly being made to eliminate racial discrimination. It is the official policy of the U.S. Government, as expressed on many occasions by President Truman, that the remaining imperfections in our practice of democracy, which result from the conduct of small groups of our people, must be corrected as soon as possible.

Increased activity in the political life of our country has been characteristic of Negro Americans. They have become a vital factor in the life of our local, State, and National Government. A reflection of this is seen in the number of Negroes holding Government Civil Service appointments. In 1938 there were 80,000 Negroes holding such appointments; this number has increased to 270,000. Not only has there been an increase in the number of such appointments, but also they are constantly assuming more and more responsible positions in the Government.

Negroes in the United States are voting in increasing numbers in all sections of our country.

It was suggested here that in certain places they were still having difficulty under the poll-tax laws. Those laws are rapidly being changed and in many parts of the country where it was not possible it is now possible for Negro citizens to vote.

In addition, the years from 1940 to the present have seen the election of Negro citizens to a number of important local, state, and national offices.

At the same time I wish to point out we do not claim to have reached perfection. We feel that our recognition of how much more yet remains to be done is a source of strength to us because it serves as a stimulant to press ahead with our task in this respect.

It so happens that the very countries which are criticizing the United States in this Committee are not themselves progressing in the fields of human rights and fundamental freedoms in their own countries. That may be only because of the difficulty of communication, but it seems to us that there is a great silence among the people of those countries. It is the silence of a people shut up behind an Iron Curtain where human rights and life are being stifled.

I will not take the time of the Committee to list all the many economic and social advances taking place in my country. They are well-known to all of you even though the five countries to whom I am addressing my remarks repeatedly disclaim knowledge of these facts. Many of you have traveled in the United States. I will simply mention, however, one point—the number of hours per week that the working man is now working in my country. The Federal Fair

Labor Standards Act has established a standard workweek of 40 hours by requiring penalty payments for overtime labor. The average of hours worked in all manufacturing industries has now declined to 40 hours a week. In the railroad transportation industry, the average is 40 hours a week. In power laundries 42 hours a week is the average. In textile mills, production workers average 41 hours a week. In printing and publishing, workers average slightly less than 40 hours a week.

The charge has also been made that the United States favors two covenants on human rights instead of a single covenant because the United States does not favor economic and social progress in other countries. This is obviously a ridiculous and false argument. It perhaps is unnecessary to answer this argument, since its falsity is so obvious; yet, I should stop for a few minutes to answer it frankly, since from time to time by the repetition of a particular argument, its falsity may soon be forgotten and the fact that it has been repeated so many times without answer tends to lull some into thinking that there perhaps is some merit to the assertion.

What does the record show?

The United States Government, in the course of the past 6 years, has made available over 30 billion dollars in the form of loans and grants to various countries. Of this amount, a total of over 5 billion dollars had been made available to countries in underdeveloped areas. This financial assistance by the U.S. Government does not include our subscription of 635 million dollars to the International Bank. Nor does it include contributions which we have made to U.N. programs such as the International Children's Emergency Fund, the International Refugee Organization, Relief and Rehabilitation for Refugees of Palestine, and the U.N. expanded Technical Assistance Program, contributions which have in large part been used to assist in the improvement of economic and social conditions in underdeveloped areas.

During the fiscal year 1951 alone, the U.S. Government made available on a grant basis over a quarter of a million dollars for programs of technical and economic assistance of underdeveloped areas.

As is well-known in this Committee, of the total financial contributions to UNICEF—some 155 million dollars—the United States has contributed about 100 million dollars.

Of the 5 billion dollars made available to underdeveloped areas during the past 6 years by the United States, almost 1 billion dollars was made available by the U.S. Export-Import Bank. This assistance has been in the form of loans for economic-development purposes to Latin America, the Near East, Africa, and Asia. During a recent period of one year, the Bank loaned over 395 million dollars. Of this amount over 96 percent went to underdeveloped areas.

Meeting the needs of underdeveloped areas for basic facilities in such fields as transportation, power, communications, and public health serves as a springboard for attaining higher standards of living for the people in these areas.

I have cited these figures of capital made available for economic development from the United States not for the figures themselves, nor for self-praise. I have cited them only as concrete evidence that the Government and people of the United States are very much interested in the economic development of other countries—and in more than an academic way.

The Congress of the United States this year decided to increase the lending authority of the Export-Import Bank an additional 1 billion dollars. This brings the basic lending capacity of the bank up to 4 billion dollars at the present time.

In addition, Congress recently appropriated over 400 million dollars to support a widespread program of economic and technical assistance to agriculture and industry in the Near East, Africa, Latin America, and Asia. These funds are to be made available almost entirely on a grant basis.

The U.S. Technical Cooperation Administration, established about a year ago, has been constantly gaining momentum. During the first year of its expanded program, almost 500 requests for technical assistance were approved. By August of this year, programs were underway in 36 countries in every part of the world.

In addition, Congress has provided that up to 13 million dollars may be available as the United States contribution to the United Nations expanded Technical Assistance Program for the next fiscal period.

I might also mention that the United States share of the 1950 gross assessment budget of the many specialized agencies, including the International Labor Organization, the International Children's Emergency Fund, and the Palestine Refugee Organization, is always a good and fair share. I would like to point out that no contributions to these organizations have been made by the nations attacking the United States.

We understand the difficulties faced by the Soviet Union in rebuilding her economy after the war. We also understand that she is expending funds to assist the countries along her borders whose economy she is now dominating. But if the Soviet Union would cut down the large expenditures she has continued to make since the end of the war for her large armed forces, she would have more funds and resources with which to build a peaceful economy and to assist other countries.

I am not suggesting that the Soviet Union undertake to assist the economic development of other countries as much as the United States is doing—that would not be possible since our economy is so much stronger than that of the Soviet Union—but I am suggesting that the Soviet Union should make some contribution to the many economic and social programs of the United Nations and the specialized agencies, to show in practice as well as in their speeches that it has a real interest in the economic and social progress of other nations, particularly of underdeveloped countries.

I hope, Madame Chairman, that I have made it amply clear that the support of my delegation for two covenants on human rights does not stem from any lack of interest in the economic and social progress of people in our own country or any disinterest in the economic and social progress of other countries.

The United States supports two covenants because we believe that two covenants would constitute a practical approach to the question before us. We do not believe it advisable as proposed by some delegations that everything go into one covenant. For all the reasons I have previously stated in this Committee, we would make much greater progress in the achievement of human rights and freedoms in the world by the simultaneous completion of two documents—one on civil and political rights and the other on economic, social, and cultural rights, and the attacks of the countries which I have been answering have not changed my point of view on this subject. □

5. "UN: Good U.S. Investment"

Foreign Policy Bulletin, October 1, 1952

So much has been said lately about the failures of the United Nations that some people in the United States have begun to feel the UN is only a burden to them, a cost in taxes for which they receive nothing in return.

Because of this I think that, particularly during UN week, October 19 to October 25, we should look first at what the UN really is, what it has done and what our share in this undertaking has brought us.

What is the United Nations? It is an organization of 60 sovereign nations which have agreed to abide by the articles of the UN Charter in an effort to live in a more peaceful world atmosphere among the peoples of the world. Each nation retains its sovereignty. It can withdraw from the society of nations at any time. The effort is made to conduct the business of the UN in as democratic a fashion as possible, and the will of the majority is respected, but none of the members can force any nation to do anything it does not wish to do. The best illustration of this is that the United States has just announced that henceforth it will not pay as high a percentage of UN expenses as it had agreed to pay in the past, and will start the reduced scale in 1952, although American representatives had previously accepted this obligation on the assumption that our Congress, which has the final word in matters of finance, would agree to pay on the old scale for another year. No matter what this may mean in curtailing the work of the UN, if the United States sticks to its decision there is no way of coercing us and there would be no way to coerce any other nation.

Russia, as we all know, decided that the North Koreans were not behaving in an aggressive manner when they crossed the 38th Parallel in Korea and tried to take over South Korea, and the UN has not been able to force Russia to change its position.

So the UN remains a voluntary aggregation of nations, primarily affected by the climate of world opinion.

It is the desire of our nations themselves to increase good will in the world. This perhaps seems a weak reed to lean on, but so far I think the acceptance of decisions made by the UN shows we can count on the fact that world opinion will carry weight, and for the greater part we can count on good will among the nations.

The specialized agencies of the UN were set up as independent agencies reporting back to the UN Economic and Social Council so that it would be possible for them to have either more or less members than the UN and to function independently. The specialized agencies have done more than any other organs of the UN to promote better understanding and good will.

For example, through the work of the World Health Organization we are gradually learning a great deal more about the needs of our fellow human beings around the world whose populations are not properly fed and not protected against diseases which are now well enough understood to be prevented. The WHO is putting on a campaign on a world scale against malaria and tuberculosis. This is important, because until people have enough health and energy to work they cannot accomplish any of the things that are essential to raising their standard of living and improving their material condition to the point where they may consume such things as are manufactured by the more highly developed peoples.

Another specialized agency, the Food and Agriculture Organization (FAO), is gradually putting together for us a picture of the world food situation and promoting greater knowledge of agriculture.

None of these agencies alone could meet any of the world problems, but joined together and working in cooperation they will succeed in doing a tremendous job that will not only benefit the underdeveloped nations but also the de-

In 1940, ER testified before Congress in support of federal aid to migrant workers. (FDR Library)

"I want to say an urgent word for a group of workers which is always left out when social legislation is written. They are the expendables. The ones who are bargained out of a piece of social legislation as the price for getting something else in. I am speaking of farm workers, including the migratory agricultural workers and their families. Today they compare economically to the workers in the industrial sweatshops of the early 1900s."

Elinor Morgenthau and Jane Addams visited ailing settlement activist Lillian Wald. (FDR Library)

"When you talk about the welfare state, as a rule people think that is a rather derogatory term— that a welfare state is not a good thing. But if we could change it around a little and say that we believed that society included the government, the individuals themselves as individuals, and all other groups . . . if we thought of them as working together to increase the welfare of the individual, then we would cease, I think, to have fear of just the mere words 'welfare state.' We would have a truer conception of what the words really mean."

Shortly after becoming first lady, ER visited the Bonus Army encampment. (FDR Library)

"We often make the mistake of believing that what happens at the bottom makes no difference. As a matter of fact, it is what we do at the bottom which decides what eventually happens at the top. If all the way down the line every able-bodied citizen attended to his duties, went to community meetings, tried to find out about the people who were going to hold office, knew the questions that came before them, there would be a radical change in the quality of people who take active part in political work."

In 1941, ER addressed a DC meeting on "should women be allowed to work." (FDR Library)

"Is it wise to lay down laws and regulations about any particular group? If we begin to say that married women cannot work, why shouldn't we say next that men with an income of more than a certain sum shall not work, or that your people whose parents are able to support them have no right to look for jobs? It seems to me that it is the basic right of any human being to work."

In 1943, ER began her tour of the Pacific front by visiting Pearl Harbor. (FDR Library)

"If human beings can be trained for cruelty and greed and belief in power which comes through hate and fear and force, certainly we can train equally well for gentleness and mercy and the power of love which comes because of the strength of the good qualities to be found in the soul of every individual human being."

After joining the American delegation to the UN in 1945, ER took an active role in floor debates. (FDR Library)

"If I can reach only one person with my message about the importance of the United Nations, I feel that my efforts were rewarded and my time not wasted."

In 1951, ER chaired the UN Human Rights Commission charged with implementing the Universal Declaration of Human Rights. (FDR Library)

"I do not believe that oppression anywhere or injustice which is tolerated by the people of any country toward any group in that country is a healthy influence. I feel that unless we learn to live together as individuals and as groups, and to find ways of settling our difficulties without showing fear of each other and resorting to force, we cannot hope to see our democracy successful."

In 1952, ER visited "the awakening East" where she conferred with Indian Prime Minister Nehru and Madame Pandit. (FDR Library)

"The democracy that India is building will probably never be exactly like ours. There is no reason why it should be, for her history, cultural background and needs are completely different from those that dictated our form of democracy and guided its development. What the leaders of India want and are determined to have is a democracy that is indigenous to their own country."

In 1954, ER and Yugoslavian leader Marshal Tito debated plans to curtail Soviet expansion. (FDR Library)

"We sat down to talk and I studied his face. His chin is firmly molded, he looks at you without evasion, and the lines in his face attest experience a younger man would not have had. He is not tall, but his is a commanding figure. When he speaks to give an order, there is no question that he knows what he wants."

In 1953, ER met with young women wounded by the atomic bombing of Hiroshima. (FDR Library)

"We must cooperate for our mutual good. . . . The easy answer is to all that is human nature is such that we cannot do away with war. That seems to me like saying that human nature is so made that we must destroy ourselves."

In 1955, ER visited a Moroccan refugee camp where she talked eye to eye with a child en route to Israel. (FDR Library)

"If we relate the immediate problems of the child to the problems of the family as a whole, we will find ourselves concerned with housing, medical and dental care, education and recreation. We will be interested in wages and hours for labor, and we will try to figure out an adequate family income."

ER at Val-Kill, 1957. (FDR Library)

"Somehow or other, human beings must get a feeling that there is in life a spring, a spring which flows for all humanity, perhaps like the old legendary spring from which men drew eternal youth. This spring must fortify the soul and give people a vital reason for wanting to meet the problems of the world today, and to meet them in a way which will make life more worth living for everyone. It must be a source of inspiration and faith."

In 1957, ER invited labor organizers to hold their training session at Val-Kill.

"It is not only physical courage which we need, the kind of physical courage which in the face of danger can at least control the outward evidence of fear. It is moral courage as well, the courage which can make up its mind whether it thinks something is right or wrong, make a material or personal sacrifice if necessary, and take the consequences which may come."

In 1958, ER toured the International Exhibition in Brussels with Harry Belafonte. (FDR Library)

"If we do not see that equal opportunity, equal justice, and equal treatment are meted out to every citizen, the very basis of which this country can hope to survive with liberty and justice for all will be wiped away."

After the *Dennis* decision, ER became more outspoken in defense of unregulated debate. (FDR Library)

> *"We must be able to disagree with people, and to consider new ideas, and not be afraid. The day that I am afraid to sit down in a room with people that I do not know because perhaps five years from now, someone will say, 'You sat in the room and five people were Communists, and so you are a Communist," that day will be a bad day for democracy."*

In October 1960, ER overcame her reluctance and campaigned for the Kennedy-Johnson ticket. (Library of Congress)

> *"I think Senator Kennedy is anxious to learn. I think he is hospitable to new ideas. He is hard-headed. He calculates the political effect of every move. I left my conversations with him with the feeling that here is a man who wanted to leave a record of not only having helped his countrymen, but having helped humanity as a whole."*

In 1962, ER and Esther Peterson introduced the report of the President's Commission on the Status of Women. (FDR Library)

> *"Women must become more conscious of themselves as women and of their ability to function as a group. At the same time they must try to wipe from men's consciousness the need to consider them as a group or as women in their everyday activities, especially as workers in industry or the professions."*

Eleanor Roosevelt, 1962.

"The thing that counts is the striving of the human soul to achieve spiritually the best that it is capable of, and to care unselfishly not only for personal good but for the good of all who toil with them upon the earth."

veloped nations which need markets for their goods. Their cooperation will lead to the purchase of raw materials by the developed nations, which can then sell the finished goods to the less industrialized countries.

The specialized agency known as UNESCO—the educational, scientific and cultural organization—has perhaps been more violently attacked than any other for the reason that its task was less easy to perform.

Education is essential to both health and the improvement of the world food supply. Controversies can develop, however, as to the methods which shall be employed to give that education. Any organization which really sets out to do something in the intellectual field where it not only touches governments but directly affects the peoples of the world is bound to have a controversial task. In any country differences of opinion as to what are the aims of education and how they shall be achieved are constantly discussed, but when an organization tries to find answers and work on a world scale it is dealing with a very difficult problem. To awaken interest in the interchange of thought and intellectual knowledge must be a concern of UNESCO, and some nations will resent and resist these efforts.

I am sure in the long run we are going to discover that we would never have reached a level of better understanding without the aid of UNESCO, but we must be patient and wait for results, for this work, like all other international work, is experimental.

I wish that everyone in the United States would take the trouble to write to the UN and get its booklets telling of the work of the specialized agencies and, where possible, get its film strips, because everyone can understand pictures and it is thus easier to see what is really being accomplished.

Some people are disappointed because peace hasn't fallen upon us like manna from heaven. There is still fear and misunderstanding in the world, and I am afraid we must all make up our minds that peace will require as much hard work as winning a war and that we must use the UN and back it up loyally and enthusiastically, or else its efforts for gradual improvement in understanding will fail. It is the only machinery we have through which we can acquire greater knowledge of other peoples and they can acquire knowledge and understanding of us.

The return for our investment is that communism has been prevented from overrunning the world. We have allies and friends and a place where we can work together and grow to better understanding. Many misunderstandings have been cleared up short of war, and where there is war we do not stand alone. From my point of view our membership in the United Nations is a good investment. □

6.   "The Universal Validity of Man's Right to Self-Determination"

Department of State Bulletin, December 8, 1952

Before giving the views of my delegation on the question of the self-determination of peoples, I should like to reserve my delegation's right to reply at a later stage to the misstatements and distortions of fact about the United States, particularly with reference to territories under U.S. administration, contained in the statements of the representatives of Byelorussia and Poland, as well as to any other such misstatements that may be made in the course of this debate.

The desire of every people to determine its own destiny, free from dictation or control by others, is one of the most deep-seated of all human feelings. Throughout history groups of individuals having common bonds of language, religion, and culture have developed a sense of solidarity as a people and have tended to resent any effort of the outsider, the foreigner, to interfere with them. So strong is this feeling that men of many peoples have at various times been willing to lay down their lives to be free from domination by others.

The fact that wars have sometimes resulted from the failure of one people to respect the wishes of another led us all as members of the United Nations to agree that one of our major purposes is "to develop friendly relations among nations based on respect for the principle of equal rights and self-determination of peoples." In our present discussion we find ourselves faced with the problem not only of giving greater moral weight to this principle but at the same time giving it clearer definition so that it may have universal validity in the complex world of today.

While the underlying concept of self-determination is, I suppose, as old as human society, the term "self-determination" is relatively new. It appears to have been used first with regard to the nineteenth-century struggle of certain European peoples for a separate national existence. It occurs in the writings of the radical German philosophers of 1848 as *Selbstbestimmungsrecht,* which was translated into English as "the right of self-determination of nations" in a resolution adopted by a Conference of European Socialists in 1915. As a number of speakers, including the representatives of Egypt and the United Kingdom have pointed out, this phrase was given wide currency as a principle of international diplomacy by an American President, Woodrow Wilson. However, as several speakers have also reminded us, Woodrow Wilson from the beginning recognized that the principle of self-determination has its limitations. Because I think it important that we keep President Wilson's thought in this matter clearly in mind, I should like to quote again the statement he made in setting forth his "four principles" before the U.S. Congress on February 11, 1918. He asserted that all well defined national aspirations shall be accorded the utmost satisfaction that can be afforded them without introducing new, or perpetuating old, elements of discord and antagonism that would be likely in time to break the peace of Europe and consequently the world.

Today we discuss the question of self-determination in quite a different and much more complex setting. The stage is no longer Europe alone; it is worldwide. In a single resolution of a few paragraphs, we are setting forth certain guidelines for the respect of a principle, not only in Europe but in Asia, Africa, and the Americas as well. Consider for a moment the wide variety of cultures of the peoples with whose self-determination we are concerned—the culture of the spear and the earthen hut, the culture of vast rural peasantries, the complex culture of industrial cities, and confused combinations of culture. The complexity would seem to me enough to make us cautious lest we be too precise, narrow, or rigid in drawing up rules for promoting respect for the principle of self-determination.

In this debate, as with any resolution we adopt, we are molding for generations to come a principle of international conduct. If self-determination is a right which belongs to all people, it is inappropriate for us to express ourselves here in a general resolution with respect only to certain people. Our words and phrases must be made to apply as much to those who once exercised the right and had it snatched from them as to those who have never possessed it.

We, like others before us, would ask ourselves, therefore, what may constitute a "people" to whom the principle of self-determination shall be applied. What are their characteristics? What are their cultural or political or geographical boundaries?

In our search for an answer we find the very concept of a "people" undergoing rapid evolution. Possibly the very first group of human beings seeking to maintain itself as an entity free from the control of others was the family or kinship group. The trend of history, in varying degrees and with numerous setbacks, seems to have been that larger and larger groups of once separate peoples have been formed and have come to think of themselves as a single people. Almost every nation represented at this table is composed of disparate elements of population that have been combined in one way or another into a unified or federated political system.

Here differences among formerly separate peoples either have been or are being submerged and new and larger peoples are emerging. This process of evolution and merger is still going on. It is a trend which diminishes the possibilities of conflict. Must we not exercise the greatest care lest anything we do here tend to freeze the pattern of peoples along present lines and thus instead of promoting the unity of mankind, emphasize certain obstacles to such unity?

We in the United States have gained the conviction from our own experience that the combination of peoples is a process of enrichment. Right here in New York City the number of persons of Irish descent total nearly 550,000, more than in the city of Dublin; the Italian population, similarly defined, is well over 1,000,000 and exceeds the population of Naples. New York has more people of Jewish origin than all Israel. Our 12,000 Arabic-speaking people are the equivalent of a small Middle Eastern city. Yet, as I am sure you have seen demonstrated many times, their children are not Irishmen, Italians, Jews or Arabs. They are Americans.

We do not claim for one moment that the process of creating a new people is easy or that we have fully succeeded in doing so for all elements of the population, but we know it can be done and we are convinced that this process is to be preferred to clinging overzealously to the separateness of peoples.

At the same time we believe it is possible and desirable to retain a good deal of diversity within large political entities. Through our federated system of government, each state and each community preserves for its people the maximum voice in their own affairs. Louisiana has continued its legal system adopted from France, passed on from the earliest settlers of the region. Arizona and New Mexico have Spanish as one of the official languages of their legislatures. Throughout the country, people worship in Norwegian and Russian, publish newspapers in German and Greek, broadcast over the radio in a variety of tongues. In every state, county, and town the people decide for themselves who shall teach in their schools and what shall be taught. Their policemen come from their own communities and are subject to their control.

This is self-determination exercised to a high degree, yet without sacrificing cooperation in the larger fields of common interest. Each element of the national community contributes to the national government, takes part in it, and helps to shape the decisions which lead to a national destiny. Yet it must be equally clear that to grant the automatic exercise of the absolute right of political self-determination to every distinct section of our population would be detrimental to the interests of the population as a whole. And such considerations would apply to the territories whose future rises or falls with ours.

In this context we might ask ourselves: Does self-determination mean the right of secession? Does self-determination constitute a right of fragmentation or a justification for the fragmentation of nations? Does self-determination mean the right of people to sever association with another power regardless of the economic effect upon both parties, regardless of the effect upon their internal stability and their external security, regardless of the effect upon their neighbors or the international community? Obviously not.

As I have suggested, the concept of self-determination of peoples is a valid and vital principle, but like most other principles it cannot be applied in absolute or rigid terms. Surely it is not consonant with realities to suggest that there are only two alternatives—independence or slavery. Just as the concept of individual human liberty carried to its logical extreme would mean anarchy, so the principle of self-determination of peoples given unrestricted application could result in chaos. Is either principle thereby invalidated? Certainly not! On the contrary, we feel sure that human freedoms can find their fullest expression only in the context of responsibility.

The resolution before us, in at least one other respect, raises the question of absolutes. It speaks of granting the right of self-determination, upon a "demand for self-government," by ascertaining the wishes of the people through a plebiscite.

We are compelled to ask, is this not an extremely limited concept of self-determination? Is the demand for self-government the only question on which the people should be consulted? Is the plebiscite the only method of consultation?

Were self-determination synonymous with self-government, we would find these questions easier to answer. But self-determination, as applied to non-self-governing territories, whose peoples have not had the opportunity to attain their full political growth, is a much more complicated matter. It has application at all stages along the road to self-government.

Self-determination is a process. It is in essence the process of democracy as contrasted with the process of dictation in any society developed or underdeveloped. It is, as has been said by other speakers, a process which involves responsibilities as well as rights. It is the process by which people develop their own laws and provide their own justice. This means not merely the right to compose a code of law, nor even the actual writing of a code; it also means general agreement to abide by the laws in the interests of society as a whole, even though one's individual or group freedoms are thereby limited. Self-determination is the process by which people agree to finance their own affairs, spread their burdens among themselves, and see that individual contributions to the common good are made. Self-determination is the building of roads and schools; not just deciding to build them, but finding the engineers, the money, the workmen, the teachers, and seeing the job through.

These matters are the essence of self-determination. If self-determination can be increasingly developed in all phases of the life of a people, their self-governing or independent institutions, when achieved, will be strong and lasting. If we conceive of self-determination as synonymous with self-government, we ignore the nature of the process by which true self-government is attained. Mistaking the form for the substance, we might in fact jeopardize the very rights we seek to promote.

There are not only many aspects of the life of any people to which the principle of self-determination can be applied; there are also many ways of learning the wishes of the people, and they must be appropriate to the question involved, as well as to the literacy and understanding of the citizens.

Furthermore, as I indicated a moment ago, it would be unfortunate if we limited our concept of self-determination to the non-self-governing world. We have seen in our own time flagrant examples of peoples and nations, vigorous and proud and independent, which have been overrun by a conqueror and subjected to his dictatorial control. These peoples and nations are entitled to the restoration of their independence.

At a time in history when the freedoms of so many individuals and peoples have been destroyed or are seriously threatened, it is, in the view of my delegation, important that the United Nations reaffirm the principle of self-determination and promote international respect for it. It is important that it do so for *all* peoples, and not solely for peoples in some form of colonial status. In considering the recommendations to this end drafted by the Commission on Human Rights, my delegation would strongly urge that we consider them within the framework of universality and of responsibility lest we frustrate the very purpose for which the principle of self-determination was set forth in the charter— that is, "to develop friendly relations among nations."   □

7.   "U.N. Deliberations on Draft Convention on the Political Rights of Women"

Department of State Bulletin, December 31, 1951

Statement of December 12

As most of you know, the subject of this convention—equal suffrage for women—is very close to my heart. I believe in active citizenship, for men and women equally, as a simple matter of right and justice. I believe we will have better government in all of our countries when men and women discuss public issues together and make their decisions on the basis of their differing areas of experience and their common concern for the welfare of their families and their world.

In the United States, and in most countries today, women have equal suffrage. Some may feel that for that reason this convention is of little importance to them. I do not agree with this view. It is true, of course, that the first objective of this convention is to encourage equal political rights for women in all countries. But its significance reaches far deeper into the real issue of whether in fact women are recognized fully in setting the policies of our governments.

While it is true that women in 45 of our 60 member nations vote on the same terms as men, and in 7 more already have partial voting rights, too often the great decisions are originated and given form in bodies made up wholly of men, or so completely dominated by them that whatever of special value women have to offer is shunted aside without expression. Even in countries where for many years women have voted and been eligible for public office, there are still too few women serving in positions of real leadership. I am not talking now in terms of paper parliaments and honorary appointments. Neither am I talking about any such artificial balance as would be implied in a 50–50, or a 40–60 division of public offices. What I am talking about is whether women are sharing in the direction of the policy making in their countries; whether they have opportunities to serve as chairmen of important committees and as cabinet ministers and delegates to the United Nations.

We are moving forward in my country in this regard, for we have had women in all these posts, but not enough of them, and they do not always have a full voice in consultation. I do not expect that there will ever be as many women political leaders as men, for most women are needed in their homes while their children are small and have fewer years in which to gain public recognition. But, if we are honest with ourselves, we know that all countries have a long way to go on these matters. I believe it is this situation, far more than the continued denial of equal suffrage in a few countries, which has spurred interest in this convention and brought it before our Committee today. This situation cannot be changed entirely by law, but it can be changed by determination and conviction. I hope we will use this discussion to deepen these convictions in ourselves and in our governments.

This convention is the result of work in the Commission on the Status of Women. The United States is proud of the contribution it has been able to make to this Commission through the participation of our representatives, Judge Dorothy Kenyon and Mrs. Olive Goldman.

The terms of the draft convention before us are simple. Articles 1 and 2 provide for the right to vote and to be elected to publicly elected bodies, such as parliaments, established by national law. These are the basic rights which all people must have to express their interest and protect themselves against discrimination or deprivation of liberty. The Charter of the United Nations reaffirms in its preamble the principles of equal rights for men and women. The first General Assembly endorsed these rights when it unanimously adopted the resolution recommending that all member states, which had not already done so, adopt measures necessary to fulfill the purposes and aims of the Charter in this respect by granting to women the same political rights as men. This convention spells out this recommendation in clear and practical terms, on which all parties in a country can unite.

I think I am correct in saying that 24 countries have taken action to extend suffrage rights for women since the Charter was signed in 1945. The most recent of these changes have been in Lebanon and Bolivia. Important gains have been made within the past few years in a number of other countries—Greece, for instance, and in Haiti.

Article 3 of this convention goes beyond the basic rights in articles 1 and 2 into the matter of public office. It provides that women shall be entitled to hold public office established by national law on the same terms as men, and to exercise all public functions in the same way. The object of this article—to encourage opportunities for women in government service—has my hearty endorsement, and that of my Government. Women today hold many important Government posts and an increasing number are in executive positions and in Foreign Service. The wording of article 3 presents certain problems that I believe we should discuss, and in a moment I will go into them in more detail. In principle, however, I am sure we are all in agreement with article 3.

We are also asked to consider formal clauses to complete the convention, on the basis of texts proposed by the Secretary-General. The United States is in general agreement also with these proposals. This is a very simple convention, and it would seem to us that the formal clauses should be limited to the fewest necessary to make the convention effective. These would presumably be those providing for ratification or accession, entry into force, settlement of disputes, notification, and deposit. The Secretariat has proposed certain other clauses which, of course, can be included if the Committee desires, but they do not seem to me to be essential. The simpler and shorter we can keep this convention, the more readily people will understand it and the more effective it will be.

There are other questions we will no doubt want to debate in regard to this convention. I hope, however, that in our debates we will never lose sight of the significance and importance of our objectives.

Now I want to go back to article 3. This is a very interesting article, for the right to "hold public office" includes both elective and appointive office. The right to be *elected* to public office has usually been recognized along with the right to vote. For instance, the Inter-American Convention on the Granting of Political rights to Women, formulated at Bogotá in 1948, includes the right to vote and to be elected to national office. Article 2 of this convention covers a part of this right, the right to be elected to such bodies as parliaments. However, the right to be *appointed* to public office has not previously been included in an international convention, so that we are now considering its expression in treaty terms for the first time.

In relation to appointive office, the language in article 3 is very broad. The term "public office" is taken to include appointments to posts in the (1) civil service, (2) foreign (diplomatic) service, and (3) judiciary, as well as (4) posts primarily political in nature, such as cabinet ministers or secretaries. The number of appointive offices established by national law is usually large, far larger than the number of offices filled by election, and the tasks to be performed by appointive officers are likely to vary widely in substance and in level of responsibility.

Article 3 specifies offices are to be held "on equal terms with men." This is also an inclusive phrase, covering such matters as recruitment, exemptions, pay, old age and retirement benefits, opportunities for promotion, employment of married women. All these are important matters on which women have sought equality for many years.

As I said before, in the United States women have the rights specified in this convention, including the rights we believe article 3 is intended to cover, and we have long urged that women in all countries have similar opportunities. A question does arise, however, as to whether the term "public office" is intended to include military service. My delegation believes it is not so intended. Almost all countries make some distinctions in the kinds of military duty they regard as suitable for women. The most usual distinction, and a natural and proper one, is that women are not used as combat troops and are not appointed to certain posts which might involve the direction of combat operations. Our attitude toward article 3 is, therefore, based on the understanding that it does not include military service.

The United States also has some difficulty with the phrase "public functions," which occurs in the second part of article 3. The U.S. law "Public Office" covers all public posts and this may be true in other countries. The term "public functions" accordingly does not seem to add anything to the text. The phrase might be clarified, however, if the words "related thereto" were inserted after "public functions." This would make it quite clear that no traditional or legal limitation on women in any country, such as restrictions on a woman's right to serve in certain professions or to bring suits at law would interfere with her capacity to serve in public office.

If the phrase is retained in its present form, the view of the United States would be that the public functions referred to in this convention are coterminous with public office.

This convention on political rights of women is not in itself an answer to the problems of modern government. But it points up, I believe in useful ways, how governments can expand their resources by taking full advantage of the energy and experience of their women citizens. Women's organizations throughout the United States have stated their belief in its principles and its value. The convention is a symbol of the progress women have made in the past 100 years, and a challenge to them to claim and make full use of the political rights they achieve. It is for these reasons that the United States hopes that this Committee may agree on a text to which we can give unanimous endorsement.

Statement of December 15

I want first to say just a little about the statements which the distinguished delegate of the Soviet Union and several of her colleagues have made on the situation of women in the United States. These delegates seem concerned, for instance, that in most of our States women share the domicile of their husbands and vote from it as their legal residence. Of course, this is true also of the men; their legal residence is the family domicile shared by their wives. In the United States we assume that husbands and wives wish to live together, and we protect their right to do so, and to share in the management of family affairs and the guardianship of their children. If the woman desires to be separated from her husband, she can set up a separate domicile. The courts also decide how best to protect the welfare of children of separated couples, and unless there is good reason to the contrary, the mother is almost always preferred to take care of young children.

A great many of the other comments which have been made seem to spring from the same source—a difference of opinion, really, as to the importance of the family in all our relationships, including our responsibilities as individuals toward our governments. We were struck, for instance, with the distinction the distinguished delegate of Byelorussia made Saturday afternoon. She said, I believe, that one of the great values in the provision of crèches and nursery schools in the Soviet Union was that it permitted a woman to fulfill her role as mother and at the same time share in the public life of her country. We do not think of the "role of mother" in our country as separating women or denying women a full share in our public life. We feel rather that it is the family which is the center for men and women alike, and for their children, and we try to make it possible for the father of the family to earn enough so that the woman can stay home and care for their children if she wishes. At the same time, as you all know, American women participate fully in all professions and public activities, and more than half our employed women are married women.

Our family relationships result in a number of legal and judicial distinctions which limit the husband as well as the wife. Our laws are changed if these distinctions become unjust to either party, and changing conditions, particularly in modern business, have led to various changes. But the family is still the center of American living.

I am puzzled by certain other comments that have been made because, so far as I can see, what my Soviet colleagues wish us to do is to discriminate against men.

For instance, people in the United States speak many languages. Here in New York you will hear many different languages in the streets and restaurants. In some of our states, however, one seldom hears any language but English. In those States, voters are usually required to be literate in English. But in others—for instance, our Southwestern States, where Spanish is frequently spoken—voters may qualify in either language. In our courts, interpreters are always provided for those who cannot speak or understand English. In no case is there discrimination against women as such.

The distinguished representatives of Czechoslovakia and the Soviet countries have spoken also of the situation of Negro voters in the United States. As you know, great progress has been made in recent years in assuring Negro voters full security in casting their votes. Many more Negroes voted in this past election than ever before in our Southern States as well as Northern. The figures these delegations quoted seemed to be somewhat out of date in this regard. It was implied that the difficulty Negro women have experienced in regard to suffrage is connected with the existence of a poll tax in some of our Southern States. The poll tax is a per capita tax, once usual in many countries, but it is now being replaced almost everywhere by other forms of taxation. It now exists in only five of our States. It applies equally to all people, whites as well as Negroes. However, since it applies equally to men and women, I do not see how any provision on the poll tax could be included in this convention without its resulting in discrimination against men.

I have been glad to hear that Soviet women hold many public offices and participate widely in public life. I have been glad to note this year that the Soviet Union, the Ukraine, and Byelorussia have included women on their delegations to the General Assembly. There have been very few women on these delegations in the past—in fact, I do not recall any since the first General Assembly in 1946. I hope that this convention may lead to greater participation by women in the true organs of power in the Soviet Union, such as the Presidium and the Secretariat of the Central Committee of the Communist Party, in which I understand no women are now included. The experience women have achieved in the more formal and subsidiary bodies throughout the Soviet Union should entitle them to recognition also in bodies which determine the major policies of their Government.

The Soviet Union has brought in a number of amendments, and I want also to discuss these briefly. I understand those on the first three articles of the convention are similar to those presented in sessions of the Commission on the Status of Women and in the Economic Council. Both the Commission and the Council rejected the changes and additions in these proposals on the ground that they are unnecessary in so simple a convention as this one. I would like to point out, however, that the language proposed by the Soviet Union, presumably to assure application of this convention "without discrimination," is in fact very discriminatory, because it enumerates only a few grounds and omits others. The most notable omission is in regard to political opinion. The Soviet amendment also omits the phrase "without discrimination of any kind," which might otherwise cover "political opinion." It seems to me that in a convention on political rights, if you are going to provide any guaranties against discrimination, the most important one would be freedom for all types of political opinion. But, as I said before, the intent of this convention to apply to all women is entirely clear, and we believe any such additional clause would be confusing and might in fact have the result—as the Soviet proposal does—of limiting its effect.

The proposal to expand article 2 by enumerating certain other bodies also seems unnecessary, since all those mentioned in the Soviet draft are included within the phrase "publicly elected bodies" already in article 2. Neither does it seem necessary to add their proposed article 4, calling for implementing legislation. In so simple an agreement as this, the convention itself is sufficient.

Another proposal has to do with the proposed clause on settlement of disputes and provides for arbitration rather than a reference to the International Court of Justice. The United States regards this proposal as a departure from the procedures already approved as part of our UN structure and will oppose it accordingly.

Several countries have proposed that the convention include a clause on the extension of the convention to non-self-governing and trust territories. Women in all territories under the administration of the United States have the rights in this convention, and we believe all women everywhere should have them. As I said earlier, this is a very simple convention, and the simpler and briefer we can keep the formal clauses, the easier it will be for people to understand it and the more effective it will be. However, the United States has no objection to the addition of such a clause, if the majority desire it.

We have been listening with great care to the statements on this convention, because, you remember, the United States indicated in its statement that we do not believe the convention applies to military service, and asked whether that was the general opinion among the delegates. We, therefore, appreciated greatly the strong expression of agreement with our position by the distinguished delegate of France, and also various other statements which supported this view. I believe no contrary view has been expressed and take it there is general agreement that the present convention does not include military service. As I said earlier, the United States regards the obligation it would undertake under this convention with regard to "public functions" as coterminous with "public office" . . . .   ☐

8.   "Eisenhower Administration Rejects Treaty"
My Day, April 8, 1953

New York—I was not really surprised when I read in the paper last night about Secretary Dulles' testimony on the subject of executive agreements and treaties. I had heard rumors that this abandonment of the Human Rights Covenants was to be the position of the State Department and the Administration but it was hard to believe that it would be done in quite the way it has been done. It is quite evident as the Secretary of State said that executive agreements are necessary for the safeguarding of the country in certain situations and to prevent them or insist that they only be accomplished in cooperation with the Senate would be endangering the working of our foreign relations. To say, however, that it is improper to have a treaty which is going to change the social customs of a country and its legal practices as regards the protection of its individual citizens and their civil liberties seems to me an utterly strange position to take. I wonder if all of the Republicans will agree with this stand on the Human Rights Covenants. I am very happy to say that present administration did not carry on the bipartisan policy followed by the Democratic administration in the immediate past by which many Republicans were given opportunities for service and gained experience. Had the present administration carried on this bi-partisan policy, I might have been asked to finish out my last year on the Human Rights Commission. Had I been asked I probably would have felt obligated to accept and now I would be in the unpleasant position of having to resign in the face of the administration's attitude toward these Covenants. Mrs. Lord must find it a curious position to be in, to join 17 other nations in Geneva to draft two covenants which her government has announced it will not present to the Senate.

It would seem more logical to withdraw from the Human Rights Commission if this is to be the U.S. attitude. Even the Soviets, though many of us are fairly sure they will not ratify, have not announced through their government that they will not ratify, so their representatives are not quite in as awkward a position as those from the U.S. True, this attitude will not take away from us in this country our social, political or civil rights but there are many areas in the world where our leadership, even if it had been confined to civil and political rights, might have helped vast numbers of people to gain these rights. In spite of all that has been said we would have been in no danger of losing any of our rights and there were many ways, either through reservations, through working for a federal state clause, or improving the wording of the present articles, in which we could have made it possible to ratify the Covenant on Civil and Political Rights but we are not even going to try. We have sold out to the Brickers[1] and McCarthys. It is a sorry day for the honor and good faith of the present administration in relation to our interest in the human rights and freedoms of people throughout the world.

---

[1] In 1951 Senator John Bricker (R, Ohio) proposed a Constitutional amendment requiring that any treaty operating with the nation be supported by laws "which would be valid in the absence of a treaty." The amendment failed in the Senate by one vote in 1954.

9.   ER's Response

My Day, April 9, 1953

New York—I read with great interest this morning President Eisenhower's letter to the UN Commission on Human Rights meeting in Switzerland, which he sent through the U.S. Representative, Mrs. Oswald B. Lord. He
states that freedom is indispensable for the achievement of a stable peace, that
people everywhere are seeking peace and freedom, that we must press ahead to
broaden the areas of freedom. He regrets the fact that in totalitarian governments there is no respect for freedom or for the dignity of the human person
and considers this a basic cause of instability and discontent in the world today.
These are wonderful sentiments and entirely true statements but they give no
indication of how those people or we ourselves with them are going to work together to attain the ends desired.

The Secretary of State's letter to Mrs. Lord is a clearer statement. In brief he
says that no legal instrument capable of wide ratification in the world today
would have any value since it could not be as good as the actual practice in the
advanced democracies and would have no advantage in the countries where the
people have few, or none, of the traditional human rights, nor could it be applied
in totalitarian states. We can take it, I imagine, that the Secretary looks upon the
Universal Declaration of Human Rights in somewhat the same category as the
Emancipation Declaration by Abraham Lincoln. It was of value to declare the
slaves free and it was of value to put down in the Universal Declaration, even
though it had no legal binding value, a set of standards from Human Rights and
Freedoms throughout the world and to accept the resolution saying we would
try to attain these standards and we would acquaint our people throughout the
world with these desirable human rights and freedoms. No one will deny that
writing these Covenants was difficult. Great Britain recognized this a long while
ago and I imagine they are relieved that the burden of having to make a decision
as to what their attitude will be, has now been taken over by the U.S. since they
can simply say now that they follow our position. The Soviets will excoriate us
unless the dove of peace is very strongly flying toward the U.S. at this time and
they feel they must appease us. In the old days they would have said we had no
interest in the well being of people throughout the world. It will be interesting
to see what their delegates actually say at the present meeting. The representatives of many other nations will feel lost and perhaps a little contemptuous of
our fears. We are not willing to sign anything which binds us legally in the field

of human rights and freedoms. Yet we in the U.S. find legal decisions helpful in gaining rights for our own people. Other nations may bind themselves if they wish, but we feel that it is impossible "to codify standards of human rights as binding legal obligations" and the administration does not want to fight a section of the American Bar Association, or the isolationists, or those who might vote for the Bricker Amendment. In other words, we use high sounding phrases but we are afraid, afraid to tackle a difficult thing and try to improve it and accept it ourselves as far as we are able.

The papers say Mrs. Lord need not feel embarrassed and I quite agree with them. She need not feel embarrassed but the administration and our statesman should feel somewhat embarrassed.   □

10.   "Where Do Human Rights Begin?"
Remarks at the United Nations, March 27, 1953

Where, after all, do universal human rights begin? In small places, close to home—so close and so small that they cannot be seen on any map of the world. Yet they *are* the world of the individual person: The neighborhood he lives in; the school or college he attends; the factory, farm, or office where he works. Such are the places where every man, woman, and child seeks equal justice, equal opportunity, equal dignity without discrimination. Unless these rights have meaning there, they have little meaning anywhere. Without concerted citizen action to uphold them close to home, we shall look in vain for progress in the larger world.   □

PART V

The Cold War Abroad: 1945–1963

1. Revisiting Yalta

My Day, June 1, 1945

Hyde Park—Yesterday I wrote about one of the points raised in Secretary of State Stettinius' recent speech, and today I would like to continue with a discussion of the Polish issue.

It is evident that the Yalta agreement, as far as Poland is concerned, became difficult to carry out and the much-to-be desired creation of a new government was not accomplished. Poland has a right to freedom. But it is evident, too, that Russia, in return for her valiant fighting, has a right to feel that her European doorway is safe. That being the case, the type of government which exists in Poland and the boundaries which are finally agreed upon will be of greater concern to Russia than to any of their other Allies. Some compromise will have to be reached. It is not yet clear what can or should be done, but I think it is good that Secretary Stettinius spoke out and did not treat these subjects as something which the people of this country were not concerned with.

All thoughtful people agree that Russia, Great Britain and ourselves must cooperate in peace as we have cooperated in the war, if the world is to have peace. Therefore, I like very much the plain speaking on the part of our Secretary of State, which emphasizes for all of us the fact that machinery cannot make peace. Only the good will of peoples and their leaders can develop understanding and create an atmosphere in which peace can exist.

We might as well frankly face the fact that in this country there are many people who do not like the British empire. Sometimes this feeling may be a carry-over for old world backgrounds; sometimes it is still our Revolutionary War; sometimes it is a sense of inferiority, which makes us insist on our own superiority and look down on anything which is different from our own habits and customs.

Fundamentally, however, I think it is most often the type of dislike which exists in families now and then. The various members will call each other names, but they do not like it when outsiders do it. I do not think there is any real fear in this country of war between the English-speaking nations of the worlds.

Our feeling toward Russia, however, is different. She is an unknown quantity. Her strength is not yet measured. The fact that she has done in some 25 years what the rest of Europe has taken several hundred years to do gives many a sense of insecurity. We know how rapidly her people have become literate. We know their fanaticism in defense of their form of government and of the leaders who have turned medieval conditions into a modern industrial civilization. We often do not understand that such rapid development means uneven development. I am told that throughout Russia you often hear the phrase, "It will be better." That is a sign that they know their full accomplishment is not yet achieved. Something great has happened, nevertheless. We, in this country, do not quite understand it as yet, and there lies one of the reasons for our uncertainty.

With both Great Britain and Russia, however, we must decide that peace is worth the effort we must make in order to understand and like each other, and that effort must be extend to all other countries as well.   ☐

2.   ## "The Russians Are Tough"

Look, February 18, 1947

I was leaving in the early morning by Army plane for Berlin. The argument on displaced persons had dragged itself out until a very late hour. When the vote was finally taken and adjournment was finally announced, I made my way over to my opponent, Mr. Vishinsky, the delegate from the USSR. I did not want to leave with bad feeling between us. I said, "I hope the day will come, sir, when you and I are on the same side of a dispute, for I admire your fighting qualities." His answer shot back: "And I, yours."

That was February, 1946. When I saw Mr. Vishinsky again, it was October, 1946. He came to join his delegation at the second session of the United Nations General Assembly in Flushing, New York. I realized that we might again have some acrimonious discussions. But I had no personal bitterness. I have never had any personal bitterness against any of the people in any of the Eastern European group. I have had, nevertheless, to argue at some length with them because we could not agree on fundamental problems.

I have found that it takes patience and equal firmness and equal conviction to work with the Russians. One must be alert since if they cannot win success for their point of view in one way, they are still going to try to win in any other way that seems to them possible.

For example, the Eastern European group has but one interest in the International Refugee Organization set up to deal with displaced persons in Europe: the repatriation of as many of their nationals as possible. We, on the other hand, while agreeing that repatriation is desirable, feel there will be people who do not wish to return to their home countries. And our belief in the fundamental right of human being to decide what they want to do must impel us to try to prevent any use of force against displaced persons. We must find the opportunity, if we possibly can, for people to carry out new plans for resettlement somewhere in the world.

I have worked over this and similar questions with the Russians at two meetings of the General Assembly of the United Nations. They are a disciplined group. They take orders and they carry them out. When they have no orders they delay—and they are masterful in finding reasons for delay. They are resourceful and I think they really have an oriental streak—which one finds in many people—which comes to the fore in their enjoyment of bargaining day after day.

When they find themselves outside their own country in international meetings or even in individual relationships, they realize they have been cut off from other nations. They are not familiar with the customs and the thinking of other peoples. This makes them somewhat insecure and, I think, leads them at times to take an exaggerated, self-assertive stand which other people may think somewhat rude. I think it is only an attempt to make the rest of the world see that they are proud of their own ways of doing things.

I always remember that my husband, after one effort to make me useful since I knew a little Italian, relegated me to sightseeing while he did the buying in old bookshops in Italy. He said I had no gift for bargaining! Perhaps that is one of my weaknesses. I am impatient when, once I think the intention of a thing is clear, the details take a long time to work out. Gradually, however, I am coming to realize that the details of words and expressions are important in public documents.

I admire the Russians' tenacity, though it is slightly annoying to start at the very beginning each time you meet and cover the same ground all over again. I have come to accept this as inevitable. It means one hasn't convinced one's opponent that the argument presented was valid. It is perhaps only fair, therefore, that they should go on until they either decide it is useless to continue or one is able to convince them that the opposing stand has truth in it.

I can point to a resolution which was presented after we had finished our discussion on the International Refugee Organization charter and the vote had been taken. Some seventy-odd amendments had been presented and considered. Apparently, it was all over. Then our Yugoslav colleague presented a resolution.

In many ways that resolution tried to do the things which the Eastern European group felt essential regarding displaced persons. Its passage would have nullified many of the things accepted. Our committee voted down the first parts of the resolution, but the third paragraph had in its first line the word "screening," which represented something everybody could agree on.

I think most of our colleagues did not want to show prejudice against the Yugoslav representative. So without reading beyond the first line, they voted "yes" on this paragraph. The last few lines, however, referred back to the former paragraph which we had voted down. It was not until the vote came to the Netherlands that a "no" was heard. He gave no explanation and the "yes" continued to be voted until it came to me. I voted "no" saying, "voting 'yes' on this paragraph makes no sense." I was greeted with laughter. But when they came to read the paragraph, it could only make sense if the preceding paragraph was attached. This paragraph, however, we had voted down!

It was a triumph for our Yugoslav colleague. I hope he realized that the committee desired to show some personal friendliness to him as an individual.

There are many factors which make working with representatives of the USSR difficult. Their background and their recent experiences force upon them fears which we do not understand. They are enormously proud to be Russians and are also proud of the advance of their country over the past 25 years.

They also labor under one great disadvantage. Communism started out as a world revolution and undoubtedly supported groups in the other nations of the world which were trying to instill communist beliefs. Leaders of communism today in Russia may or may not believe the whole world should hold the same political and economic ideas. They do realize that for the time being, they have all that they can well do in their own areas. Though they wish to influence the governments of neighboring states to insure safety from aggression, they no longer think it possible to convert the world to communism at present.

It is unlikely that the Russian leaders today would actively encourage groups to work within other non-communist nations. In fact I think they find it embarrassing to have these groups active. It not only creates in the democracies an active desire to fight back, but extends very often to a general feeling against the USSR.

I feel sure that the representatives of the USSR in this country have little desire to be associated with the American communist groups. One of the difficulties arising here is that among our own citizens we have disagreements about situations in their native lands. For instance, we have Poles who support the present government which is friendly to the USSR. We have Poles who oppose the Russians and probably would support the old regime in Poland.

There are Russians here who left Russia after the first revolution. There are some who left more recently from Ukraine or from the Baltic states. They all form groups here supporting different groups in Europe.

This makes for us a complex situation. It must make it difficult for representatives of existing governments when they come here.

These differences will eventually be resolved. It is fairly obvious that if existing governments continue to be supported by their people, the rest of the world will have to accept what those people have accepted and learn to work with those governments.

In working with the USSR, we will have to divorce our fear and dislike of the American communists, as far as possible, from our attitude as regards the representatives of the Soviet government. We will have to insist that the Soviet government give no help or comfort to a communist group within our country. I think when this is clearly established, we can work with Russia as we have with the socialist government in Great Britain. Both differ from our political and economic views, but these views are not static anywhere.

Words alone will never convince the Soviet leaders that democracy is not only as strong as, but stronger than communism. I believe, however, that if we maintain as firm an attitude on our convictions as the Russians maintain on theirs, and can prove that democracy can serve the best interests of the people as a whole, we will be giving an effective demonstration to every Soviet representative coming to this country.

We know that democracy in our own country is not perfect. The Russians know that while communism has given them much more than they had under the Czar, it's still not perfect.

The question is, which group will fight more earnestly and successfully for its beliefs? We must come in contact with each other. Therefore, the battle is an individual battle to be fought by every citizen in our respective countries. The language barrier is, of course, one of the things which makes it difficult to work with the Russians. More and more they speak English. I wish I could say that more and more we speak Russian! . . .

Talking through an interpreter never encourages friendly relations. I think we feel that it is more difficult to know the representatives of the USSR and of the Eastern European group than it is to know someone, for instance, from France, Great Britain, Italy, or any of the South American countries.

It is true, I believe, that official representatives of the USSR know that they cannot commit their country without agreement with the Kremlin on some special program of action. It makes them extremely careful in private conversation. We who feel we can express our opinions on every subject find a Soviet representative unsatisfactory on a personal basis. This might not be the case if we met just plain, unofficial Russians who felt they had no responsibility and could converse freely on any subject with a plain American citizen!

We undoubtedly consider the individual more important than the Russians do. Individual liberty seems to us one of the essentials of life in peacetime. We must bear this in mind when we work with the Russians; we cannot accept their proposals without careful scrutiny. . . . But I am hoping that as time goes on, the differences will be less important, that we will find more points of agreement and so think less about our points of disagreement.

On the higher levels, where questions of expansion of territory, trade and influence have to be settled, I think we have to remember our own young days as a new Republic, and that Russia is a young, virile nation. She has to be reminded that world cooperation, international ownership and activity seem more important than any one country's interests. Not an easy lesson for any of us to learn, but one that is essential to the preservation of peace.   □

3.   # The Korean War

My Day, February 2, 1951

. . . . I have come to the conclusion that the nation as a whole has a very short memory. A number of people lately have asked me how we happened to be in Korea and why did the President start the war there? These seem to me almost impossible questions.

Anyone remembering back to the last war should know that the Japanese occupied Korea, and when we conquered Japan, we took the country over from them. They should also remember that Russia came into the war as our ally against Japan some months earlier than had been expected. It was originally understood at Yalta that the Soviets could not fight on two fronts, but would come in just as soon as the war in Europe ended. Instead of that they came in ahead of schedule, perhaps because they felt they must guard their Asiatic interests.

In any case, when we took over Korea, Russia quite naturally claimed a part of the responsibility and an arbitrary line was set up—the 38th Parallel. North of that was Soviet responsibility, south of that was ours.

The United Nations was asked by us to supervise a free election in South Korea. Syngman Rhee, while out of the country during the Japanese occupation, had been constantly agitating for Korean freedom. Since this was the first election participated in by the Korean people, it was perhaps understandable that they voted for this man whom they considered the leader for Korean independence. I am told that under him some steps toward a free and democratic government have been taken.

On the other hard, the Soviets refused to allow any interference and set about militarizing the North Koreans. When they were ready, they invaded South Korea. The South Koreans resisted. Immediately our President asked the UN to take action. It did so promptly, and the call went out for volunteers to enforce the UN stand against aggression.

This is the history of how we happen to be in Korea and how this whole situation came about. And this is why, having branded the North Koreans as aggressors, we also had to brand the Chinese Communists as aggressors. Whether you are a big or a small nation, aggression must be called by the same name.

If the Russians had not been the ones responsible for the North Koreans' preparation, one might hope that the Chinese had suffered anxiety in seeing us so near their Manchurian border. But I am quite sure the Soviets know that we are a peace-loving people and the Chinese Communists know it, too. Had they listened to what we said—and believed us—they would know that we had no intention of invading China, that we are only anxious to see Korea become a peaceful country with a government the people themselves have chosen.

That is our aim and the aim of the UN. I hope it can be carried out. □

4. ## Truman's Dismissal of MacArthur

My Day, April 8, 1951

New York—I have a very great admiration for General MacArthur as a soldier and from all I hear he has been a good administrator in Japan and made some wise and far-reaching reforms. I feel that this country owes him a debt of gratitude for the part he played in World War Two and I hope when he comes home he will be received with the honors due one of the great Generals of the United States in World War Two.

I cannot feel, however, that a Commanding General in the field, particularly when he commands for a group of nations, should take it upon himself to announce the policy that in his opinion should be followed in the areas of the world where he is commanding troops. I can not speak for any other citizen of the United States and I know there are Representatives in the House and in the Senate who are in complete sympathy with the things that have been said lately by General MacArthur but for myself I am unhappy about them.

As a citizen I have two great concerns at the present time; first, it is that the United States policy and the United States troops should continue to support the United Nations in an effort to clearly show the world that aggression by any nation is going to be withstood by the UN as a whole. Secondly, my concern is that we, as a nation, should do all we can to bring about a peaceful world. We will not help in that direction if any overt act is taken or anything is said by responsible officials which can give communist China an excuse for saying that we are aiding and abetting aggression against the communist Chinese government or against USSR controlled territory in Asia. Why should we, at this juncture, ally ourselves with any portion of the Chinese people? Whatever difficulties now exist in China must be settled by the Chinese people themselves. It may be they can settle their difficulties without further internal strife. Certainly that is a solution to be desired, but that we should in any way support a government that could not remain in control of the Chinese people because it was unable to bring about a unified government, or the reforms threat would give the people hope of a better life in the future, seems to be a mistake.

Again we seem to be lining up on the side of reaction simply because we can not approve of communism which is on the opposite side. I think we would be justified in refusing to recognize the communist Chinese government for some time. In any case, I would think we could not recognize them until they did represent all the Chinese people and had proved their ability to accept the requirements that go with becoming a member of the United Nations. If the Chinese people as a whole live under a communist regime, I think that regime will either have to satisfy some of their needs or it will cease to be acceptable to the people. Chinese people are a patient people and Heaven knows they have lived with civil war a long time, but having made up their minds to get some reforms I think they will be critical of any sham reforms and will be quick to resent anything which gives them reforms only in name and not in actual fact. To accept the suggestions made for our foreign policy by General MacArthur seems to me to put us in a very equivocal and undesirable position.   □

5.   China and the Korean War

My Day, April 12, 1951

Yesterday the news came that General MacArthur had been replaced in the Pacific areas by General Ridgway. It was the only thing, I think, that the President could do under the circumstances, which were very unfortunate, and I thought the President's message was a very kind message, stating that as one of the great Generals, General MacArthur had earned his place not only in history but in the hearts of his countrymen. Unfortunately he has felt apparently that he had certain rights that have never belonged to a military officer, and therefore he could not continue in this post. It is quite natural that the Republicans should consider it a tragedy and play up in their statements their feelings against the President and his policies.

I was glad to see that Senator Flanders, at least, said that General MacArthur should have resigned and then spoken. No one would deny him that right, but it saddens one that for political partisan reasons the Republicans will stand back of a policy which so evidently would make trouble with our Allies, would make diplomatic action practically impossible and would start World War Three in the Pacific area. I feel that we have more chance for peace than we have had, for the USSR knows well that they will still face a resolute General who has been very successful in holding them in check. The hope is that the Chinese Communists and the USSR will recognize that what they have paid in losses is too great a price and see that they must revise that policy since it is evident that they miscalculated both the ability and the determination of the United Nations in Korea.

I would disagree with the British in their desire to recognize the Chinese Communist government, at least for the present. I still believe that it makes sense to let the Chinese who are accustomed to trading with each other use diplomacy to settle their own difficulties. I can not understand why the British want to settle the Chinese difficulties for them unless their interests in Hong Kong make them cling to the hope that in this way they will succeed in bringing about a more friendly and cooperative attitude towards themselves in the Chinese communist government.

It would seem to me that we have learned by now that no appeasement earns any concessions for USSR controlled governments. Any signs of weakness or conciliation bring more stubborn resistance on their part. Only when we act from strength, saying our position is such, that we hope they will consider settling peacefully the problems between us, do we get any kind of reasonable cooperation from them.

Look at the length of time it has taken to discuss an agenda at the meeting of Foreign Ministers. The USSR wanted this meeting but they have done what they always do—made all the difficulties they could and delayed conclusions because time means nothing to them. When they think the patience of the Allies is worn too thin then they make a concession and keep the discussions going. Those are old tactics and we should have learned how to face them by this time. If they can wait, we can wait, but while we wait we must never let up on preparations for defense.

6.   "First Need: Resettlement"

The Nation, June 7, 1952

The subject of the evening is one in which I am very much interested because I have just been briefly in three Arab states and in Israel. I could not possibly know a great deal after the short time that I was there, but I have had considerable contact with people from those countries in the United Nations and through that contact I have learned some things.

Reason no longer really operates when you arrive at a point of emotion such as has been reached between the Arab States and Israel. Israel, strangely, is more objective—though perhaps it is not really so strange, because it is always easier for persons to remain objective when they have the edge in their favor. And I think that, in the war between the Arabs and Israel, probably Israel had the edge in its favor.

I sit in a United Nations committee, the Humanitarian, Educational and Cultural Committee, where, I think, we should behave as charitably as possible and at least preserve the amenities. The USSR and the USA representatives manage to say good morning to each other, even though as a rule between times, we attack each other quite vigorously. The Israeli delegate sits between two Arab delegates and I have never known the Arab representatives to say good morning, or apparently to recognize that the Israeli delegate exists. That is not exactly conducive to the best sort of cooperation.

But once you have been in the Near Eastern countries, the impression you come away with is that if the United Nations succeeds in resettling those poor, wretched Arab refugees, who are in worse camps than almost any I have ever seen, then there would be a chance of getting somewhere. And there is nothing to be done *but* to resettle them. They have been trained both by Communists who have come in and by the Arab leaders to get hold of you wherever you meet them and to tell you: "We want to go home." You know it is a slogan, because they say it in unison. Most of them do not talk English, but you walk into a schoolroom and all the little boys get up together and say, "We want to go home." And you know quite well there is no home for them to go to in most cases.

If finally they are resettled, I think the logic of the situation will gradually bring about Arab-Israel cooperation. And nothing is more desirable, because Israel has a great deal of administrative and organizing ability, and would be in a position to help.

In the Arab states there is a stirring. Here are countries that have just recently become free; they are very nationalistic because their freedom is a new thing. The leaders have not had much training as yet in administration and organization. Their people as a whole want not just to exist any longer; they want to live. Their governments know that, but they do not quite know how to meet these desires for an improved standard of living. I think if one could just transfer a little of the ability to administer and organize into the Arab governments, their business circles, their agriculture, one would find the problems of the Arab countries solving themselves very rapidly.

Israel at present probably has the greatest capacity in the area for using any aid that comes to it, and if the Israelis could help in the development of other countries, I think it would be the way to remove the fear that the Arabs have. The Arabs are not very logical because in one breath they tell you, "We are impressed by the fact that Israel is receiving all this immigration. Israel is a very small country and some fine day they are going to be crowded and they are going to take us over." Then in the next breath they say, "Ah, but the Arabs have long memories and someday we will drive the Israeli people into the sea." Well, the two just do not go together. It is not logical.

So you are left with the feeling that you have to live through the present period, you have to put everything you can into trying to clear up the refugee situation, and then, perhaps, with help from the rest of the world, you may get the cooperation which will make of the Near East a stabilizing element which is badly needed in this area. Once you have cooperation, I believe Israel can make its best contribution and the Arab States can develop and be a real factor for peace in the world.   □

7.   "The Changing India"

From *India and the Awakening East*, Harper and Row, 1953

. . . . One of the things we of the West who are attempting to understand India must realize is why the Communist philosophy is perhaps easier for them to accept than our own.

It is a fact that very few of them know what we are talking about when we speak of freedom in the abstract, as we are accustomed to in the United States or Great Britain or other European countries. They have had no experience with the reality; for they have hardly ever been free. It is only in the last six years that they have had their own government; and they held their first election only a year and a half ago. The great majority of them have been hungry all their lives; indeed, they have been hungry for generations, and they will become hungrier as their population increases, unless drastic measures are taken.

But their poverty has been made more bearable by their religion which reaches the worthlessness of material possessions and the virtue of voluntary renunciation, and promises to the upright the reward of a better life in the next incarnation. For it is part of the Hindu belief that when a person dies he is reborn again in some other form; and whether that form is higher or lower in the scale of existence depends upon his conduct in his present life.

In effect, what it means to a starving Hindu peasant in the Madras, to a Hindu dweller in the slums of Bombay, to a Hindu refugee sleeping in the streets of Calcutta is that since he cannot eat and must go without, he can at least go without voluntarily and patiently, and thereby store up treasures for the life to come.

So they have gone on, these masses of people, living closely together, suffering together and sharing a deep sense of brotherhood and a common reverence for those who are willing to renounce the good things of the world and to join with their brothers in suffering. It is not unusual for a prince, when he feels he is approaching his last years, to give away all he has and retire to a mountain top or a cave, placing his begging bowl where the poor can put in it their offerings of food from their meager stock, knowing that having become a holy man he can repay them by prayer. Holy men with their begging bowls are fairly common sights in India.

The appeal renunciation has for the Indian people was borne out by something told me by Dr Katju, the cultured and charming Cabinet minister who showed us about Allahabad. The morning we went out on the river I asked him about the significance of the different emblems on the flags that floated above the huts and tents of the holy men along the banks. He explained to me that Hindus believe in the existence of one Supreme God, Brahma, who however has various aspects and who manifests himself in various ways. These different aspects have been personified in a number of lesser gods, who are represented by images. Each family has its own particular household god, whom it worships, but all these gods are simply different manifestations or expressions of the one Universal God. Then he told me a story of Krishna, the warrior hero who is worshiped as the human embodiment of the great god Vishnu the Preserver. Vishnu, Brahman the Creator, and Shiva the Destroyer are the three principal gods of the Hindu trinity. In a way, the tale is reminiscent of some of the old Greek myths. Krishna left his wife for a journey to far away places and was gone many years. After he left she bore him a son of whose coming Krishna knew nothing; and she brought the boy up to guard the house and to let no one enter it. One day, without notice, Krishna returned. His son barred the entrance and Krishna, incensed, cut off the boy's head. Finding his wife within, he demanded to know who it was that had dared to deny him entrance, and whose head he had cut off. His wife in horror told him that it was his own son. Grief-stricken, and desiring to make amends, Krishna killed and cut off the head of an elephant which he brought back and put on his son. To this day Ganesh—the god with the elephant's head—is the defender of all homes; and all over India you see his image on little plaques fastened over or near the doors of the houses.

Dr. Katju finally turned to me and said: "Those flags are there to guide the pilgrims, so each of them will know where to find the holy man who represents his special household god." Then he added, rather sadly, I thought: "You know, Mrs. Roosevelt, if I were to give up my position in the Cabinet and give away everything I have made in my life and sit with a begging bowl under one of those flags, I would have one hundred times more influence with the people than I have today."

I thought then of Gandhi who gave up his considerable income as a lawyer and everything he had and chose instead the simple life of an ashram. The people loved him for his sacrifice and renunciation; it was, largely, the secret of his enormous influence with them and was what made it possible for him to become a national leader.

In my mind's eye I saw a picture of the home for Untouchable boys that Gandhi had founded on the outskirts of New Delhi and of the bare little room on the second floor that he used when he went there to stay with them. I saw the room when we were in New Delhi, and I stood at the entrance awed by the thought of the power of the man who had lived there. All there was in that room is still there—a rug, a rolled-up pad that was used at night as a bed, a pillow. People who came to see him sat cross-legged on the floor before him, as I should certainly have had to do had I ever had the good fortune to be received by him. . . .

We in the West do not demand or expect such austerity and self-denial in the lives of our public men, and though we might respect them for it, it would not greatly enhance their influence. But the hungry people of India were won by Gandhi's life of voluntary renunciation and service, and they followed him as long as he lived.

The philosophy of renunciation, combined with appalling poverty, has created a situation made to order for the Communists, who have shaped their propaganda cleverly. They do not promise fantastic material rewards; they say something like this—"Your lives have been difficult. You have known only hardship and poverty. If you will surrender your will to the state, which labors for the good of the people as a whole, the state will see that all of you have worked to do for which you are compensated; and all of you will have something to eat. It may not be as much as you would like, but you will be assured of enough to keep body and soul together. And you will have the satisfaction of knowing that throughout the Communist world all your brothers will share equally with you, and are also enjoying the fruits of their own labor."

Freedom to eat is one of the most important freedoms; and it is what the Communists are promising the people of India.

Our Western doctrines are less easy to grasp. We strive for great prosperity; we want to be free to progress as far and as rapidly as we can, and we have enough confidence in ourselves not to want to be restricted to a minimum. Our laws may set certain minimum standards, but none of us wants to be kept by law from working for better things.

To the Indians, however, we seem to be interested in material gains only. Moreover what we offer, what we assure them is possible, is so far removed from anything within the experience—or even the knowledge—of most of them that it sounds, quite simply, fantastic, not believable. We cannot be sincere, they think. But what the Communists offer is entirely understandable. The possibilities they hold out have the advantage of being something the Indian people can imagine achieving; that they can see as not too far removed from the pattern of their past or from their vision and hope for the future. Yes, they say, this much possibly is within our reach. They have no background of knowledge that would enable them to detect the speciousness of the Communist promises; they do not realize that the Communist system is a brake not only on material but spiritual advance; they have not yet made the connections between freedom and not just less hungry stomachs but full stomachs.

There is no question in my mind that Prime Minister Nehru is trying to develop a democracy that, though perhaps not exactly like ours, will ensure all the people personal freedom. But if an accompanying material prosperity is also to be achieved—and the government will not be successful unless it can demonstrate certain progress on the material side—considerable education and re-education of the people will be necessary. For a belief in the virtue of renunciation is not an incentive to hard work for material gain; but only hard work by all the people is going to bring any real betterment of their living conditions. Somehow a spiritual incentive, a substitute for renunciation, will have to be found. Somehow they must be made to realize the living and exciting possibilities of the freedom and democracy their new government offers them.

These ideas had been gradually forming in my mind as I traveled about India, and in my last talk with Prime Minister Nehru the night before I left Calcutta, I tried to put them into words for him. I asked him first whether my feeling about the Indians' great admiration of renunciation was correct, and I told him what Dr. Katju had said. He was quick to answer that he thought the Indian people wanted their public men to do their work; but then he added: "They do admire renunciation," and from the tone of his voice I gathered that he admired it too.

I went on to ask whether there were not two separate lines that would have to be pursued before the goals of the Five Year Plan could be achieved. One was of course the line of material progress, involving the procurement of the material aid, technical assistance, supplies and machines needed to develop India's agricultural and industrial economy and trade. With, in the meantime, enough food grains to keep the people from starving. These things the technically advanced countries of the West could help them with.

But the other requisite of the success we could not help with—to discover an equivalent to renunciation. Only the Indian leaders, especially Nehru himself, with his deep understanding of the Indians' inner needs, could judge what spiritual incentives would induce them to make the effort necessary to obtain material satisfaction.

Our material wealth has come to us almost as a by-product of our effort to fulfill our spiritual and democratic ideals and as a result of our philosophy of work. But our ideals are peculiar to our culture; they satisfy us, but they would not necessarily satisfy the Indian people. . . .

My own feeling is that with their religious and cultural background something different will be required to spark in them the conviction that the modern struggle of a highly technological developed state is worth while.

I do not know whether my analysis is right or whether I am simply imagining a situation; yet when I was talking to Nehru that night, he gave me no feeling I was wrong.

I think it is well for all of us as we size up the effect of the Communist promises in this area of the world, and the possible success of our own conception of democracy, to bear in mind that our world and way of life is an unknown quantity to the people of the East. This is one of the hurdles we will have to get over before we can hope fully to understand each other. . . .   ☐

---

8.   "Soviet Attacks on Social Conditions in U.S."

Department of State Bulletin, January 13, 1953

After the speakers' list was closed, the Committee heard the distinguished delegates of the Ukraine, Soviet Union, Poland, and Byelorussia talk at great length about social conditions in the United States. These four speakers, like another speaker earlier in the debate, made many allegations about declin-

ing standards of living in this country, about our inadequate facilities for housing, education, health, and social welfare, about racial discrimination, and about
the high cost of living in the United States. These speakers all asserted that the
defects in American life are due primarily to the preparations of our Government for war.

This is the seventh year in which I have heard these same old, stale charges
hurled against the United States. On several previous occasions I have replied to
these charges, point by point, with the true facts. But, after all, no one ever ex-
pects replies to Soviet slanders to have any effect whatsoever on their representatives. Each year I present the facts about the situation in the United States; and
then the next year these representatives offer up the same old distortions of fact.

The Committee is so far behind in its schedule that I will not delay it today
with any detailed rebuttal. I should like merely to summarize what I have said on
six previous occasions, knowing full well it will not prevent this group of representatives from saying the same thing all over again next year.

First, the U.S. Government and the American people do not want another
world war; they are not preparing for another world war; they are doing, and
will do, everything in their power to maintain international peace and security
and to resist aggression.

Second, social conditions in the United States are not perfect and the standard of living of large numbers of the American people is far from satisfactory.
It does not require this annual shower of crocodile tears by this group of representatives to make me aware of the defects in American life. I am fully aware
of these defects, for I have spent the better part of my life fighting to help correct them.

Third, despite the fact that the standards of health, education, social welfare,
housing, and race relations are not as high in the United States as we Americans
would desire, they are much higher than the distinguished delegate of the Soviet Union and her colleagues would lead the Committee to believe.

Every year, the distinguished delegate of the Soviet Union and her colleagues
quote a long list of figures to show what a small part of the *Federal* budget of the
United States is devoted to education, health, social insurance, and similar activities. Every year I have to remind these delegates that the major expenditures
in our country for education, health, social insurance, and similar activities
comes not out of the Federal budget, but from the States, the counties, the
cities, and the towns, and from private sources of many kinds. Let me cite just
one figure, for probably the seventh time, to show the utter falseness of all these
charges. The distinguished delegate from the Soviet Union stated that less than
one percent of the budget of the Federal Government in the United States is de-

voted to education. That is a correct statistic because education is not the primary responsibility of the Federal Government, but that statement gives a completely false impression. The States, local communities, and private institutions are primarily responsible for education in the United States. In the fiscal year 1950–51 our State and local governments spent a total of $7,500,000,000 on education, or 34.1 percent of their total expenditures; and our private institutions in addition spent many millions of dollars on education.

Fourth, despite all the imperfections in our American society and despite all I have heard about the perfect paradise that exists in the Soviet Union, Poland, Byelorussia, and in certain other countries—I am sure every person with decent instincts still prefers to live in imperfect freedom than in a propaganda paradise without freedom. For the last 20 years in this country, the Republican Party, a majority of our newspapers, and millions of our citizens have been criticizing and denouncing the Government; and for the next 4 years, the Democratic Party, many of our newspapers, and millions of our citizens will be criticizing and denouncing the new Administration. Yet not one Republican politician or diplomat has been imprisoned or hanged for his opposition to the Government in power. Not one newspaper has been suppressed. Not one citizen has been shipped off to a slave-labor camp. Nor will anything of this kind happen in the next 4 years to any American who happens to disagree with the Republican Administration.

In conclusion, Mr. Chairman, we in the United States know better than these critics the many things that are lacking in our country. We have done much in the past, and we are doing much today, to correct these injustices and these low standards. We would be doing even more today if we were not compelled by the aggression in Korea and by the threat of aggression elsewhere to help strengthen the free world and to preserve the peace.   □

9.   "Why Are We Cooperating with Tito?"

Look, October 8, 1954

In charting our diplomatic and military defensive against Soviet communism, we in the United States have, officially, embraced a Communist state and a dictator who looks upon communism as a particularly endowed means of governing. The state is Yugoslavia. The man is Marshal Tito.

Perhaps there is no more contradictory situation in our postwar diplomacy. Certainly, in my travels around the United States, there is no question on international affairs which I am asked more often than: "Why are we doing business with Tito?"

In practical terms, of course, there is no real question on why we support President Josip Broz (Tito) today. He and his regime are against the Soviets, and, in the temper of these times, this puts Tito and Yugoslavia on the same defensive footing as we of the Western world are. In simple realism, more people in the United States are more afraid of the Soviets than are afraid of Yugoslavia.

Yugoslavia, for its own part, has aligned itself more closely with the West through a pact with Greece and Turkey. These three nations have pledged to defend themselves together against attack from without. This has drawn them more closely to the Atlantic Pact defense system, and to the West as a political unit, than ever before.

With the very forthright idea that whoever is against the Soviets is our friend, many people in this country have accepted Yugoslavia as an ally. This large group of Americans thus agrees to support Tito with military and economic aid, but still has reservations on whether this democratic nation should be doing business with a one-man regime. The problem is that most of us in this country do not understand how Tito's communism differs from the Russian variety.

As the guest of Tito and his wife at their summer villa on the island of Brioni in the Adriatic, I devoted several long conversations to trying to place this man, his ideas and his system of government into perspective.

I entered the long reception room the morning he first received me, and I could not help thinking that it required only a great desk at the far end of the room to resemble the places where Mussolini and Stalin greeted their guests—making the visitor walk the entire length of the room to be received. But Tito arose and came forward quickly. He seemed friendly, and appeared genuinely kind and warm.

We sat down to talk, and I studied his face. His chin is firmly molded, he looks at you without evasion, and the lines in his face attest experience a younger man could not have had. He is not tall, but his is a commanding figure. When he speaks to give an order, there is no question that he knows what he wants and that he does not expect to be misunderstood or misinterpreted.

Our discussions turned almost at once to the relationships between his country and Russia, as to forms of government, as to viewpoint, as to aims. He talked first of Russia, cautioning against the West's overestimating the occasional apparent signs of weakness in the Soviet Union. He kept reminding me that there was a great army in Russia. He pictured the Soviets as always pretending to the role of protectors of weaker nations, so as to keep their influence in the satellites intact. He emphasized that any apparent threat against Russia itself would serve only to unite the Russian people.

I probed particularly for his real thoughts on communism as it is practiced in Yugoslavia. His reply was quick, and to the effect that communism existed nowhere, least of all in the Soviet Union, which he called an imperialist state with state capitalism. He pictured communism as an ideal which could only be reached when people ceased to be selfish and greedy and when everyone would be willing to see each individual receive according to his needs from communal production. But that condition, he told me, was a long way off.

Once I asked him to classify himself in governmental philosophy. Tito smilingly said he supposed he might call himself a social democrat. The Marshal explained that practically everything in Yugoslavia was nationalized, but he did not believe that everyone liked that. He said all the people lived on the salaries they earned, but there was a belief in private property—as in a house or a small farm not exceeding 20 acres.

Tito dislikes what is evolving in Yugoslavia being called communism. He also objects to calling it Titoism or Yugoslavianism. His theory is that every country should develop according to its own needs, and he does not want his methods held up as an example for another country where they might not work at all.

Eventually, we turned to his own role and I found him adamantly opposed to being called, or thought of, as a dictator. He told me of his colleagues, a group of World War II partisans like himself, who worked together to develop each phase in the reshaping of Yugoslavia. He proudly told me how they would draft a new law and have it printed in the press, and how the government would hold up applying the law until reaction had been measured. Individual letters concerning the new law would be analyzed, and the proposal then would be redrafted and resubmitted for comment. This process of steady and continuing referendum he took as proof that he was not running a one-man show.

I was moved to the conclusion that Tito conceives of his as popular government, not too far removed in his mind from that of our country. Of course, the basic difference is that it is government from the top down rather than from the bottom up—and that's the difference between day and night. In speaking of these processes of referendum, he was quite expansive—almost as a father toward a favorite child. I realized that he felt this was a government of transition—a step toward a more elaborate system to meet the needs of people coming out of a monarchy until they should become more educated to the methods of self-government.

We got around to talking about his concept of internal communism. I asked him about the one-party system, and was told that more than one candidate for an office always was put up—so the people had a choice (as in a primary). Then he added with a smile: "There is no great difference between your system and ours. We have one party and you have only two—just one more!"

There are sharp differences, I think, between the peoples of Yugoslavia and Russia. The Russian peasants for years were unprotesting slaves, and when they were driven to seek any measure of improvement, these revolts were led by the intellectuals. On the other hand, the Yugoslav groups have been constantly in revolt, constantly fighting for freedom. This has produced in them a character far different from that of the Russians. I think that it must be conceded that Tito himself has this basic difference in quality, and that he recognizes it in his people—which may be the great reason for the split between Yugoslavia and the Cominform.

As we chatted about Yugoslavia's break with the Cominform, I pressed the Marshal for an answer to one question which lurked in my mind. Although he had rebelled at Russian efforts to impose the Kremlin's will in Yugoslavia's internal affairs, he had never repudiated, to my knowledge, the concept that the Cominform was designed to spread world communism.

Tito thought there was a trend in the world toward socialism, but he insisted that nations must develop in their own way, without others trying to impose plans and methods upon them.

This led to a sore point. I gathered at once that he felt quite strongly that the great powers in the West should no more interfere in the way other nations wished to carry on their affairs than should other nations interfere in the affairs of the Western nations. I explained to Tito that many Americans understood that his country needed economic aid and that I had been impressed by the gratitude shown for that aid. But I told him flatly that I felt that such gratitude did not prove that, when the aid was no longer needed, his government might not return to Stalinist methods.

The Marshal was shocked—as much apparently by the implication that there were many other Americans with such reservations as by the fact that I told him this. He emphatically assured me that the break with the Cominform had brought an end, for good and all, to Stalinist methods in Yugoslavia. He repeated an earlier assurance to our then Ambassador, Mr. George Allen, that regardless of whether we extended aid or not, the attitude of Yugoslavia toward the Cominform and the Soviet Union would not change.

From Tito on down, nowhere in Yugoslavia did I find any evidence of any intention to rejoin the forces of world communism. From the Ministry of the Interior, I inquired about the secret police and about the rumors one hears of political prisoners and various other types of prisoners. There I was told that the secret police make arrests every month, but that the search is for Soviet infiltration and Soviet agents who are attempting to win over the Yugoslav people to collaboration with Russia. This sort of infiltration just is not allowed in Yugoslavia, any more than it is allowed in the United States.

Tito and the people I met and talked with in Yugoslavia seemed to have the warmest feelings toward the United States. That doesn't mean that we always will agree on methods, since Yugoslavia is a socialist state, at the present time extremely concerned with its own internal economic and social affairs, and ours is a representative republic with a capitalist economy.

Tito's Yugoslavia, despite its break with the Soviets, remains part of the Communist world. Let us not fool ourselves that it has any sympathy for, or understanding of, our free-enterprise system. But also, let us not become so obsessed with the words that we disregard Yugoslavia's importance to us as a powerful enemy of the Soviet imperialism which is the greatest menace to our free world.   □

10.   Tensions in the Middle East

My Day, November 2, 1956

San Francisco—I was very much interested the other day in a statement made by the new King of Saudi Arabia to the effect that 10 million Arabs should be sacrificed to get rid of the Israelis. In one way I imagine the people of Israel should be proud of the fact that the Arabs estimate they will need 10 million to be sacrificed in a war to subdue a couple of million people.

In another way it seemed to me, as a citizen of the United States believing in the United Nations and in the hope of a peaceful world, that his was a shocking statement. The United Nations resolution dividing Palestine did not please many of the people immediately interested, but the Israelis have accepted it and gone ahead and built on that tremendous influx of immigration from the Arab states and Europe which includes many people who have become a burden on the country. Still, democracy has been preserved and economic and political stabilization are moving forward.

The problems are great in Israel but they are being met and conquered, and since in that area of the world this one of the strongholds of democratic government it would seem that it was a paramount interest to the countries of the West to support and help it grow.

This in no way means antagonism or unwillingness to help the Arab states to grow, but two of the Arab States, Egypt and Syria, are under a dictatorship. Even though that dictatorship may have been necessary and may be the most benevolent government that can be developed at present, it still means that these states are not democratically governed and may still have political and military upheavals. This group of Arab states has expressed its loss of confidence in the United States and in the West by remaining strictly neutral in the differences between the Soviet Union and the United States. As far as the Korean War is concerned, they have shown in every possible vote their mistrust of the UN case in Korea.

Many people deplore the loss of friendship for the United States in the Arab states and feel it is due to the fact that the United States was willing to back the United Nations proposal for the division of Palestine. Whatever the cause, the results are deplorable and the policies now pursued are far more disturbing than the creation of the government of Israel.

It seems to me a most shocking thing for the head of a government in these days of tension to announce what is tantamount to a verbal declaration of war. For the United States, therefore, to contemplate giving arms to the Arab countries seems to me to be a highly questionable policy. I am sure we have the most laudable intentions, first of showing that we are willing to help both Israel and the Arab states on an equal basis. Next, we are undoubtedly hoping that these arms will make the Arab states feel that they can put up some fight if the Soviet Union should decide to attack them.

I can see no reason whatsoever which will prevent the Arabs from using these arms against Israel, if they are so inclined, and once that happens a bitter war will ensue in that area of the world and we will be forced to take a stand which would certainly complicate matters considerably and face us with an increasingly difficult problem. ☐

11.   "What Are We For?"

From *The Search for America*, Prentice-Hall, 1959
Eleanor Roosevelt and Huston Smith

Less than fifteen years ago the United States stood on top of the world, its reputation as unrivaled as its power. As C. L. Sulzberger has observed, we were almost in a position to dictate a *pax americana*.

Today our security is in jeopardy and our principles on the defensive. In the years since World War II the initiative has slipped from our grasp to the point where, as Walter Lippmann has concluded, the North Atlantic community is "no longer the political center of the world." George Kennan is not an alarmist, but even he has reported the United States to be the object of world obloquy, disapproval, and "in some cases of outright hatred," to a degree unprecedented in our history. A decade of anti-American demonstrations in Paris, bombs in the American library in Athens, outrages against Vice-President Nixon in South America, and a world-circling trail of broken plate glass in front of offices of the United States Information Service form a sobering backdrop to his observation.

Why this severe decline in our world stature and prestige? Many factors have contributed, of course. Some of them may have been unavoidable. American G.I.'s have belted the world, and soldiers are never a nation's best ambassadors. Our superior wealth and power may have provoked envy regardless of how we behaved. Perhaps the world simply expected more of us than any nation can provide and we are feeling the backwash of its disenchantment.

But in the end, such explanations are excuses. The major responsibility for the decline in our world position lies with the way we have conducted our foreign affairs. And back of this lies the question of what we have wanted our foreign policy to accomplish.

I

During the first hundred years of our national life we wanted little more from the world than that it leave us alone. So adequate was our continent for our needs, so engrossed were we in building it up, that our prime request of the world was that it not distract us from our indigenous tasks. During the next fifty years, the years that led up to World War II, we passed from being a debtor to a creditor nation. This transition led us to want more from the world. We now wanted it to provide us with a field in which we could expand economically, for raw materials and markets, and safe foreign investments had become important to our economic life. Since World War II our basic objective has again shifted. In this period we have wanted above all else to keep the world from falling into Communist hands. Each of these periods has had its slogans: "no entangling alliances" and "isolationism" for the first; "Open Door," "Manifest Destiny," and "dollar diplomacy" for the second; and "Communist containment" for the third.

Each of these objectives continues to have some relevance for today. We still want a world which will permit us to work out our national life in our own way, which will be conducive to our economic development, and which will stand up to Communism. But none of these former objectives provides an adequate keystone for our present foreign policy.

We need to see this clearly. So, having noted the continuing truth in these former objectives, let us note their deficiencies.

Isolationism, which advocates an essentially "live and let live" approach to the world, may have sufficed in our past. But quite apart from the question of whether it is even logically feasible in a world as interrelated as ours, two things should be obvious: one, that for such an approach to succeed, all nations possessing any power at all must subscribe to it; and two, that the contemporary world contains at least one such nation that hasn't the slightest interest in doing so. From the beginning of the Communist epoch, the Soviet Union has geared itself for world outreach. In part this thrust roots from historic centrifugal forces that have been pressing outward for a hundred years, to the Pacific, the Balkans, and the Middle East. But this is not the whole story; we deceive ourselves if we miss the extent to which the Soviet outreach springs from a sense of mission. . . . A Communist isolationist is a contradiction in terms. While Soviet missions are busy in Latin America trading machinery and oil for wool and coffee, Arab and Asian students are being trained in Moscow, Russian teachers are touring West Africa, and technical advisers are dispatched to India, Burma, and Indonesia.

Faced with such a rival who is out to remake the world in its image, it is obvious that if we want a world different from that of the Communists, we shall have to work for it. To put the matter paradoxically, even if we should want nothing more than a "live and let live" world, we would now have to exert our influence in every land to insure its continuance or evolution. And we would have to exert this influence with as much force and ingenuity as the Soviets.

It may be supposed that our commitments around the world and the regularity with which we now vote a substantial portion of our annual budget to programs of foreign aid is evidence that we have put isolationism behind us. But this is only partially correct. Certainly raw, crude, "Fortress America" isolationism is dead. Two and a half world wars and the continuing cold one have taught us that we must take the world seriously and work with it intimately. But isolationism is not completely routed by involvement. There remains the question of what engagement is for. In its subtle form isolationism admits that we have no alternative to being deeply involved with the world, but it holds that the purpose of this involvement is to preserve a world in which we can still substantially go our own way. This sophisticated variety of isolationism still characterizes our outlook. We go forth to the ends of the earth, but not to remake the world toward goals we believe are relevant to all human living. We go to hold back our antagonists.

. . . . Our goals should differ from those of the Communists, but they should embrace the world as wholeheartedly. They should be as clear as the Communists' goals, and we should work as hard in their behalf, using, of course, means that are consonant with them. The ease with which such words can be written belies the wrench from our past that will be required if we take them seriously. For if we accept the fact that we not only have world goals, but that they must henceforth take precedence over national ones because we can no longer have the kind of nation we want unless we have the kind of world we want, our foreign policy ceases to be primarily defensive—a shield for our security. It becomes instead a channel through which we pour our resources and energies to remake the world. For too many years already, while the Soviet Union has pegged its goal at international proportions we have conceived our goal parochially—to build here, in this sweet land, the good society. To lift our sights to world proportions is a staggering assignment. It will take money, resolution, and a shift in our total national attitude toward the world. But there is no reason to regard the shift with dread. . . .

If isolationism has ceased to be an adequate guide for our foreign policy, so has economic expansion. Obviously we should continue to work for a world that will provide us with raw materials, markets, and secure investments, but we cannot permit mercantile interests to dictate or even dominate our foreign policy. The Biblical dictum to "seek first the kingdom and all these things will be added unto you" is relevant here. Insofar as we succeed in building a world that is stable and prosperous, we shall prosper too. . . . So what begins by sounding like moralism turns out to be stark realism, for it is one of the undernoticed phenomena of our times that we are at one of those unusual junctures in history where, internationally speaking, what is good for us and what is good for others very nearly coincide. Unless the world prospers, it will not be able to buy from us as we wish. And unless justice is effected, passions will erupt into a war which is likely to destroy everything.

The greatest need of our foreign policy, however, is to transcend the "Communist containment" objective that has obsessed us for the last decade. Communism needs to be contained. But to make its containment our top and direct objective is a mistake.

There are at least two reasons for this. One is that "containment" is a negative objective, and these can never match the appeal of positive ones. People live by affirmations, not negations. The late Alfred North Whitehead put this succinctly when, in another context, he pointed out that "if man cannot live by bread alone, still less can he live by disinfectants." Most of the world's population wants change, and if we knew their lot we would not blame them. If, then, we put ourselves in the position of resisting change while our opponents advocate it, we proceed under a hopeless handicap. . . .

The second defect of our "containment" policy really concerns the means by which we have sought to effect it. These means have been preponderantly military; the ratio of our military to our economic aid to foreign countries shows this quite clearly. But since Korea, the Communist offensive has not relied on military advances. It has switched to economic maneuvers and internal subversion against which our airstrips and missile ramps have stood starkly impotent. In some cases our preoccupation with answering Communism with might may inadvertently have encouraged its spread, for military bastions tend to increase local burdens rather than alleviate them, contributing thereby in impoverished countries to the desperation on which Communism feeds. Is not this in part the story of the Baghdad Pact and the Eisenhower Doctrine that now lie virtually in ruins amidst Communist advances in the strategic Middle East? Military power must play a part in our international dealings, but we have banked on it in recent years for more than it can deliver, at the same time underrating what can be achieved through wise diplomacy and imaginative nonmilitary use of our economic resources especially through the joint agencies of the United Nations.

II

The argument up to this point can be summarized in three propositions:

1. United States foreign policy should shed the remnants of its isolationism and direct itself to achieving world goals.

2. The world goals toward which our policy is directed should not be weighted to our advantage at the expense of other nations and peoples.

3. The goals must be positive rather than negative ones. We must break the present image in which we give the world the impression that whereas the Chinese and Russians have something to believe in, Communism, we have something to *dis*believe in, also Communism.

It might help us break out of this predominantly negative approach if we ask: Suppose Communism were to evaporate overnight. What would we do? . . .

It ought not to be difficult for us to formulate constructive goals. . . .

There seem to be no slogans today to take the place of those of yesteryears— "the war to end all wars," "the war to make the world safe for democracy," "the four freedoms," "the century of the common man." But in prose if not in poetry we can specify the ends toward which our foreign policy should be directed. The aim of the United States should be to build a *peaceful* world of *autonomous, prospering democracies*. As all the peoples of the world would benefit from the realization of these goals, perhaps the phrase "world welfare" can serve to summarize them here.

Obviously we are not going to get such a world at once, and in the give and take of international negotiations, one or more of the objectives listed in the preceding paragraph must often yield for the time being to others. In such cases, it would seem wise as a rule to give priority to the objective appearing earlier in the sentence.

Peace must come first because the prospect of the world being reduced to radioactive dust is so awful that we must be patient about other objectives if pressing for them would throw the world into total war. Even peace cannot be absolutized, for if the Soviets were to demand our capitulation, we would fight. But peace comes first in the sense that our pressures for the autonomy, prosperity, and democratization of other lands must not be impetuous to the point of bringing the world to war.

Autonomy will in certain cases have to wait. This is true both for nations like Hungary or Tibet which are under Communist hegemony, and for the few remaining nations in which political consciousness has not matured to a point where independence is feasible. Somaliland is an example here, with a population of one and a half million, of which perhaps fifty are literate. In cases like these, we should make clear that we favor not only independence when political maturity has developed but also steps which will hasten such maturity.

Tibet illustrates why, even in poverty-stricken regions of the world, autonomy should generally take precedence over increased prosperity. The Chinese went to Tibet offering industrialization and a higher material standard of life. It was assumed that to people as poor and illiterate as these simple peasants who live on the roof of the world and have nothing to lose but their yaks this "argument of the stomach" would prove conclusive. But their brief, sad revolt, fought with such great courage and so little hope, has proved how limited is the doctrine of "economic man."

Democracy in our list of objectives means the presumption of freedom for individuals within their nations. Such freedom has three components: personal, political, and economic. Personal freedom involves the individual's right to think for himself, to express his opinions vocally and in print, to live under the authority of law rather than personal whim, to have a fair trial if he violates this law, and to be educated. Political freedom involves the individual's right to affect his government's actions and procedures by electing those who will rule over him and voting directly on measures of special import. It is the application of the concept that as protection against the abuse toward which power inclines, this power should be distributed broadly among the populace. Economic freedom involves the citizen's right to choose his field of employment, to improve his income by merit and exertion, and to initiate enterprises of his own and realize profits therefrom.

The urge for this freedom which democracy seeks to safeguard appears to be innate in the human makeup. Hold the arms and legs of an infant and he will struggle to be released. Similarly peoples, though subjugated for years or generations, will reach out for freedoms if they become possible. The young Hungarians had known nothing but tyranny. They had received the full measure of Soviet indoctrination. Yet when the restraining pressures slackened, they fought for freedom as if they had known nothing else. When post-Stalin Russia and Mao's "let a hundred flowers bloom" China gave hints that freedom of opinion might be tolerated, political commentaries in the form of articles and wall newspapers blossomed overnight as if to prove that freedom's flower, though dormant through a long winter, was far from dead.

By defining democracy as the presumption of freedom we guard against the notion that freedom can be absolutized. When absolutized it jams and becomes nonfreedom: political freedom founders in anarchy (France before the return of DeGaulle was almost an example of this); civil liberties slip into license, and economic freedom moves toward monopoly, exploitation, and unemployment. In this respect freedom, as Gide has remarked, is like a kite that cannot rise on the wind unless restrained. When freedom is presumed rather than absolutized it carries no implication that governments are best which govern least. On the contrary, it accepts Lincoln's principle that government must do for the people what needs to be done but what they cannot do at all for themselves or cannot do as well. Specifically in our own case this involves accepting social security and a host of governmental policing and regulating measures as supports of freedom. In doing so, however, it remains aware on the one hand of freedom's worth and on the other of the way in which concentrations of power, both political and economic, can choke this freedom. Consequently it prefers that things be done nongovernmentally where they can be done as well this way; it leans toward letting its citizens follow, alone or in groups, where their minds and spirits will lead them until evidence arises that their freedom is interfering with the freedom of other citizens. . . .

Even qualified as "the presumption of freedom," democracy must take last place on our list of world objectives. There are places in the world where, if political power were distributed among citizens, they would be too inexperienced to run their nations effectively: the reversion of Indonesia, Burma, and Pakistan to dictatorships within the last year is evidence of this general point. Similarly with respect to economic freedom: where capital is nonexistent and centralized planning and government operation is needed to get the process of industrialization off the ground, to hold out for economic freedom in any sense that resembles capitalism in our own country may thwart development intolerably. Yet democracy with its three ingredient freedoms remains an important part of our creed, for though we admit that there are situations in which it is currently inapplicable, we profoundly believe that it is the noblest form of political life man has yet devised. Where conditions such as poverty and illiteracy make it inappropriate, therefore, these stand as calls to us to do what we can to alleviate such conditions.

III

No statement of objectives provides a simple criterion by which decisions can be made. This is especially true in international relations where ambiguities, paradoxes, and compromises must inevitably abound. The clearest present example of such ambiguity is to be found in our alliances. Our military pacts often strengthen governments that work against our democratic and humanitarian principles. Few would argue that Jeffersonian principles are furthered by buttressing Franco's despotism, the dictatorships of Chiang Kai-shek and Syngman Rhee, or King Saud's slaveholding absolute monarchy. Yet to say we ought therefore not to have entered into these alliances would be to forget that autonomy precedes both prosperity and democracy among our objectives. For all their odious aspects, these pacts have helped to retain the independence of nations that would otherwise have fallen before the Communist advances.

When security is threatened, our differences must usually take a back seat. But this does not mean that they need have no seat at all. Our fault lies not in allying ourselves with governments with which we ideologically differ. Our fault lies in becoming so preoccupied, even obsessed, with matters of immediate military security that we let our other objectives go by the board completely. There is a text for this point too if we want it: "these ought ye to have done, and not to leave the other undone." Concern for the autonomy of western Europe may require that we include Spain in our military alliances, but it does not require that we do nothing to induce General Franco to use our support to increase freedom and prosperity of his people, especially in view of their complaint that the actual effect of our dollars and tanks is just the reverse: to shore up a regime which would otherwise have to reform or be overthrown. Sometimes we give the impression that we are willing to accept any terms such countries dictate as long as they stay on our side, as though, as Mr. Kennan has remarked, "it was we, rather than they, who had the most to lose if they went too far in the relations with Moscow."

. . . . Where mutual security is not at stake there is even less excuse for supporting oppressive dictatorships and stagnant feudalisms. Cuba, Venezuela, the Dominican Republic, and Haiti are cases in point. In Haiti every leading newspaperman if not already killed is in jail, yet we continue to supply the country with military aid which has no effect on the balance of world power but serves only to bolster a vicious dictatorship. No wonder we are developing a "lover of dictators" reputation in South America. Our relations with these countries are not even dominated by "containment" considerations but rather by short-range economic advantage as seen by powerful American industries. Japan provides another example in the category of economic shortsightedness. All four of the world welfare goals we have proposed require freer trade to help her out of her truly appalling straits, but we bow to narrow sectional interests in our country and keep our barriers high.

The only conclusion possible is that our foreign policy has . . . been dominated by objectives of communist containment, economic advantage, or indifference—a dimension of isolationism; objectives which are proving themselves increasingly inadequate to the needs of our time. The people of the United States are beginning to recognize this and throughout the nation there is a groundswell of restiveness with our present approach. What remains lacking is a leader with imagination great enough to see the convergence of our national interest with *world* welfare defined in terms of peace, autonomy, prosperity, and democracy, and who possesses the leadership ability to translate his vision into concrete policies that will carry the support of the people.

Never has our nation stood in greater need of such a man.   □

12.   ## The Bay of Pigs and the Congo

My Day, April 24, 1961

New York—From the newspaper accounts it would seem that our Central Intelligence Agency was not very well-informed as the internal situation in Cuba. Once account suggested that on the one hand we had underestimated Castro's hold on the people of Cuba, and, on the other, that those who might

have wanted to revolt would be unable to do so, since the government had become a police state.

I wonder if we are not falling back on this second idea and ignoring the fact
that there may be groups of people in Cuba who find themselves in better condition today than they were under Batista. It is difficult, of course, to find out.
Yet, from what one reads, the exiles seem to be drawn largely from the intellectual and business groups of Cuba, whereas conditions among the poorer people may be such that Castro has been able to improve the hopes they hold for a
better life. In that case, the greater number of people would not be inclined to
join with the rebels. Since a successful invasion in this instance depended upon
an uprising among the masses in Cuba, it should have been evident to our people that this undertaking was premature.

Lies are evidently easy to fabricate in the present atmosphere of Cuba. Dr.
Raul Roa of Cuba charged the Sherman tank was involved in the landing on
Giron Beach, but it now turns out that the tank was actually one of Russian
make. Again, an American Social Security number, given as proof that it was an
American pilot who was shot down in Cuba this week, turns out to a number
belonging to a Connecticut cabinetmaker who has never flown a plane and says
he has no interest in Cuban politics.

On the whole, it seems to me that even though the President's statement was
correct that no American would take part in a Cuban landing, still we were involved in a way. This is perhaps not conductive to giving other nations the feeling that we are actually going to consult with the other Latin American states on
all matters concerning our neighbors in this hemisphere, and that we will not act
on our own.

Certainly, the votes in the UN have not been encouraging. We lost on the resolution to have the inter-American organization use their good offices to negotiate their difficulties between Cuba and ourselves, and even more serious than
that our Latin American friends refused to go along with the resolution for financial support to the UN in the Congo situation.

As far as one can see, this leaves no alternative to the Secretary-General but
to lay the question before the Security Council. If no one will pay for the military operations, then it may well come to any end in the Congo. This is what the
Soviets have been trying to bring about from the very beginning. If will make it
possible for the Belgians to move back, for the Soviets to bring in whatever they
wish, and I am very much afraid that the chaos that will come about if the UN
troops are withdrawn will mean bitter hardships for the people of the Congo and
no coordinated effort for steady improvement.

France is also confronted by a very difficult problem since the rebel forces of the French Army have seized power in Algiers and declared a state of siege in the whole of Algeria. The only encouraging work so far as I could see Saturday was that the Soviet Union and Great Britain had come to a "general agreement" to call for an end to the hostilities on Monday, which would bring about a cease fire and a study for a truce.   ☐

13.   "What Has Happened to the American Dream?"

Atlantic Monthly, April 1961

On January 4, 1961, the New York *Herald Tribune* carried . . . a news item from Russia. It described the new propaganda drive which is in line with the world Communist manifesto recently published. This manifesto declared "the United States is the bulwark of world reaction and the enemy of all the peoples of the globe."

Writers, lecturers, and agitators are being trained in special schools to spread this propaganda wherever they can. How many Americans read that news item? How many of them glanced at it and shrugged or laughed and dismissed it from their minds? How many of them were aware of the slow and relentless effect of Soviet propaganda among the uncommitted nations of the world and its effect on our standing among many peoples? I don't know, but I am sure that there were not enough. Not nearly enough. We are facing the greatest challenge our way of life has ever had to meet without any clear understanding of the facts.

There is in most people, at most times, a proneness to give more credence to pleasant news than to unpleasant, to hope that, somehow or other, things "will come out all right." But this was not the frame of mind that created the United States and made it not only a great nation but a symbol of the way of life that became the hope of the world. One can fight a danger only when one is armed with solid facts and spurred on by an unwavering faith and determination.

On my first visit to Russia I had watched the training of small babies. On my second trip, I studied the older children, their conditioning, their discipline, their docility, their complete absorption in the Communist system. Every child learns his Marxism backwards and forwards. By the time he leaves school, he is prepared to take not only his skills but his political ideas with him, wherever he may be sent, to whatever part of the world.

Wherever I went in Russia I found no personal hostility. But there was an unshaken conviction that the United States not only threatens but actually desires and seeks war. Here we are, equipped with the best communications in the world, and yet we have not learned how to use them in a way that can reach people.

Today, we are one of the oldest governments in existence. . . . And yet we are supinely putting ourselves in the position of leaving the leadership to the Russians, of following their ideas rather than our own. For instance, when the Russians set up a restriction on what visitors to the country may be allowed to see, we promptly do the same thing here, in retaliation. Whenever we behave in this manner, we are copying the methods of dictatorships and making a hollow boast of our claim that this country loves freedom for all. We owe it to ourselves and to the world, to our own dignity and self-respect, to set our own standards of behavior, regardless of what other nations do.

By practicing what we preach, putting democracy to work up to the very hilt, showing the world that our way of life has the most to offer the men and women and children of all countries, we may regain our lost leadership. Against those mindless millions we can oppose the unleashed strength of free men, for only in freedom can a man function completely.

When I visited Morocco in 1958 I had my first opportunity to see for myself the difficulties that arise in the transition stage between colonialism and independence. The troubles that Morocco was encountering were, it seemed to me, fairly typical of the basic difficulties of all young nations in transition.

As the French withdrew from Morocco, taking their nationals along, the villages found themselves stripped of teachers and doctors. Countless villages were without a single person trained to give medical assistance. The Moroccans themselves were not yet prepared to replace the doctors, the teachers, the civil service employees with their own men. It may be decades before they are ready to do so. Where, then, are the necessary people to come from? I feel that in that answer lies the key, or one of the major keys, to the future.

The great problems seem to be that, while people may be able to fight successfully for freedom, they may not yet be prepared to set up a stable and functioning independent government. The French pulled out, but the Moroccans had no one to replace them. They were totally unprepared for self-government. They were, in fact, much worse off than they had been a year before.

Today, this is happening again, in the Congo with the withdrawal of the Belgians. The time for colonization has gone forever, but some intermediate transition system is essential if chaos is not to follow.

A recent Afro-Asian resolution in the United Nations reveals the difficulty of the position by these words: "Inadequacy of political, economic, social or cultural preparedness" shall not serve as a pretext for denying independence. Now, it is certainly true that such a pretext has often been used in denying the right of self-determination. But it is equally true that without some basic qualifications, self-determination will lead to self-destruction.

In the Near East one finds the fluctuating and uncertain position of young countries which are in transition from the ways of the past to those of the future, with no certain path to tread and with the ultimate goal still obscure. That is becoming the situation of an increasing number of infant nations as they shake off the fetters of colonialism, of the ancient laws and customs, and grope for their own place in the sun. And what that goal is to be, what kind of place they are to occupy, what political philosophy they will choose in the long run will depend in great part on how we, in this country, prepare to meet the challenge.

Is what we are doing good enough? Have the changes that have revealed themselves in recent years, particularly in Africa and the Near East and the Latin American countries, shown overwhelming evidence that we are doing an intelligent job, an adequate job? I am afraid not. Genuinely afraid.

To me, the democratic system represents man's best and brightest hope of self-fulfillment, of a life rich in promise and free from fear; the one hope, perhaps, for the complete development of the whole man. But I know, and learn more clearly every day, that we cannot keep our system strong and free by neglect, by taking it for granted, by giving it our second-best attention. We must be prepared, like the suitor in *The Merchant of Venice*—and, I might point out, the successful suitor—to give and hazard all we have.

Man cannot live without hope. If it is not engendered by his own convictions and desires, it can easily be fired from without, and by the most meretricious and empty of promises.

What I learned on these trips around the world has been much on my mind. Why, I wondered, were we not more successful in helping the young nations and those in transition to become established along democratic lines? Why was it that the Russians were doing so much better? The answer can be oversimplified, and an oversimplification is false and misleading. But part of the answer, and I think a major part, is that Russia has trained its young people to go out into the world, to carry their services and skills to backward and underdeveloped countries, to replace the missing doctors and teachers, the scientists and technicians; above all, to fill the vacant civil service jobs, prepared not only by training for the job itself, but by learning the language, by a complete briefing in the customs, habits, traditions and trend of thought of the people, to understand them and deal with them. Where the young Russians go, of course, they take with them their Marxist training, thinking, and system.

And our young Americans? Are they being prepared to take their faith in democracy to the world along with their skills? Are they learning the language and the customs and the history of these new peoples? Do they understand how to deal with them, not according to their own ideas but according to the ideas of the people they must learn to know if they are to reach them at all? Have they acquired an ability to live and work among peoples of different religion and race and color, without arrogance and without prejudice?

Here, I believe, we have fallen down badly. In the last few years I have grasped at every opportunity to meet with the young, to talk with college students, to bring home as strongly as I can to even young children in the lower grades our responsibility for each other, our need to understand and respect each other. The future will be determined by the young, and there is no more essential task today, it seems to me, than to bring before them once more, in all its brightness, in all its splendor and beauty, the American dream, lest we let it fade, too concerned with the ways of earning a living or impressing our neighbors or getting ahead or finding bigger and more potent ways of destroying the world and all that is in it.

No single individual, of course, and no single group has an exclusive claim to the American dream. But we have all . . . a single vision of what it is, not merely as a hope and an aspiration, but as a way of life, which we can come ever closer to attaining in its ideal form if we keep shining and unsullied our purpose and our belief in its essential value.

That we have sometimes given our friends and our enemies abroad a shoddy impression of the dream cannot be denied, much as we would like to deny it. . . .

They often do not know the language of the country; they are not familiar with its government or its officials; they are not interested in its customs, or its point of view.

The Russians, and I say it with shame, do much better. They are trained in the language, history, customs, and ways of life of a country before they go to it. . . .

When we look at the picture of Russian greed in swallowing one satellite nation after another and contrast it with the picture of American generosity in giving food, clothing, supplies, technical and financial assistance, without the ulterior motive of acquiring new territory, it is stupid and tragic waste that the use of incompetent representatives should undo so much useful work, so great an expense, so much in the way of materials of every kind.

Of course, what the Russians have accomplished in training their young people for important posts in the underdeveloped countries—which, I must repeat, may affect the future course of these countries—has been done by compulsion. That's the rub. For what we must do is to achieve the same results on a voluntary basis. We do not say to our young people: "You must go here and take such a job." But we can show them that where we fail, the Russians will win, by default.

Perhaps the new frontier today is something more than the new revolution in textiles and methods and speed and goods. It is the frontier of men's minds. But we cannot cast an enduring light on other men's minds unless the light in our own minds burns with a hard, unquenchable flame.

One form of communication we have failed in abjectly: that is in the teaching of languages. Most school children have several years of inadequate teaching in one language or another. I say inadequate because the study of a language, after all, is inadequate if one cannot learn to read and write it, to speak and to understand it. . . .

It seems to me so obvious that it should not need to be said that we must increase and improve the teaching of languages to our young people, who will otherwise find themselves crippled and sorely handicapped in dealing with people of foreign races and different cultures.

These are things our children should be told. These are the conditions they are going to have to meet. They ought to be made to understand exactly what competition they will encounter, why they must meet it, how they can meet it best. Yet I rarely find, in talking with them, that they have been given the slightest inkling of the meaning of the Soviet infiltration of other countries, or that the future the Soviets are helping to build is the one with which they will have to contend. I rarely find that anyone has suggested that our own young people should have any preparation whatsoever to cope with the problems that are impending.

That is why, in the course of the past several years, I have fitted into my schedule, whenever I could, occasions to talk with the young. Sometimes they come up to Hyde Park by the busload to ask questions or to discuss problems. Sometimes I talk at their schools or colleges.

The other night, three boys from Harvard, one of them my grandson, came to see me. The head of the temporary government of Tanganyika had requested that some American students be sent there to teach English to their students, so that when the latter came to America to study they would be able to understand and communicate without difficulty. The young American students were also to participate in work projects and live in the native villages, where they could study conditions.

Thirty Americans, as a pilot project, were needed, and the cost for each was estimated at $1500. There was, I am happy to say, no problem in getting recruits. The difficulty came in raising money. The big foundations turned them down. . . .

I was greatly interested, for it is out of such undertakings that bridges of understanding are built. I urged them to draw up the clearest possible statement of their plan and then to ask for scholarships. Certainly there must be thirty people willing to finance one scholarship each, in order to establish bonds of friendship and cooperation with a young nation.

Of course, there are great numbers of American college students with little information about and even less interest in the world in which they live. They are absorbed in their own concerns. . . . All this is natural enough. The trouble is that, on the whole, college students in some other countries start much earlier to relate themselves to their world and to become informed about the conditions which they must learn to meet in life.

What can we do to prepare young people to carry the American dream to the world in the best possible way? What I would like to say is this:

Today, our government and the governments of most of the world are primarily concerned—obsessed—by one idea: defense. But what is real defense, and how is it obtained? A certain amount of military defense is necessary. But there comes a point where you must consider what can be done on an academic and cultural basis.

It seems to me that, in terms of atomic warfare, we should henceforth have a small professional army of men who have voluntarily chosen this profession as an obligation to their country. But what then? What about the hundreds of thousands of young people who leave school every year, either from high school or college? Are they, from now on, to have no participation in contributing to the welfare of their country?

Far from it. As matters stand now, we draft young men into service, train them until they are useful, and then let them go. This seems to me monstrous waste.

It is my own personal conviction that every young person should be given some basic military training that might, eventually, be useful to his country. This could easily be handled either in school or at college. Instead of calling up all young men for compulsory military service, why should it not be possible to offer a counterproposal along these lines:

If you do not want to spend two years of compulsory military training, here is an alternative which is open to you. Whether you finish college or high school, you may decide what country you would like to spend two years in. You will be given two years of basic training, either during school hours or in the evenings. If you want to go, . . . , you will, from the age of fifteen or seventeen, be taught the language, the history, the geography, the economic background of the country. You will be prepared to take with you a skill, or be trained for the most crying need in many transition nations—to fill the civil service jobs that Russia is now so rapidly filling. Or, if you are preparing for a profession, you may make use of that. New industries are needed in these countries; there are technical needs in almost all areas. The economy has to be bolstered in countless ways. New techniques are required in agriculture. And nearly all of these countries need teachers badly.

For people in young nations, which are still in a transition stage and setting up governments, such a course of action on our part could be more valuable than a large standing army or economic aid, particularly when in the new country there is no one capable of administering the aid effectively. . . .

If we achieve—and why not?—a cooperation between universities and government, we might be able to equip some of our young people to take up the slack in underdeveloped countries and to bring our skills and our attitudes and our principles to them as free men.

These two-year volunteers could be doctors, engineers, teachers, scientists, mechanics, and administrators. It is possible that a system of scholarships might be worked out, which would enable us to use some of our young talent and ability in helping young countries get established. In such cases, there should be some sort of guarantee, some sort of facilities put at the use of these people when they return to their own country, to enable them to get jobs at home. This service, of course, could be in lieu of military service, but, it seems to me, it would be far more valuable.

The present long period of basic military training, which removes our young men from civilian life for two years and then returns them to it, seems to me a wasteful and pointless procedure. Certainly it could be made possible for them to have much of this basic military training that is required while they are in school. But military service, in an atomic, specialized age, should, like other professions, be on a voluntary basis and become a chosen career.

I have said that the Russians have accomplished by compulsion what we must accomplish voluntarily. But there is one element of this Russian training that is of paramount importance. They have taught their young to feel that they are needed, that they are important to the welfare of their country. I think that one of the strongest qualities in every human being is a need to feel needed, to feel important. Too often, our own youngsters do not feel that they are really essential to their country, or to the scheme of things. We have not had enough imagination to show them how very much we need every one of them to make us the kind of country that we can be.

If many of our young people have lost the excitement of the early settlers, who had a country to explore and develop, it is because no one remembers to tell them that the world has never been so challenging, so exciting; the fields of adventure and new fields to conquer have never been so limitless. There is still unfinished business at home, but there is the most tremendous adventure in bringing the peoples of the world to an understanding of the American dream. In this attempt to understand and to give a new concept of the relationships of mankind, there is open to our youngsters an infinite field of exciting adventure, where the heart and the mind and the spirit can all be engaged.

Perhaps the older generation is often to blame with its cautious warning: "Take a job that will give you security, not adventure." But I say to the young: "You have no security unless you can live bravely, excitingly, and imaginatively; unless you can choose a challenge instead of a competence."   ☐

PART VI

The Cold War at Home: 1945–1963

1.   Full Employment

Correspondence with Harry Truman, November 20, 1945

Dear Mr. President:

I hope you will forgive my writing you this letter, but I, like a great many other citizens, have been deeply concerned about the situation as it seems to be developing both at home and abroad. I have a deep sense that we have an obligation first of all, to solve our own problems at home, because our failure must of necessity, take away hope from the other nations of the world who have so much more to contend with than we have.

It seems to me, therefore, that we must get to work.

The suggestion that was made the other day that survey of our resources be made on which we base not only our national economy, but what we lend to other nations, would seem to me sound, if the person making the investigation had sufficient standing to be accepted by management and labor as well.

In situations of this kind, my husband some times turned to Mr. Bernard Baruch, because of his wealth of experience and his standing with the industrialists of the country. At the same time, I think that even the young labor leaders, like Walter Reuther and James Carey, believe in his integrity. If it could be possible to get the Detroit situation started up by giving both management and labor something so they would at least agree to work until, let us say, next October on condition that Mr. Baruch was asked to gather a staff of experts, I feel he would consult with both sides as he always has in the past.

If there was a limit for the time of the report, I think labor would not feel that it was being taken for a ride.

When it comes to lending money, it seems to me that we should lend other nations equally. If we lend only to Great Britain, we enter into an economic alliances against other nations, and our hope for the future lies in joint cooperation. If we could only lend in small amounts at present, until we get into production we can not sell to any of these countries in great quantities and there is no value in their having the money unless they can use it, it would be helpful. They would also profit by this type of survey and we would be making no promises we could not carry out.

If you talk to Mr. Baruch, I think you must do so only if you yourself, feel confidence in him, because once you accept him you will find, as my husband did, that many of those around you will at once, cast doubts upon whatever he does, but that would be true even if the job were given to the Angel Gabriel.

I think Mr. Baruch has proved in the past, his ability to see things on a large scale, and where financial matters are concerned, he certainly knows the world picture which is what we need at the present time.

I am very much distressed that Great Britain has made us take a share in another investigation of the few Jews remaining in Europe. If they are not to be allowed to enter Palestine, then certainly they could have been apportioned among the different United Nations and we would not have to continue to have on our consciences, the deaths of at least fifty of those poor creatures daily.

The questions between Palestine and the Arabs, of course, has always been complicated by oil deposits, and I suppose it always will. I do not happen to be a Zionist, and I know what a difference there is among such Jews as consider themselves nationals of other countries and not a separate nationality.

Great Britain is always anxious to have some one pull her chestnuts out of the fire, and though I am very fond of the British individually and like a great many of them I object very much to being used by them. . . .

Lastly, I am deeply troubled by China. Unless we can stop the civil war there by moral pressure and not by the use of military force, and insist that Generalissimo Chiang give wider representation to all Chinese people, which will allow the middle of the road Democratic League to grow, I am very much afraid that continued war there may lead us to general war again.

Being a strong nation and having the greatest physical, mental and spiritual strength today, gives us a tremendous responsibility. We can not use our strength to coerce, but if we are big enough, I think we can lead, but it will require great vision and understanding on our part. The first and foremost thing, it seems to me, is the setting of our own house in order, and so I have made the suggestions contained in the first part of this letter. I shall understand, however, if with the broader knowledge which is yours, you decide against it, but I would not have a quiet conscience unless I wrote you what I feel in these difficult times.

With every good wish, I am,

Very cordially yours   □

Truman's Reply

November 26, 1945

Dear Mrs. Roosevelt:

Thanks very much for your letter of the twentieth, to which I have given much thought.

I have particularly had under consideration for some time the suggestion about a study of our national resources with a view to what we can afford to do. I think that it is a very good suggestion, and expect to take some action on it.

I doubt very much whether that kind of study, however, would have much to do with the immediate situation in Detroit, although it is barely possible that it might influence the ultimate conclusion in a great many labor situations.

With respect to our foreign loans, I am sure that you have a deep appreciation of the reasons for our policy. We feel that it is necessary not only for the welfare of Great Britain but for our own welfare and for the welfare of the entire world that the British economy be not allowed to disintegrate. Equally important is the necessity of reestablishing world trade by helping the British expand their own trade instead of talking refuge in a tightened sterling bloc.

What we hope to do for Great Britain we also hope to do eventually for Russia and our other Allies, for it will be impossible to continue a stable world economy if a large part of the world has a disordered economy which would result in bitter trade rivalries and impassable barriers.

I am very hopeful that we really shall be able to work out something in Palestine which will be of lasting benefit. At the same time we expect to continue to do what we can to get as many Jews as possible into Palestine as quickly as possible, pending any final settlement.

In China, as you know, a definite commitment was made by the three major powers to support the Central Government in disarming and removing the Japanese troops now in China. I know you realize how important to the future peace in the Far East and throughout the world is this objective. All of us want to see a Chinese government eventually installed and maintained by free elections—one which will include all democratic elements, I do not see how we can do that unless we first help clear the land of the Japanese aggressors.

All of these things take a great deal of time as you know from personal experience. I am sure that it was the late President's experience, as it is mine, that we are very apt to meet criticism in the press and often in the Congress from those who are unfamiliar with the facts and to whom the facts cannot be disclosed. He often talked to me about how difficult that part of the Presidency was. However, I feel proud that our objectives are the same as those which actuated your late husband. Indeed I have no aim other than to carry them out.

I want you to now how much I appreciate your writing to me from time to time, and hope you will continue to do so.

With kindest regards,

Very sincerely   □

2.   Price Controls and Postwar Production

My Day, March 22, 1946

En Route to Los Angeles—In one of my lectures recently, I happened to mention the fact that production was extremely important to the world at the present time. During the question period, I was asked whether production in itself was sufficient or whether any other considerations were necessary to make production effective. This led me down some fascinating paths.

What do we mean when we talk about production? We do not mean, of course, merely creating things that have no value. We must produce things that people really need. Or, when you go beyond actual needs, production must be justified through its contribution to better living and the enjoyment of the finer things of life.

For production to have real value, it must also come up to certain standards. Just to multiply the things in the world, unless they meet the needs for which they are produced, would be a rather stupid procedure. People everywhere soon discover whether they are receiving value for their investment. Though, for the moment, we are probably the only source from which people can obtain certain essentials with which to rebuild their economic life, it would be foolish to believe that we can let down on the quality of our production. Sooner or later, someone would step in and do better.

We in this country, however, have always believed that, in ordinary times, volume production was what we were after, since that would bring down the cost and therefore make it possible for more people to enjoy more things. This belief of ours is one reason why we want to avoid a depression if possible. During a depression, less money is in circulation. The prices of things drop because fewer people spend money. Fewer things are produced, fewer men are employed, and the cycle of a contracting economy is upon us, which requires different and sometimes drastic measures to change the trend.

We hope, that having learned how this comes about, we will never allow it to happen in our country again. But when I see the National Association of Manufacturers demanding that we remove price controls before we are in full production, I wonder whether our greed makes it impossible for us to profit by the lessons of the past. If we were to remove price controls now, when there are so few goods on the market, we would force prices sky-high and compete against each other. The rest of the world would also compete because, without certain essentials, they cannot start producing certain things for themselves. Price controls can be removed when there are enough goods on the market for us all to obtain what we need, but to say that these controls should be removed now as an incentive to production is courting disaster.

My questioner the other night suggested that production applied to many fields besides the manufacture of goods, and of course, in that he is entirely correct. But I think that, if we remember that in every field quality is as important as quantity, it will help us not to go astray. Of course, in the fields of the arts, mass production can never be considered. In any creative art, it is beauty of execution and individual expressions which is of value and each product bears the stamp of the artists—something that can never be mass produced.

That does not mean, however, that each artist should not produce for his own satisfaction and the joy of those who appreciate his work. This brings us, I think, to the ultimate reality that each one of us, in our own way, must be a productive member of society. If our job is to scrub the floor, and we do it with the sprit of

the artist or the skilled worker, in our own little sphere we have done our part
of the world's production.   □

3.   "Why I Do Not Choose to Run"

Look, July 9, 1946

There has been some curiosity as to why I am not knocking at the
door of the members of my political party, who make up the slates for candidates
for office, in order to obtain a nomination for some elective office.

At first I was surprised that anyone should think that I would want to run for
office, or that I was fitted to hold office. Then I realized that some people felt that
I must have learned something from my husband in all the years that he was in
public life! They also knew that I had stressed the fact that women should accept
responsibility as citizens.

I heard that I was being offered the nomination for governor or for the United States Senate in my own state, and even for Vice President. And some particularly humorous souls wrote in and suggested that I run as the first woman President of the United States!

The simple truth is that I have had my fill of public life of the more or less
stereotyped kind. I do believe that every citizen, as long as he is alive and able to
work, has an obligation to work on public questions and that he should choose
the kind of work he is best fitted to do.

Therefore, when I was offered an opportunity to serve on the United Nations
organization, I accepted it. I did this, not because I really wanted to go to London last January, but because it seemed as though I might be able to use the experiences of a lifetime and make them valuable to my nation and to the people
of the world at this particular time. I knew, of course, how much my husband
hoped that, out of the war, an organization for peace would really develop.

It was not just to further my husband's hopes, however, that I agreed to serve
in this particular way. It was rather that I myself had always believed that women
might have a better chance to bring about the understanding necessary to prevent
future wars if they could serve in sufficient number in these international bodies.

The plain truth, I am afraid, is that in declining to consider running for the
various public offices which have been suggested to me, I am influenced by the
thought that no woman has, as yet, been able to build up and hold sufficient

backing to carry through a program. Men and women both are not yet enough accustomed to following a woman and looking to her for leadership. If I were young enough it might be an interesting challenge, and we have some women in Congress who may carry on this fight.

However, I am already an elderly woman, and I would have to start in whatever office I might run for as a junior with no weight of experience in holding office behind me. It seems to me that fairly young men and women should start holding minor offices and work up to the important ones, developing qualifications for holding these offices as they work.

I have been an onlooker in the field of politics. In some ways I hope I have occasionally been a help, but always by doing things which I was particularly fitted by my own background and experience to do. My husband was skilled in using people and, even though I was his wife, I think he used me in his career as he used other people. I am quite sure that Louis Howe, who was one of the most astute politicians as well as one of the most devoted of friends, trained me and used me for the things which he thought I could do well, but always in connection with my husband's career.

In the last years of his life, Louis Howe used to ask me if I had any ambitions to hold political office myself. I think he finally became convinced that though I understood the worst and the best of politics and statesmanship, I had absolutely no desire to participate in it.

For many years of my life I realized that what my husband was attempting to do was far more important than anything which I could possibly accomplish; and therefore I never said anything, or wrote anything, without first balancing it against the objectives which I thought he was working for at the time. We did not always agree as to methods, but our ultimate objectives were fortunately very much the same.

Never in all the years can I remember his asking me not to say or to write anything, even though we occasionally argued very vehemently and sometimes held diametrically opposite points of view on things of the moment.

I think my husband probably often used me as a sounding board, knowing that my reactions would be the reactions of the average man and woman in the street.

My husband taught me that one cannot follow blindly any line which one lays down in advance, because circumstances will modify one's thinking and one's actions. And in the last year since his death I have felt sure that our objectives would remain very much the same. But I have known that I was free and under compulsion to say and to do the things which I, as an individual, believed on the questions of the day. In a way it has lifted a considerable weight from my shoulders, feeling that now, when I speak, no one will attribute my thoughts to someone holding an important office and whose work may be hurt and not helped thereby. If people do not like what I say nowadays, they can blame me, but it will hurt no one else's plans or policies.

There is a freedom in being responsible only to yourself which I would now find it hard to surrender in taking a party office. I believe that the Democratic Party, at least the progressive part of the Democratic Party, represents the only safe way we have of moving forward in this country. I believe that the liberal-minded Democrats hold to the only international policy which can bring us a peaceful world. I will work for the candidates of my party when I think they offer the best there is in the field of public service, and I will even accept mediocre men now and then if I feel that the rank and file of the Party is strong enough in its beliefs to make those inadequate leaders do better than their own ability gives promise of in the way of achievement.

However, if I do not run for office, I am not beholden to my Party. What I give, I give freely and I am too old to want to be curtailed in any way in the expression of my own thinking.

To be entirely honest I will have to confess that I thought at first one of my reasons might be that I did not want to engage in the rough and tumble of a political campaign. This, of course, would be rank self-indulgence and I should be the last one to allow myself to decline to run for public office because of any such reason, since I have urged on other women the need for developing a less sensitive spirit and for learning to give and take as men do.

I do not think that this consideration really enters into my decision. I have lived long in a goldfish bowl, and my husband's death does not seem in any way to have altered the attacks which come upon one from certain quarters. So I do not think that running for office would have brought me any more of the disagreeable things which we must learn to endure. In the long run, the mass of the people are likely to form a fairly truthful estimate of people who are before them in public life.

Had I wanted to run for office, therefore, I imagine in many ways I could have stood up under all types of attack and suffered less than most people. But I would rather help others, younger people, whose careers lie ahead of them and who have years in which to achieve their objectives. What I do may still be important, but it won't last long enough.

In the meantime, I shall be glad to serve wherever my past experiences seem to fit me to do a specific job.

Many people will think that these are all very inadequate answers and that when you are told that you might be useful, you should accept the judgments of others and go to work. All I can say in reply is that during a long life I have always done what, for one reason or another, was the thing which was incumbent upon me to do without any consideration as to whether I wished to do it or not. That no longer seems to be a necessity, and for my few remaining years I hope to be free!   □

4.   Loyalty Oaths

My Day, March 27, 1947

New York—I was asked about the President's executive order to prevent disloyal employees from working for the Government. I was asked also about the proposals, which are coming up in several parts of the country, for outlawing the Communist Party. I was asked whether I thought it was necessary to take these steps. Therefore, I've decided to write today on the feeling I have about all repressive measures.

Such measures always are a sign of lack of confidence in ourselves. If we were sure that our citizens understood the value of democracy and were clear in their minds on the subject, I doubt if we would need such an investigation as the President has ordered. It would be quite easy to eliminate from the Government, by the usual legal process, anyone who was proved to be disloyal. Naturally, any order of this kind carries a certain amount of danger with it, in that it may be possible to misuse its provisions, If a wave of hysteria hits us there will be very little protection for anyone who even thinks differently from the run-of-the-mill.

Political conditions in the USSR today still do not recognize the right of individuals to think differently. Only here and in other free democracies can we criticize our Government and have the freedom to think independently. It is, I believe, a very precious freedom, but it requires of us something more than apathetic citizenship. We must really believe in democracy and in our objectives. We cannot live in fear of either Fascism or Communism. We have to be certain that the majority of our people recognize the benefits of democracy and therefore are loyal to it.

Proposals to outlaw the Communist Party seem to be another evidence of a feeling of insecurity. I can imagine nothing stupider than to believe that the mass of people of this country would really find Communism a greater advantage to them than our own democratic system. The danger in outlawing the Communist Party is that we would set a precedent which might work gains any change or difference of opinion in the future.

I do not know why we are so prone to fears at the present time. Some people are so afraid of Russia that they are suggesting that perhaps, since we cannot hope always to be the only nation possessing the atom bomb, we should use it fairly soon to wipe out all opposition. That sounds ludicrous, but it has actually been said to me by some people.

Others fear that we cannot manage our economy so as to avoid a major depression. Still others think that it will be impossible ever to make the United Nations strong, because we are all too much afraid of each other to trust in joint action.

All of these attitudes are attitudes of fear. They show lack of confidence in ourselves and in others. For the leading democracy in the world to indulge in them is a very great danger, not to us alone but also to the world.   □

5.   Taft-Hartley Act
My Day, June 10, 1947

New York, Monday—I suppose it is impossible for any Congressional bill to be put into language which the people can understand. It will be difficult for the average worker to understand the legal language of the Taft-Hartley labor bill passed by Congress last week.

In many ways I think labor leaders have themselves to blame for some of their present difficulties—John L. Lewis chief among them, because the people as a whole have come to dread what he can do to our economy. And there are certain union rules which irk the people and which I do not think really help organized labor. These regulations have made the relations between the public and the unions increasingly unsympathetic, and should have been studied and corrected long ago.

The Congress of Industrial Organizations should have got rid of Communist leaders wherever they existed. The people of this country are more than willing to work with the Russians if they recognize on the part of the Russians a willingness to work side by side with other forms of governments and ways of life. However, the constant activity of American Communists, who evidently get their financial support as well as their political directions from Russia, creates suspicion and antagonism here and in some other counties as well.

If the Russian Government still hopes for world revolution brought about by representatives in other countries guided from Russia, it cannot be honest in trying to work cooperatively with other governments as they now exist. I am more than willing to believe that circumstances may modify the way of life and the forms of existing governments in many countries in the years to come, but the changes must come from the free will of the people, not from infiltration of ideas through the influence of outside governments. This is why union leaders known to be Communists should not have been allowed in our labor movement.

Nevertheless, the Taft-Hartley bill is a bad bill, even in its final modified form. I think it will make the work of the National Labor Relations Board practically impossible, and it opens a wide field of labor activities to federal injunctions. I see nothing gained by taking the Conciliation Service out of the Department of Labor. It seems to me that this bill is weighed in favor of the employer. For instance, the bill requires the NLRB to obtain federal injunctions against certain union practices, but there is no provision that the board obtain injunctions against employer practices.

I have not room here to go into this bill in detail, but analyses of it are available and people should study it. I was in complete accord with the labor-reform suggestions made in the President's message, but this bill goes so far beyond that, if it becomes law, it will affect adversely the lives of many people.   □

6.   Correspondence Regarding Taft-Hartley

Correspondence with Albert Harris

August 28, 1947

Dear Mrs. Roosevelt:

I wish to take issue with you as to some of the statements in your column "Nobody's Business" as reported in the New York World Telegram on August 25, 1947.

You object to labor leaders being compelled to declare themselves communists and state "we had better do the same for the heads of business." Since communists are certainly the enemies of democracy, we certainly ought to list those enemies where those communists are labor union leaders or business leaders. If there were any danger at the present time or if there is any such danger that business leaders are dangerous to democracy either as communists or fascists, they should certainly be listed.

You also object to the Taft-Hartley Act limiting the union's right to expel members to the ground of non-payment of dues and claim that management has dismissed employees because of union membership. Certainly under the Wagner Act and the other government regulations, management has been prevented or punished for dismissing "employees because of union membership." This limitation on management's powers was quite proper because of the abuse of management of its powers. Your illustration is obviously not in point because management does not have the power you claim. You claim in effect that because y wrong is allowed, therefore, x wrong should be allowed, but y wrong is punished. In addition one would expect you to take the position that all wrong should be punished wherever found and if certain wrongs are not punished, that should be no reason for permitting other wrongs to the unpunished.

You claim that it is an "infringement of our liberties, to set up for a union, in the matter of health and welfare funds, restrictions for the administration of these funds." Then you state "the employer contributes toward them, but he contributes in order that his employees may be able to accomplish through their organization the things that they desire." Your statement is not just so. The contributions made by the employer are made under agreements which provide that the money is to be used for certain specific purposes and the union has agreed to apply the funds for the specific purposes. Employers have always objected to being blackjacked into paying funds into union treasuries which may be used for any purpose whatsoever determined by the union membership by the union officials who have achieved control of union treasuries. The only "infringement of our liberties" is the infringement of violation of contract. If the union membership should contribute its own funds to a union fund and give the union officials complete liberty of disposal of the funds, then the employers and even the union membership might not be privileged to object, but when employers contribute funds for specific purposes, it is certainly an infringement upon the liberties of the employers to be deprived of the right of compelling the unions to abide by their express agreements.

Very truly yours,

Albert Harris

ER's Reply

September 8, 1947

My dear Mr. Harris:

I think I must have been a little careless or perhaps I took it too much for granted that anyone reading my recent column on the Taft- Hartley Bill would have read my previous columns on this subject. In those I made my position very clear as to the need for labor to clean house—the AFofL to get rid of its racke-teers, the CIO to get rid of its communist leaders.

I do not want communists leading our labor unions and the majority of the labor people do not want them either, but that to my mind does not justify set-ting labor apart as a group that must give certain assurances. From my point of view that is not the American way of doing things. We should all have to do it, or we should not expect any particular group to do it.

I know quite well that it was against the law to dismiss employees for union membership but there were many ways which were used to dismiss people and though that was the reason given, it was the real reason and you know this as well as I do.

I do not think that two wrongs make a right and I think abuses on the part of union and on the part of management should both be condemned.

Labor is partly responsible for the passage of the Taft-Hartley Bill because of its failure to clean house, but that does not make the Taft-Hartley Bill perfect nor does it absolve us from stating why we think it is wrong.

I know that contributions made by employer are made under agreements and I think those agreements should be lived up to and they have been in the past. If agreements are made whereby money will go into certain things, there is no more reason why the trade unions' books should be open for examination than why management's books should not be open to the trade unions for examina-tion. It should be turn and turn about and equal handed justice for all.

Very sincerely yours,   □

7. # House Committee on
    # Un-American Activities

My Day, October 29, 1947

New York—I have waited a while before saying anything about the Un-American Activities Committee's current investigation of the Hollywood film industry.

I would not be very much surprised if some writers or actors of stagehands, or what not, were found to have Communist leanings, but I was surprised to find that, at the start of the inquiry, some of the big producers were so chicken-hearted about speaking up for the freedom of their industry.

One thing is sure—none of the arts flourishes on censorship and repression. And by this time it should be evident the American public is capable of doing its own censoring. Certainly, the Thomas Committee is growing more ludicrous daily. The picture of six officers ejecting a writer from the witness stand because he refused to say whether he was a Communist or not is pretty funny, and I think before long we are all going to see how hysterical and foolish we have become.

The film industry is a great industry, with infinite possibilities for good and bad. Its primary purpose is to entertain people. It can do many other things. It can popularize certain ideals, it can make education palatable. But in the long run, the judge who decides whether what it does is good or bad is the man or woman who attends the movies. In a democratic country I do not think the public will tolerate a removal of its rights to decide what it thinks of the ideas and performances of those who make the movie industry work.

I have never liked the idea of an Un-American Activities Committee. I have always thought a strong democracy should stand by its fundamental beliefs and that a U.S. citizen should be considered innocent until proven guilty.

If he is employed in a Government position where he has access to secret and important papers, then for the sake of security he must undergo some special tests. However, I doubt whether the loyalty test really adds much to our safety, since no Communist would hesitate to sign it and he would be in good standing until he was proved guilty. So it seems to me that we might as well do away with a test which is almost an insult to any loyal American citizen.

What is going on in the Un-American Activities Committee worries me primarily because little people have become frightened and we find ourselves living in the atmosphere of a police state, where people close doors before they state what they think or look over their shoulders apprehensively before they express an opinion.

I have been one of those who have carried the fight for complete freedom of information in the United Nations. And while accepting the fact that some of our press, our radio commentators, our prominent citizens and our movies may at times be blamed legitimately for things they have said and done, still I feel that the fundamental right of freedom of thought and expression is essential. If you curtail what the other fellow says and does, you curtail what you yourself may say and do.

In our country we must trust the people to hear and see both the good and the bad and to choose the good. The Un-American Activities Committee seems to be better for a police state than for the U.S.A.   □

8.   "Plain Talk About Wallace"
        Democratic Digest, April 1948

So Henry Wallace is really going to head a third party and run for President in 1948! What strange things the desire to be President makes men do! He has probably forgotten, but I remember his coming to see me in the summer of 1945 in Washington. At that time, I felt very strongly that it would be good for the country if Henry Wallace, whom we all believed in and admired, would leave active politics and become the leader of the independents of the country. Their vote had increased greatly in the years between 1929 and 1945, but they needed leadership and organization.

They were neither Republicans nor Democrats. They were primarily interested in getting the kind of leadership which would keep them free of economic depressions. And they wanted to continue what had been a peaceful but steady revolutionary movement which had given us, over the years, a greater number of people in the middle-income brackets and fewer people in the millionaire group or in the substandard-income groups. . . .

At that time, Henry Wallace told me he believed it was his duty to stay and work in the Democratic Party. I knew then, as I know now, that he was doing what he thought was right. But he never has been a good politician, he never has been able to gauge public opinion, and he never has picked his advisers wisely.

All of these things might have been less important if he had been a disinterested, nonpolitical leader of liberal thought, but as a leader of a third party he will accomplish nothing. He will merely destroy the very things he wishes to achieve. . . .

I read with great care Henry A. Wallace's speech in Chicago Monday. Affirmatively, he stands for "a positive peace program of abundance and security, not scarcity and war. We can prevent depression and war if we only organize for peace in the same comprehensive way we organize for war."

There is no country in the world where the people would not agree they wished to organize for peace and abundance and security. But in this speech Mr. Wallace oversimplified the problems that face us today. . . .

To begin with, let us take the political situation which a third party faces. No one in this country wants a third party as much as the Communists do. All over the world they are working for confusion because that is the way to create economic chaos and political weakness, and this is their one hope of defeating democracy in the world and proving that communism is the only thing people can turn to.

The American Communists will be the nucleus of Mr. Wallace's third party. I know all the old arguments in favor of working with people who want the same objectives as you do. But I have worked rather more steadily and closely with the representatives of the USSR than has Mr. Wallace. I like all those I know and I hope that we can get on with them in a peaceful world, but I know that our only approach is an economic approach . . . they understand strength, not weakness. . . .

When Mr. Wallace assumes that by changing certain of our policies until we resemble Mr. Chamberlain, hat in hand, approaching Hitler, we will have the results which he calls "peace and abundance," I am afraid he is doing more wishful thinking than realistic facing of facts.

A totalitarian government, whether it is Fascist or Communist, has certain earmarks. Secret police rule is one of them. Another is benefits to the people but no freedom. We live, in fact, in a much more complicated world than Mr. Wallace seems to understand. . . .

Henry Wallace says he is in favor of helping Greece and he believes in the humanitarian side of the Marshall Plan, but that he would turn the aid program over to the United Nations and that aid should be given without consideration of political beliefs, on a basis of need, with the only strings attached being that nothing be used for preparation for war.

Let's look at that program. Most of the aid for Europe has to come from us or through arrangements which we make with other nations. We have no means for inspection. How would we know that none of the aid we sent was used for war preparation?

We have offered a perfectly fair system for control of atomic energy by the UN and for inspection of all the nations under that plan. The people who have stymied it right along are the Russians. . . .

Neither Great Britain nor the U.S. has such great military power in Greece that the Greeks are under any compulsion to have a government of which they do not approve. The "government" established recently by the guerrillas is led by a known Communist. Certainly the Greeks have a right to ask for help in remaining a democratic state; and certainly the steady progress of the USSR's political influence over every state which they have taken over shows that they have every intention of spreading communism wherever they can. . . .

Oh, Mr. Wallace, if you were President you would not have such pat sentences to offer us! You would find it far harder to act constructively than you suggest in your speeches! □

9.   "Liberals in This Year of Decision"

The Christian Register, June 1948

The role of the liberal today is a very difficult role, particularly in this country. We acquired through the fortunes of war the position of being the leading democracy in the world. We didn't like it very much; we have no particular desire to be responsible for what happens in the rest of the world. But because we were left in an economic position which no other country in the world could approximate, because we did not have to rebuild our cities, and our factories; because our civilians, at least, did not suffer as civilians suffered in most of the other countries where war had come to them, we find ourselves as the great democracy on which all other eyes are turned, and it has brought us a searching which I think probably we would far prefer to escape.

But whether we like it or not, that is the position we find ourselves in, and those of us who are liberals find that we are put in the position very often in international meetings of explaining the weaknesses of our democracy. Now you can explain them and excuse them, but you just can't say those weaknesses don't exist, because they do. It is a little trying, because we need very badly a unified country, and at the moment our country is very far from unified. We need that unity because of the position of leadership in which we find ourselves.

We are in a world where force still is the ultimate way of deciding questions. It should be law, but it still isn't law; it still is force. And yet we personally are very averse to acknowledging that force is still such an important factor. Being less touched than other countries by the war, we wanted as quickly as possible to forget about it and get back to normal. So we reduced our forces; we did away with as many of the restrictions as possible; and we tried to feel that the rest of the world would get back to normal as easily as we would get back to normal.

I think that it has been rather a shock to all of us to find that you cannot fight a war of complete destruction in part of the world for four years, and then settle down as though nothing had happened. Now we have to face the facts, and because we have these conditions and these facts to face, the role of the liberal is twice as difficult.

We feel strongly the desire to think the best of other people—by thinking the best, to draw out the best. It doesn't always work that way. We find that in our own country fears have grown. If they have grown here they probably have grown in other countries just as much, probably more; and we keep wondering what happens from fear and what happens from real malevolence. We watch our own country and we find things happening that we would like to denounce, and, yet, we don't know quite how far to go in denouncing those things.

I'll give you an example. As a liberal, I don't like loyalty tests at all. I have a feeling that it's much more important for us to find out why we believe in democracy and really to know why we believe in it, and to put as much into it as the USSR puts into its Communism, because I have always found that you get a great deal more out of the things you can be positive about. I don't think we should have in the government people whose loyalty we really question handling documents which should be secret documents. I think that would be terrible. But, on the other hand, it doesn't seem to me quite democratic to brand people as disloyal before you give them a chance to bring witnesses and answer their accusers. And so with all the feeling I have that we must not have disloyalty, I am also torn as to whether we really are building up our democracy and doing the positive things that we ought to be doing, or whether we're just tearing our democracy down.

The role of the liberal is hard and decisions are terribly difficult in these days. In the world picture there is no question but that the discrimination in this country hurts our position. It has been up to this time a domestic question. I felt that we could take time about it—time for white people to adjust; time for colored people to become educated, or, referring to other types of racial and religious discrimination, I felt that there was time, and that we needn't move too fast, that we could do it step by step, and gradually. I don't know whether we can now. Never, since I started to work in the United Nations, has there been a meeting where the question of our discrimination has not been brought up, and where we haven't had to answer for our country. It comes up on all kinds of things—it comes up on the question of freedom of information.

I was making what I thought was a perfectly safe speech, explaining why I thought freedom of information was valuable, and why I thought it was far better to have all kinds of opinions printed in the press and have an educated people that would make their decisions on what they read, than it was to have censorship, particularly government censorship. A gentleman whose country does have government censorship, said, "Madam, do you mean that in countries where there is a so-called free press there is no discrimination?" I had to say "touché." Nevertheless, I still believe in a free press because it does allow those of us who would like to fight discrimination to know where it exists, and we can get at the facts.

The very fact that we have discrimination and that we are the leading democracy, brings the whole of democracy into question. It is brought up against us in practically every meeting. I have come to feel that, as a liberal, wanting to defend democracy, we can no longer think of this question purely as a domestic question. We have to think of it in the implication of what it means to our world leadership, and that is very difficult to do at the present time.

I think, too, that probably one of the most difficult things we face is wanting peace, as undoubtedly all the people of the world want it. We still find ourselves in the position where, having set up machinery in the United Nations to create an atmosphere in which peace can grow, the will of the peoples for peace seems to be lacking. We find ourselves increasingly having decisions to make between the USSR and ourselves.

At home, we have certain people who say "we are the only true liberals in the country" and "we will not say that communism is bad. We will work with communism when it agrees with us." That sounds like a good, liberal way to feel. But then your actual experience makes you doubt whether that really is the way that you can feel. I've had quite a long experience with American Communism, because I began with youth groups in '34, and it has been very interesting. My first real disillusionment came when I found they wouldn't tell me the truth, and then, later, when the youth groups, led by the communist element, were picketing the White House. Then suddenly, when Russia was invaded, they had another meeting, and they sent me a telegram saying, "Now we can work together because now we are for preparedness for war," and I had to send the word back to them, "I am sorry but you lied to me and I can't work with anyone who lies." It was one of the most useful things that I ever did, because I learned all the communist tactics.

Many times in our United Nations meetings I have found that if there is a subject up that the USSR wants to get a certain vote on, you won't be able to get a vote easily, and you wonder why the delay. You go on and on until everybody is very tired and they drift out as groups do in these meetings, and if you don't watch, the move will be made for a vote and they will have won the vote while everyone was drifting out. I learned that a long while ago in one of our meetings. Everyone went scurrying to get the people back because the vote was going to be taken and we would have lost.

You learn that dealing with the Russians is not at all a question of "sweetness and light and sense." It is a question of strength. I don't happen to believe that it is a question only of economic and military strength, though I have come to believe that those two are controlling factors. But it's also a question of the strength of individuals and their convictions. . . . And that's one of the places where we're not quite as strong as we should be. In a democracy, we allow such latitude for argument on slight differences of opinion, that to get a feeling of a unified backing for certain big things is quite a problem. The lack of such latitude is, of course, the strength of a totalitarian dictatorship.

There isn't a single representative on any of the committees from the USSR, or from any of the satellite states who doesn't know how he's going to vote right straight down the line when he comes into that meeting. Everyone is going to vote just exactly as he was told to vote. He is going to attack just as he was told to attack—and nothing you say is going to make any dent, then. Six months from now, after it has gone back to the Kremlin, to the Politburo, that attitude may be changed. But it's awfully trying, and annoying, and enraging to find yourself answering first, the USSR. Then perhaps the Byelorussians say something and make the same attack and you have to answer them, too. During this last Assembly at one of the committees, I didn't answer the second time. I thought, "Well, I answered it once; I don't have to answer it each time," and the next day the delegate from the USSR got up and said, "Mrs. Roosevelt didn't answer this yesterday, so of course it must have been true!" so I discovered that each time I would have to get up. We had four attacks, exactly the same, and every time I had to say the same thing all over again. That's very enraging, and you wonder why grown people should want to do anything as time-consuming and as stupid. But that's the way it is and you just have to learn.

And, for the liberal, who wants to believe that people are all more or less the same, that they have the same motivations, and that they respond to fair and decent treatment, it is really a very disillusioning thing to work in that fashion with the USSR because you are tempted to come to the conclusion that it isn't important to do what you feel is right. You may have been brought up to believe that if you say you are going to do something, it's important that you do it for your own self-satisfaction. But you wake up to find that you are going to get cooperation only because you are stronger than they are. Now that's a rather awful thing for a liberal to have to face in this world of today, and I think a good many people probably now feel that I am not a liberal in my attitude towards the USSR.

I believe very strongly that while we have to be strong, we also have to be friendly; and that's one of the most difficult things in the world because they are so irritating. However, if you can remember the fact that they are not acting as individuals; that they are acting as government representatives, and they talk as government representatives, then you cannot dislike them as individuals. You keep your sense of liking them as people, even if you dislike their attitude and dislike what they stand for.

I think we might do some things that we haven't done so far. I think our attitude at times has been highly stupid. We do not recognize very often the fact of how sensitive they are because of insecurity. Many times and in many little ways we do not realize their insecurity and we do things that bring about bitterness, very often in little ways that are not important but have important results.

I have discovered often in working with them on committees that they respect the fact that you are not tired, that you can stand up to them, that you will put them through what you had intended to have them do. The Russians respect this. We as liberals need to make our country understand clearly that we feel our sense of security, that we are sure our democracy can be what we want it to be, and that we are going to work to make it what we want it to be. I think that is as important as the economic and military strength.

There is no doubt that we have to have the economic strength. The economic strength is the point from which we should work with Russia because it is the point where she has a tremendous respect for us. But to get that respect depends upon the liberals in this country, those among us whose convictions can make them believe that democracy is going to bring to the greatest number of people the greatest possible opportunity—those who really know that we want justice and opportunity for all the peoples. I think the liberals must accept the fact that force is still here in the world, and yet be strong enough to watch their own country so that force doesn't go to its head, which is always a danger. At the same time we must work to improve what we have and feel about it as the Communists do. They really have a crusading spirit. They really feel. And when you talk to them you understand why they feel the way they do.

In twenty-five years they have taken a people that was ninety percent illiterate and made it ninety percent literate. They haven't been able to become experts in a lot of things, and that is the cause of one of their greatest feelings of inferiority. They have been unable to join a lot of the organizations like UNESCO, for instance. They say that they won't join UNESCO because it is too expensive to join all those specialized agencies. But the truth is they haven't got the people to put there. Moreover, they always have two representatives instead of one, because no USSR representative goes alone. And, of course, when you have to have two, always, instead of one, that doubles your expense. You very soon know when you are working with people that are not at all qualified in many fields—they are not prepared for the work they have to do. In twenty-five years you don't create experts in every field. . . .

They are still 200 years behind us in many things. But they are a strong and a very young nation. They haven't much more than they ever had before, and when you compare it with what we have, they are awfully afraid of the comparison. I think they were terribly worried about their soldiers who had to go into decadent democracies and see that life was so much easier than they had it at home. . . . On the other hand, they feel they have gained a great deal and in some ways the government has given them a great deal. Far more people, for instance, go to the opera in Russia, probably, than ever go here. Certainly more people go to plays and sit through Shakespeare from beginning to end, uncut. The government has done that with the idea of taking them out of the misery in which most of them still lived. Nonetheless we are dealing with people who are ruthless at times, and we are dealing with people who are hard and who do believe in force—and, yet, who have given their people a sense of crusading. With all our years of civilization in back of us, I think we have got to face the situation as it is and we've got to know that this requires moral and spiritual leadership. It requires a friendly spirit. But it also requires the facing of realities and the knowledge that anything which can be used against us will be used against us. They believe in their way of life and if we believe in ours we've got to fight for it. We've taken it pretty much for granted up to this time.

We liberals, being liberals, are divided. We all like to go off on our own little tangents and just work on the things we are particularly interested in. There is no question in my mind but the things we do at home in a year which is a decisive year are probably very decisive in the international picture, too. There isn't anyone, I think, today—particularly among the young people, who is not really worried whether we are going to be at war in a short time or not. There is no question but what we have people in the government, and certain people outside, who feel that it would probably be much simpler to drop a few bombs on Russia right now than to wait until she is stronger. I have a lot of people say to me, "Really and honestly, now, don't you think it would be a lot better if we wiped up Russia right now?" The trouble with that, from my point of view, is that we would not really settle anything. We could destroy her cities—but she is a whale of a country. And, having once used atom bombs none of us would sleep very peacefully from then on, because somebody someday is going to have atom bombs just as we have them, and if we get into the habit of using them sooner or later we are going to be destroyed. Nobody wins a modern war.

I think that it is the major job of a liberal, if he can get together sufficiently with other liberals to do a job, really to see to it that his community does think through problems, knows what they really are, has a plan and elects people in Congress and then keeps in touch with them. Of course, that is a difficult thing to do. We've taken our rights too loosely, and we haven't thought so much about the fact that we have to preserve them, and now we are facing the need to preserve them. They are at stake. I am much more interested in seeing the liberals achieve a positive program than seeing them just on the defensive. Just being on the defensive is not going to win a peace; I think the other people of the world must feel very strongly about this, too. It's a question of letting government get out of hand.

Now it's very true that the Russians can't control their government, but if we don't control ours it will be because those of us who are liberals don't do the job. Yes, the role of the liberal in this decisive year is a hard one. We've got to do our job at home as we've never done it before in many long years. And we've got to be willing to subordinate these differences among us in order to be able to do it. We've got to be willing to sacrifice. And probably the only thanks we will get is that many people will say that we are not doing the right thing, that we are making many mistakes. They can say so many things. But I think perhaps we had better forget about what people are going to say and try as hard as we are able in the way we think is right to keep the world at peace, to keep ourselves strong in every possible way, and not to be fooled. That is as important as anything else. We can be fooled. I think Henry Wallace is being fooled. I have always been very fond of Henry Wallace, but he never has had to work with the Russians, and I have. And I don't feel that just "sweetness and light" by itself is going to win a just peace. I think we need clear facing of facts and holding on to our own ideals, and trying to bring the world to a sense of our strength in all ways. Without it I don't see any reason why we should win against the other great power that stands out against us today.   □

10.   Dispute with Francis Cardinal Spellman

My Day, June 23, 1949

New York—The controversy brought about by the request made by Cardinal Spellman that Catholic schools should share in Federal aid funds forces upon the citizens of the country the kind of decision that is going to be very difficult to make.

Those of who believe in the right of any human being to belong to whatever church he sees fit, and to worship God is his own way, cannot be accused of prejudice when we do not want to see public education connected with religious control of the schools, which are paid for by taxpayers' money.

If we desire our children to go to schools of any particular kind, be it because we think they should have religious instruction or for any other reason, we are entirely free to set up those schools and to pay for them. Thus, our children would receive the kind of education we feel would best fit them for life.

Many years ago it was decided that the public schools of our country should be entirely separated from any kind of denomination control, and these are the only schools that are free, tax-supported schools. The greatest number of our children attend these schools. They receive free materials and free books and, when necessary, transportation is arranged for them. That is because in this nation we believe that free education should be available, according to the means available to the nation on a constantly improving basis.

In the early days elementary schools alone were provided. Today an increasing number of children go through high school. I believe that the time will come when free higher education will be available, even through professional courses, to such students as how the ability to use such education well. Also, I think we may soon be considering whether to provide living expenses to these students, since there might be loss of valuable material to the nation if such students did not feel that they were no longer a drag upon their families after they had reached the time when ordinarily they could go to work.

This should be done to develop those who show intelligence among our citizens, for this group is of the greatest importance in the progress and defense of civilization.

It is quite possible that private schools, whether they are denominational schools—Catholic, Episcopalian, Presbyterian, Methodist, or whatever—or whether they are purely academic, may make a great contribution to the public school systems, both on the lower levels and on the higher levels. They will be somewhat freer to develop new methods and to try experiments, and they will serve as yardsticks in the competitive area of creating better methods of imparting knowledge.

This, however, is the very reason why they should not receive Federal funds; in fact, no tax funds of any kind.

The separation of Church and State is extremely important to any of us who hold to the original traditions of our nation. To change these traditions by changing our traditional attitude toward public education would be harmful, I think, to our whole attitude of tolerance in the religious area. If we look at situations which have arisen in the past in Europe and other world areas, I think we will see the reasons why it is wise to hold to our early traditions.

11.   Correspondence with Cardinal Spellman

July 21st, 1949

Dear Mrs. Roosevelt:

When, on June 23 in your column MY DAY, you alligned [sic] yourself with the author and other proponents of the Barden Bill and condemned me for defending Catholic children against those who would deny them their constitutional rights of equality with other American children, you could have acted only from misinformation, ignorance or prejudice, not from knowledge and understanding! It is apparent that you did not take the time to read my address delivered at Fordham University; and, in your column of July 15th you admitted that you did not even carefully read and acquaint yourself with the facts of the Barden Bill—the now famous, infamous bill that would unjustly discriminate against minority groups of American children. Unlike you, Mrs. Roosevelt, I did not make a public statement until I had studied every phrase of the Barden Bill; nor did I take issue with a man because his faith differed from mine. We differed, Congressman Barden and I, over the unimpeachable issue of equal benefits and equal rights for *all* American's children.

I had intended ignoring your personal attack, but, as the days passed and in two subsequent columns you continued your anti-Catholic campaign, I became convince that it was in the interest of all Americans and the cause of justice itself that your misstatements should be challenged in every quarter of our country where they have already spun and spread their web of prejudice. I have received hundreds of messages from persons of all faiths demanding that I answer you. I am, therefore, not free to ignore you.

You say you are against religious control of schools which are paid for my taxpayers' money. That is exactly what I, too, oppose. But I am also opposed to any Bill that *includes* children who attend parochial schools for the purpose of receiving funds from the Federal Government while it excludes these same children from the distribution and benefits of the funds allocated. I believe that if the Federal Government provides a bottle of milk to each child in a public school it should provide milk for all school children. I believe that if Federal Funds are used to transport children to public schools they should be used to transport parochial school children. I believe if through the use of Federal funds the children who attend public schools are immunized from contagious disease that *all* children should be protected from these diseases.

"Taxation without representation is tyranny" was the cry that roused and rallied our pioneer Americans to fight for justice. *Taxation without representation* should rouse today's Americans to equal ardor to protest an injustice that would deprive millions of American children from the health and safety benefits to which *all* our children are entitled. And the Supreme Court of the United State has declared that health and transportation services and the distribution of non-religious textbooks to pupils attending parochial schools do not violate our Constitution.

"The separation of Church and State is extremely important to us who hold to the original traditions of our nation," you continue. But health and safety benefits and the provision of standard non-religious textbooks for all American children have nothing to do with the question of separation of Church and State!

I cannot presume upon the press to discuss, analyze or refute each inaccuracy in your columns—for they are manifold. Had you taken an objective, impersonal stand, I could then, in the same impersonal manner, answer you. But you did not. Apparently your attitude of mind precluded you from comprehending issues which you either rigorously defended or flagrantly condemned while ignorant of the facts concerning both the Barden Bill and my own denunciation of it.

American freedom not only permits but encourages differences of opinion and I do not question your right to differ with me. But why I wonder do you repeatedly please causes that are anti-Catholic? Even if you cannot find it within your heart to defend the rights of innocent little children and heroes, helpless men like Cardinal Martyr Mindszenty, can you not have the charity not to cast upon them still another stone?

America's Catholic youth fought a long and bitter fight to save all Americans from oppression and persecution. Their broken bodies on blood-soaked foreign fields were grim and tragic testimony to this fact. I saw them there—on every fighting front—as equally they shared with their fellow-fighters all the sacrifice, terror and gore of war—as alike they shared the little good and glory that sometimes comes to me as together they fight and win a brutal battle.

Would you deny equality to these Catholic boys who daily stood at the sad threshold of untimely death and suffered martyrdom that you and I and the world of men might live in liberty and peace? Would you deny their children equal rights and benefits with other sects—rights for which their fathers paid equal taxation with other fathers and fought two bitter wars that all children might forever be free from fear, oppression and religious persecution?

During the war years you visited the hospitals in many countries, as did I. You too say America's sons—Catholic, Protestant and Jew alike—young, battered, scarred, torn and mutilated, dying in agony that we might learn to live in charity with one another. Then how was it that your own heart was not purged of all prejudices by what you say these, our sons, suffer?

Now my case is closed. This letter will be released to the public tomorrow after it has been delivered to you by special delivery today. And even though you may again use your columns to attack me and again accuse me of starting a controversy, I shall not again publicly acknowledge you. For, whatever you may say in the future, your record of anti-Catholicism stands for all to see—a record which you yourself wrote on the pages of history which cannot be recalled—documents of discrimination unworthy of an American mother!

Sincerely yours,

Francis Cardinal Spellman

Archbishop of New York

ER's Reply

July 23, 1949

Your Eminence:

Your letter of July 21 surprised me considerably.

I have never advocated the Barden Bill nor any other specific Bill on education now before the Congress. I believe, however, in federal aid to education. I have stated in my column some broad principles which I consider important and said I regretted your attack on the Barden Bill because you aligned yourself with those, who from my point of view, advocated an unwise attitude which may lead to difficulties in this country, and have created, as a result, the exact things which you and I would deplore, namely, the increase in bitterness among the Roman Catholic groups, and the Protestant and other religious groups.

I read only what was in the papers about your address and I stated in my column very carefully that I had not read the Barden Bill or any other Bill carefully because I do not wish to have it said that I am in the favor of any particular Bill.

If I may, I would like to state again very simply for you the things I believe are important in this controversy. In the early days in this country there were rather few Roman Catholic settlements. The majority of the people coming here were Protestants and not very tolerant, but they believed that in establishing a democratic form of government it was essential that there be free education for as large a number of people as possible, so there was a movement to create free public schools for all children who wished to attend them. Nothing was said about private schools. As we have developed in this country we have done more and more for our public schools. They are open to all children and it has been decided that there should be no particular religious beliefs taught in them.

I believe that there should be freedom for very child to be educated in his own religion. In public schools it should be taught that the spiritual side of life is most important. I would be happy if some agreement could be reached on passages from the Bible and some prayer that could be used. The real religious teaching of any child must be done in his own church and in his own home.

It is fallacious, I think, to say that because children going to public schools are granted free textbooks in some states, free transportation, or free school lunches, that these same things must be given to children going to private schools. Different states, of course, have done different things as they come under majority pressure from citizens who had certain desires, but basically by and large, throughout the country, I think there is still a feeling that if the public school is the school which is open to all children, then it should not be tied in with any school. At present there are physical examinations for children in public school which are provided without cost to the parents but there is nothing to prevent people who send their children to private schools from making arrangements to pay for similar examinations for their children.

I should like to point out to you that I talked about parochial schools and that to my mind means any schools organized by any sectarian group and not exclusively a Roman Catholic school. Children attending parochial schools are, of course, taught according to the tenets of their respective churches.

As I grow older, it seems to me important that there be no greater stress laid on our divisions, but that we stress as much as possible our agreements.

You state: "And the Supreme Court of the United States has declared that health and transportation services and the distribution of non-religious textbooks to pupils attending parochial school do not violate our Constitution." None of us will presume to decide questions which will come up before the Supreme Court of the United States, but all of us must think seriously about anything which is done, not only in relations to the specific thing, but in relation to what may follow after it and what we think will be good for the country.

Anyone who knows history, particularly the history of Europe, will, I think, recognize that the domination of education or of government by any one particular religious faith, is never a happy arrangement for the people. Spiritual leadership should remain spiritual leadership and the temporal power should not become too important in any church.

I have no bias against the Roman Catholic Church and I have supported Governor Smith as governor and worked for him as a candidate for the office of President of the United States. I have supported for public office many other Roman Catholic candidates.

You speak of the Mindszenty case. I spoke out very clearly against any unfair type of trial and anything anywhere in any country which might seem like attack on an individual because of his religious beliefs. I can not, however, say that in European countries the control by the Roman Catholic church of great areas of land has always lead to happiness for the people of those countries.

I have never visited hospitals and asked or thought about the religion of any boy in any bed. I have never in a military cemetery had any different feeling about the graves of the boys who lay there. All of our boys of every race, creed and color fought for the country and they deserve our help and gratitude.

It is not my wish to deny children anywhere equal rights or benefits. It is, however, the decision of parents when they select a private or denominational school whether it be Episcopalian, Wesleyan, Jewish or Roman Catholic.

I can assure you that I have no prejudice. I understand the beliefs of the Roman Catholic Church very well. I happen to be a Protestant and I prefer my own church, but that does not make me feel that any one has any less right to believe as his own convictions guide him.

I have no intention of attacking you personally, nor of attacking the Roman Catholic Church, but I shall, of course, continue to stand for the things in our government which I think are right. They may lead me to be in opposition to you and to other groups within our country, but I shall always act, as far as I am able, from a real conviction and from honest belief.

If you carefully studied my record, I think you would not find it one of anti-Catholic or anti-religious group.

I assure you I have no senses of being an "unworthy American mother." The final judgment, my dear Cardinal Spellman, of the worthiness of all human beings is in the hands of God.

With deepest respect, I am

Very sincerely yours,

Eleanor Roosvelt

P.S. I haven't as yet, given this letter to the press. I am, however, entirely willing to have you do so.   ☐

12.   Address to Americans for Democratic Action

Reprinted in *The Congressional Record*, April 1, 1950

Mr. Chairman, ladies and gentlemen, it's a very inspiring thing these days to come to a meeting such as this and find so many people coming together to discuss and make plans for an organization devoted to obtaining in our country as good a government as we can have. This organization is made up of both Democrats and Republicans.

. . . I think the thing that makes one happy about ADA is that it really has convictions. And the people who belong, belong because they want to find a way to put those convictions to work. They recognize . . . that our democracy is not perfect. But they also know that it's working to improve democracy. That is the important thing. Those who are satisfied—those who feel that there is nothing they can do—they are the people who will do harm to the Government and the citizenship in the United States.

We live in a time when every single one of us must realize that what actually is important in a democracy is that sense of individual responsibility. And there are certain things here in our country that I think we must watch very carefully. It is true, as has been said, that there is a sense of insecurity—I might almost say a sense of fear—among many people in this country of ours. With some people it's a fear of the possibility of war; with others it's a fear of what the new weapons of war may mean if we should come to war; with others it's a fear of what may happen to them personally if by chance they offend in any way. That is the fear that bothers me most—the fear of people who are afraid to be themselves, to hold convictions, to stand up for them—because that fear, I think, is the fear which can really hurt our democracy more than any other.

This is a time when it takes courage to live. It takes the kind of courage that it took in the earliest days of our history. . . . I'm sure that there have been other times in our history which have looked black indeed to the citizens of the country and its leaders. But at present we need all the courage that our forefathers had and perhaps a little more, because we have a job to do at home and a job to do in the world.

The job at home has to be done, and has to be done first. We have to be unafraid. And we have to realize that here is where we as individuals have to fulfill our belief in democracy. If we cannot prove here that we believe in freedom, in the ability of people to govern themselves, if we cannot have confidence in each other, if we cannot feel that fundamentally we are all trying to retain the best in our democracy and improve it, if we cannot find some basic unity even in peace, then we are never going to be able to lead the world. This is the problem that is before us today. If we do not lead the world, who is going to lead it? We have to accept the fact that it's what we do here that makes us fit to lead the world. So every day in our daily lives as citizens we are building our world leadership.

Our great struggle today is to prove to the world that democracy has more to offer than communism. You can't just say that anyone who understands communism must be against it. You have to face the fact that this is a struggle, and a very great struggle. If we want to win the cold war, if we want to reach a greater security—I think it's going to take us a long time, and I think we have to develop a courage and a staunchness that perhaps we have never had. If we want to achieve it, then we must prove to the world what we can offer. That means we have to take certain definite steps. We have, for instance, to make sure that we have civil rights in this country. There was a time when we could look on that question as a purely domestic one—that we could take all the time we wanted to educate ourselves to solve the problem. It isn't any longer a domestic question—it's an international question. It is perhaps the question which may decide whether democracy or communism wins out in the world.

I sit in the United Nations; have sat in the General Assembly since 1946, and I sit in the Human Rights Commission. Over and over again the failures of democracy are pointed out to me in terms of specific instances of things that have happened in our country. I don't try to say they didn't happen, because usually I know that they did. All I can say is that we know about them, and those of us who really care, work to improve our democracy. Therefore, we must actually look at ourselves with more critical eyes than we have in the past.

Where do we fail, and how hard do we try to live up to the things we've given lip service to? It's not a domestic question; it's a question that perhaps is one of the most important factors in the winning of the struggle. Of course, economic questions enter into this struggle, too. We cannot be complacent about the unemployment in our country—about injustices. Not long ago I remember hearing in a certain city that the papers actually printed what certain rather well-paid officials would have as pensions in an industry, and yet when it came to the point of pensions to the workers, that was too heavy a burden for the industry. Well now, I'm not a Socialist. I'm a very practical capitalist, I'm sure. But if we want to keep capitalism, we in this country have got to learn that there must be a real sharing, a real understanding, between management and labor. They must plan together because their interests are really identical. But both sides must realize it.

Now, the answer to unemployment. I didn't get an answer when I asked some of our Democratic Senators the other day, "What is the answer to unemployment?" I doubt if many people know. I think it's one of the things that perhaps we need to experiment, and perhaps it may be tied up, too, with some of our decisions in the realm of foreign affairs. Perhaps backing the United Nations with our own four-points program, seeing what can be done through them, to work with other nations in the world, that may have some tie with unemployment. There may be other things that I know nothing about, but I never like to feel that we don't face problems and that we don't set people to work on finding the answers. There's no reason why we shouldn't say we don't know the answer now; there's every reason why we shouldn't say we're not trying to find out. It is essential, I think, to our winning this struggle that we actually find answers, because in this economic area communism has a program. And democracy has to have a better one. If it doesn't, we're being judged before the bar of the world, and we have to win. We have to win because we have a conviction that democracy does offer people something that no other form of government and no other way of life can offer.

There's one thing that always strikes me, and that is that the Communist representatives in the United Nations never talk about liberty; they never mention it. On one occasion when Mr. Vishinsky was forced to do so, he said that was a foolish thing to talk about because no one could have liberty. Well, you and I know quite well that everyone's liberty is conditioned by the rights of other people. But we must think about liberty, because that is really one of the basic reasons why we prefer democracy to communism. And somehow we must keep ourselves free from fear and suspicion of each other. I sit with people who are representatives of Communist countries, and to sit with them is a lesson in what fear can do. Fear can take away from you all the courage to be an individual. You become a mouthpiece for the ideas which you have been told you must give forth. I have no feeling of real antagonism toward these representatives because, poor things, they can do no other. They must do that; their lives depend on it.

Now, it seems to me that the ADA is an organization that has thinking people in it, and we must preserve the right to think and to differ in the United States. We must be able to disagree with people, and to consider new ideas, and not to be afraid. The day that I am afraid to sit down in a room with people that I do not know because perhaps 5 years from now, someone will say, "You sat in the room and five people were Communists, and so you are a Communist," that day will be a bad day for democracy. We must be sure enough of ourselves, of our own convictions, to sit down with anyone and not be afraid of listening to what they have to say, and not be afraid of contamination by association. It's true that the company you keep may say something about what you are. But to be able to meet with people and argue your own point of view, and to meet with people whom you do not have to screen beforehand to be sure they are safe to meet with—that must be a part of the freedom of every citizen in the United States.

So I'm grateful that ADA prods us to think that it has an opportunity to bring before us the ideas that seem important, that it also has the opportunity of backing people in elections who promise to be good public servants. I'm grateful that it is representative of people in both political parties, and I'm grateful for the numbers that have come today. I think it shows that we as a Nation are waking up to the need to preserve our basic ideas in our Republic, that we are waking up to the fact that we have to live those ideals, and that we have to improve our democracy by the way we live. To do that we must come together, and consult together, and get other people to help us where we need help. There must be no one who fights the battle of good government, of freedom of thought, of real democracy, with a sense of doing it alone. That is the value of ADA—you do not have to be alone . . . .   ☐

13.   "If I Were a Republican Today"

Cosmopolitan, June 1950

If I were a Republican today, I think I would ask my party to take a clearcut stand. At present, it is *not* clearcut. They say, for instance, they're *against* the present Administration's health bill because it is "socialized medicine," but they acknowledge that we *need* more medical care throughout the country, and so they are vaguely for better medical care without specifying exactly how it is to be accomplished. They are for freedom as against socialism, but no one in the Democratic Administration is a Socialist.

The Republicans believe in a bipartisan foreign policy. They complain that the Administration has of late laid down the policy and consulted the Republicans after the policy was made and not before. They *could*, however, suggest machinery by which they could take part in all this policy-making either by returning to the former practice of legislative representation in the delegation for the United Nations General Assembly, or by some type of close coordination between the State Department and the foreign relations committees in both the Houses of Congress.

If I were a Republican, I would want my party to formulate exactly *what* it stood for in foreign affairs and state *why* it was for certain policies and against others, so that it would not be *quite* so difficult for the public to understand just what the Republican stand on foreign policy actually is. Their program as recently stated is curiously evasive. I would want my party to state what kind of peace policies it would pursue in *contrast* to those of the present administration. I would want a clearcut statement on the defense of my country, which is closely tied to the policy of peace. The present statement is in very general terms, and it does not face the realities of the situation.

In the last campaign for the presidency, the Republican candidate came out *against* certain types of farm aid. If I were a Republican, I would want my party's stand on price support and handling of surplus crops, etc., very *clearly* stated. I would also want to know in unmistakable terms my party's stand on conservation and development of natural resources, because in the place where we are today, the development of water power, the control of floods, and soil and forest conservation are of primary importance to the future of the people of the country.

Both parties state we must have civil rights for all regardless "of race, religion, color, or country of origin." When it comes to making these words effective in *law*, both parties are divided and a coalition of Democrats and Republicans prevents any legislation from becoming law.

It used to be said of the two political parties that the Republican Party believed in looking after the interests of the people at the top. If they prospered, the prosperity would carry on down to all the people; on the other hand, that the Democratic Party believed that they had to look after the well-being of the people at the bottom, and that if they prospered and had a satisfactory life, the people at the top would also prosper.

These are two basically different theories, but today you can find people in both parties who believe in either one or the other theory. If I were a Republican, I think I would consider it *important to have that point cleared up* so that one could choose the philosophy one felt was the most sound. If we have reached a point in our economic development where it is clear to all of us that the interests of the top and the bottom are so closely tied that they must be mutually developed, then I think it would be well for either party, or both parties, to state that as a new policy.

As I read over the Republican pontifical bible as it has just been issued, it seems to me that they have gone over the things that they think elected President Truman, and they have accepted them all, saying: "Gentlemen, we will do all of these things and more, and we will reduce your taxes, which will give you more money to spend as you wish." This *may* fool the voters but I do not *think* it will, and I, for one, would like both parties to be clear and explicit in the philosophy that underlies whatever they do. Then we would not get out the confused vote, and we would have the kind of participation by the voters one saw in the last election in Great Britain. We never get as big a percentage of the vote out as they did, and that is largely, *I think, because the policies of the two major parties are at present so lacking in clarity* that the people wait and make their final decision on the candidates and what each says in the campaign. Many people do not vote because they honestly do not understand what the policies back of the oratory are, and they decide that it will not matter much *which* party wins, and therefore they stay away from the polls.

In this country we believe in a two-party system, but in the past few years it has sometimes, it seems to me, been difficult to form a clearcut idea of what the two political parties actually represent. I believe it is important always to have a strong opposition party no matter *which* party is in power, and that is why the issues should be clear.

As a Democrat, I would say that the majority of the Democratic Party is more liberal and progressive than the majority of the Republican Party, but the Dixiecrats, for instance, line themselves up with the most reactionary element in the Republican Party, and it must be difficult for some of the Republican liberals when they see their proposals more frequently urged by the Democratic Party than by the Republican majority.

A short time ago, on my television program, Senator Wiley of Wisconsin read me the new Republican Party platform, and I could not help thinking that it has some curiously reminiscent planks that might almost have made their first appearance in the New Deal. The Republicans say they are for a reduction in taxes but are not for a reduction in any of the services rendered the people! The services are all to be met by more economical administration of government! That, of course, is always the slogan of the party out of power because it is not in the position of administering these agencies of government, and when you are not actually doing the job it is always easier to say it could be done more economically. But the history of the Republican Party is not the history of retrenchment in government personnel or expenditure.

It is true that services to the people usually have been started in Democratic Administrations and then adopted and continued in Republican platforms.

It is true that the cost of government goes up with these services. However, I do not think it will be proved by close scrutiny of our past history that the Republicans employ any fewer Republicans than the Democrats employ Democrats in political places.   □

14.   Senator Joseph McCarthy

My Day, August 29, 1952

Hyde Park—I have a rather interesting letter from a lady today and I would like to answer it in my column. She says: "In view of your past record of sponsoring organizations with Communist leanings, some of which even booed

266 SENATOR JOSEPH MCCARTHY

your late husband, I cannot conceive of your making a speech against a red-blooded American like Senator McCarthy. He has earnestly tried to free our government of Communists. What have you done in that line?"

First, I would like to point out that I have not as yet made a speech against Senator McCarthy.

The only organization I ever sponsored which had any degree of Communist control was the American Youth Congress in the early thirties. There was a very good reason for working with those young people and the bulk of the membership was not then, and never was later, Communistic.

A group among them were Communists then and perhaps may have remained so—that I do not know. But I would like to remind people in general and especially my correspondent that this was a particularly difficult period for young people.

They were coming out of college in great numbers and finding no jobs. Democracy was failing them and many of the most intelligent thought Communism would solve their problems.

Sooner or later many of them found out how intolerable Communist control was and they became better citizens of our democracy than ever before. They did not inform against their former colleagues, they simply gave up Communism and went to work as citizens of our democracy.

They were the more valuable because they knew what was wrong with Communism and they understood and cherished the democratic form of government and the democratic way of life.

Back in the thirties, however, these young people—even those who booed the President—needed friends. They were rude, true, but also desperately unhappy and frustrated. It was fortunate that the White House understood this.

My devotion to my country and to democracy is quite as great as that of Senator McCarthy. I do not like his methods or the results of his methods and I would like to say to my correspondent that I think those of us who worked with young people in the thirties did more to save many of them from becoming Communists than Senator McCarthy has done for his fellow citizens with all his slurs and accusations.

I know the dangers of Communism. I know it perhaps better than many other American citizens because for nearly five months of every year for the last six years, I have sat in meetings with the Communist representatives of the USSR.

I despise the control they insist on holding over men's minds. And that is why I despise what Senator McCarthy has done, for he would use the same methods of fear to control all thought that is not according to his own pattern—in our free country!   □

15.   Alger Hiss

Correspondence with Arthur Grafflin

November 14, 1953

Dear Madam:

The corrosive dry rot and encouragement of treason in this country began and was fostered by Franklin and Eleanor Roosevelt, and has been fostered and in many ways encouraged since then by Eleanor Roosevelt.

That is a very grave charge, but is not made lightly. It is not suggested for a moment that either of you were or are deliberate traitors to this country, but is suggested that there was on the part of both of you, and is now on yours, a far too great lack of understanding of many subversive influences and efforts in this country, and a far too easy tolerance of or indifference to their menace, especially on your part as you have given so much incomprehensible encouragement to so many undesirable individuals and causes. In your undoubtedly well-intentioned but certainly very muddleheaded "thinking" and expression of opinions about almost everything on earth, and your easy tolerance of so many intolerable things, I believe it entirely true to say that you have been and are one of the most pernicious influence in this country today.

One of the worst and most indefensible of your recent utterances is your reference to the "alleged" treason of Alger Hiss. It was a shameful, utterly stupid—and I choose that word very carefully for no other seems to suit as well—and disgusting statement for you or anyone other than an out-and-out Communist to have made, and clearly indicates the trend on caliber of your 'thinking.'

Please, Mrs. R., can't we possibly have the great boon and solace of your silence for a while in this country? We are very, very tired of your shallow opinion, as well as evasions of truth and fact.

Very Truly Yours,
A. G. Grafflin

ER's Reply

November 19, 1953

Dear Mr. Grafflin:

May it be possible that you have forgotten that we do not state a person is guilty until he is proved guilty? And have your forgotten that Mr. Hiss was convicted of perjury and not of treason?

I have not said that Mr. Hiss may not be proved guilty but so far he has not been and in accordance with our ancient custom, those of us who adhere to the ways of American justice do not condemn him.

You are entitled to your opinion of my husband and myself but I am also entitled to disagree with you.

Very Sincerely yours,

Mr. Grafflin's Reply

November 23, 1953

Dear Mrs. Roosevelt:

I appreciate your courteous reply to my admittedly somewhat heated recent letter.

Of course I do not feel that any person should be adjudged guilty until he has been proved so. What I think you completely overlook in the case of Alger Hiss is that the very perjury of which he was convicted was in connection with treasonable acts of his which the perjury conviction established, and that the sole reason he was not directly tried on charges of treason and spying and conspiracy was because of the statute of limitations which applied in the matter under existing laws. To me, such a limitation is absurd, for treason is certainly as reprehensible and vicious as murder, on which there is properly no limitation.

I do not feel, however, that you or anyone else, because of personal prejudices, should conveniently hide behind a technicality in such a clear-cut case as that of Alger Hiss, in casting such unwarranted reflection upon our very courts, after the extremely fair trail he had, by still attempting to excuse his treasonable actions as "alleged" treason. My prime criticism of you is based upon your far too easy tolerance of and sympathy with many intolerable things and causes and persons, which seem so very misguided, however well intended. For some strange reason, you always seem to be or to wind up on the side of so many wrong people and causes. No one in his sense would suggest that you or the late President were or are deliberately and actively in sympathy with or indifferent to the really vicious things which Communists and their activities represent in the world, but there certainly appears to have been throughout an incredible unawareness and gullibility and even indifference about the menace of such things, which have caused great harm in this country.

That is why, frankly, I suggested the "great boon" of your silence about such matters for a while, because it honestly seems to me that you are again and again muddying waters which ought not to be stirred up as you do. How much more honest it would be, and how much better for the country, if obvious mistakes were admitted, instead of trying to cloud them over by indirection or, as in the case of Mr. Truman, by vicious invective and mis-statements of fact, or omission of vital facts.

Very truly yours.

ER's Reply

December 3, 1955

Dear Mr. Grafflin:

I have never questioned Alger Hiss' conviction for perjury but many people who really knew him, which I did not, have felt that he actually had not committed treason. Therefore, until it is proved it is better for those of us who do not want to add to the present hysteria, not to go on accusing him.

You forget that when my husband was alive we were fighting a war with Russia as our ally. We knew quite well that Russia had accepted Germany as an ally until Germany turned against her, but we needed Russia in the war. She saved us many men. Fortunately for both of us at that time we did not have to be suspicious of everyone we knew. I think that is one of the sad things that have happened to us.

I believe if the F.B.I. had been allowed to continue its work, being strengthened if necessary, without interference by congressional committees, we would not have reached the hysteria and discontented situation in which this country now finds itself and which to my mind is far more dangerous than the feeling that the F.B.I. would not be able to protect us as it did between World War I and World War II. I feel this so deeply that I would think I was doing the country a great injustice if I kept silent as you suggest.

I do not think I have made any mistakes or done the country any harm.

Very sincerely yours,   ☐

---

16.   "Social Responsibility for Individual Welfare'

From *National Policies of Educational, Health and Social Services*, Edited by James Russell (New York: Doubleday, 1955)

I am happy that in this remarkable conference that has been called to celebrate and to deepen the thinking and knowledge of our people throughout the country on these subjects, we should have the stress laid on this particular subject: "Social Responsibility for Individual Welfare."

. . . . Now, it has come about that when you talk about the welfare state, as a rule people think that that is a rather derogatory term—that a welfare state is somehow not a good thing. But if we could just change it around a little and say that we believed that society included the government, the individuals themselves as individuals, and all other groups—universities, the people who form the policies, the industrialists, the people who guide commerce, industry, and agriculture—if we thought of them altogether as working together to increase the welfare of the individual, then we would cease, I think, to have fear of just the mere words "a welfare state." We would have a truer conception of what the words really mean.

It is basic in a democracy that leadership for the welfare of the people as a whole must come from government. It is true that we pride ourselves on holding the reins of government, but we need leadership. We need a voice to define our aims, to put into words the things we want to achieve; and so we look to government to do just that—so that we do not stand still but move forward. Just as Alice in Wonderland had to run very fast to stay in the same place, we must run even faster to stay in the same place, and we have to do even more in order to go forward. We will go backward unless we go forward.

My husband used to say that we progressed by crises, that when the crisis was so bad that we wondered how we were going to meet it, then we were ready to try something new, to try something that perhaps we would otherwise have hesitated to undertake.

When sometimes I hear it said that in my husband's time we started something dreadful, something which they called "creeping socialism," I wonder whether instead we didn't really face the fact that a democracy must meet the needs of its people, and whether what we did was not actually to save democracy, to save free enterprise, to keep for ourselves as much freedom as we possibly could. Had we not met the needs of the people, we might have waked up and found ourselves not just in creeping socialism, but perhaps going actually to the far extremes of either fascism or communism, because we could not find a way to meet the needs of the people.

As I have been around the world it has seemed to me that we in this country, when we talk of capitalism or free enterprise, should explain what we mean, because there are many areas of the world in which it is not at all understood what we actually mean when we talk of our own capitalism, of our own development in the past thirty years or forty years, let us say.

We have had great changes, but they have been the changes which had to come if our people were to have a chance for full development. To be sure, some of the things were very new; now they seem very old. I can remember when we started old-age pensions. Now the idea is not very shocking to us—a mutual contribution towards this security in old age. We started care for the blind and the crippled. Many said that it was simply a humanitarian gesture, but it was more than that. It is real insurance so that they will not remain a burden on society. That is why we continue to develop the employment of the crippled and the blind. We continue to find useful ways of using people, even handicapped people.

Old-age pensions, as now accepted, are contributed to throughout the working life of every individual. Care for the blind and the crippled may sound completely humanitarian, but on the contrary it is really an insurance so that society will not have an obligation to carry handicapped people as a complete burden. In the underdeveloped areas of the world the only thing open to the handicapped individual is to beg. We not only try to extend the best medical care but we try to train these individuals to earn a living, and we are constantly working with industries to open occupations to trained handicapped people, while many industries also have undertaken training programs of their own. This whole program eliminates a burden from society, just the same as pensions do which are paid for during the working life of an individual.

We believe in unemployment insurance. We know that it is not perfect in operation. We know that a number of things that are done for general welfare are not perfect in the way they work out, but that it would be unwise to wipe out the whole of something because there needed to be certain reforms and changes. It was felt that as we went along we would realize that unemployment insurance was not just for the benefit of the individual; it was for the benefit of our economy. It was to try to keep us from having debacles, from actually having buying power so reduced as to hurt the economy of the nation as a whole. It is part of our economic insurance.

There are many things that, just like freedom, we must constantly be studying and watching when we do things for the welfare of people, because we do not want to remove from people their sense of responsibility and initiative. We want them to feel that they are partners in each thing that we do, that if they function in a democracy, then what their government does comes from them. They acquiesce, they work it out, and they must not lose initiative.

We have not completely solved the unemployment problem because it is still open to abuses. It is safeguarded to some extent by the fact that government offices try to find jobs for people within their range of employment, which they are expected to accept. But many people have had the experience of knowing individuals who took advantage of unemployment insurance when they really could have obtained work. The law was not written to encourage such people, and so ways should be sought to eliminate existing loopholes so that it would be impossible to get unemployment insurance unless one is unable to find work in a field where one is competent.

All these social measures were designed to protect society from sudden fluctuations in the economy and to protect the individual from situations beyond his control which he could not completely handle by himself. They were designed as cooperative measures between the individual and his government, which, I think, is a step forward. They should not tend to remove initiative from people nor keep them from feeling a sense of individual responsibility and ambition.

The advantage of a democracy over the socialist state would seem to be a greater freedom, which provides for the development of the individual for free choice of a way of life and for a sense on the part of the individual of participation in the decisions made which affect his life and his future. His government tries to remove from the individual a fear of want so that he may be freer to fully develop, but it does not countenance a stepping in of government to take over the major part of the responsibility for man's existence.

I was struck in France by the difference between our philosophy and theirs, which are still miles apart. They do not think that it is important that a man earn a living wage. We do. I think it is the basis of the welfare of the individual.

Under the social-security system of France nearly every employer pays his employees less than a living wage. He pays from 35 to 50 per cent of the wage, not to the employee, but into a *caisse* or fund managed by the government and distributed under government auspices to families according to their size. Under this system a man with five or six children receives a considerable sum more from the government than he earns. In a democracy like ours we think it important for industry to be so organized that a man receives wages commensurate with his work and on which he can support his family. In other words, what we hope to ensure to every individual is an ability to earn a living, and the benefits of a welfare state are simply auxiliary to meet emergencies and to help a human being to meet situations that may arise in his life which he ordinarily could not meet alone.

There I was told very calmly, "Oh, but you do not understand our system. We know we don't insist upon a living wage, but the government gives to families, according to the number of children, an allowance. If you have five or six children you might almost as well not work because the government pays you so much more than you can possibly earn."

We have to recognize that our type of capitalism in this country is different from what the same word connotes in some other countries. From the time of the last depression we have taken great strides in the recognition of the responsibility of government and industry to cooperate to prevent any disasters to the normal economy of the country. We have to be prepared to meet disasters caused by nature. These we expect the government to cooperate in meeting, but we recognize the responsibility of industry today as well as of the individual. We believe that together we should strive to give every individual a chance for a decent and secure existence, and in evolving our social patterns we are trying to give both hope for better things in the future and security from want in the present.

Basically, all of us believe that where the people feel they have justice, opportunity, and freedom and can actually rely on the interest of their government and on the attitudes of society to help them achieve stabilization and as much security as one can ever count on in human life, there will be belief in the government and the security that no other isms will really undermine the faith in the ideas on which this country was founded.

We believe that together we should strive to give every individual a chance for a decent and secure existence; and in evolving our social patterns we are trying to give both hope for better things in the future and security from want as far as possible in the present.

These aims should not affect either the initiative of the individual or his sense of responsibility, but should give him a feeling of partnership in his government and with the economy of his country as a whole, which we hope will be a pattern that far transcends the economic pattern and the ideological promises that are made in parts of the world by Communism.

If we live and work for the basic ideals that our country was founded on and have justice and freedom, I think we need not have loyalty boards. We need not have inquisitions. We can trust that what we believe in and stand for will be strong enough so that we can trust each other and other people as a whole.   □

17.   # Stevenson Campaign Address

Charleston, West Virginia, October, 1956

I want to tell you why I came back into active political work. I worked for the United Nations for six years and in doing that I tried to act as a representative of the American people not as a Democrat or a Republican, but for all the people of the country. I went to the first meeting in London to orga-

nize the UN and that is where I first really came to know Adlai Stevenson. I had
met him before, but never really knew him as a person. I think because I have
become conscious that we were losing, not gaining friends in the last four years
that I began to think who was the best candidate to bring us back to world thinking, and to realize that now practically all domestic problems tied into the problems of the world. At that first meeting Adlai Stevenson did all the preparatory
work since the meeting in San Francisco up to the London meeting. Every country had a group of people working in the Preparation Committee, he headed
ours and did wonderful work. He knew all the other people and told us when
we came who they were and what they did. I was worried as I was the only
woman and felt I was looked on not as "one of the crowd." Mr. [John Foster]
Dulles and Mr. [Senator Arthur] Vandenberg [R-Michigan] were not happy that
I was along, so I worked with great care and read all the time on the steamer
about the State Department position papers. They were quite hard to understand for the State Department has a language all its own devised to keep others
from understanding it, and I had to learn this new language. There were brief-
ings every day for all delegates and for the press, and other than that I spent all
my spare time reading these papers. One day I met Mr. Vandenberg in the cor-
ridor and he said "we decided to ask you to serve on Committee 3." This made
me feel that they were all meeting without me, and I had no idea what Committee 3 was, but I said I would be delighted to serve, and then went on to find
out what work Committee 3 did.

Adlai Stevenson told us about the people in the other delegations. He really
made a study of the people we would deal with, and what the setup would be
and much background information. This made all the difference in our ability to
work with the others. I watched Adlai Stevenson from then on, and he worked
on several of the Committees. Some people gain respect and others lose respect
when you are working with them. Adlai Stevenson gained. All the trips taken by
the Secretary of State have not gained friends for us—we have had four years of
dealing with crises. We have no one who has looked at the whole world and tried
to map out what we are going to do. It is not necessary to reach a crisis if you
prevent them from happening. We must have a clearcut policy and we need to
state it. Otherwise we must just drift along and hope trouble will disappear, but
it doesn't. Little things are often important in relation to other countries—
using the wrong word—handling people without understanding of background—lead to real trouble when we are trying to make them see things from
our point of view. On my trips around the world I have been confronted in country after country with stories of little things. The story of Dulles going to Egypt's
ruler just when Great Britain had finally negotiated to leave, and presented him

with two pistols. Of course Great Britain was angry. It is an amusing thing to tell, but it didn't make friends for us! And when the Secretary of State was in Israel and was presented with a remarkable Bible, beautifully bound—he said "of course this includes the New Testament?" Ben-Gurion got red up the back of his neck. These things are not really funny, as they are the things that lose friends for us in the world.

I remember after the 1952 elections Adlai Stevenson went on a trip around the world. I followed him in most places and particularly in Asia. Always I was told "We like your Mr. Stevenson—he listened to what we had to say." This taught me a lesson. If you want to learn it is a good idea to listen. I discovered that we Americans have a reputation for doing all the talking. If you don't know much about the people and their background doing all the talking and not finding out their ideas, is not a wise thing to do. One difficulty of course, is that we have become the leaders of the free world and possibly this came without our wanting it and without much preparation, so we need to learn. Adlai Stevenson took his trip to Africa because he had not seen this Continent which he realized was one area where our problems would lie in the next few years, and he felt obliged to learn about these people. A person must take the trouble to learn what he needs to know if new problems are to be solved in new ways.

How about things happening here at home? There is hardly a domestic problem that doesn't touch on international problems. Civil Rights is an example. We must use patience. We can't do everything at once, nor as quickly in every place, but we must move and we must show that we really intend that every citizen shall have equality of opportunity, recognition as a citizen and live without feeling that he is not an equal of every other citizen in our democracy. If this doesn't happen and we show that we are not in earnest, it will hurt in our world leadership. We must bear in mind that two-thirds of the world's population is colored, and we are the minority race. We have often exploited the people of other races, but this is not wise. Today they long for freedom in all areas of the world. We are the people who lead in the struggle for freedom and we can't afford to let people see any exploitation here at home. That is not the example of a nation that says everyone is created free and equal!

I am deeply concerned about education, and if you have been listening to Adlai Stevenson you will know that he too is deeply concerned in giving young people a better life. We may think this is just a domestic problem and that it doesn't tie up with the struggle between Communism and Democracy and in the defense of our country. We may think it is just a difficulty in our own community to get good teachers and more classrooms. I think we had better face the fact that if we go on not meeting the crisis in education we are losing out on the biggest challenge that Communism has put before us. Why? Because today in the Soviet Union 90% of the people can read and write. Any young person who shows an ability to use higher education can achieve it. Not only an education, but a subsidy grant while he is getting his education. Of course it is a type of education you would not like. We don't want to be regulated and indoctrinated, but it is a tremendous challenge to our system. We should know it and face it. Last year the Soviets trained 1,200,000 young engineers and physicists for export to be sent in their program of Technical Assistance to countries to whom they promised help. We trained 900,000 and our own industries took them all. Last year the *Herald Tribune* Forum had the Deputy Commissioner of Education from the Soviet Union here for a visit. She was a woman, and from peasant stock. Our State Department did nothing to plan this woman's trip, for she was not here on official business. One day I was called in New York and told about this woman and asked if I would not like to have her come for tea. I said I would be delighted, and I am glad that I did. I learned much about the Soviet teaching program. If a student is going to be sent to Brazil they are told to learn Portuguese. If they are going to Burma they are taught the Burmese dialects. Then when they go to a country they can not only offer their skills, but they have a common language so that it is much easier to import their thoughts. It means a great deal to people if you have taken the time to learn their language. You have gained much confidence for your efforts. I believe our young people should know as firmly why they believe in Democracy as the young Soviets know why they believe in Communism. We do our jobs because we understand—we believe in our democracy—we believe that individual personality is endowed by God with certain inherent freedoms and therefore we have something as individuals which we can delegate to our government which gives us a stronger basis than the Communist people. As I told the Deputy Commissioner we can demonstrate this—we are not ordered as you are, we do what we do because we want to. If we go outside of our own country to work we do so because we want to—not because our government says we must. There are large areas of the world that have never known freedom and don't know what it is, so to many it seems freedom to be allowed to have an education. When you speak of freedom you mean something your government has given you, we mean something inherent in us as a gift of God. So, this women told me her story. She is a peasant woman and did not have much opportunity and had no chance for education. She said that she had worked hard for what she had, but her government gave her every opportunity. She said "I am here because of my government. How can I separate my rights and the rights of my government?"

So, we can no longer put questions in one package and say we are just interested in more classrooms or more teachers or more schools. We must know
what the challenge is, and then have a plan for meeting it.   ☐

18.   Segregation in the South

My Day, April 30, 1957

New York—It is a relief to know Attorney General Herbert
Brownell Jr. actually and finally has asked Congress to pass the civil rights bill.

I am not familiar enough with these bills to know whether or not they give
Mr. Brownell the jurisdiction he thinks he needs to deal with such shocking cases
as he mentioned.

But if they do, we may hope to see our Justice Department moving to prevent the shame which such incidents have brought on our entire country. They
have particularly brought shame on our system of states' rights which makes it
possible for a state to violate all concepts of justice and decency and still avoid
interference by the Federal Government.

I have been reading a book called *Go South for Sorrow*, by Carl T. Rowan. I am
only half way through it but it has forced me to review what has happened in the
South since the Supreme Court decision against segregation in the schools.

It is nearly three years since the day in May when we held our heads a little
higher because the highest court in the land removed from the lives of all our
children the degradation of discrimination. And the history of our country in
these years is an appalling record of lawlessness, of contempt for our Supreme
Court and those who sit on it.

In areas of the South and in the Senate of the United States we have accepted the leadership of a man like Sen. James O. Eastland. As I read speeches in
Congress, I could hardly believe that our country would allow such a man to
lead and that our people would allow themselves to be guided by such ideas and
such untruths.

I love my country and I want to be very proud of it and in my ancestry I have
both Southern and Northern blood. I cannot disassociate myself from the things
that are done by American citizens, no matter what part of the country they
come from.

I think the time has come for all citizens who have convictions to speak out
and be counted on the side of law and decency.

In reviewing the history of these past years since May 1954 I am beginning to understand more clearly why so many in the world doubt our leadership.

We talk of brotherhood; we say that democracy means an appreciation of the importance of the human personality and of the rights of individual human beings; we say our democracy is inspired by Christianity as exemplified in the teachings of Christ.

Then we allow people such as Sen. Eastland to quote the Bible and the life of Christ as justification for doctrines entirely opposed to the whole spirit of Christianity, or ethics, or human brotherhood.

I shall force myself to read every word of Mr. Rowan's book. I do not have to go South for sorrow. I sorrow here for the shame of these past three years.   □

19.   ## The Smith Act

My Day, June 22, 1957

New York—Just at this time, when many of us have felt that the individual was losing many of his rights, it is encouraging to note the decisions of the Supreme Court upholding the Constitutional freedoms.

The Court—at least the majority on it—seems to have redefined the ancient idea that its function is to guard the rights granted to our people in the Constitution and the Bill of Rights. This it has done in reversing the contempt conviction of John T. Watkins,[1] labor leader, and the freeing of five California Communist leaders convicted under the Smith Act and the granting of a new trial for nine others.

I also am glad that, after his long fight, John Stewart Service, former Foreign Service officer, won a reversal of the judgment of the Court of Appeals which in June, 1956, held that Mr. Service had been rightfully dismissed as a security risk.

When you study the way the different Court justices acted in reversing the Communist leader's convictions, you find certain differences in their reasoning.

For instance, two of them, Justices Hugo Black and William O. Douglas, felt that the Smith Act is unconstitutional. I have not the space to discuss the legal points, but I think it is well worth everyone's time to read the varied opinions.

I for one, am glad that the Court has handed down a decision which forever

[1] The case is Watkins v. U.S. 354 U.S. 178 no. 261, which was argued March 7, 1957.

bars any Smith Act indictment under the "organize' section. The word "organize" was being construed in its narrow sense, meaning that simply bringing a Communist group into being was found to be cause for indictment. The Court held the Communist Party had been organized in its present form by 1954 at the latest and that, in 1951 when the indictment was brought against the leaders, the three year statue of limitations had run out. . . .   □

20.   # The Civil Rights Act of 1957

My Day, August 6, 1957

Hyde Park—The Senate has voted to attach a modified jury trial amendment to the civil rights bill. The amendment will permit the judge to decide in cases of civil contempt, but will require a jury trial in cases of criminal contempt.

A civil contempt case would not require a jury trial because in such a case the judge would simply be insisting that his orders be carried out. For instance, a judge might order an election official to permit a qualified Negro to register, and could jail the official for civil contempt until he permitted the Negro to register, but as soon as the official had done so he could no longer be held in jail.

A criminal case would be brought against an individual who willfully disobeyed or obstructed the purpose of a judge's order. As an example if a judge had issued an order forbidding the intimidation of voters and somebody threatened a man who was trying to vote, that somebody would be tried for criminal contempt. As I understand it, the judge would determine what is civil and what is criminal contempt.

It seems to me that in all these discussions, our lawmakers have neglected to face the fact that we have states which make it practically impossible for a Negro to register. He may be perfectly well qualified to vote, by all ordinary standards, but no one could answer some of the questions put to him. And even if he manages to answer them correctly, a Negro's application can simply be accepted, and he is told that it must come before the election board, and there the matter rests, and he never hears of it again and goes on being an unqualified Negro voter— or rather, non-voter.

I can see why many liberals are hesitant to take any action that appears to be against trial by jury, for this has always been considered one of our greatest assets in achieving justice for the individual. Yet the whole point of the Southerners' fight for the jury trail amendment is that they know a white jury will not give Negroes the right to vote. This is just a way of escaping from having to face the quite different problem of coming out against the right of Negroes to vote, which is the right of every American citizen. ☐

21. Stevenson on the Civil Rights Bill

My Day, August 9, 1957

Hyde Park— I had the pleasure of seeing Mr. Adlai Stevenson for a short time the other afternoon, just after he had faced a mammoth press conference. It is rather hard, I think, to be asked so many questions about the situation in the United States on the first day you are back here from travels abroad. You have hardly had time to catch your breath before you are asked about things that you have only seen reported in foreign papers, and it is extremely difficult to be prepared to answer.

I agreed entirely, however, with what Mr. Stevenson said on the civil rights bill. He would prefer to have even the little that will come with this bill than to have nothing.

In his travels, he has had the opportunity to see the change that is coming about, even in the last two years, among peoples in many areas of the world. As in central Africa, for instance. Mr. Stevenson knows, therefore, how important what we do there is for our position in countries where people want freedom and respect as human beings and a chance to grow. Little as this civil rights bill seems to do, it will at least give us some chance of growing, in this country.

I think the Southern Senators, led by Senator Lyndon Johnson and Senator Richard Russell [D-Georgia], have won a costly victory—because this fight for civil rights is not going to stop. If the people of Africa are on the move, the people of the United States are also on the move. Our people are not going to be satisfied with crumbs such as this civil rights bill gives them. It will bring us no peace, but it is better to pass it and see what we can achieve with even this slight change.

I hear from Washington, however, that the Republicans, in all probability, will just let it lie over and do nothing, and then will try to use it as an issue in the next campaign. Vice-President Richard Nixon and Senator Johnson both are trying to

fool the people, white and colored people alike. It will be interesting to see how
far they succeed.   ☐

22.   Correspondence with Lyndon Johnson
       Regarding the Above Column

August 17, 1957

Dear Senator Johnson:
    I am sorry that you are disappointed in my support but you must realize that
I understand very well your extremely clever strategy on the Civil Rights Bill.
You may not have been "trying to fool the people" but you chose the one point
on which good people might have some qualms and you built on that and that is
why you have a goodly company of people with you. The end result, however, is
that the Bill with this amendment will do very little since the "qualified voter"
still has to qualify according to the laws of the states and none of you have
touched on that particular point at any time. I have said that it is best to accept
this bill than to have nothing, and even the NAACP agrees on that, but it would
be fooling the people to have them think that this was a real vital step toward
giving all our people the right to vote or any other civil rights.
    I doubt if the Republicans ever really intended to do anything along this line
but I can't say that I really believe the Democrats have intended to do much either, particularly those of you who come from Southern states or borderline
states as Texas is.
    I admire your ability as a leader. You have certainly done a remarkable piece
of work and I know how persuasive you are, but it is easier to look at actual results when you sit at a distance and are not really affected by what happens one
way or another, and that is what I have been doing. I hope you pass the Bill and I
shall say that it is better because it will at least show the world that we have
moved a little but it will be a very little towards that fundamental right of every
citizen—the right to vote.
    Now may I add that I have pointed out in a column which will come out of
Tuesday that I fully expect that as Senate Leader you will cooperate with Senator [William] Knowland [R-California] and put back many of the foreign aid
cuts, if not all. If the House Bill were approved there would be real harm done

to the UN programs and foreign aid all the way down the line would suffer. I have said in this column that you and Senator [Mike] Mansfield [D-Montana] are too statesmanlike to allow this to happen though it is a perfectly natural desire to want to show up the Republicans in their leadership. You would not allow this desire to influence you in your decision as to the real good of the country.

I hope I am correct in believing this and I am sorry to have caused you disappointment for, like everyone else, I find you a delightful and persuasive person and I have great admiration for your ability, but on the Civil Rights issue I am afraid I must hold to my own opinion.

Very Cordially yours,   □

LBJ's Reply

August 22, 1957

Dear Mrs. Roosevelt:

I am not seeking to prolong an argument and I recognize that honorable people can always draw different conclusions from the same set of facts. But I am afraid that someone has misled you on one of the basic factors involved in the bill.

No one touched upon the point that voters will have to qualify under the laws of the individual States simply because that could be effected only by changing the Constitution itself and the facts are that no Constitutional amendment on that question could be attempted at this time. It would encounter strong opposition—not just from the South but from all sections of the country.

However it has been pretty well agreed that it is not the State laws which prevent people from voting but the administration of the State laws. The bill definitely gives the Federal government power to intervene whenever the laws are being maladministered to deprive people of the right to vote. It would definitely cover the cases that were presented to the House Committee by the Justice Department during the course of the hearings.

Of course, the bill will not help anyone vote if it is not passed. At the present time, those who seek an issue rather than a bill are grabbing all possible sources of ammunition to prevent passage.

I am hoping that the Senate will restore a considerable part of the mutual security money that was cut by the House. However, it will be extremely difficult simply because the case of the money has not been presented properly by the Administration. The officials of the government who are explaining the measure to the Appropriations Committee seem to think that Madison Avenue slogans are a substitute for cold, hard facts and they are not very helpful to those of us who do not want to see America's foreign policy go down the drain.

I wish that the program had been handled more forthrightly all along. We would not be facing some of our difficulties if there had been more candor as to the real problems of the last few years.

Sincerely,

23.   "Ike—'Nice Man, Poor Leader'; Nixon— 'Anything to Get Elected'"

Interviewed by Carl Rowan

Minneapolis Morning Tribune, September 13, 1957

Eleanor Roosevelt's opinion of Dwight David Eisenhower as a president is a bit less than flattering.

Her opinion of Richard Nixon, the man she fears will be the next president, is decidedly bad.

And her opinion of John Foster Dulles, Ike's Secretary of State, probably would be said in language the lady doesn't use.

Mrs. Roosevelt sees Dwight Eisenhower as a nice man who sincerely hates war, but she said he's too poor a leader to move a confused world toward peace.

And this "new Republicanism" is mostly talk, she says, "for when it comes to a basic change in GOP economic theory, Ike certainly has none of his own."

Mrs. Roosevelt confesses that "I'm very prejudiced where Nixon is concerned. I don't believe that he really has any convictions of his own. I get the feeling that he is displaying and will display whatever policies will get him to the White House."

"Actually, since his strongest conviction seems to be to do what the most voters want strongly, this may turn out to be an advantage if he is the next president, as is very possible."

Mrs. Roosevelt's assertion that Nixon will "do anything to get elected" stems primarily from her contention that he "employed a Communist issue he knew to be false" in 1950 when he defeated Mrs. Helen Gahagan Douglas, an old friend of Mrs. Roosevelt's, in the California Senate race.

Mrs. Roosevelt says Nixon accused Mrs. Douglas of being a Communist "because he knew that was how he would be elected" even though "he knew quite well that she was not a Communist."

She said she always has felt that "anyone who wanted an election so much that they would use those means did not have the character that I really admired in public life."

Mrs. Roosevelt says President Eisenhower has failed abysmally to give leadership to a country trying to lead the world—and this is why she steadfastly opposed making a military man president.

"Any military man in a civilian post of that kind is at a disadvantage," she explained. "A military man has been led to expect certain codes of conduct from every one in a military regime. But this is not always present in a civilian regime."

She recalled that of all the military men she knew during FDR's and Truman's regime, Gen. George C. Marshall was the best civilian administrator.

He was "remarkable as secretary of state," she says, yet things went wrong in some important diplomatic dealings, and Marshall was stunned because subordinates gave neither the loyalty nor the performances he had expected as a matter of routine.

"President Eisenhower also has the disadvantage of not getting from his staff—as he would in the military—the facts on which to act," Mrs. Roosevelt continued.

"In civilian cases, too much evaluation involves personal political and other prejudices, and unless a president is able to back up reports given to him with his own knowledge and evaluation, he is at a sad disadvantage."

"Mr. Eisenhower's knowledge is not adequate to meet the situations he has faced and will face," she added.

Mrs. Roosevelt cited foreign affairs as a most critical area in which poor advice and a personal lack of knowledge have made it impossible for Mr. Eisenhower to lead properly.

"He is taking Dulles' advice on whatever the foreign affairs situation might be, and I have felt that the failure that we have seen in our foreign affairs is a failure to act fast enough to forestall crises," she said.

"When crises are upon us, we then meet them in any way that we can—sometimes well, sometimes badly—but they are forced upon us by someone else's action. . . . well the Suez crisis is the best example of that.

"We asked Britain to withdraw her troops from Egypt. The supposition was that in doing that we had a very definite policy of how we would then move to make it possible to keep the Suez canal open and get another agreement that would really lead toward a settlement of difficulties in that area.

"Instead, we could only dillydally.

"We didn't communicate with our allies, so they became frustrated and despondent and felt that nothing was happening even though their vital interests were at stake and the whole economy of western Europe was going down hill.

"I was told after the invasion of Egypt that had the British and French waited two weeks more we hoped to have an understanding with Nasser.

"Well, why on earth hadn't we kept our allies in close touch?

"We have allowed things to just happen without being prepared to deal with them.

"I don't think that's real statesmanship. I think that's neglect."

Intimates say there is a long-standing mutual lack of admiration between Mrs. Roosevelt and Dulles, brought to a peak near the end of Mrs. Roosevelt's tour of duty as a United Nations delegate.

They say the best way to get a bona fide belly laugh out of her is to mention that November day in 1948 when the United States mission of the U.N. got ready for a briefing sessions in Paris with all eyes still glued on the late election returns from the United States.

Some eager beaver on the staff was so sure Dewey had been elected president and that John Foster Dulles was of that moment a sort of secretary of state-designate that he switched the chairs around to give Dulles the "spot of honor" at the head of the briefing table.

Just as the mission members assembled word came through that Truman apparently had won and there was a mad scramble to put Dulles down the table where he was before.

Mrs. Roosevelt says shortly after Mr. Eisenhower's election in 1952, even before Dulles had become secretary of state, he wrote her that her services would not be needed on the next United States delegation to the U.N.

Mrs. Roosevelt replied that she was aware "that all ambassadors submit their resignations on Dec. 31, and mine will be in."

Ike's troubles with Congress stem directly from his lack of leadership, particularly where severe cuts were made in foreign aid and in funds for the United States Information Agency, Mrs. Roosevelt says.

"Congress is very economically minded, largely because they are discouraged with the results of much of our spending," she asserted.

"Congressmen don't realize that we should review our whole foreign aid program. We have put too much of our foreign aid into military assistance.

"All the military assistance given to states in the Near East is utter and complete waste because unless you raise the level of daily life for the people of many of these countries they have nothing worth fighting for."

Mrs. Roosevelt thinks congress has yielded to "a feeling of frustration," that like the ordinary citizen, the congressman is asking what we have accomplished with our aid money in recent years.

"Many people write me asking if we have bought friendship," she added. "It seems perfectly obvious that you never buy friendship; you may buy certain attitudes for a while, but never real friendship.

"Our aid is meant to give people the strength to stand up with dignity and to follow leadership that they respect.

"But all is lost, of course, if we give them no leadership to follow."   ☐

24.   "Why I Am Opposed to 'Right to Work' Laws"

American Federationist, February 1959

I am frequently asked why I oppose laws which certain groups are trying to enact in our states under such slogans as "right to work," "voluntary unionism" and the like.

I am glad to give my views because much confusion as to the wisdom of this legislation has resulted from misrepresentations by its sponsors.

I feel that if I can help clear away the fog, I will have performed a useful service to my fellow Americans.

If our nation is to meet the needs of today and continue to go forward, all of us must be able to distinguish that which is good for the general welfare from that which is bad. I consider "right to work" laws to be bad for the individual states and bad for the nation.

They are bad not just for working people but for employers as well, many of whom shortsightedly support this legislation.

Such laws would impose grave injustices on all working people. But employers would suffer, too, for the end result would be not only lower wages but a shrinking national economy and a drying up of purchasing power for America's mass production economy.

This would mean that our farmers also would be hurt. Everybody would be harmed in one way or another.

Most people realize we are a nation of workers and that whatever is harmful to the majority of our citizens is hurtful to the whole nation. It follows, then, that every man and woman who is dependent upon a job for his livelihood should understand the time bomb that is concealed in these laws under plausible-sounding but untruthful slogans and labels.

The labels "right to work," "voluntary unionism," "voluntary union membership" and the like are misnomers, of course.

They are the sugar coating to make palatable the bitter pill of the real intent of the laws which, I am afraid, most people do not take the time to read.

The "right to work" label is an implied promise that the legislation does not carry out. Such laws do not guarantee anyone a job or even the right to have a job.

The "voluntary union membership" slogan is another deceptive distortion to divert attention from the fact that this legislation makes legal a compulsory open shop, destroying the right of employers and employees to agree mutually on a union shop at the collective bargaining table.

This right is, of course, a key provision of the federal Taft-Hartley Act. Therefore, the agitation to enact state "right to work" laws is a highly suspect maneuver to override and nullify federal law.

As simply as I can say it, I am opposed to "right to work" legislation because it does nothing for working people, but instead gives employers the right to exploit labor. Not only does it do nothing for working people, but it robs them of the gains they have made over more than a half century of bitter struggle for betterment.

These rights to a fair return for their labor and skills, to decent working hours and reasonable job security were first recognized nationally, and became federal labor policy, in the presidential administration of my late husband.

I believe the Wagner Labor Act of 1936 was, in its way, as important a contribution to human progress as the Magna Carta and our own Bill of Rights were to our forebears.

I cannot bring myself to believe that anyone in his right mind would seriously advocate abolition of the freedoms brought into being by those documents.

Nor can I believe that the majority of our people will permit a backward step through "right to work" laws toward the grinding toil and impoverishment that were the workers' lot in the past century.

I am glad that my faith in the wisdom of our people was borne out in the November election. As we all know, five out of six states where "right to work" was an issue voted overwhelmingly against it.

I thought Senator Lyndon Johnson expressed it very well when he said the election outcome showed Americans "will not veto the Twentieth Century."

The election result has taught the "right to work" sponsors at least one lesson. In New Mexico, since the election, they have changed their name from "Citizens' Right to Work Committee" to "Educational Committee for Voluntary Union Membership." But I do not believe this new slogan will deceive our citizens any more than did the "right to work" label.

As I have said, our federal laws clearly state workers have a right to a voice in determining what shall be fair pay for their labor and skills. These laws provide that a majority of workers in a plant may select a trade union of their choice to represent them in collective bargaining with management.

This certainly seems a fair arrangement to me. The workers gain strength by sticking together which they otherwise would not have. The union provides them with a voice through which to present their side.

But suppose workers had no unions to represent them. Each employee would have to make his own arrangement with his employer. What chance would one worker have in an argument with management over a pay raise or better working conditions?

And if the employer decided he could hire two young workers for the wage he was paying an older, more experienced hand, what could the older worker do about it without the collective strength of a union to protect his rights?

The federal labor-management act also provides for reasonable union security. If a majority of workers decide there should be a union security clause, and this is agreed to by management, then it becomes a part of the contract and a "condition of employment."

A worker does not have to be a member of the union to get a job. But he is expected to become a member of the union after a period of thirty to sixty days.

This gives the union fair and reasonable security to carry out its responsibilities with the employer which arise because under the Taft-Hartley Act the union must by law represent all employees in the plant.

It would not be fair to the majority of workers, who have chosen a union to represent them and pay dues to support the continuing costs of union organization, to have to pay for obtaining a wage increase, or to prevent a wage cut, for a few workers who might try to get these benefits free.

A union requires membership of all in the plant, too, to prevent watering down of its strength through normal turnover or employment expansion and to combat establishment of a company-dominated union or non-union shop.

Here, again, the principle of union security is not only recognized by federal law but is in keeping with the American system of democratic government, which says that the will of the majority shall prevail.

It is this union security clause which gives workers a fair balance with management at the collective bargaining table. Without it, the strength of the workers' union can be whittled down to the point where an employer can pay the lowest possible wages.

It is at this keystone of strength that the "right to work" sponsors have aimed their laws. When this is understood I feel sure all will agree that it shows the true purpose of these laws as seeking first to weaken and in the end to destroy all unions, and with them the whole structure of collective bargaining between labor and management.

To make this part of the American democratic system appear odious and suspect, the "right to work" sponsors use another slogan. They call the union shop clause "compulsory unionism," which, as I have explained, is not true. This is simply a demagogic maneuver by employers to play on man's natural feeling that no one should be forced to do what he does not want to do.

It is a "nice" way of putting controlling power back into the hands of employers.

The extent to which "right to work" sponsors go to try to make us believe they are something they are not would be ludicrous were the aim of their deceptions not so dangerous to the nation's welfare.

Someone sent me a copy of a recent leaflet put out over the name of a so-called "National Right to Work Committee." It has on its cover the figure of a man, obviously representing "management," shaking hands with another, obviously a worker. The caption reads: "A coalition of employers and employees united in a common cause."

The inference, of course, is that employers are sponsoring "right to work" laws to help the workers, and that workers are behind them, when nearly everyone knows this is just the opposite of fact and truth.

By now it is certainly well known that sponsorship of "right to work" laws stems from the National Association of Manufacturers, the U.S. Chamber of Commerce and the American Farm Bureau Federation which they control, and that the large amounts of money spent in various states in an attempt to force passage of the laws comes mainly from some of our large corporations.

Perhaps it is not as widely known that the National Association of Manufacturers launched its first campaign to "break" trade unions at its national convention in 1903—more than a half century ago—and has been hard at it ever since.

As to the question of whether workers look to employers or trade unions to protect their interests, we have the answer in U.S. government records.

Between 1947 and 1951 the federal government conducted 46,119 secret ballot elections on the question of whether workers want the union shop. In 97 percent of the elections the workers voted for the union shop.

I think it is not unreasonable to question the motives of the "right to work" sponsors in view of these facts.

I can best sum up my opposition to "right to work" laws in these words:

I am opposed to this legislation because it is narrow in concept, punitive and discriminatory against wage-earners, and is designed solely to benefit employers.

I am opposed to it because its real aim is to destroy American labor.

I am opposed to it because the campaign to enact "right to work" laws is based on dishonesty and deception.

I am opposed because it would upset the present balance between labor and management that has become a basic guarantee of a prosperous national economy.

I am opposed to "right to work" laws because they promote industrial strife instead of industrial peace.

It is true that unions have become powerful over the years. But we should not forget that the power of the unions is puny compared to the power that goes with the enormous wealth of Big Business. And business had power first.

Whether unions have grown and with this growth have become powerful is not the problem today.

The problem, rather, is to make both labor and business feel the responsibility that goes with power, and to use this power mutually for the benefit of all. ☐

25. ## Statement on Behalf of the National Consumers League

Before the Subcommittee on Labor and Public Welfare,
United States Senate, May 14, 1959

I am very happy to have the opportunity to talk to you gentlemen this morning, because the bill before you (S. 1046) is one about which I have very strong feelings and convictions. I was eighteen years old when I first went for the Consumers League into sweatshops in New York City. (By the way, I am speaking to you today for the National Consumers League of which for many, many years I have been a vice-president.) For the first time in my life I saw conditions I would not have believed existed—women and children working in dark, crowded, dirty quarters, toiling, I was told, all day long and way into the night, to earn a few pennies, carding safety pins or making little things of feathers.

Those conditions I can never forget. So when some twenty years ago the Congress passed and my husband signed the Fair Labor Standards Act, I rejoiced. At last we had tackled on a national scale the basic problem of poverty—the non-living wage. The minimum wages established in 1938 were low, 25 cents to begin with, later increased to 30 cents and then to 40 cents an hour. But low as they were, they provided a floor below which in those depression days no worker, covered by the Act, could legally be paid. That was a tremendous step forward and a firm foundation on which to build.

I am glad to say in the past 20 years we have made some progress. We have gone from 40 cents an hour to 75 cents, and today our minimum wage is $1.00 an hour. But the cost of living has risen too. I am sure that none of us here believes that a workman who is paid $1.00 a hour today is four times better off than he was in 1938 when his wage was 25 cents an hour. Nor do we believe it was the intent of the Congress, which passed the Fair Labor Standards Act, that the standard of living of workers at the minimum level should remain static—that the minimum wage should increase only as much as the cost of living rises. I am sure it was the hope of Congress that as we worked out of the depression into better times, the lowest as well as the highest paid workers should share in the growing national prosperity, and that as the economy can afford it the minimum wage should be increased. Certainly the present proposed increase of 25 cents an hour is modest indeed. I read only recently that a workman would have to earn $2.25 an hour in order to provide a family of four with the food, clothing, shelter and other necessities contained in a "modest but adequate" budget prepared a few years ago for a working man's family by the Department of Labor. And yet I understand that the wages of millions of workers would be increased by the adoption of the $1.25 rate.

My friends have been telling me of a recent attempt in Texas to establish a legal minimum wage in that state of 50 cents an hour. Studies showed that department stores were paying wages of $18 to $25 a week; laundries from $12.50 to $35; restaurants were paying kitchen help as little as $15 a week. The arguments raised against establishing any legal minimum wage were the same as those which have been used by employers over the past 50 years. The proposed 50-cent minimum wage would be a "socialistic toehold" toward a higher minimum. It would ruin many small businesses. The state would be taking over and ruining free private enterprise.

I have always believed that in a democracy it is the obligation of the government to give to its citizens the protection and care they need for the benefit of the individual, the family and the nation as a whole. Comparatively few workers earning less than $1.25 an hour today belong to labor unions. Therefore, they are in a very poor position to bargain individually with their employers for higher wages. For them the state and the federal governments have an obligation to set a floor below which no employer may go in setting wages. I believe a minimum wage law is a protection for decent businessmen as well, men who recognize the need and wisdom of paying adequate living wages, but who must meet the competition of less conscientious employers who use wage cutting as a means of gain. Moreover, our entire economy would benefit if millions of workers at the minimum level were enabled by a 25 cent increase in the hourly minimum wage to buy more food, clothing and medical care they so badly need.

I understand the bill Mr. [John] Kennedy and Mr. [Wayne] Morse are sponsoring would not only raise the minimum wage but would bring minimum wage protection to 7 or 8 million more workers than are now covered by the Fair Labor Standards Act. This I think is very important. There is no moral or economic justification which I can see for protecting the families of one group of American workmen against want and not protecting the others. I realize the federal government has the constitutional authority to legislate only for those industries engaged in or affecting interstate commerce. But I see no legal excuse for the Congress exempting any workers who have the constitutional right to be covered from the provisions of the Fair Labor Standards Act.

I want to say an urgent word for a group of workers which is always left out when social legislation is written. They are the expendables. The ones who are bargained out of a piece of social legislation as the price for getting something else in. I am speaking of farm laborers, including the migratory agricultural workers and their families. Today they compare economically to the workers in the industrial sweatshops of the early 1900s.

I know that the bill to amend the Fair Labor Standards Act which you are considering today does not provide protection for agricultural workers. But I understand that Mr. McNamara and Mr. Clark are sponsoring a bill in the Senate which would provide for legal minimum wages for farm laborers. I presume you will be holding hearings on Senators McNamara's and Clark's bill later on in the session. But as it may be impossible for me to appear at that time, I want to take this opportunity to tell you how exceedingly important I think it is that immediate action be taken to relieve the plight of these unfortunate citizens.

I am a member of the National Advisory Committee on Farm Labor, and have had ample opportunity to know of the misery and destitution of farm workers and their families. Poor housing, low wages, child labor, all the privations and sufferings that go with poverty. I always like to quote from government bulletins when citing figures, because I believe they seldom exaggerate a situation. So let me tell you the annual earnings reported by the Department of Agriculture last September for hired farm workers in the United States for 1958. Migratory farm workers earned on the average $745 for the year from agricultural employment. Nonmigratory farm workers earned $737. The migrants increased their earnings to $859 by working an average of 16 additional days at non-farm labor; and the nonmigrant workers by working an average of 20 days off the farm added $161 to their average annual earnings, bringing the total to $895.

These figures speak for themselves. That no family could more than subsist on such earnings is obvious. To relieve their suffering they must depend on charity in times of sickness, unemployment and other emergencies. [Labor] Secretary [James] Mitchell said at a recent meeting on the problems of farm labor:

> It is intolerable and indecent for a society to produce by overworking and under-paying human beings. Even if the product may cost more, we, in this country, usu-ally accept the difference in cost because it is the man—that counts—not the thing. . . . It is my conviction that the migrant farm worker will never take his place as a fully useful citizen, and never be able to successfully resist exploitation, until, first, federal legislation guarantees him a decent minimum wage upon which he can build a decent and independent life.

Much needs to be done for these people. They should be covered by unemploy-ment and workmen's compensation laws. The application of the Social Security Act to farm workers should be improved. Better housing, medical care, educa-tion for their children should be provided. But the most immediate need is a minimum wage law that will assure decent wages to these hard-working, ne-glected American citizens.

Hand-in-hand with a minimum wage law should go a measure to prohibit the employment of little children in commercialized agriculture. Thousands of chil-dren, 8, 9, 10 years of age and even younger work in the fields beside their par-ents day after day. One understands why such conditions seem necessary when one knows what the parents earn. Every additional penny earned relieves a bit the desperate family need. But doctors, educators, social workers all know that growing children suffer more from fatigue than do adults. The American Med-ical Association has recommended for the protection of children's health "a gen-eral 14-year minimum age requirement for the employment of children."

You know, of course, that the Fair Labor Standards Act prohibits the employ-ment of children under 16 years of age during school hours in industry. Outside of school hours the employment of youngsters under 14 years is illegal. To me the importance of extending these same regulations to the employment of chil-dren in agriculture cannot be too strongly emphasized. I am not proposing that parents living on small family farms should not be allowed to use their own chil-dren to help with the family chores. I am speaking only of children employed on commercial farms as hired labor.

I thank you, gentlemen, for this opportunity to talk to you about these serious matters which are before you, and to congratulate you on your efforts to find ef-fective ways of reducing the extent of our social and economic problems.   □

26.   ## Lyndon Johnson and the Civil Rights Act of 1960

My Day , April 11, 1960

New York—It is a good thing that the Senate has finally passed the civil rights bill after an eight-week fight, with 42 Democrats and 29 Republicans in favor. This is only the second civil rights legislation to pass the Senate since the Reconstruction Era. The first civil rights act of 1957 was also a voting rights measure. Already those who want a really fair bill giving the Negroes their full rights are denouncing this bill, and I am quite sure that it will continue to be denounced. But I hope that it is at least a step in the right direction.

All of us in the Democratic party, I think, owe Senator Johnson a vote of thanks. He has risked repercussions among his Southern colleagues and among his own constituents. He has made it possible for the Democrats to claim equal, if not more, responsibility for the passage of the bill which of course should never have had to be passed—for the right to vote should be something which every citizen of this country enjoys without any question. Since it was necessary to pass the bill, however, we are fortunate to have had a parliamentary leader with the skill of Senator Johnson.

My own fear is of intimidation which I feel sure will be tried to prevent Negro citizens in the South from registering and voting. I hope the Attorney General can find ways of protecting the registration and of preventing retaliation when the Negro citizens of the South exercise their constitutional right. . . .   □

27.   ## Stevenson, Kennedy and the 1960 Democratic Convention

My Day, July 12, 1960

Los Angeles—I am glad that Adlai Stevenson has said that if nominated he would campaign vigorously. I hope it will be the kind of campaign which he made in 1952.

In 1956, I felt that he and Sen. Estes Kefauver had worn themselves out in the primary campaign and that the campaign against their real rivals, the Republican candidate, was thereby weakened. As a result, they listened to advisers without really asserting their own natural tendencies.

Mr. Stevenson was a better campaigner in 1952 than in 1956, and if he should be nominated, I hope he will campaign as he did in 1952.

From the pre-convention reports, I gathered that with Sen. Lyndon Johnson's arrival in Los Angeles he had begun to attack Sen. John Kennedy as his main rival. I do not feel that Sen. Stuart Symington has enough strength to be of much importance in the fight between the two main contenders.

If it should turn out that Senator Johnson can really bring about a stalemate, then, it seems to me, it is obvious Senator Kennedy, with his liberal feelings, will have to turn to Mr. Stevenson. He cannot allow what might be called the more conservative wing of the party to really win, even if he himself is obliged to take second place.

I personally do not think Senator Kennedy's age should be attacked, but we want the best ticket we can have because we want to win as strongly as possible in November. Without a question that ticket seems to me to be Stevenson and Kennedy.

With such a ticket, labor will know that its interests are safeguarded. And business will know that they have an administration that will analyze financial and economic problems and deal with them in a careful and imaginative way.

Men like Chester Bowles, Hubert Humphrey and the better leaders in labor and in all the religious and racial groups also will know that they are dealing with men who believe that the good of human beings has to be considered, and that the future well-being of the United States, economically and socially, lies in our understanding of our own interests in the context of the world situation.

A Stevenson-Kennedy ticket, with the men they would draw around them, would give confidence to the world in a way that no other ticket I can think of would do. It would probably not please the conservative Republicans nor the reactionary Democrats, and as a ticket it would mean that reactionary elements of the South would be very unhappy.

These reactionaries would know that law enforcement would be considered important and, while common sense would be used, there would certainly be a steady pressure for the acceptance of the fact that our attitude on civil rights is of paramount interest because it affects our leadership throughout the world.

We could not successfully fight the battle against communism in the world unless at home we demonstrated that we believed in equal opportunity for all our citizens and that in a democracy each individual had equal rights and dignity before the law.   □

28.   # Campaigning for Kennedy

Four Selections

My Day, August 17, 1960

New York—In my conversation with Sen. John Kennedy at Hyde Park Sunday, I was anxious, needless to say, to find out if he and Adlai Stevenson had planned to work closely on foreign affairs during the campaign.

I knew there would be no question of Rep. Chester Bowles working closely with the Senator, because it was for this purpose that he withdrew as a candidate for re-election to Congress. And I felt sure that it would be easy for Senator Kennedy and Representative Bowles to work together.

Senator Kennedy has a quick mind, but I would say that he might tend to arrive at judgments almost too quickly. Therefore, it seemed important to me that he should have a good relationship during the campaign with Mr. Stevenson, thereby demonstrating that their philosophies are sufficiently similar so that they could work well together in the future, even though Mr. Stevenson has a more judicial and reflective type of mind.

I was pleased to learn that the Senator had made plans much along these lines. It gave me a feeling of reassurance.

Our Democratic candidate is a likeable man with charm, and I think that already, since the convention, the difficulties and responsibilities that the future may hold for him as President have opened up new vistas for him and brought about a greater maturity.

I think Senator Kennedy is anxious to learn. I think he is hospitable to new ideas. He is hard-headed. He calculates the political effect of every move. I left my conversation with him with the feeling that here is a man who wants to leave a record of not only having helped his countrymen, but having helped humanity as a whole.

I had withheld my decision on joining Herbert Lehman as honorary chairman of the Democratic Citizens Committee of New York until I had a chance to see and talk with our Democratic candidate. After Senator Kennedy's visit, I telephoned my acceptance to serve with Mr. Lehman, and I told Senator Kennedy that I would discuss what help in the campaign I could give, for I have come to the conclusion that the people will have in John F. Kennedy, if he is elected, a good President.

As the weeks go by I hope I will have an opportunity to see our candidate more and to know him better, but I have enough confidence in him now to feel that I can work wholeheartedly for his election. . . .

My Day, November 11, 1960

Castine, Maine—Here it is Thursday morning and still the popular vote count is not fully in from California nor from one or two other doubtful states. But the electoral vote is firmly for Sen. John F. Kennedy, so we can say that as a nation we will embark on a new course.

Already Senator Kennedy has said that he counts on moving swiftly after the inauguration on January 20. I hope, however, that he will take no responsibility for policy before he is able also to be responsible for personnel and for methods by which any policy is carried out. I am sure he will obtain as quickly as possible all the information the President has promised to share with him to help in an orderly change of administration. The responsibility remains with the President and the Republican Party until Inauguration Day.

The President-elect will need all the youth and energy and health, which fortunately he seems to have, to meet the problems that are going to engage him from the first day of his responsibility. In his favor, too, will be a Congress of his own party. And if there still remains the possibility of a coalition of reactionary Republicans and certain reactionary Democrats, there also can be a coalition of progressive Republicans and Progressive Democrats. So I think with his great power as President and the prestige of winning in this close election, Mr. Kennedy will be able to carry out his pledge to "the long-range interests of the United States and the cause of freedom around the world."

There is one important goal I hope he can achieve, and that is to develop among the people of the country a sense that he is their man and that he is working for them and needs their help. It will take the best that is in the people of this country to uphold him and make him a strong President and a strong leader of the whole United States.

. . . . It will be a good example to many parts of the world that such a close election can be accepted and be followed by closing our ranks behind the new President. In some areas of the world such a result might well mean a revolution and a refusal to accept the verdict on the part of the loser.

We are the example of a democracy in action as a government. Vice-President Richard M. Nixon has behaved in the best tradition. He must, of course, be bitterly disappointed. But he will have the opportunity to function in the business groups which he believes in, and he may well find that this world outside of politics may be more suited to his talents than the political world in which he has tried hard to rise. He, of course, still will have considerable power in his own party because of his heavy popular vote.

The real question for the people of the United States is whether they are prepared to face the fact that for the past eight years they have been sleeping; they
have not been told clearly enough that they are in a struggle for survival and
that either our system of freedom will prevail in the world or that the Soviet
system of communism will prevail. If we waken to the real challenge of the
world of today and put all that is best in us into our struggle at home and abroad
we can win. . . .

My Day, November 14, 1960

. . . Senator Kennedy took a risk in his campaign when he telephoned and
promised to help the Rev. Martin Luther King. He might have lost those Southern states he so sorely needed in the campaign. But he took the risks and he did
not lose those states. It may well be that similarly risks will have to be taken to
save humanity from itself. If so, I hope they will be taken with the same background of principle and high purpose, because that is the only way in which the
people can be brought to understanding and to action of their own in support of
their leaders.

My Day, December 27, 1960

. . . I think the storm of protest which has been aroused by the appointment of
Robert Kennedy to the Attorney-Generalship is beginning to seem foolish.
Granted that he is young, granted that he has no long experience as a lawyer behind him, he nevertheless has integrity. His ability seems to be unquestioned and
it is just possible that he understands certain phases of his brother's programs
better, and has a more comprehensive knowledge of them, than anyone else that
the President-elect has been able to find.

In this case, I doubt whether the President-elect is choosing his brother. I
think he is choosing a man whom he believes will get some of the things done
which he wants to accomplish.

With an Attorney General who will use his powers to the limit, a good deal can
be accomplished along the lines that I am sure the future President wants. Much
can be done for civil rights, something can be done to control the racketeers.

It may well be that after careful thought and search the President-elect has
decided that the qualities needed to carry through this job are found in his
brother. This judgment may be good or bad, but it seems to me that we might

wait with a little more calm to find out whether President-elect Kennedy's objectives are better obtained through the way he has chosen, or whether he
should have observed the unwritten tradition that having members of your
family in positions of government where they carry real responsibility is
dangerous.   ☐

29.   Presidential Commission on the Status of Women

My Day, February 16, 1962

Paris—Before coming over here my last two days in the United
States were spent largely in Washington, D.C., and I want to tell you about them
before writing about my current month-long trip.

On last Monday morning in the White House the President opened the first
meeting of the Commission on the Status of Women. . . .

We kept ourselves strictly on schedule all day and opened our afternoon
meeting promptly at two o'clock at 200 Maryland Avenue, below the Capitol,
where the Commission on the Status of Women will have its permanent office.

We soon began to discuss the best way to organize to achieve the maximum
of work not only on the six points laid down in the President's directive to the
commission but in other situations which will certainly arise. The commission
will try to make its influence felt concerning women's problems not only in the
Federal area but in state and local areas and in industry as well as in women's
home responsibilities.

The effort, of course, is to find how we can best use the potentialities of
women without impairing their first responsibilities, which are to their home,
their husbands and their children. We need to use in the very best way possible all our available manpower—and that includes womanpower—and this
commission, I think, can well point out some of the ways in which this can be
accomplished.

I was glad to hear brought up the question of part-time work for women and
of better training in certain areas because the possibilities available to women
could be more widely publicized and education could be directed to meet and
prepare for these new openings. . . .   ☐

30.   "The Social Revolution"

Tomorrow Is Now, Harper and Row, 1963

Be an opener of doors for such as come after thee, and do not try to make the
universe a blind alley.

—RALPH WALDO EMERSON

The economic revolution is bringing with it social changes that are
being felt everywhere. As the life of human beings is lifted above the animal
level, they become aware of new aspirations, beyond the immediate and pressing need for food to eat, and develop a passionate longing for independence.
What is stirring like yeast everywhere is the revolution of equality, the assertion
by men and women of their human dignity, and their demand for its recognition
and acceptance by others.

Certainly it is this particular revolution which the United States should be able
to win, hands down, because this is the concept upon which our life is based.

"We know," Barbara Ward wrote recently, "that the passionate desire of men
to see themselves as the equals of other human beings without distinctions of
class or sex or race or nationhood is one of the driving forces of our day."

We know—yes. But what are we doing about it? We are dealing today with
millions upon millions of people of diverse religions. That should be easy for us.
This country, after all, was founded upon the principle of religious freedom. But
how is it working out in actual practice?

Many of us still remember, with shame, the burning crosses, the revival of the
Ku Klux Klan that accompanied Al Smith's campaign for the Presidency. All of
us remember, more recently, during John Kennedy's campaign, the fantastic
claims that, if a Catholic were elected to the Presidency, the Pope would take
over the direction of the policies of the nation. Even now when this nonsense has
been shown to be without foundation, I know of no one who has withdrawn his
original cry of alarm or admitted that he was mistaken.

In a very real sense, the United States is the world's show window of the democratic processes in action. We know, too well, what people see when they
look in that window. They see Little Rock and Baton Rouge and New Orleans.
They see Albany, Georgia. They see the deep-rooted prejudice, the stubborn ignorance of large groups of our citizens, which have led to injustice, inequality,
and, sometimes, even brutality.

I think what most of us remember most vividly about the riots and the cruelty of Little Rock, Baton Rouge, and New Orleans is the pictures we saw in our

newspapers, pictures which gave us a tremendous shock when we realized what ugliness and degradation mass fear could bring out in human beings.

Grown women wanted to kill one poor little nine-year-old girl, one of the children going into the Little Rock school. The cold fact is hard to believe that anywhere in our country women would be screaming for the death of a child because she was going into a white school. Yet this is what happened. This was the result of mass fear and mass psychology.

The beast in us is something we have to learn to control. It would be wise if we came to realize how it functions on many different levels. Habit is one of the controlling factors. If we can learn to subdue the emotions arising from prejudice, if we can learn that the social revolution in which we are engaged should, among other things, provide all our people with an equal opportunity to enjoy the benefits that have been the privileges of a few, we are going to be astonished to discover that many whom we considered incapable of development were only underprivileged; that given the opportunity for education there are latent endowments which will be valuable not only to these people in themselves but to their country and the world as well.

It is this minority of strident and prejudiced people, with their unwillingness to accept race equality—at whatever cost—who provide the Communists with most of their ammunition against the democratic system, who are loudest in their expression of hatred for Communism.

One of the most difficult experiences I have ever been through was that of serving as Chairman for the Commission of Inquiry into the Administration of Justice in the Freedom Struggle, held in Washington in May of 1962. I found it difficult—and intolerably painful—to accept the fact that things such as I have described could happen here in these United States. This was the kind of thing the Nazis had done to the Jews of Germany—and there, also, as a misguided effort to demonstrate their race superiority.

Only by focusing the attention of the nation as a whole upon this situation can we find a remedy for it. The overwhelming pressure of public opinion would accomplish more than any other single factor to rectify the condition and to help eliminate it.

What emerged, of course, was that, as had been true since before the Civil War, it was largely whites whose economic condition was little better than that of the Negroes who represented the most virulent element, concentrating the chief hatred, prejudice, and—yes, downright brutality. It was, perhaps, the only way in which they could proclaim their superiority. They appeared to be terrified for fear the Negroes would be permitted to stand on their own merits, and might, in many cases, leave them far behind.

302 THE SOCIAL REVOLUTION

And here, too, emerged another and unmistakable similarity to the Nazism we had believed destroyed—at least in Germany. Most of the dictators of the West—Franco, Mussolini, Hitler—claimed that they were "saving" their lands from the threat of Communism. Today, as I have learned over and over to my cost, one needs only to be outspoken about the unfair treatment of the Negro to be labeled "Communist." I had regarded such expression to be the only honorable and civilized course for a citizen of the United States.

To digress for a moment, this recurring matter of labeling "Communist" anyone who does not agree with you is essentially an act of dishonesty and it should be nailed every time for what it is. Few of the Southern politicians who resented my stand on integration ever troubled to examine it. Instead they said "Communist." The Nazis excelled at this sort of thing. It has no place in America.

To return to the Commission of Inquiry, there appeared before us a succession of people who had set out to test the operation of the laws in regard to civil rights. The methods they used were peaceful enough. Some of them indulged in public prayer; some of them rode on buses to see whether segregation was still practiced on buses and in terminal facilities; some of them sat in at lunch counters for the same purposes; some of them picketed a segregated lunchroom for *one minute and a half!* And one young man was teaching Negroes, who had been driven from their farms for attempting to register to vote, how to make a kind of leather tote bag so that they could earn enough money to hold back starvation.

These were the people who suffered indignity, danger, arrest on preposterous charges; people who are even now facing incredibly long prison sentences; people who, in some cases, were treated with a brutality that sickens one to think of. . . .

I'd like to look for a moment at a few of these cases, at conditions that could only have existed because, as a people, we are paying only lip service to our democratic principles; we have, at least in this area, been tending to lose our social revolution.

Ronnie Moore was one of those who sat in at a lunch counter; one of those who participated in the picketing which lasted just one minute and a half. He was arrested and had to raise a cash bond of $1,500. Rearrested, the charge became "conspiracy to commit criminal mischief." There was an additional $2,000 bond. After serving twenty-one days in jail, he was released, and this time arrested for "criminal trespassing and disturbing the peace." (He was taking shelter from the rain.) By now the bond was up to $6,500.

For fifty-eight days, Ronnie and another young man were kept in a seven-by-seven-foot cell, without a window; and taken out only twice a week for a shower.

After his release there was a new charge, "criminal anarchy," and the bond had now reached a total of $16,500.

Let's take another case, that of a young Negro minister with a group of students who intended to pray and sing in protesting the arrest of the picketers. They sustained a barrage of forty-seven tear gas bombs; police dogs attacked them. Later, three hundred young students had to be treated for dog bites and tear gas, and for having been trampled upon.

A white boy named John Robert Zellner, the young son of a Methodist minister in south Alabama, was arrested for protesting the expulsion of a colored girl from a high school. The charge, ironically enough, was "disturbing the peace and contributing to the delinquency of a minor."

While he was a prisoner in the white section of the jail, the other white prisoners, furious because he was attempting to help Negroes, "threatened me with castration . . . said if I went to sleep I'd wake up with a knife in my back."

"I thought," Robert commented during his testimony, "it was quite ironic that the United States was able to launch a man into space and let him go around the world three times and yet they weren't able to take care of a small human relations problem."

Frank Nelson, another white man, who had been a student in engineering at Cooper Union and then served with the United States Coast Guard as a civil engineer, was asked: "Why are you, as a white person, participating in these activities?"

"Actually," he answered, "it was just a matter of getting down to finally doing what just about everybody thinks is correct and I . . . got tired of sitting around in the living room and discussing how bad things were . . . and finally decided to see if I could perhaps do something to change things."

How much must be changed was made clear in the repeated pictures of brutality: of policemen directing some of the vandalism, of the police dogs and the tear gas, of the young man who was blackjacked and had to have fifty-seven stitches taken in his head; of the white boy on whose hand they put what they called a "wrist breaker," a metal clamp which they tightened until the victim fainted several times from pain.

Then—unspeakable ugliness in this our own country—"An electric shock probe, used in stockyards to shock cattle and make them move along, was used around the private parts. It was very painful stuff. I was picked up and held in the air by the private parts." This was the young man who had attempted peacefully to teach the dispossessed Negroes to earn a living by making tote bags.

It was because of such people as this that Gerald Johnson, a Negro student, answered as he did when he was asked, "What made you get in all this trouble?"

"I have grown up under segregationist rule . . . and I didn't like the way things

worked. . . . When I heard people like Bob Zellner . . . the things that they have
been through for people like me . . . I couldn't face sitting back doing nothing,
and I don't want my children to grow up under something like that."

"In other words," he was asked, "you wanted to fight on the home front for
some of the liberties and privileges of American citizenship that the Negro soldiers fought overseas to guarantee to the rest of the world?"

"Right," he said.

When I first introduced this painful and shameful subject, I said that its solution rests with public opinion. So it does. The President of the United States can
lead only if he has followers. It is the voice of America that he must hear clearly.

Realizing at the inquiry that many of the young victims of race prejudice and
savagery were bitter about the kind of judges before whom their cases were
heard, I tried to make the following point:

I think you have to realize that under our political system, judges have to be
endorsed by the senators and congressmen of their district.

Now, unless you can awaken public opinion to have some effect in the South,
you are asking the President to risk very often a vote on his Administration's policy bills and perhaps not get them passed because he has refused to follow recommendations of the elected representatives of the district.

This points up, I think, the need for the individual citizen to be awakened and
held responsible, because it is the people in these areas who are really responsible.

They elect their representatives. They are the ones who feel this way and I think
they will respond to the real feeling of the rest of the country, if it is brought out
and crystallized and made clear what they are doing to their country in the eyes of
the world and in the eyes of their own nation and of their own people.

The great Russian pianist Anton Rubinstein once said hotly, "Despots never
think the people ripe enough for freedom." We still have too many people in this
country who feel that the Negro is not ripe for equality, in education, in the
economy, in housing, in opportunity.

If this is our lesson to the nations who are trying to bridge the gap between
primitive living and the age of nuclear fission, and to those other nations whose
culture was already old while ours was primitive, they can only reject it entirely. In making their great transition to the modern world, these people need all
the help we can give them; they need our respect; they need our recognition of
their essential dignity as human beings. But while we fail in such recognition to
those of our own people whose skins are colored—as are the skins of two out of
three of all the peoples of the world—they will never believe in our sincerity,
never believe that we pay more than lip service to the ideals of democracy which
we claim to defend.

One of our blind spots comes with the persistent and fondly cherished idea that, because some peoples have lagged behind in civilization and in cultural development, they are congenitally incapable of that development. This has been disproved over and over by such anthropologists as Margaret Mead. It can be disproved almost daily if we look about at some of the magnificent achievements of Negroes.

"You can't," say the people who take comfort in speaking in clichés, "change human nature."

Now the only way we can judge human nature is by human behavior, and behavior is modified and changed and developed and transformed by training and surroundings, by social customs and economic pressures. When we wince, sickened, at some of the grosser violence of an Elizabethan play, we are simply indicating that our "human nature" has undergone some drastic alterations in the past three hundred years.

Some years ago, I studied a snapshot which I have never forgotten. It was a picture showing two men standing outside a primitive grass hut in the Philippines. One of the men was naked except for a loincloth. He had wild bushy hair. In either hand he held a skull. He was a headhunter from the bush.

The young man beside him wore a white suit and glasses. In his hand he carried a small professional bag. He was a trained physician, working in the field of public health. He was the headhunter's son!

That transition, from headhunter to scientist, was not even the work of one generation; it was the work of perhaps fifteen years at the outside. What had been required to "change human nature" and make the leap from the Stone Age to the present? Opportunity, education, recognition of his human potentialities and a chance to be trained for a job in the field for which he was best suited.

But we must not overlook the operative factor. The young scientist had been trained. Too often, we tend to expect too much of people to whom we have given no training.

As far back as I can remember every attempt at improvement in the standard of living for Negroes was met by complaints that they were not ripe for equality. Because I was interested in housing, I was involved many years ago in one of the first slum clearance projects. People said, "It is ridiculous to give a bathroom to these people. They don't know how to use it. Some of them are keeping coal in the bathtub."

Our answer to that was to put a director in charge who helped people to learn about their new surroundings and to adapt to them. As soon as they became familiar with the various conveniences they used them properly.

Of course, difficulties are apt to develop if people are provided with modern conveniences without being given any guidance or instruction in their use. Certainly it is unfair to expect people without training to use properly what they have never encountered before.

And here, I think, there is a responsibility both for the whites and the Negroes. Too often, it is true, Negroes from underprivileged areas move into apartments or neighborhoods and, because they have been taught no better, clutter the hallways with filth and arouse reasonable resentment and alarm in the white tenants, who naturally do not want to see their way of life deteriorate. The function of democratic living is not to lower standards but to raise those that have been too low. . . .

If we are going to belong to our world we must take into account the fact that the majority of the peoples of the world are non-whites. We must learn to surmount this deep-seated prejudice about color. Certainly we must face the evidence that the color of the skin does not regulate the superiority or inferiority of the individual.

Now and then, when I have pointed out example after example of non-whites whose superiority in their fields cannot be challenged, I am told, "Oh, but those are exceptions." The same thing may be said of superior people among the white population. . . .

It is interesting to study our own racial problems and to compare them with the problems that exist in Africa. The basic issues are quite different. I have had African nationals tell me that the struggle for the liberation of the Africans from colonial powers was initiated by the efforts of the Africans themselves. Here in America, they said, it has nearly always been the whites and not the Negroes who saw the injustices and tried to correct them. Indeed, it is the success of the Africans in attaining their liberty, and the dignity that has grown out of their new status, that has lent a new spirit to our own Negroes.

Of course, one of the stumbling blocks in creating this equality in our own social revolution is another cliché like the one "You can't change human nature." This is used as a final stopper to any discussion of the subject. "Would you," these people ask, "like to see your daughter marry a Negro?"

Now this is a red herring if I ever saw one. Racial intermarriage is not involved in job equality, in educational equality, in housing equality. In fact, I strenuously doubt that any father who ever asked that challenging question had the slightest fear that his daughter wanted to marry a Negro. Nonetheless, the inference from his question is that his daughter is quite likely to do so unless she is prevented by the enforced segregation of Negroes.

All this is really preposterous. No one knows it as well as the person who clings to his question as though it were actually an answer to the problem. The immense majority of people instinctively seek their own kind. . . . The issue of intermarriage is used as a stumbling block in the path of human justice; it is used to hold back opportunity for millions of our citizens to develop their full potentialities in an ambience of mutual respect.

True, there are occasional—but very rare—cases of great attraction between different races. There are some successful marriages; for instance, those of Walter White with a white woman and Marian Anderson with a white man. And I know of others. But these, of course, are exceptional people, strong enough to escape the aura of martyrdom that so often hamstrings such a marriage.

But I still contend that the use of this fatuous question to prevent the development of the Negro race is essentially an act of dishonesty. It is used, like sleight of hand, to distract our attention from inequalities in wages, in living quarters, in education, that are an ineffaceable disgrace to us as a people.

It often seems to me that prejudice so blinds us that we see only what we expect to see, what we want to see. . . .

While it is essential for us to cope at once with the social revolution in this country we must, at the same time, learn to adjust to the social revolutions in other parts of the world. This is not only a matter of common decency, it is a matter of common sense. If there were no desire on the part of the African peoples to enter the modern world we would not be able to develop new markets for ourselves.

These people are looking for guidance on that long and difficult climb, a climb that they must make swiftly. . . .

Where are the Africans to turn for guidance? To the Eastern world or to the Western world? One thing is sure. We cannot convince them of the value of our ideas, our principles, and our ideals unless we know clearly what they are, unless we are able to express them, unless we are prepared to implement them. And we cannot address any people successfully unless we know and understand—and respect—that people.

We can no longer oversimplify. We can no longer build lazy and false stereotypes: Americans are like this, Russians are like that, a Jew behaves in such a way, a Negro thinks in a different way. The lazy generalities—"You know how women are. . . . Isn't that just like a man?"

The world cannot be understood from a single point of view.

If we cannot understand the people who make up our own country, how are we going to understand the people we are trying to lead in the world as a whole? The Soviets tell them that they are better suited to be of assistance to them because they are closer to their problems than we are. Our simple assertion that this is not true is meaningless. We must prove that it is not true.

How? Well, the Soviets invite people to their country and show them what they want them to see. But our country is open to all who wish to move around. They can judge for themselves. Both the good and the bad are open for inspection.

And, on the whole, even our bad spots are not as bad as most visitors have been led to believe. Often the reality of a situation will seem much better than the fantastic tales that have grown up about what actually goes on in our country. For instance, a few years ago, the idea of most Africans about what happened to the colored people in this country was so completely erroneous and exaggerated that the stories were unrecognizable. Whatever visitors from these countries saw here was a vast improvement on what they had been told. Nonetheless, our obligation to improve our own conditions is not diminished.

One thing is certain: in this modern world of ours we cannot afford to forget that what we do at home is important in relation to the rest of the world. The sooner we learn this, the sooner we will understand the meaning of our social revolution.

It is not too much to say that our adjustment to our own social revolution will affect almost every country in the world. Nor is it too much to say that we should be able to make our adjustment with comparative ease. What is required of us is infinitesimal compared to the adjustments that are to be made in the backward nations—in prejudice, in superstition, in ignorance, in habits and customs. They are coming out of the bush; we have only to come out of the darkness of our own blind prejudice and fear into the steady light of reason and humanity.

You will tell me, perhaps, that to cope successfully with our social revolution we must bring about a revolution in the mentality of the American people. While there is much truth in this, it is well to remember that, in many respects and in many areas of the United States, that revolution has been fought—and won. In his first inaugural my husband said, "We do not distrust the future of essential democracy."

The ensuing years, up to the Second World War, revealed that, when they had taken a wrong turning, the American people were willing to shift their position, to look freshly at conditions, and to find new methods of tackling them. And they were able to do this within the framework of the American system; they were able to find a middle course that upheld the capitalistic system at a time when most of the world seemed to have adopted the policy of extremes—either the extreme right of Nazism or the extreme left of Communism.

What we have failed too often to do is to appeal to this capacity for flexibility in the people. . . .

In using the term, I do not mean adjustment merely to the dramatic and obvious physical changes: to modern transportation and electrical gadgets and all the scientific inventions that have transformed our world. Within an incredibly short time, . . it simply becomes one more convenience.

No, the basic change in the social revolution has been the change in values. To my mother-in-law, for instance, there were certain obligations that she, as a privileged person, must fulfill. She fed the poor, assisted them with money, helped them with medical expenses. This was a form of charity required of her.

The point of view that she simply could not accept was my husband's. He believed—as I trust most civilized people believe now—that human beings have rights as human beings: a right to a job, a right to education, a right to health protection, a right to human dignity, a right to a chance of fulfillment.

This is the inevitable growth in our thinking as a nation—the practical application of democratic principles. No one today would dare refer to the mass of the people, as Alexander Hamilton once did, as "that great beast." And that, perhaps, is a minor victory in the long battle for human rights.   □

A Comprehensive Bibliography of the Articles of Eleanor Roosevelt

(Excluding "My Day")

1921
"Common Sense Versus Party Regularity." News Bulletin (League of Women Voters of New York State) (16 Sept. 1921).

1922
"The Fall Election." *L. W. V. Weekly News* (New York League of Women Voters) (1922).
"Organizing County Women for a Political Party." *L. W. V. Weekly News* (New York League of Women Voters) (1922).

1923
"American Peace Award." *Ladies' Home Journal* 40 (Oct. 1923): 54.
Untitled. *L. W. V. Weekly News* (12 Oct. 1923).
"Why I Am a Democrat." *Junior League Bulletin* 10 (Nov. 1923): 18–19.
"I Am a Democrat." *Women's Democratic Campaign Manual, 1924.* Washington: Democratic Party, National Committee 1924–1928, 1924. 85

1924
"How to Interest Women in Voting." *Women's Democratic Campaign Manual, 1924.* Washington: Democratic Party, National Committee 1924–1928, 1924. 102–3.

"M'Adoo [*sic*] Mobilizes His Forces Here." *New York Times,* 8 June 1924: 5.
"Statement of Policy Committee." *The Winning Plan Selected by the Jury of the American Peace Award.* New York: n.p., 1924. 4–6.
"What Has Politics Gained by the Women's Vote?" *National Democratic Magazine* 1 (Apr. 1924): 21.

1925
"New York Rebuilt." *Women's City Club Bulletin* (June 1925): 5–6.
Women's Democratic News. Ed. Eleanor Roosevelt.

1926
"The Democratic Platform." *Women's City Club of New York* (Oct. 1926): 14–15.

1927
"As a Practical Idealist." *North American Review* 224 (Nov. 1927): 472–75.
Congressional Record (6 Jan. 1927): 1154.
L.W.V. Weekly News (New York League of Women Voters) (Dec. 1927).
"On Albany Hill." *Quarterly* (Women's City Club of New York) (June 1927).
"What I Want Most Out of Life." *Success Magazine* 11 (May 1927): 16–17, 70.
"What Is Being Done in Albany." *Quarterly* (Women's City Club of New York) (Mar. 1927): 10–11.

1928
"Committee on Legislation." *Quarterly* (Women's City Club of New York) (June 1928): 28–29.
"Governor Smith." *Junior League Magazine* 15 (Nov. 1928): 23, 110.
"Governor Smith and Our Foreign Policy." *Woman's Journal* n.s. 13 (Oct. 1928): 21.
"Jeffersonian Principles the Issue in 1928." *Current History* 28 (June 1928): 354–57.
"News of Democrats and Their Activities." *Bulletin* (Women's National Democratic Club) 3 (Dec. 1928): 18–19.
"Women Must Learn to Play the Game as Men Do." *Red Book Magazine* 50 (Apr. 1928): 78–79, 141–42.
"The Women's City Club at Albany." *Quarterly* (Women's City Club of New York) (Mar. 1928): 16–17.

1929
"Education for Girls." *Independent Education* 3 (Dec. 1929): 7–8.

1930
"Building Character." *Childhood and Character* 7 (May 1930): 6–7.
"Good Citizenship: The Purpose of Education." *Pictorial Review* 31 (Apr. 1930): 4, 94, 97.
"The Ideal Education." *Woman's Journal* n.s. 15 (Oct. 1930): 8–10, 36.

Introduction. *Margaret Fuller.* By Margaret Bell. New York: Boni, 1930, 13–14.

"Mrs. Franklin D. Roosevelt Looks at this Modern Housekeeping." *Modern Priscilla* 44 (Apr. 1930): 13, 64.

"Servants." *Forum* 83 (Jan. 1930): 24–28.

"A Summer Trip Abroad." *Women's Democratic News* 5 (Apr. 1930): 2, 12, 16; 6 (May 1930): 6, 13; 6 (June 1930): 16; 6 (Aug. 1930): 6, 16; 6 (Oct. 1930): 14, 24; 6 (Dec. 1930): 16; 6 (Feb. 1931): 14; 6 (Apr. 1931): 7, 16; 7 (May 1931): 16; 7 (July 1931): 2.

"What Is a Wife's Job Today?" *Good Housekeeping* (August 1930): 34–35, 166, 169–73.

"Women in Politics." *Women's City Club of New York Quarterly* (Jan. 1930): 5–7.

1931

"Building Character: An Editorial." *Parents' Magazine* 6 (June 1931): 17.

"How I Make My Husband Happy: An Interview." *Babylon (N.Y.) Leader* (November 30, 1931).

"Let Every Child Have His Own Library." *Wings* (Literary Guild of America) 5 (Jan. 1931): 16–17.

"Mrs. Franklin D. Roosevelt Tells the Story in a Nutshell: A Word to the Woman in the Home and to the Woman in Business by the First Lady of New York." *Baltimore and Ohio Magazine* 19 (May 1931): 21.

"Ten Rules for Success in Marriage." *Pictorial Review* 33 (Dec. 1931): 4, 36.

"This Question of Jobs." *Junior League Magazine* 17 (Jan. 1931): 14.

"Travels of a Democrat." *Women's Democratic News* (February, March, and April 1931).

1932

Introduction. *Alice's Adventures in Wonderland, Through the Looking-Glass, and The Hunting of the Shark.* By Lewis Carroll. Washington: National Home Library Foundation, 1932. [2].

Babies—Just Babies. Ed. Eleanor Roosevelt. 1–2 (Oct. 1932-June 1933).

"Be Curious—and Educated!" *Liberty* 9 (2 July 1932): 30–31.

"Children of School Age." *School Life* 18 (March 1933): 121–122.

"Christmas." *New York American* 24 Dec. 1932.

"Economic Readjustment Necessary." *Democratic Bulletin* (August 1932): 14, 27.

"Grandmothers Can Still Be Young." *Liberty* 9 (20 Feb. 1932): 38–40.

"Grow Old Gracefully." *Reader's Digest* 21 (Sept. 1932): recto and verso of back cover.

"How to Choose a Candidate." *Liberty* 9 (5 Nov. 1932): 16–17.

Introduction. *John Martin's Book: Tell Me a Story.* Jacket Library, 1932.

"Make Them Believe in You: An Editorial." *Babies—Just Babies* 1 (Nov. 1932): 3.

"Merry Christmas! An Editorial." *Babies—Just Babies* 1 (Dec. 1932): 3.

"Preparing the Child for Citizenship." *New York Times,* 24 Apr. 1932, sect. 3: 7.

"Presenting 'Babies—Just Babies.'" *Babies—Just Babies* 1 (Oct. 1932): 5–6.

"Today's Girl and Tomorrow's Job." *Woman's Home Companion* 59 (June 1932): 11–12.

"What Are the Movies Doing to Us?" *Modern Screen* 4 (Nov. 1932): 26–27, 102.

"What Religion Means to Me." *Forum* 88 (Dec. 1932): 322–24.

"What Ten Million Women Want." *Home Magazine* 5 (Mar. 1932): 19–21, 86.
"Wives of Great Men." *Liberty* 9 (1 Oct. 1932): 12–16.
"Women's Political Responsibility." *Democratic Bulletin* 7 (Jan. 1932): 12.

1933
"The Camp for Unemployed Women: A Novel American Experiment Under the Relief
    Administration." *World Today: Encyclopedia Britannica* 1 (Oct. 1933): 1.
"A Child Belongs in the Country: An Editorial." *Babies—Just Babies* 1 (Apr. 1933): 3.
"Consider the Babies: An Editorial." *Babies—Just Babies* 2 (May 1933): 3.
"A Happy New Year: An Editorial." *Babies—Just Babies* 1 (Jan. 1933): 3.
"Has Life Been Too Easy for Us?" *Liberty* 10 (4 Feb. 1933): 4–7.
"I Answer Two Questions." *Woman's Home Companion* (Dec. 1933): 24.
"I Want You to Write to Me." *Woman's Home Companion* (August 1933): 4.
"In Appreciation of Anne Alive!" [Foreword] *Anne Alive! A Year in the Life of a Girl of New York
    State*. By Margaret Doane Fayerweather. New York: Junior Literary Guild & Mc-
    Bridge. 1933, vii-ix.
"Lives of Great Men: An Editorial." *Babies—Just Babies* 1 (Feb. 1933): 3.
"The Married Woman in Business." *Woman's Home Companion* (Nov. 1933): 4.
"Mobilization for Human Needs." *Democratic Digest* 8 (Nov. 1933): 3.
"Mrs. Roosevelt Replies to the Letter of an Unknown Woman." *McCall's* 60 (Mar.
    1933): 4.
"Mrs. Roosevelt Urges Women to Have Courage of Convictions and to Stand on Own
    Feet." *Clubwoman GFWC (General Federation of Women's Clubs)* 13 (Feb. 1933): 10.
"On Girls Learning to Drink." *Literary Digest* (January 1933): 3.
"Passing Thoughts of Mrs. Franklin D. Roosevelt." *Women's Democratic News* 8 (February
    1933): 6.
"Passing Thoughts of Mrs. Franklin D. Roosevelt." *Women's Democratic News* 9 (June
    1933): 6–7.
"Ratify the Child Labor Amendment." *Woman's Home Companion* (September 1933): 4.
"Recreation as a Preparation for Life." *Recreation* 27 (Nov. 1933): 374, 394.
"Setting Our House in Order." *Woman's Home Companion* (October 1933): 4.
"Should a Wife Support Herself?" *Every Woman* 1 (July 1933): 9.
"The State's Responsibility for Fair Working Conditions." *Scribner's Magazine* 93 (Mar.
    1933): 140.
"What I Hope to Leave Behind." *Pictorial Review* 34 (Apr. 1933): 4, 45.
"When Nature Smiles: An Editorial." *Babies—Just Babies* 2 (June 1993): 3.
"White House to Mrs. Roosevelt." *New York Times*, 2 Apr. 1933, sect. 2: 1–2.

1934
"Adventures with Early American Furniture." *House & Garden* 65 (Feb. 1934): 21–23.
"Appreciations." *Miss Wylie of Vassar*. Ed. Elisabeth Woodbridge Morris. New Haven: Yale
    University Press for the Laura J. Wylie Memorial Associates, 149–55.

"By Car and Tent." *Woman's Home Companion* (Aug. 1934): 4.

"Exposition Farms: A New Idea in Experimental Farming." *Consumers' Guide* 1 (13 Aug. 1934): 3–4.

"First Lady Pleads for Old Age Pensions." *Social Security* 8 (Feb. 1934): 3–4.

Foreword. *Getting Acquainted with Your Children.* By James W. Howard. New York: Leisure League of America, 1934. 5–6.

"I Have Confidence in Our Common Sense." *Woman's Home Companion* (June 1934): 4.

"Learning to Teach." *Virginia Teacher* 15 (May 1934): 100–101.

"Let Us Be Thankful." *Woman's Home Companion* (Nov. 1934): 4.

"Living and Preparation for Life Through Recreation. *Recreation* 28 (Nov. 1934): 366–369.

"A Message to Parents and Teachers." *Progressive Education* 11 (Jan. 1934): 38–39.

"The National Conference on the Education of Negroes." *The Journal of Negro Education* 3 (Oct. 1934): 575–575.

"The New Governmental Interest in the Arts." *American Magazine of Art* 27 (Sept. 1934): 47.

"On Education." *School Life* 19 (Jan. 1934): 102–3.

"Our Island Possessions." *Woman's Home Companion* (Oct. 1934): 4.

"The Power of Knowledge." *Woman's Home Companion* 3 (Mar. 1934): 5.

"Recreation." *Woman's Home Companion* (Jan. 1934): 4.

"The Right to Give." *Woman's Home Companion* (Dec. 1934): 21.

"Subsistence Farmsteads." *Forum* 91 (Apr. 1934): 199–201.

"Too Old for the Job." *Woman's Home Companion* (Feb. 1934): 4.

"Traditional Holidays." *Woman's Home Companion* (Sept. 1934): 4.

"Youth Facing the Future." *Woman's Home Companion* (May 1934): 4.

"What Does the Public Expect from Nursing?" *American Journal of Nursing* 34 (July 1934): 637–640.

"The Woman's Crusade." *Daughters of the American Revolution Magazine* 68 (Jan. 1934): 8–1.

"The Women Go After the Facts about Milk Consumption." *Consumers' Guide* 1 (28 May 1934): 3–5.

1935

"Because the War Idea Is Obsolete." *Why Wars Must Cease.* Ed. Rose Young. New York: Macmillan, 1935, 20–29.

"Building for the Future." *Woman's Home Companion* (Feb. 1935): 4.

"Can a Woman Ever Be President of the United States?" *Cosmopolitan* (Oct. 1935): 22–23, 120–21.

"Children." *Hearst's International Cosmopolitan* (Jan. 1935): 24–27.

"Facing Forward." *Woman's Home Companion* (Jan. 1935): 4.

"Facing the Problems of Youth." *National Parent-Teacher* 29 (Feb. 1935): 30.

"Facing the Problems of Youth." *Journal of Social Hygiene* 21 (Oct. 1935): 393–94.

"Five Years: What Have They Done To Us?" *Hearst's International Cosmopolitan* (Jan. 1935): 24–27, 146–147.

"Gardens." *Woman's Home Companion* (March 1935): 4.

"In Defense of Curiosity." *Saturday Evening Post* 208 (24 Aug. 1935): 8–9, 64–66.

"In Everlasting Remembrance." *Woman's Home Companion* (May 1935): 4.

"Jane Addams." *Democratic Digest* 12 (June 1935): 3.

"Maternal Mortality." *Woman's Home Companion*. (July 1935): 4.

"Mountains of Courage." *This Week* (4 Nov. 1935): 7, 25.

"Mrs. Roosevelt Believes in Paroles and Providing Jobs for Released Men." *Periscope* (U.S.N.E.P. Lewisburg, Pa.) 3 (Oct. 1935): 5–6.

"The Place of Women in the Community." *National Education Association Proceedings.* 1935: 313–316.

"Traveling Thoughts of Mrs. Franklin D. Roosevelt." *Women's Democratic News* 11 (Oct. 1935): 6–7.

"Tree Worship." *Woman's Home Companion* (July 1935): 4.

"We Can't Wait for the Millennium." *Liberty* (1935): 18–20.

"We Need Private Charity." *Current Controversy* (Nov. 1935): 6, 47.

"Woman's Work Is Never Done." *Woman's Home Companion* (April 1935): 4.

1936

"About State Institutions." *Caswell News* (Caswell Training School, Kinston, N.C.) 1 (May 1936): 3, 8.

"Are We Overlooking the Pursuit of Happiness?" *Parents' Magazine* 11 (Sept. 1936): 21, 67.

Bulletin (National Committee on Household Employment) 4 (Jan. 1936).

"A Fortnight in the White House." *Women's Democratic News* (New York State Section of the *Democratic Digest*) (Feb. 1936): 3–4.

"Goal Kicks for '36." *School Life* 21 (Jan. 1936): 105.

"The Homesteads Are Making Good." *Democratic Digest* 13 (Mar. 1936): 10.

"A Month at the White House." *Women's Democratic News* (New York State Section of the *Democratic Digest*) (June 1936): 3.

"The Negro and Social Change." *Opportunity* (Jan. 1936): 22–23.

"Persistence Wins." *School Press Review* (Oct. 1936): 1–2.

"Safeguard the Children." *American Child* 18 (Jan. 1936): 1.

"The Unemployed Are Not a Strange Race." *Democratic Digest* (June 1936): 19.

"What Libraries Mean to the Nation." *American Library Association Bulletin* (June 1936): 477–79.

"The White House and Here." *Women's Democratic News* (New York State Section of the *Democratic Digest*) (July 1937): 2.

1937

"A Busy Month in and out of the White House." *Women's Democratic News* (New York State Section of the *Democratic Digest*) (July 1937): 2.

"A Christmas Letter." *Post-Intelligencer* [Seattle, Wash.], 25 Nov. 1937.

"A Christmas-Spirited Housecleaning." *Reader's Digest* 31 (31 Dec. 1937): verso of front cover, recto and verso of back cover.

"Highlights of a Busy Month." *Women's Democratic News* (New York State Section of the *Democratic Digest*) (May 1937): 2.

"Highlights of a Month at the White House." *Women's Democratic News* (New York State Section of the *Democratic Digest*) (Aug. 1937): 2, 4.

"Highlights of the Past Few Months." *Women's Democratic News* (New York State Section of the *Democratic Digest*) (Mar. 1937): 2.

"In Praise of Molly Dewson." *Democratic Digest* 14 (Nov. 1937): 15.

"A Month in the White House." *Women's Democratic News* (New York State Section of the *Democratic Digest*) (Apr. 1937): 2, 4.

"My Month." *Women's Democratic News* (New York State Section of the *Democratic Digest*) (Dec. 1937): 3.

"A Peaceful Month in the Country." *Women's Democratic News* (New York State Section of the *Democratic Digest*) (Oct. 1937): 2, 4.

"Questions." *Progressive Education* 14 (Oct. 1937): 407.

"Should Wives Work?" *Good Housekeeping* 105 (Dec. 1937): 28–29, 211–12.

"South by Motor and West by Plane." *Women's Democratic News* (New York State Section of the *Democratic Digest*) (July 1937): 2.

"This Is My Story." *Ladies' Home Journal* 54 (Apr. 1937): 11–13, 48, 50, 53, 55; 54 (May 1937): 14–15, 47–48, 50, 52–53; 54 (June 1937): 14–15, 100, 102–4, 106–7; 54 (July 1937): 22, 76–80; 54 (Aug. 1937): 29, 68–70, 72; 54 (Sept. 1937): 30, 52–53, 55–56; 54 (Oct. 1937): 18, 88, 90, 93, 95; 54 (Nov. 1937): 19, 55–56, 58–60, 63; 54 (Dec. 1937): 29, 49, 51–52, 54–55; 55 (Jan. 1938): 23, 55–57.

"A Vacation Month Spent in Guest House at the Val-Kill Cottages." *Women's Democratic News* (New York State Section of the *Democratic Digest*) (Sept. 1937): 2, 4.

Foreword. *The White House: An Informal History of Its Architecture, Interiors and Gardens.* By Ethel Lewis. New York: Dodd, Mead, 1937, v-vi.

"When the First Lady of the Land Entertains: An Interview." *Democratic Digest* 14 (Sept. 1937): 16–17.

1938

"Americans I Admire." *Woman's Day* 1 (Sept. 1938): 4–5, 43–44; 2 (Nov. 1938): 8–9, 42; 2 (Jan. 1939): 8–9, 43; 2 (Mar. 1939): 16, 49.

"Cherry Blossom Time in Washington." *Reader's Digest* 32 (Apr. 1938): 57–58.

"Cherry-Blossom Time." *Reader's Digest* 82 (Apr. 1963): 228c.

"A Christmas Letter." *Post-Intelligencer* [Seattle, Wash.], 24 Nov. 1938.

"Divorce." *Ladies' Home Journal* 55 (Apr. 1938): 16.

"Education, a Child's Life." *Progressive Education* 15 (Oct. 1938): 451.

"Henry Street's Pioneer." Rev. of *Lillian Wald: Neighbor and Crusader* by R. L. Duffus. *Survey Graphic* 27 (Dec. 1938): 616.

"Lady Bountiful Rolls Up Her Sleeves." *Reader's Digest* 32 (Mar. 1938): 53–55.
"Mrs. Roosevelt Answers Mr. Wells on 'The Future of the Jews.'" *Liberty* 15 (31 Dec. 1938): 4–5.
"My Children." *McCall's* (Apr. 1938): 4, 75.
"My Day." *Consumers' Cooperative* 24 (Feb. 1938): 19.
"My Days." *Quote* 1 (Nov. 1938): 36–37.
"My Home." *McCall's* (Feb. 1938): 4, 46, 132.
"My Job." *McCall's* (Mar. 1938): 4, 68.
"My Month." *Women's Democratic News* (New York State Section of the *Democratic Digest*) (Feb. 1938): 2, 4.
"On Teachers and Teaching." *Harvard Educational Review* 8 (Oct. 1938): 423–24.
"Resolutions I Wish Consumers Would Make for 1938: A Dozen Targets for Consumers Who Want to Make Their Buying Power Count Toward a Better New Year." *Consumers' Guide* 4 (3 Jan. 1938): 3–8.
"Seeking a Place in Community." *Southern Workman* 67 (June 1938): 165–171.
"Should Married Women Work? A Californian Asks Mrs. Roosevelt to Explain Her Statement in the Democratic Digest." *Democratic Digest* 15 (May 1938): 24.
"Success Formula for Public-Spirited Women." *Democratic Digest* 15 (Aug. 1938): 39.
"Trialog on Office Holders." *Independent Woman* (Jan. 1938): 17–18.
"Two Paths to Peace." *Democratic Digest* (Aug. 1938): 19.
"Youth." *Hearst's International Cosmopolitan* (Feb. 1938): 26–27, 134–36.

1939
"Adventures with Early American Furniture." *House and Garden* (Feb. 1939): 21–23.
"American Democracy and Youth." *New University* (Mar. 1939): 7–8.
"Challenge." *The Guardian* (Dec. 1939): 1–2.
Common Sense Neutrality. Ed. Paul Comly French. New York: Hastings, 1939. 182–97.
"Conquer Fear and You Will Enjoy Living." *Look* 3 (23 May 1939): 6–11.
"Current Quotations." *Education Digest* 4 (May 1939): 7.
"Do Our Young People Need Religion?" *Liberty* 16 (17 June 1939): 12–13.
"Eleanor Roosevelt Says." *Educational Music Magazine* 18 (Jan./Feb. 1939): 6–7.
"Flying Is Fun." *Collier's* 103 (22 Apr. 1939): 15, 88–89.
"Food in America." *Woman's Day* (Oct. 1939): 27–29, 33.
"Good Manners." *Ladies' Home Journal* 56 (June 1939): 21, 116–17.
"Government Becomes Alive." *Daily Times* [Chicago, Ill.], 6 Sept. 1939: 55.
"Keepers of Democracy." *Virginia Quarterly Review* 15 (Jan. 1939): 1–5.
"Mrs. Roosevelt Awards Medal." *Crisis* (Sept. 1939): 265, 285.
"Mrs. Roosevelt Counsels Women." *Democratic Digest* 16 (Jan. 1939): 11.
"Mrs. Roosevelt on Democratic Women's Day." *Democratic Digest* 16 (Dec. 1939): 29.
"Our American Homes." *Child Study* 16 (May 1939): 182.
"Security Begins Beyond the City Limits." *Hearst's International Cosmopolitan* 106 (May 1939): 38–39, 90–91.

"Security for Youth and Age." *Time* (March 6, 1939): 11.

"Talk to Birds." *Good Housekeeping* 109 (Dec. 1939): 27–29.

To Enrich Young Life: Ten Years with the Junior Literary Guild in the Schools of Our Country. Garden City: Junior Literary Guild, 1939. 24.

"A Vision for Today." *New York Times Magazine,* 24 Dec. 1939: 4.

"War! What the Women of America Can Do to Prevent It." *Woman's Day* 2 (Apr. 1939): 4–5, 46–47.

Introduction. *Washington, Nerve Center.* The Face of America. By Edwin Rosskam; Ruby A. Black, co-editor. New York: Alliance, 1939. 5–6.

"Why I Am Against the People's Vote on War." *Liberty* 16 (8 Apr. 1939): 7–8.

"Why I Am a Democrat." *Junior League* (Sept. 1939): 29, 60.

"Women in Politics." *Democratic Digest* 16 (July 1939): 13–14.

"The Women of America Must Fight." *This Week Magazine* 16 (2 July 1939): 7.

"You Can Prevent Crime." *Woman* (Nov. 1939): 36–37.

1940

"The American Home and Present Day Conditions." *What's New in Home Economics* 4 (April 1940): 1, 11.

"Art and Our Warring World." *Round Table* (November 24, 1940).

Foreword. *American Youth: An Enforced Reconnaissance.* Ed. Thacher Winslow and Frank P. Davidson. Cambridge: Harvard University Press, 1940, ix-xi.

Foreword. *American Youth Today.* By Leslie A. Gould. New York: Random House, 1940, vii-viii.

"Christmas 1940: A Short Story." *Liberty* (28 Dec. 1940): 10–13.

"Christmas—A Story." *Eleanor Roosevelt's Christmas Book.* New York: Dodd, Mead. 1963. 3–5.

"Civil Liberties, the Individual and the Crisis." *Reference Shelf* 14 (1940): 173–182.

"Eleanor Roosevelt on Recreation." *Recreation* 34 (Dec. 1940): 570.

"Farm Youth of Today." *American Farm Youth* 6 (Nov. 1940): 3.

"Fear Is the Enemy." *Nation* 150 (10 Feb. 1940): 173.

"A Guest Editorial." *Opportunity* 18 (Mar. 1940): 66.

Foreword. *Happy Times in Czechoslovakia.* By Libushka Bartusek. New York: Knopf, 1940, [iii].

"Helping Them to Help Themselves." *Rotarian* 56 (Apr. 1940): 8–11.

"Helping People to Help Themselves." *Ladies' Home Journal* 57 (Aug. 1940): 12.

"Homes for Americans: An Editorial." *Woman's Day* 3 (Apr. 1940): 3.

"In Appreciation." *Synagogue Light* 8 (Oct. 1940): 4.

"Insuring Democracy." *Collier's* 105 (15 June 1940): 87–88.

"Intolerance." *Cosmopolitan* (Feb. 1940): 24–25, 102–3.

"The Man from Jail." *World Digest* 12 (June 1940): 61–62.

"Men Have to Be Humored." *Woman's Day* 3 (Aug. 1940): 12–13, 58.

"Mrs. Roosevelt's Advice on Public Speaking." *Democratic Digest* 17 (Feb. 1940): 3.

"Mrs. Roosevelt Speaks." *Democratic Digest* 17 (Aug. 1940): 16.
"My Advice to American Youth." *Look* 4 (27 Aug. 1940): 56–58.
"Read the Bill of Rights." *Democratic Digest* 17 (Jan. 1940): 12.
"Shall We Enroll Aliens? No." *Liberty* 17 (3 Feb. 1940): 13.
"Sixty Years Consecutive ORT Work." *ORT Economic Bulletin* 1 (Nov. 40): 1–2.
"A Spanking." *Liberty* 17 (22 June 1949): 6–8.
"Twenty-four Hours." *Ladies' Home Journal* 57 (Oct. 1940): 20, 58, 60.
"What Can We Do for Youth?" *Occupations* 19 (Oct. 1940): 9–10.
"What Value Has the Ballot for Women?" *Democratic Digest* 17 (June/July 1940): 25.
"The White House Speaks." *Ladies' Home Journal* 57 (June 1940): 21, 121–24.
"Why I Still Believe in the Youth Congress." *Liberty* 17 (20 Apr. 1940): 30–32.
"Women in Politics." *Good Housekeeping* 110 (Jan. 1940): 8–19, 150; 110 (Mar. 1940): 45,
    68; 110 (Apr. 1940): 45, 201–3.
"Women in Politics." *Woman's Press* (Y.W.C.A.) (Apr. 1940): 165.
Foreword. *Youth—Millions Too Many? A Search for Youth's Place in America.* By Bruce L.
    Melvin. New York: Association Press, 1940, 5–6.

1941

[Review]. *The American Presidency: An Interpretation.* By Harold J. Laski. *Harvard Law Review*
    54 (June 1941): 1413–14.
"Appreciating the Great Outdoors." *Student Life* 7 (May 1941): 2.
"Defense and Girls." *Ladies' Home Journal* 58 (May 1941): 25, 54.
"Girls and National Defense." *Women in America: Half of History.* Ed. Mary Kay Tetreault.
    Chicago: Rand McNally, 1978, 60–64.
"First Lady Addresses Workers' Wives." *Trade Union Courier* 6 (1 Sept. 1941): 6.
"First Lady in Her Own Right." *Echo.* (March 1941): 3–5.
"If I Were a Freshman . . ." *Threshold* 1 (Oct. 1941): 5–6.
"Important as Ever." *Our Bill of Rights: What It Means to Me, a National Symposium.* By James
    Waterman Wise. New York: Bill of Rights Sesqui-centennial, 1941. 116.
"An Inspiration to All." *Opinion* 12 (Nov. 1941): 12.
"Know What We Defend." *Democratic Digest* 18 (May 3, 1941): 12–13.
"Larder for the Democracies." *Democratic Digest* 18 (Oct. 1941): 7.
"My Week." *Our Country* 1 (May 1941): 16.
Foreword. *The New Program of the United States Committee of International Student Service.*
    New York: The Committee, 1941, 4–5.
"Our Widening Horizon." *Democratic Digest* 18 (Feb. 1941): 9.
"Shall We Draft American Women?" *Liberty* 18 (13 Sept. 1941): 10–11.
"Social Gains and Defense." *Common Sense* 10 (March 1941): 71–77.
"Speech Training for Youth." *Quarterly Journal of Speech* 27 (Oct. 1941): 369–71.
"Tower Club." *The Tower: Yearbook of the Tower Club, Ohio State University, 1941,* 2.
"Weaving: An Old American Handicraft." *Woman's Day* (Feb. 1941): 27–28.

"What Does Pan-American Friendship Mean?" *Liberty* 18 (4 Oct. 1941): 10–11 and *Congressional Record Appendix* (22 Oct. 1941): A4784–85.

"What Is the Matter with Women?" *Liberty* 18 (3 May 1941): 12–13.

"What Must We Do to Improve the Health and Well-Being of the American People?" *Town Meeting* (December 8, 1941): 13–22.

"What's Wrong with the Draft." *Look* 5 (15 July 1941): 23–25.

"Women in Defense: A Script by Mrs. Roosevelt." *New York Times Magazine,* 7 Dec. 1941: 6–7.

1942

"Attitudes of Youth and Morale." *The Family in a World at War* edited by D. M. Gruenberg. Harper and Brothers, 1942.

Foreword. "Born in the USA." *Baby Talk* 7 (July 1942): 11.

"The Community and Morale." *Educational Record* 23 (Jan. 1942): 63–68.

"The Democratic Effort." *Common Ground* 2 (Spring 1942): 9–10.

"Education Is the Cornerstone on Which We Must Build Liberty." *Education for Victory* 1 (1 Apr. 1942): 1.

"For American Unity." *American Unity* 1 (Oct. 1942): 3.

"How about Your Vacation?" *Cosmopolitan* (Apr. 1942): 28–29.

"The Issue Is Freedom." Rev. of *American Unity and Asia.* by Pearl Buck. *New Republic* 107 (3 Aug. 1942): 147–48.

"Let Us Earn a True Peace." *Country Gentleman* 112 (Dec. 1942): 9, 52–53.

"Let Us Have Faith in Democracy." *Land Policy Review* 5 (Jan. 1942): 20–22.

"Marching . . . with Eleanor Roosevelt: This Month Your Government Asks That You . . ." *McCall's* 69 (Mar. 1942): 57.

"Messages." *Free World* 4 (Oct. 1942): 7–18.

"Mobilizing Human Skills." *Common Sense* 11 (July 1942): 240–42.

"Mrs. Roosevelt Sends Columbus Day Message to Jewish People Through Jewish Mirror." *Jewish Mirror* 1 (Oct. 1942): 3.

"Must We Hate to Fight? No." *Saturday Review of Literature* 25 (4 July 1942): 13.

"My Day." *Democratic Digest* 19 (Sept. 1942): 14.

"My Day—The Polish Day." *Pulaski Foundation Bulletin* 1 (Dec. 1942): 3.

"Race, Religion and Prejudice." *New Republic* 106 (11 May 1942): 630.

Preface. *Refugees at Work.* Comp. Sophia M. Robinson. New York: King's Crown, 1942, [v]-vi.

Special Issue on Morale. Ed. Eleanor Roosevelt. *Saturday Review of Literature* 25 (4 July 1942).

"To Care for Him Who Shall Have Borne the Battle." *Collier's* 110 (28 Nov. 1942): 20.

"War Work Is Not Enough." *Democratic Digest* 19 (Oct. 1942): cover, 10, 14.

"What Is Morale." *Saturday Review of Literature* 25 (4 July 1942): 12.

"What We Are Fighting For." *American Magazine* 134 (July 1942): 16–17, 60–62.

1943
"Abolish Jim Crow!" *New Threshold* 1 (Aug. 1943): 4, 34.
"The Four Equalities." *Negro Digest* 1 (Sept. 1943): 81–83.
"The Case Against the Negro Press. Con." *Negro Digest* 1 (Feb. 1943): 53.
"A Challenge to American Sportsmanship." *Collier's* 112 (16 Oct. 1943): 21, 71.
"Eleanor Roosevelt Visits the South Pacific: As the First Lady Views It." *Democratic Digest*
	20 (Sept. 1943): 8–9.
"First Lady on Home Safety." *Home Safety Review* 1 (May/June 1943): 10, 15.
"Freedom: Promise or Fact." *Negro Digest* 1 (Oct. 1943): 8–9.
"How Britain Is Treating Our Soldier Boys and Girls." *Ladies' Home Journal* 60 (Feb. 1943):
	24–25, 125–26.
"It's a Ladies' Fight." *Kelly Magazine* (San Antonio Air Service Command) 1 (Christmas
	1943): 7.
"It's Patriotic to Teach." *Educational Leadership* 1 (Oct. 1943): 3 and *Teacher's Digest* 4 (Feb.
	1944): 56.
"A Message to the Mountain Folk." *Arcadian Life Magazine* 2 (Spring/Summer 1943): 5.
"Monthly Posters Are Vital in War Bond Sale." *Minute Man* 2 (15 May 1943): 5.
"Noted Women Write on World We Want—First Article by Mrs. Roosevelt." *Christian*
	Science Monitor 5 Jan. 1943, Atlantic ed.: 8.
"The World We Want." *Letter from America* 13 (22 Jan. 1943): 1.
"The Red Cross in the South Seas." *Ladies' Home Journal* 60 (Dec. 1943): 30, 158–60.
"Studying Spanish." *Saturday Review of Literature* 26 (10 Apr. 1943): 10.
"They Talk Our Language Differently." *Collier's* 111 (27 Feb. 1943): 18, 20, 22.
"Trained Minds and Trained Hearts." *Smith Alumnae Quarterly* 34 (May 1943): 125.
"Women at War in Great Britain." *Ladies' Home Journal* 60 (Apr. 1943): 22–25, 70, 72.
Women Students—the Men Are Counting on You!" *Intercollegian* 61 (Dec. 1943): 7.
"Your New World." *Life Story* 7 (Feb. 1943): 33.

1944
"American Red Cross 'Down Under.' " *American Lawn Tennis* 37 (Apr. 1944): 16–17.
"The American Spirit." *Congressional Weekly* 11 (June 9, 1944): 10–11.
"American Women in the War." *Reader's Digest* 44 (Jan. 1944): 42–44.
"As Johnny Thinks of Home: He Idealizes What He Left Behind." *Social Action* 10 (15 Mar.
	1944): 5–7.
"Eleanor Roosevelt Says." *Ammunition* (UAW-CIO) 2 (Aug. 1944): 1.
"Equality Is Labor's Cause." *Workmen's Circle Call* 12 (July 1944): 10.
"Henry Wallace's Democracy." Rev. of *Democracy Reborn* by Henry Wallace. *New Republic*
	111 (7 Aug. 1944): 165–66.
"How to Take Criticism." *Ladies' Home Journal* 61 (Nov. 1944): 155, 171.
"If You Ask Me." *Reader's Digest* 45 (Sept. 1944): 100–101.
"In Unity There Is Strength." *Workmen's Circle Call* 12 (July 1944): 10.
"Is the Human Race Worth Saving?" *Liberty* 21 (23 Dec. 1944): 15, 54.

"It's Patriotic to Teach." *Teacher's Digest* 4 (Feb. 1944): 56.

"New Stepping Stones in the Pacific." *Survey Graphic* 33 (Jan. 1944): 5.

"Our Homes in the Post-War World." *National Parent-Teacher* 38 (June 1944): 22–23.

"The South in Postwar America." *Southern Patriot* 2 (June 1944): 1–2.

"To the Women of the B & O Family." *Baltimore and Ohio Magazine* 30 (June 1944): 3.

"We Must Have Compulsory Service." *Parents' Magazine* 19 (Nov. 1944): 16–18.

"Should the U.S. Adopt Peacetime Compulsory Military Training? Pro." *Congressional Digest* 24 (Jan. 1945): 16.

"What I Saw in the South Seas." *Ladies' Home Journal* 61 (Feb. 1944): 26–27, 88–90.

"What Kind of World Are We Fighting For?" *Canadian Home Journal* (Jan. 1944): 12–13.

"What Will Happen to Women War Workers in Post-War America." *Southern Patriot* 2 (Apr. 1944): 1–2.

"What Will Victory Bring?" *Argosy* 318 (Apr. 1944): 16–17.

"Woman's Place After the War." *Click* 7 (Aug. 1944): 17–19.

"Women at the Peace Conference." *Reader's Digest* 44 (Apr. 1944): 48–49.

Foreword. "Women in the Postwar World." *Journal of Educational Sociology* 17 (Apr. 1944): 449–50.

"Young Men Must Look Forward." *Future* 6 (June 1944): 9.

1945

"Address to Conference on Educational Programs for Veterans." *Education for Victory* 3 (April 1945): 1–3.

"From the Melting Pot—An American Race." *Liberty* 22 (14 July 1945): 17, 89.

"If You Ask Me." *Negro Digest* 3 (Feb. 1945): 9–10.

"Milestone in Human Relations." *Council Women (National Council of Jewish Women)* 7 (May/June 1945): 4–5, 16.

"One of Many." *Reader's Digest* 46 (June 1945): 26.

"Personal Sorrow Lost in Humanity's Sadness." *Democratic Digest* 22 (June 1945): 9.

"Mrs. Roosevelt Says." *Bayonet* 1 (Jan. 1945): 16.

"Music in the White House." *Your Music* (Nov. 1945).

"Now for the World We Are Fighting For." *Modern Mystic and Monthly Science Review* 5 (July 1945): 124–25.

"Tolerance Is an Ugly Word." *Coronet* 18 (July 1945): 118 and *Negro Digest* 3 (Oct. 1945): 7–8.

Introduction. *The White House Conference on Rural Education, October 3, 4, and 5, 1944.* Washington: National Education Association of the U.S., n.d. 11–13.

"You Can't Pauperize Children." *Ladies' Home Journal* 62 (Sept. 1945): 128–29.

1946

"American Women in the War." *Reader's Digest* (Jan. 1946): 42–44.

"Can America Be Prosperous in a Sea of Misery?" *Ladies' Home Journal* (May 1946), 35, 131–132, 134.

Foreword. *As He Saw It.* By Elliott Roosevelt. New York: Duell, Sloan and Pearce, 1946, vii-ix.

Congressional Record (18 July 1946): 9401.

"Eleanor Roosevelt to the German American." *German American* 5 (15 Oct. 1946): 3.

"For an International Bill of Rights." *Democratic Digest* 23 (July 1946): 4–5.

"Human Rights and Human Freedom." *NewYork Times Magazine,* 26 March 1946: 21.

"If You Ask Mrs. Roosevelt." *Practical English* 2 (17 Mar. 1947): 7.

"Importance of Background Knowledge in Building for the Future." *Annals of the American Academy of Political and Social Science* 246 (July 1946): 9–12.

Preface. *The Jew in American Life.* By James Waterman Wise. New York: Messner, 1946, 5–6.

"A Message to American Girls." *American Girl* 29 (Feb. 1946): 4.

"The Minorities Question." *Toward a BetterWorld.* Ed. William Scarlett. Philadelphia: Winston, 1946. 35–39 and in *Christianity Takes a Stand: An Approach to the Issues of Today, a Symposium.* Penguin, 612. Ed. William Scarlett. New York: Penguin, 1946, 72–76.

"The Refugees Place in American Life." *Talks (CBS)* IV (January 1946): 28–29.

"Mrs. Roosevelt Speaks." *Summary* (Elmira, N.Y. Reformatory) 64 (29 Mar. 1946): 2.

"My Father and I." *NewYork Times Magazine,* 16 June 1946: 28.

"The People Interview Mrs. Roosevelt." *Saturday Review of Literature* 29 (23 Mar. 1946): 24.

"The United Nations andYou. *Vital Speeches of the Day* 112 (May 1, 1946): 444–45.

"U.S. Position on International Refugee Organizations." *Department of State Bulletin* 15 (Nov. 24, 1946): 935–38.

"Why I Do Not Choose to Run." *Look* 10 (9 July 1946): 25–26.

"Why I Travel." *Holiday* (Apr. 1946): 24–26.

1947

Foreword. *F.D.R. Columnist: The Uncollected Columns of Franklin D. Roosevelt.* Ed. Donald Scott Carmichael. Chicago: Pellegrini & Cudahy, 1947, [ii-iii].

Foreword. *F.D.R.: His Personal Letters, Early Years.* Ed. Elliott Roosevelt. New York: Duell, Sloan and Pearce, 1947. xv-xvi.

"Getting Over Having a Baby." *Babies Keep Coming: An Anthology.* Ed. Rebecca Reyher. New York: Whittlesey House-McGraw-Hill, 1947, 400–1.

"I Tell My Life Story in Pictures." *Look* 11 (16 Sept. 1947): 26–33.

"If I Had It All to Do Over Again." *Babies Keep Coming: An Anthology.* Ed. Rebecca Reyher. New York: Whittlesey House-McGraw-Hill, 1947, 321–23.

"In Pursuit of Happiness." *Woman's Journal* 11 (Aug. 1947): 20.

"International Bill of Human Rights." *MethodistWoman* 8 (Nov. 1947) 14.

"Message from Mrs. Franklin D. Roosevelt, Chairman, Commission on Human Rights." *United NationsWeekly Bulletin* 2 (25 Feb. 1947): 170.

"Roosevelt Christening Charm." *Babies Keep Coming: An Anthology.* Ed. Rebecca Reyher. New York: Whittlesey House-McGraw-Hill, 1947, 123–24.

"The Russians Are Tough." *Look* 11 (18 Feb. 1947): 65–69.

"Should a Negro Boy Ask a White Girl to Dance?" *Negro Digest* 6 (Dec. 1947): 41–42.
"Women and the United Nations." *General Federation Clubwomen* 27 (Sept. 1947):17–18.

1948

"Acceptance Address." *Bryn Mawr Alumnae Bulletin* 28 (April 1948).
"A Comment by the Commission Chairman: Mrs. Franklin D. Roosevelt." *United Nations Bulletin* 5 (1 July 1948): 521.
"A Decade of Democratic Women's Days." *Democratic Digest* 25 (Aug. 1948): 16.
Foreword. *F.D.R.: His Personal Letters, 1905–1928*. Ed. Elliott Roosevelt and James N. Rosenau. New York: Duell, Sloan and Pearce, 1948. xvii-xix.
"He Learned to Bear It." *The Roosevelt Treasury*. Ed. James N. Rosenau. Garden City: Doubleday, 1951, 74–75.
"Letters from Our Honeymoon." *Ladies' Home Journal* 65 (Dec. 1948): 42–43, 95–97, 99, 102, 104–105.
"Liberals in This Year of Decision." *The Christian Register* 127 (June 1948): 26–28, 33.
"Plain Talk about Wallace." *Democratic Digest* 25 (Apr. 1948): 2.
"The Promise of Human Rights." *Foreign Affairs* 26 (Apr. 1948): 470–77.
"Toward Human Rights Throughout the World." *Democratic Digest* 25 (Feb. 1948): 14–15.

1949

Editorial. *ADA World* 3 (20 Apr. 1949): 2.
Introduction. *Freedom's Charter: The Universal Declaration of Human Rights*. Headline Series, 76. By O. Frederick Nolde. New York: Foreign Policy Association, 1949, 3–4 and Headline Series, 76. By O. Frederick Nolde. Millwood: Kraus Reprint, 1973, 3–4.
"Human Rights." *Peace on Earth*. New York: Hermitage House, 1949, 65–71.
"If You Ask Me." *Negro Digest* 7 (July 1949): 20–23.
"Importance of the Covenant." *United Nations Bulletin* 7 (1 July 1949): 3 and *The Covenant on Human Rights*. By Charles Malik and Mrs. Franklin D. Roosevelt. New York: International Documents Service, 1949, 4–5.
Foreword. *Mark Twain and Franklin D. Roosevelt*. By Cyril Clemens. Webster Groves: International Mark Twain Society, 1949, [11].
"International Children's Emergency Fund." *Relief for Children*. Department of State Publication 3415, International Organization and Conference Series III, 24. (Feb. 1949): 1–8.
"Making Human Rights Come Alive." *Phi Delta Kappan* 31 (Sept. 1949): 23–28.
"A Message to College Men." *Prologue* (Bowdoin College) 2 (May 1949): 7.
"Messages on Human Rights." *United Nations Bulletin* 7 (15 Dec. 1949): 743–45, 747–49.
"The Rights of Assembly." *United Nations Bulletin* 6 (Jan. 1, 1949): 5.
"This I Remember." *McCall's* 76 (June 1949): 11–15, 116–28, 138–39, 141–42, 144–49, 156, 159, 163–64; 76 (July 1949): 16–19, 95–98, 101–2, 109–12, 120, 123–24, 127–28; 76 (Aug. 1949): 14–15, 99–102, 109–13, 116, 119–20, 123–24, 127–28; 76 (Sept. 1949): 16–17, 111–16, 128, 130, 132–39, 143–45,

148; 77 (Oct. 1949): 18–19, 33–34, 36–8, 40–42, 44, 46, 59–60, 62, 66–70, 80; 77 (Nov. 1949): 20–21, 112–26, 136; 77 (Dec. 1949): 20–23, 80, 82, 84, 86, 88–89, 91.

"Universal Declaration of Human Rights." *School Life* 31 (Mar. 1949): 8–10.

"What I Think of the United Nations." *United Nations World* 3 (Aug. 1949): 39–41, 48.

"Eleanor Roosevelt: The United Nations." *Annals of America.* Vol. 16. Chicago: Encyclopedia Britannica, 1968, 613–17.

1950

"A Brief History of the Drafting of the Universal Declaration of Human Rights and of the Draft Covenant on Human Rights." *Negro History Bulletin* 14 (Nov. 1950): 29–30, 46.

"Continue the Fight for Better Schools." *School Life* 33 (Dec. 1950): 33–34.

Foreword. *F.D.R.: His Personal Letters, 1928–1945.* Ed. Elliott Roosevelt and Joseph P. Lash. New York: Duell, Sloan and Pearce, 1950, xvii.

"A Front on Which We May Serve." *United Nations World* 4 (June 1950): 50–51.

"If I Were a Republican Today." *Cosmopolitan* 128 (June 1950): 29, 172.

"A Message to Boys' Village . . . and You!" *Southwest Louisiana Boys' Village News* 3 (Aug. 1950): cover.

"Mrs. Roosevelt Discusses Human Rights." *United Nations Reporter* 3 (Apr. 1950): 3.

Foreword. *Pandit Nehru's Discovery of America.* By Philip Pothens. Madras: Indian Press, 1950), 9.

"The Real Perle Mesta." *Flair* 1 (Oct. 1950): 31, 110.

"Reason . . . Must . . . Dominate . . ." *United Nations Bulletin* 8 (1 Apr. 1950): 327.

"This I Believe about Public Schools." *The Nation's Schools* 45 (March 1950): 31–36.

"This I Remember." *Omnibook* 12 (May 1950): 1–45.

"United Nations: All of Us Can Help." *Book of Knowledge 1950 Annual.* New York: Grolier Society, 1950, 161–62.

"What Liberty Means to Me." *Liberty* (1950) and *The Liberty Years, 1924–1940.* Ed. Allen Churchill. Englewood Cliffs: Prentice-Hall, 1969, 426–27.

"Women Have Come a Long Way." *Harper's* 201 (Oct. 1950): 74–76.

Introduction. *The World We Saw.* By Mary Bell Decker. New York: R. Smith, 1950, 3.

1951

"A Collector's Characteristics." *The Roosevelt Treasury.* Ed. James N. Rosenau. Garden City: Doubleday, 1951, 199–201.

"The Elementary Teacher as a Champion of Human Rights." *Instructor* 61 (Sept. 1951): 7.

"The Faces of the People." *The Roosevelt Treasury.* Ed. James N. Rosenau. Garden City: Doubleday, 1951, 445–49.

"Franklin Was a Practical Politician." *The Roosevelt Treasury.* Ed. James N. Rosenau. Garden City: Doubleday, 1951, 380–81.

"He Disliked Being Disagreeable." *The Roosevelt Treasury.* Ed. James N. Rosenau. Garden City: Doubleday, 1951, 155–57.

"The Home: A Citadel of Freedom." *Jewish Parents Magazine* (Apr. 1951): 4–5.

Introduction. *No Time for Tears.* By Charles H. Andrews. Garden City: Doubleday, 1951. 7–8.

"Redrafting the Human Rights Covenant." *United Nations Bulletin* 10 (15 Apr. 1951): 386.

"Report on the Covenant." *United NationsWorld* 5 (Aug. 1951): 17–18.

"A Report on the Covenant of Human Rights." *Delhi Mirror* 1 (24 Feb. 1952): 4, 13.

"The Role of the Elder Statesman Appealed to Him." *The Roosevelt Treasury.* d. James N. Rosenau. Garden City: Doubleday, 1951, 190–92.

"The Seven People Who Shaped My Life." *Look* 15 (19 June 1951): 54–56, 58.

"Statement on Draft Covenant on Human Rights." *Department of State Bulletin* 25 (13 Dec. 1951): 1059, 1064–66.

Foreword. *The Story of My Life.* By Helen Keller. 1951 and New York: Dell, 1961, 7–8 and 1972, 7–8.

"That Was Characteristic of Franklin." *The Roosevelt Treasury.* Ed. James N. Rosenau. Garden City: Doubleday, 1951, 116–17.

"To My Complete Surprise." *The Roosevelt Treasury.* Ed. James N. Rosenau. Garden City: Doubleday, 1951, 186–87.

"A World for Peace." *International Home Quarterly* 15 (Summer 1951): 136–40.

1952

Foreword. *Beauty Behind Barbed Wire: The Arts of the Japanese in Our War Relocation Camps.* By Allen H. Eaton. New York: Harper, 1952, xi-xii.

"Communist Charges vs. US Territorial Plans." *Department of State Bulletin* 27 (27 Dec. 1952): 1032–37.

"Convention Headlines." *Democratic Digest* 29 (Aug. 9, 1952): 10.

Introduction. *The Diary of a Young Girl.* By Anne Frank. Garden City: Doubleday, 1952, 7–8.

Foreword. *A Fair World for All: The Meaning of the Declaration of Human Rights.* By Dorothy Canfield Fisher. New York: Whittlesey House, 1952, 5–6.

"Restlessness of Youth: An Asset to Free Societies." *Department of State Bulletin* 26 (21 Jan. 1952): 94–97.

"Growth That Starts from Thinking." *This I Believe [1]: The Living Philosophies of One Hundred Thoughtful Men and Women in All Walks of Life.* Ed. Edward P. Morgan. New York: Simon & Schuster, 1952, 155–56.

Foreword. *To Win These Rights: A Personal Story of the CIO in the South.* By Lucy Randolph Mason. New York: Harper, 1952, [ix] and Westport: Greenwood, 1970. [ix].

"UN: Good U.S. Investment." *Foreign Policy Bulletin* 32 (1 Oct. 1952): 1–2.

"The United Nations and You." *See* 11 (Nov. 1952): 10–13.

1953

"The Education of an American." *House & Garden* 104 (Aug. 1953): 60–61.

"The Japan I Saw." *Minneapolis Sunday Tribune Picture Roto Magazine,* 11 Oct. 1953: 4–5.

"The Need for Intellectual Freedom." *Say* 5 (Spring 1954): 4.

Foreword. *Peace Through Strength: Bernard Baruch and a Blueprint for Security.* By Morris V. Rosenbloom. Washington: American Survey Association—Farrar, Straus and Young. 1953, 23–26.

Foreword. *Roosevelt and the Warm Springs Story.* By Turnley Walker. New York: Wyn, 1953, [v].

"Should UN Remain a Major Plank in U.S. Policy?" *Foreign Policy Bulletin* 33 (15 Oct. 1953): 4–5.

"Some of My Best Friends Are Negro." *Ebony* 9 (Feb. 1953): 16–20, 22, 24–26 and *White on Black: The Views of Twenty-one White Americans on the Negro.* Ed. Era Bell Thompson and Herbert Nipson. Chicago: Johnson, 1963, 3–17.

"Speaking of Teaching." *National Parent-Teacher* 48 (Nov. 1953): 20.

"To Answer Their Needs . . ." *United Nations Bulletin* 14 (15 Jan. 1953): 92.

"U.N. and the Welfare of the World." *National Parent-Teacher.* 47 (June 1953): 14–16.

1954

Foreword. *The Captains and the Kings.* By Edith Benham Helm. New York: Putnam's, 1954, v-vii.

"Churchill as a Guest." *Churchill by His Contemporaries.* Ed. Charles Eade. New York: Simon and Schuster, 1954, 186–92.

Foreword. *G. P. A. Healy, American Artist: An Intimate Chronicle of the Nineteenth Century.* By Marie De Mare. New York: McKay, 1954. xv-xvi.

Foreword. *The Man Behind Roosevelt: The Story of Louis McHenry Howe.* By Lela Stiles. Cleveland: World, 1954, [vii].

"Memo to the Field." *AAUN News* 26 (Nov. 1954): 7.

"Mrs. Roosevelt and Mr. Dies Debate." *US News and World Report* 37 (27 Aug. 1954): 94–95.

"The Need for Intellectual Freedom." *Say: The Alumni Magazine of Roosevelt College* 5 (Spring 1954): 4.

"Negotiate with Russia: Never Use the H-Bomb." *Time* 64 (30 Aug. 1954): 16.

"Patience, Persistence, Vision and Work." *The Christian Register* 134 (July 1955): 17–18.

"Roosevelt Day Greetings." *ADA World* 9 (Feb. 1954): 2M.

"Should You Help Your Children?" *Lifetime Living* 3 (Dec. 1954): 26.

"The U.S. and the U.N." *Guide to Politics, 1954.* Ed. Quincy Howe and Arthur M. Schlesinger, Jr. New York: Dial, 1954, 60–64.

"Why Are We Co-operating with Tito?" *Look* 18 (5 Oct. 1954): 80, 82–83.

1955

"Children of Israel." *Midstream* 1 (Autumn 1955): 110–11.

"In the Service of Truth." *Nation* 181 (July 9, 1955): 37.

"Is a UN Charter Review Conference Advisable Now?" *Congressional Digest* 34 (Nov. 1935): 275–277.

"Memo from the Field." *AAUN News* 27 (Mar. 1955): 7.
"Memo from the Field." *AAUN News* 27 (May 1955): 7.
"Memo from the Field." *AAUN News* 27 (June 1955): 7.
"Memo from the Field." *AAUN News* 27 (Sept. 1955): 7.
"Memo from the Field." *AAUN News* 27 (Oct. 1955): 7.
"Memo from the Field." *AAUN News* 27 (Feb. 1955): 7.
"Obligation of Leadership." *Childhood Education* 32 (Sept. 1955): 2–3.
"Report to the Membership." *AAUN News* 27 (Dec. 1955/Jan. 1956): 1.
"Social Responsibility for Individual Welfare." *National Policies for Education, Health and Social Services*. Ed. James Earl Russell. Columbia University Bicentennial Conference Series. Garden City: Doubleday, 1955, xxxv-xxxvii.
"Your United Nations." *Bulletin of the American Library Association* 49 (Oct. 1955): 491.

1956
"Age, Health and Politics: An Interview." *Journal of Lifetime Living* 21 (April 1956): 24–27.
"Attorney General's List and Civil Liberties: Replies to an Anvil Questionnaire." *Anvil and Student Partisan* 7 (Spring/Summer 1956): 17.
"Do the Kind Thing." *Every Week* 23 (15–19 Oct. 1956): 48.
"If You Ask Me." *Ladies' Home Journal Treasury*. New York: Simon & Schuster, 1956. 314–16.
"Memo from the Field." *AAUN News* 28 (Mar. 1956): 7.
"Memories of F.D.R." *Look* 20 (17 Apr. 1956): 101.
"Mrs. Roosevelt Applauds Labor's Strength and Unity." *Railway Clerk* 55 (Jan. 1, 1956): 3.
"Prayer for a Better World." *Parents' Magazine* 31 (June 1956): 76.
"The Right to Vote." *Voting Guide, 1956: How to Make Your Vote Count*. Washington: Americans for Democratic Action, 1956, 4–5.
"Roosevelt Day Greetings." *ADA World* 11 (Feb. 1956): 2M.
"Salute to Montgomery." *Liberation* 1 (Dec. 1956): 4–5.
"This Is My Story." *Ladies' Home Journal Treasury*. New York: Simon & Schuster, 1956, 262–67.

1957
"F.D.R. as Seen by Eleanor Roosevelt." *Wisdom* 2 (July 1957): 30.
"From the Wisdom of Eleanor Roosevelt." *Wisdom* 2 (July 1957): 31.
Introduction. *Letters from Jerusalem*. By Mary Clawson. London, New York: Abelard-Schuman, 1957, xiii.
"Roosevelt Day Greetings." *ADA World* 12 (Feb. 1957): 2M.
"Schoolday Tips from Mrs. Roosevelt." *Sunday Star Magazine* [Washington], 25 Aug. 1957: 28–29.
Foreword. *300,000 New Americans: The Epic of a Modern Immigrant-Aid Service*. By Lyman Cromwell White. New York: Harper, 1957, ix.

Introduction. *Youth Aliyah: Past, Present and Future.* By Moshe Kol. F.I.C.E. Documents 1, Israel. Jerusalem: International Federation of Children's Communities, 1957, 7–8.

1958
"Among My Favorites: A Massachusetts Coast Scene by Ludwig Bemelmans." *Art in America* 46 (Spring 1958): 39.
"A Brief Message to Japanese Women." *Today's Japan* 3 (Sept. 1958): 16.
"How to Get the Most Out of Life." *Star Weekly Magazine* [Toronto], 30 Aug. 1958: 3–4.
"Mrs Roosevelt: An Interview." *Equity* 43 (Oct. 1958): 10–14.
"On My Own." *Saturday Evening Post* 230 (8 Feb. 1958): 19–21, 66, 68–70; (15 Feb. 1958): 32–33, 106–8; (22 Feb. 1958): 30–31, 56–57, 60–62; (1 Mar. 1958): 30, 95–96, 98; (8 Mar. 1958): 32–33, 72–74.
[Foreword]. *The Shook-up Generation.* By Harrison E. Salisbury. New York: Harper & Row: 1958, [5].
Foreword. *Talks with Teachers.* By Alice Keliher. Darien: Educational Publishing, 1958. 3–4.
"The Value of Human Personality." *Intercollegian* (YMCA) 76 (Sept. 1958): 4.
"Values to Live By." *Jewish Heritage* 1 (Spring 1958): 44–45, 54.
"We Can Meet the Soviet Challenge." *New Lincoln School Conference News* (Spring 1958): 3.
Foreword. *World Youth and the Communists: The Facts about Communist Penetration of WFDY and IUS.* By Nils M. Apeland. London: Phoenix House, 1958, 7–8.

1959
"A Dessert Mother's Helper Can Prepare." *Kids' Stuff* (Fall 1959): 11.
Preface. *From the Morgenthau Diaries, Years of Crisis, 1928–1938.* By John Morton Blum. Boston: Houghton Mifflin, 1959, [v].
Introduction. *Give Us the Tools.* By Henry Viscardi. New York: Eriksson, 1959, xvii–xix.
"Is America Facing World Leadership?" *Journal of the American Association of University Women* 53 (Oct. 1959): 7–11.
"The Meaning of Freedom." *This Week Magazine* (3 May 1959): 2.
"Mrs. Roosevelt Reports on Her Trip to Russia." *Equity* 44 (May 1959): 3.
"On Reaching Her 75th Birthday Eleanor Roosevelt Praises Television's Contribution to the Senior Citizen." *TV Guide* 7 (17 Oct. 1959): 6–8.
"Segregation." *Educational Forum* 24 (Nov. 1959): 5–6.
"What Are We Here For?" By Eleanor Roosevelt and Huston Smith. *The Search for America.* Ed. Huston Smith. Englewood Cliffs: Prentice-Hall, 1959, 3–12.
"Where I Get My Energy." *Harper's* 218 (Jan. 1959): 45–47.
"Why I Am Opposed to 'Right to Work' Laws." *American Federationist* 66 (Feb. 1959): 5–7.

1960
"Education Is Essential." *Bryn Mawr Alumnae Bulletin* 40 (Winter 1960): 7.
[Foreword]. *FDR Speaks.* Ed. Henry Steele Commager. Washington: Washington Records, 1960, 3.

"Mrs. Roosevelt's Page." *Woman* 47 (26 Nov. 1960): 17; 47 (3 Dec. 1960): 21; 47 (10 Dec. 1960): 25; 47 (17 Dec. 1960): 21; 47 (24 Dec. 1960): 47 (31 Dec. 1960): 23; 48 (7 Jan. 1961): 23; 48 (14 Jan. 1961): 16; 48 (21 Jan. 1961): 18.
"My Advice to the Next First Lady." *Redbook* 116 (Nov. 1960): 18–21, 95–96.
"You Learn by Living." *True Story* 83 (Oct. 1960): 37, 112–16; 83 (Nov. 1960): 56–59, 98.

1961
[Review]. *Dag Hammarskjold: Custodian of a Brushfire Peace*. By Joseph P. Lash. Garden City: Doubleday, 1961. On dust jacket.
"The Joy of Reading." *Coronet* 50 (Sept. 1961): 74–75, 80.
"A Policy Toward Castro's Cuba." *Current* 14 (June 1961): 19.
"A President's Planning." *Saturday Review* 44 (8 July 1961): 10.
"Social Responsibility for Individual Welfare." *National Policies for Education, Health and Social Sciences*. Russell and Russell: 1961.
"What Has Happened to the American Dream?" *Atlantic* 207 (Apr. 1961): 46–50.

1962
Introduction. *The Adventure of America*. By John Tobias and Savin Hoffecker. New York: Geis, 1962, vii.
Foreword. *Brutal Mandate: A Journey to SouthWest Africa*. By Allard K. Lowenstein. New York: Macmillan, 1962, [v]-vi.
Foreword. *From the Eagle's Wing: A Biography of John Muir*. By Hildegarde Hoyt Swift. New York: Morrow, 1962, 7–8.
Foreword. *The Long Shadow of Little Rock: A Memoir*. By Daisy Bates. New York: D. McKay, 1962, xiii-xv.
"Modern Children and Old-Fashioned Manners." *Redbook* 119 (Oct. 1962): 47, 122, 124–25, 127–28.
Foreword. *The Road to the White House. F.D.R.: The Pre-Presidential Years*. By Lorena A. Hickok. Philadelphia: Chilton, 1962, vii-viii.
"Statement of Mrs. Eleanor Roosevelt, Chairman of the President's Commission on the Status of Women." *Congressional Record* (15 Feb. 1962): 2281.
"The Teaching Challenge of the Future." *Graduate Comment* (Wayne State University) 6 (October 1962): 12–15, 23.
Foreword. *This Is Our Strength: Selected Papers of Golda Meir*. Ed. Henry M. Christman. New York: Macmillan, 1962, ix-xiv.
"To All AAUN Members West of the Mississippi." *AAUN News* 34 (Mar. 1962): 6.
"A Woman for the Times." *Boston Sunday Globe Magazine*, 27 May 1962: 3.
"What Can I Do about Peace and People?" *Bookshelf* (National Board of the YWCA) 45 (Summer 1962): 1, 10.
Introduction. *You're the Boss: The Practice of American Politics*. By Edward J. Flynn. New York: Collier, 1962, 7–9.

1963

"Eleanor Roosevelt from This Is My Story." *A Reader for Parents: A Selection of Creative Literature About Childhood.* New York: Norton, 1963, 61–69.

"I Remember Hyde Park: A Final Reminiscence." *McCall's* 90 (Feb. 1963): 71–73, 162–63.

"Israel Will Become a Great Nation.: *The Mission of Israel.* Ed. Jacob Baal-Teshuva. New York: Speller, 1963, 32.

Introduction. *My Darling Clementine: The Story of Lady Churchill.* By Jack Fishman. New York: McKay, 1963, 1–5.

Foreword. *Planning Community Services for Children in Trouble.* By Alfred J. Kahn. New York: Columbia University Press, 1963, vii-viii.

"Tomorrow Is Now." *Ladies' Home Journal* 80 (Sept. 1963): 39–45.

"A Visit to Campobello." *Ford Times* 56 (Apr. 1963): 2–6.

"My Day" columns may be found in the following newspapers:

Atlanta Constitution
Kansas City Star
Milwaukee Journal
New York World Telegram
New York Post (1957–1962)

INDEX

Brkish, Dusan: on Human Rights
    Commission, 156
Brotherhood: democracy and, 57
Brotherly love: need for, 100
Browder, Earl: rights of, 122, 122n1
Brown, Laura S.: Veterans
    Administration, 62n4
Brownell, Herbert, Jr.: and Civil Rights
    Bill of 1957, 277; as Attorney
    General, 277
Brown Shirts: intolerance and, 121
Brown vs. Topeka Board of Education: history
    of, 277–278; resistance to, 277
Broz, Josip. See Tito
Bryan, William Jennings: impracticality
    of, 96
Buck, Pearl: praises Polish women, 107
Buddha: as model democrat, 53
Burma: dictatorship in, 219–220;
    Soviet advisors in, 215
Business: limits of influence, 146;
    responsibility of, 290; Wallace on,
    146
Byelorussia: as "propaganda paradise,"
    208; criticism of U.S. policy
    toward women, 185; criticisms of
    U.S. by, 206–208; on UNDHR,
    157, 158, 168; response to criti-
    cism by, 176; UN behavior of,
    250–251; women's political
    participation in, 186; women's
    role in, 185

Cadden, Joe: AYC and, 126, 127
Cain, Harry, 9
Calcutta (India), 203, 205
California: Japanese Americans banned
    from, 143; regional interests of,
    84
Capitalism: as middle course, 308;
    explanation needed for, 270;
    uniqueness of American, 272

Caraway, Hattie (D-Ark.): career of, 59
Carey, James: Baruch and, 232
"Cash and carry," 7; ER's support for,
    101–102
Cassin, Rene: on Human Rights
    Commission, 156
Castro, Fidel: influence of, 221–222;
    opposition to, 222
Catholicism: discrimination against,
    121; see also Parochial schools;
    Roman Catholic Church; Francis
    Joseph Spellman
Catholics: war service of, 256
Catt, Carrie Chapman, 7; as role
    model, 58n1
Cellar, Emmanuel (D-NY): Polish Jews
    and, 111
Central Intelligence Agency (CIA), 12;
    Cuba and, 221–222
Chamberlain, Neville: suggestions of,
    101; Wallace as, 246
Chamber of Commerce: and right to
    work laws, 289; religious dis-
    crimination within, 121
Chang, Peng-chan: chair of Human
    Rights Commission, 157
Charleston (WVa.), 13; Stevenson
    campaign in, 273
Chicago Civil Liberties Committee:
    ER's address to, 130–132
Child custody: in U.S., 184
Child Health Week: response to ER's
    address regarding, 19
Child labor: AMA on, 293; Fair Labor
    Standards Act and, 293; farm labor
    and, 293; in migrant communities,
    292; menace of, 75; prevalence of,
    75
Children: community responsibility
    toward, 73–75; labor problems
    and, 74; needs of, 71; problems of
    as family problems, 74; rights of,

Dewey, Thomas: election of 1948 and,
285
Dewson, Molly: career of, 61; leadership
skills of, 61; praised by ER, 61
Dictatorship: Chiang Kai-shek and,
220; Franco and, 220; in Burma,
219–220; in Cuba, 221; in
Dominican Republic, 221; in
Haiti, 221; in Indonesia, 219- 220;
in Pakistan, 219–220; in South
America, 221; in Venezuela, 221;
King Saud and, 220; Syngman
Rhee and, 220; U.S. relationship
with, 220–221
Dies Committee. *See* House Un-
American Activities Committee
(HUAC)
Disabled: employment of, 271
Discrimination: UNDHR guarantees
against, 151–152; UNDHR
sanctions against, 161; *see also*
Racial discrimination; African
Americans; American Indians;
Japanese Americans; Jews
District of Columbia: old-age pension
proposals, 21
Divorce: U.S. attitude toward, 184
Dollar diplomacy, 214
Domestic policy: as foreign policy, 308;
personal impact of, 29; U.S.
failures regarding, 308–309
Dominican Republic: dictatorship in,
221
Douglas, Helen Gahagan: Nixon's
defeat of, 283; red-baiting of, 283
Douglas, William O.: on Smith Act, 278
Draft: wastefulness of, 228
Draft International Covenant on
Human Rights: writing of, 163
Dublin (Ireland), 178
Duels: changing attitudes toward, 82
Dulles, John Foster: attitude toward

ER, 274; election of 1948 and,
285; ER's criticism of, 189, 274,
283, 284 insults Ben-Gurion, 275;
on UNDHR, 187, 189; relationship with ER, 285; seeks ER's
resignation from UN, 285; visits
Egypt, 274

Eastland, James O. (D-MS): ER's
disdain for, 277–278
Economic policy: ER's priorities
regarding, 124; goals of, 124
Economics: interdependence and, 29
Economic sanctions: as strategy, 99
Economy Act of 1937, 5, 39–40;
revisions of, 39
Education, 5, 13, 20; American laws
regarding, 165; Arthurdale plan,
25; as deterrent to communism,
275–276; benefits African
Americans, 140; controversies
over, 175; curiosity as central to,
32, 33; ECOSOC resolution on,
164–165; ER's experience in, 33;
essential for leadership, 36; federal
aid to, 12, 253, 254, 255, 258;
foreign language and, 227; future
of, 254; importance of, 305; international need for, 229; necessity of
liberal arts curriculum, 52; rights
of, 154–155; right to, 71, 103,
136, 218, 309; separation of
church & state in, 254; shortages,
133; Soviet criticism of, 207;
Spellman on, 255; state aid to,
258; Stevenson's commitment to,
275; Supreme Court on, 255;
UNDHR on, 154–155, 160; U.S.
distrust of, 308
Education Committee for Voluntary
Union membership: in New
Mexico, 287

Federal budget: foreign aid and, 215; social services and, 207
Federal Bureau of Investigation (FBI): and internment, 141; ER's support for, 269
Federal government: functions of, 37; reorganization of, 39
Federal Theater Project (FTP): communist involvement in, 43; congressional criticism of, 42; ER's support of, 5, 42
Ferguson, Miriam, A. (D-Tex.): criticism of, 60
Film: censorship and, 244
First Red Scare, 1
Fish, Hamilton (R-NY): criticism of, 104–105
Flanagan, Hallie: ER meets with, 42
Flanders, Ralph (R-VT): on MacArthur, 199
Flushing (NY): UN meeting in, 193
Fordham University: Spellman and, 255
Foreign Affairs, 10, 156
Foreign aid: allocation of, 232; purpose of, 286; Truman on, 233; volunteers as, 229
Foreign language: essential skill, 227, 276; teaching of, 227, 276
Foreign policy (U.S.): as impacts domestic policy, 275; bipartisanship and, 188; challenges confronting U.S., 298; civil rights and, 275; conflict resolution in, 85; defensive nature of, 214; during Cold War, 191–230; economic growth and, 216; Eisenhower administration and, 285; ER's approach to, 11; foreign aid and, 281–282; goals of, 216, 217–218; history of, 214; isolationism and, 216; limits of military in, 198; mutual security money

debates and, 282; need for clearcut, 274; need for understanding of, 90; postwar goals of, 214; UNDHR and, 187; war idea and, 82; World War II and, 105; *see also* Containment
Foreign Policy Bulletin, 173
Forum, 22
France: aircraft purchase by, 101; Algerian rebels and, 222–223; anarchy in, 219; battlefields in, 84; D-Day landings in, 109, 113; ER's tour of, 84; impact of World War I in, 84; Morocco and, 224; on UNDHR, 157, 158; persecution of Jews in, 108; philosophy of, 272; political insecurity in, 50; social security system in, 272; women of compared to American women, 67; World War II and citizens of, 104
Franco, Francisco, 7; claims of, 302; despotism of, 220
Freedom: abstract nature of, 202; as security, 273; constant vigilance regarding, 271; defined, 218–219; education as, 276; Gide on, 219; individual responsibility for, 271; perceptions of, 276; Soviet vs. American, 276; UNDHR definition of, 150
Freedom from fear: in UNDHR, 149
Freedom of assembly: in wartime, 130; support for, 123; UNDHR guarantee of, 153
Freedom of belief: in UNDHR, 149
Freedom of expression: as essential, 244
Freedom of information: value of, 248
Freedom of movement: UNDHR on, 152, 161
Freedom of religion: education policy

Poll tax, 6; debated in Human Rights
    Commission, 170; elimination of,
    185- 186; opposition to, 139
Poorhouses: disadvantages of, 22
Population increase: as reason for war,
    86
Porterfield, Robert: bartering tale told
    by, 78
Poston (Ariz.), 9; internment camp in,
    141; riots in, 141
Poverty: dangers of, 220
Poverty level: establishment of, 291
Prayer: in schools, 257
Prejudice, 306; as ammunition for
    CPUSA, 301; ER's rejection of,
    259; roots of, 301
Presidential Commission on the Status
    of Women: creation by JFK, 14;
    ER's appointment to, 14; goals of,
    299; purpose of, 299
Price controls: reasons for, 235
Privacy: right to, 152
Production: and price control, 235;
    as civic duty, 147; defined, 234;
    standards, 235
Progress: roots of, 51–52
Prohibition: women's impact on, 66
Propaganda: dangers of, 117–118; ER's
    of criticism of, 8; impact of, 223;
    lure of, 223; public opinion as a
    reaction to, 30; "War of the
    Worlds" as, 117–118
Property: right to, 153
Protestantism: ER's preference for, 259
Public education: history of, 254, 257;
    see also Education
Public health: housing and, 33
Public Health Service: functions of, 37
Public opinion: as civil rights tool, 304;
    as deterrent to war, 90, 97, 99;
    dangers of, 104; essential for social
    change, 304; on isolationism, 88;

on war- related issues, 88; on
    World War II, 104
Puerto Rico, 46
Pyle, Gladys (R-SDak.): in U.S. Senate,
    59

Quakers: civic impact of, 71

Race riots: world awareness of, 300–
    301
Racial discrimination: against Chinese,
    135; against Japanese, 135; as
    threat to democracy, 248; freedom
    of the press and, 248; international
    implications of, 249; UN discus-
    sions of, 248; USSR on, 207
Racial problems: African vs. American,
    306
Racial violence: police brutality and,
    303
Racism: as threat to democracy, 47;
    compared to Nazism, 302; dangers
    of, 114; eradication of, 136; fear
    and, 301; German anti-Semitism
    as, 114; habits of, 135; irrational
    nature of, 301; Japanese Ameri-
    cans and, 143; priority concern,
    135; threat of, 52; U.S. suscepti-
    bility to, 114; see also African
    Americans; Anti-Semitism; Racial
    discrimination
Randolph, A. Philip, 6
Rankin, Jeannette (D-Mont.): antiwar
    vote of, 59
Ravensbruck Women's Preventive
    Camp: description of, 107
Reason: inherent trait, 150
Reconversion: issues to consider in
    planning, 110
Reference Shelf, 130
Refugees: ER-Vishinsky debate
    regarding, 193; Hindu, 203;